CIVIL LITIGATION

CIVIL LITIGATION

Inns of Court School of Law

 BLACKSTONE PRESS LIMITED

First edition published in Great Britain 1996 by Blackstone Press Limited,
Aldine Place, London W12 8AA. Telephone (020) 8740 2277
www.blackstonepress.com

© Inns of Court School of Law, 1996

First edition 1996
Second edition 1997
Third edition 1998
Fourth edition 1999
Fifth edition 2000

ISBN: 1 84174 056 X

British Library Cataloguing in Publication Data
A CIP catalogue record for this book is available from the British Library.

Typeset by Style Photosetting Ltd, Mayfield, East Sussex
Printed by Ashford Colour Press, Gosport, Hampshire

FOREWORD

These manuals are designed primarily to support training on the Bar Vocational Course, though they are also intended to provide a useful resource for legal practitioners and for anyone undertaking training in legal skills.

The Bar Vocational Course was designed by staff at the Inns of Court School of Law, where it was introduced in 1989. This course is intended to equip students with the practical skills and the procedural and evidential knowledge that they will need to start their legal professional careers. These manuals are written by staff at the Inns of Court School of Law who have helped to develop the course, and by a range of legal practitioners and others involved in legal skills training. The authors of the manuals are very well aware of the practical and professional approach that is central to the Bar Vocational Course.

The range and coverage of the manuals have grown steadily. All the manuals are updated annually, and regular reviews and revisions of the manuals are carried out to ensure that developments in legal skills training and the experience of our staff are fully reflected in them.

This updating and revision is a constant process and we very much value the comments of practitioners, staff and students. Legal vocational training is advancing rapidly, and it is important that all those concerned work together to achieve and maintain high standards. Please address any comments to the Bar Vocational Course Director at the Inns of Court School of Law.

With the validation of other providers for the Bar Vocational Course it is very much our intention that these manuals will be of equal value to all students wherever they take the course, and we would very much value comments from tutors and students at other validated institutions.

The enthusiasm of the staff at Blackstone Press Ltd and their efficiency in arranging production and publication of the manuals is much appreciated.

The Hon. Mr Justice Elias
Chairman of the Board of Governors
Inns of Court School of Law
August 2000

CONTENTS

CONTENTS

CONTENTS

CONTENTS

CONTENTS

PREFACE

Virtually everybody who picks up this Manual for the first time will have had previous, perhaps considerable, experience of the study of the law. However, since there is no standardisation of legal education, it is quite possible that many students will, so far, have approached the law from a purely academic premise. Others may have followed courses which have a more practical orientation. Both have their advantages and drawbacks.

The vocational course is, however, designed to prepare the aspiring barrister to meet the disciplines of everyday professional life at the Bar, and this Manual has been prepared with that purpose in mind.

This Manual deals with many of the major aspects of civil litigation with which an aspiring practitioner needs to be familiar. It must be stressed that this Manual is intended to be a practical introduction to civil procedure, but as you progress on the course you will also have to become familiar with the 'White Book' and 'Green Book' for more detailed guidance on the practice in the High Court and County Courts respectively.

It is hoped that this Manual will provide a means of understanding the concepts of civil litigation, rather than being a mere statement of its constituent 'nuts and bolts'. It has been designed with the hope, as has been said, of promoting an understanding of fundamental principles involved, so that the various Orders and Rules which govern civil litigation can the more easily be digested.

This new edition has been substantially revised and rewritten to ensure that its contents are as up-to-date as possible. However, it is essential that you look out for the new rules which are due to come into force next year. It is hoped that this work will continue to provide an invaluable source of reference well after the (hopefully successful) conclusion of the Bar Vocational Course.

TABLE OF CASES

TABLE OF STATUTES

TABLE OF STATUTORY INSTRUMENTS

ONE

INTRODUCTION

This Manual describes the way in which disputes are resolved through litigation in the civil courts of England and Wales. This chapter will first outline the steps that are normally taken in a case, from the moment a client consults a solicitor to the enforcement of any judgment obtained. It will then deal with a number of matters of general principle.

Commentary on how to draft court documents for use in litigation can be found in the **Drafting Manual**, and will not be discussed here. Regarding applications for orders in court, this Manual will describe the procedure and the principles that are applied, sometimes in some depth. However, guidance on how to present such applications is contained in the **Advocacy Manual**.

Various forms, documents and orders are referred to in this Manual. You will be supplied with examples of most of these at the start of the course, and these should be used in conjunction with this Manual.

The law is stated as on 2 May 2000. It should be noted that the civil justice system underwent a fundamental change with effect from the 26 April 1999, when the present rules governing civil proceedings were introduced. These new rules are the Civil Procedure Rules 1998 ('CPR'), which have statutory force as they are made by statutory instrument. They lay down a detailed procedural code covering all proceedings in the County Courts, the High Court, and the Civil Division of the Court of Appeal. They replace the former rules dealing with civil proceedings in the High Court and the Civil Division of the Court of Appeal (the Rules of Supreme Court 1965, the 'RSC') and a second set of rules dealing with cases in the County Courts (the County Court Rules 1981, the 'CCR'). A huge body of case law developed dealing with the old RSC and CCR. Some of it remains relevant (particularly where what may appear to be procedural cases turn on points of substantive law, see *Malgar Ltd v R E Leach Engineering Ltd*, *The Times*, 17 February 2000), but one of the main ideas behind introducing the new system was to enable the courts to break free from the technical approach adopted in a lot of the old cases. Consequently, cases decided under the old rules need to be treated with a great deal of caution.

1.1 Outline of the Usual Steps in a Case

1.1.1 OVERVIEW OF STAGES IN A COMMON LAW ACTION

Figure 1.1 illustrates the main stages in a common law action, whether commenced in the High Court or a County Court.

Figure 1.1 Main stages in common law actions

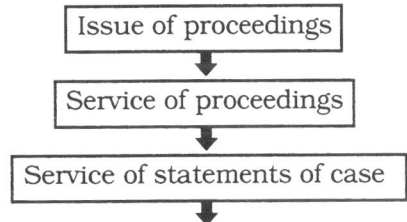

This Manual will cover all of these stages. At this point it is helpful to provide an outline of the steps in a possible case. The steps which follow are based on a personal injury claim in the County Court.

1.1.2 THE INITIAL ROLE OF THE SOLICITOR

Let us take the example of a client who goes to see a solicitor about an accident suffered at work.

During the interview, the solicitor will need to obtain a full statement from the client. This will comprise a description of the accident, the extent of the injuries suffered, and all other relevant information, including the client's background, date of birth and National Insurance number (so the Benefits Agency can provide a certificate of State benefits paid to the client), witnesses who may be able to give evidence, etc.

Among other matters, the client will clearly want advice as to whether any claim for compensation is likely to succeed, and if so, how much is likely to be awarded. Often, this cannot be answered immediately. Before giving such advice, medical reports will usually have to be obtained, and counsel's opinion may eventually be sought. Medical reports will often be obtained as a joint exercise in conjunction with the defendant's insurers.

Another matter which may have to be investigated is whether the proposed defendant is worth suing. After all, if the person responsible is of limited means, insolvent, untraceable or unknown, then, unless there is liability insurance, further steps may simply be a waste of time and money.

1.1.3 THE COST OF LITIGATION

The client will also, not unnaturally, be concerned as to how much the action will cost, and how much, if anything, he or she will be liable to pay. Initial advice on whether the claim is worth bringing may be paid for by the provision of 'legal help' under the Community Legal Service. If proceedings are envisaged, 'full representation' may be applied for under the Community Legal Service. However, in both cases, eligibility depends on whether the client's financial resources (income and capital) are below the limits set by regulations. You will find public funding discussed in **Chapter 35**. If assistance under the Community Legal Service is not available, the litigation will have to be funded by the client or through a conditional fee agreement, unless there is a trade union or insurance company prepared to foot the bill. Of course, if the client is ultimately successful, much (although usually not all) of his or her costs will be repaid by the other side. Normally the solicitor will give some indication of the likely cost, and will ask for a sum to be paid on account.

1.1.4   **PRE-ACTION PROTOCOL**

It is common to have a period of negotiations before proceedings are issued. If these are successful, a great deal of time and expense should be saved. A formal system for early exchange of information and evidence has been laid down for personal injuries claims likely to have a maximum value of £15,000 in the personal injuries pre-action protocol, which was published as part of the CPR. The idea behind the protocol is to promote contact and negotiation between the advisers for the two sides before proceedings start, with the aim of encouraging negotiated settlements and avoiding unnecessary litigation. Parties complying with the protocol have to provide each other with most of the relevant documentation and evidence relevant to assessing the merits of the claim and its value. It is therefore hoped that compliance with the protocol will enable the parties to settle claims on a fair and informed basis. The protocol will be considered in more detail in **Chapter 2**.

1.1.5   **LIMITATION PERIOD**

The primary limitation period in personal injuries cases is three years, and usually proceedings must be issued within that time. However, the Limitation Act 1980 (LA 1980), ss. 14 and 33, which are discussed at **23.3.3.4** and **23.5.2**, may sometimes assist a claimant who would otherwise be out of time.

1.1.6   **ISSUE OF THE CLAIM FORM**

The claimant will usually use a law stationers' form for the claim form. The nature of the claim must be indorsed on the form, together with its value. Further, full particulars of claim can be incorporated into the claim form, although these can be served separately.

The claim form is issued by being sealed with the court's seal. This is discussed further in **Chapter 3**.

1.1.7   **SERVICE OF THE CLAIM FORM**

The claimant has four months in which to serve the claim form. If any difficulty is experienced in doing so, it may be possible to have its validity extended (see **Chapter 25**). Service is usually effected by the court by posting the claim form by ordinary first class post to the defendant. In all cases it must be accompanied by a 'Response Pack' containing forms to be used by the defendant in responding to the claim. There is no need to serve the particulars of claim with the claim form, but the claimant has the option of doing so if so desired.

1.1.8   **SERVICE OF PARTICULARS OF CLAIM**

The Particulars of Claim is the document in which the claimant sets out the nature of the claim against the defendant. Briefly, it sets out the facts that the claimant alleges and which, if proved, would establish one or more causes of action against the defendant or defendants. At the end of the document it is usual to set out a 'prayer' listing the remedies, such as damages and interest, that are sought against the defendants. The contents of the Particulars of Claim must be verified by a 'statement of truth' signed by the claimant or the claimant's solicitor.

If the client's condition may deteriorate in the future, a claim for provisional damages may be made in the Particulars of Claim: see **13.7**.

As mentioned above, the Particulars of Claim may be incorporated into the claim form, or be separate but served with it, or be separate from the claim form and served later. Unless time for service is extended by agreement (which is quite common) or by order of the court, the Particulars of Claim must be served within 14 days after service of the claim form on the defendant.

Normally, Particulars of Claim stand on their own. Personal injuries cases, like the case we are considering, are an exception, and in such cases the claimant must serve two documents with the Particulars of Claim, namely:

(a) a medical report dealing with all the injuries alleged in the Particulars of Claim and on which evidence is proposed to be adduced at trial; and

(b) a schedule of the past and future expenses and losses claimed (including loss of earnings and pension rights).

1.1.9   SUBSEQUENT STAGES

Assuming the parties are unable to agree on terms of settlement, the stages of the action after service of the Particulars of Claim are usually as follows:

(a) Acknowledgment of Service within 14 days by the defendant by returning the form to the court. A defendant may ignore this step, and simply file a Defence (step (b)) within the 14 day period after service of the Particulars of Claim.

(b) Service of the Defence by the defendant. This must be done within 14 days of service of the Particulars of Claim, or 28 days if an acknowledgment of service was filed.

(c) Service of the Reply, if any, by the claimant within 14 days thereafter.

(d) Shortly after the Defence is filed the court will send allocation questionnaires to the parties. These are four-page documents asking questions about what needs to be done to prepare the case for trial.

(e) After the parties return their allocation questionnaires a District Judge at the court will decide which case management track to allocate the case to. Cases worth less than £5,000 will usually be allocated to the small claims track, those worth between £5,000 and £15,000 are usually allocated to the fast track, and those worth more than £15,000 usually go on the multi-track.

(f) At the same time as allocating a case to a track the court will usually give directions regarding the steps that need to be taken to prepare the case for trial, and which lay down a timetable within which those steps must be taken.

(g) The parties exchange lists of documents (see **Chapter 20**) in accordance with the court's directions.

(h) The parties inspect each other's documents seven days later, usually by sending copies through the post.

(i) If the claimant needs money prior to trial, for example to convert a house to provide wheelchair access or to purchase a suitable motor car, an application notice may be issued applying for an order requiring the defendant to make an interim payment on account of any damages that might ultimately be recovered at trial: see **Chapter 13**.

(j) The parties will prepare their cases for trial. They will take statements from witnesses, which will need to be exchanged (**Chapter 30**); they prepare the expert evidence in accordance with the court's directions; they may seek further information from the other side on questions of fact (**Chapter 22**); they may serve notices to admit facts and to prove documents (**Chapter 32**); and, if they may be relying on hearsay evidence, serve notices under the Civil Evidence Act 1995 (CEA 1995): see **Chapter 31**.

(k) The defendant may seek to protect its position on costs by paying money into court: see **Chapter 27**.

(l) One of the things the District Judge will have done when giving directions at the allocation stage is to decide when the parties should return listing questionnaires. This will generally be when the directions made on allocation should have been fully complied with. Listing questionnaires ask detailed questions about compliance with directions and the nature of the evidence to be adduced at trial.

(m) Usually, once listing questionnaires have been returned the court will confirm the trial date or a 'window' during which the trial will take place.

(n) Particularly in multi-track cases, but to some extent also in fast track cases, the court may hold case management hearings from time to time between filing of the Defence and trial. These can take several forms, including allocation hearings, case management conferences, pre-trial reviews and listing hearings.

(o) Prior to trial, counsel will need to be briefed, witnesses served with witness summonses if necessary (for which see **33.12.6**) and bundles of documents prepared for the court.

(p) The trial itself is almost invariably held in open court, which means the public and press may be present. It is conducted by a circuit or district judge depending on its value. Counsel are wigged and gowned, and witnesses give oral evidence on oath or affirmation.

(q) After hearing the evidence the judge gives judgment and considers the question of costs: see **Chapter 36**.

(r) The court will usually send the parties a sealed copy of the judgment, which is simply a record of the result of the trial, not the judge's reasons.

(s) The loser may consider an appeal to the Court of Appeal: see **Chapter 39**.

(t) The winner is usually entitled to an order for costs against the loser. In fast track cases costs are usually assessed by the judge there and then. In multi-track cases costs are usually subject to detailed assessment. This is a process that can take many months, culminating in a hearing before a costs officer. It is open to the losing party to seek to agree the amount of costs payable with the successful party.

(u) If the loser fails to pay the damages and/or costs, the winner may have to go on to enforce the judgment: see **Chapter 38**.

1.2 The Courts

1.2.1 JURISDICTION OF THE COUNTY COURT

1.2.1.1 Creature of statute
The County Court owes its existence to statute, and the jurisdiction exercised by its judges and officers must be derived from the CCA 1984 and the CPR, failing which it will be acting *ultra vires*. The CPR are dicussed further at **1.2.2.1** below.

Until recently it has always been thought that, being a creature of statute, the County Court had no inherent jurisdiction. Since *Langley* v *North West Water Authority* [1991] 1 WLR 697, where the Court of Appeal held that a County Court had inherent jurisdiction to make local practice directions, it has been accepted that County Courts do in fact have an inherent jurisdiction.

The Civil Procedure Act 1997, s. 5, has inserted a new section into the CCA 1984 (s. 74A) with regard to Practice Directions in the County Courts, which may only be made with the approval of the Lord Chancellor.

1.2.1.2 Lacunae in CCR

The CCA 1984, s. 76, provides:

> *In any case not expressly provided for by or in pursuance of this Act, the general principles of practice in the High Court may be adopted and applied to proceedings in a county court.*

In *R* v *Bloomsbury and Marylebone County Court, ex parte Villerwest Ltd* [1975] 1 WLR 1175 (DC) Lord Widgery CJ said:

> It is only when there is a lacuna in the County Court Rules, some general principle not dealt with at all, that one is justified in applying [section 76] and seeking inspiration from the High Court rules instead.

1.2.1.3 Remedies available in the County Court

The CCA 1984, s. 38(1), provides:

> *Subject to what follows, in any proceedings in a County Court the court may make any order which could be made by the High Court.*

County Courts have no power to order the remedies available on judicial review (mandamus, certiorari and prohibitions).

Further, the County Court Remedies Regulations 1991, made under CCA 1984, s. 38(3)(b), provide that County Courts shall not have power to grant search orders and have the power to grant freezing injunctions (see **Chapters 15** and **16**) only in limited circumstances. Exceptions where freezing injunctions can be granted in the County Court, include injunctions over the subject matter of County Court proceedings and injunctions in aid of the execution of County Court judgments. (It should be noted, however, that search orders and freezing injunctions can be granted generally in the specialist Patents County Court and the Central London County Court Business List.) Where the County Court has no power to make such an order, the proceedings are transferred to the High Court for the purpose of making the application, then transferred back to the County Court.

1.2.2 JURISDICTION OF THE HIGH COURT

1.2.2.1 General

High Court procedure is governed primarily by the SCA 1981 and the CPR. Very often the Act is expressed in wide terms, leaving the Rules Committee to control the statutory powers by rules of court and the appellate courts to establish principles for the exercise of the statutory powers. If the Rule Committee exceeds its powers, its rules may be challenged as *ultra vires*. A successful challenge against one provision was made in *General Mediterranean Holdings SA* v *Patel* [1999] 3 All ER 673. The Committee's power to make rules is derived from the Civil Procedure Act 1997, ss. 1 and 2, which is to be exercised with a view to securing that the civil justice system is accessible, fair and efficient.

Secondly, matters of practice are regulated by *Practice Directions* which supplement the main CPR.

Thirdly, the High Court can fill any gaps in the above in its inherent jurisdiction.

1.2.2.2 Inherent jurisdiction

The inherent powers of the High Court derive from the fact that it is the successor to the old common law courts. By resorting to its inherent jurisdiction the court can ensure justice is done between the parties where otherwise there might appear to be a gap in the court's powers through a situation not being covered expressly in either the SCA 1981 or the CPR. The ambit of the court's inherent powers moves with the times, so in *Harrison* v *Tew* [1990] 2 AC 523, HL, it was held that the court's inherent jurisdiction in an area may be ousted by later statutory provisions dealing with the same subject matter.

1.2.2.3 District Registries of the High Court

There are 133 District Registries, each one serving the districts of a number of County Courts. District Registries are established by SCA 1981, ss. 99–103. All actions involving disputes in London must be commenced in the Royal Courts of Justice (RCJ); elsewhere the claimant can choose between the RCJ and the local District Registry.

1.2.2.4 Masters and District Judges

Most of this Manual is concerned with various interim applications which can be made in civil proceedings. These are applications to the court, other than by way of trial or appeal, for various orders or directions. Interim procedure is dealt with in **Chapter 10**. One point that is worth mentioning here is that, apart from interim injunctions, most interim applications are made to a Master or District Judge in the first instance. Masters exercise this jurisdiction in the High Court sitting in London (both QBD and Ch.D.). District Judges perform the same function in High Court cases proceeding in District Registries. Rather confusingly, the corresponding official in a County Court is also called a District Judge, and one person may be the District Judge for both a High Court District Registry and its local County Court.

1.3 Choosing the Appropriate Court

1.3.1 WHICH COURTS HAVE JURISDICTION

Civil jurisdiction is exercised mainly by the High Court and County Courts. Magistrates' courts have limited jurisdiction over matrimonial and some other matters, and are not considered in more than outline in this Manual.

1.3.2 CHOICE BETWEEN HIGH COURT AND COUNTY COURT

For many types of proceedings the High Court and County Courts have concurrent jurisdiction. The decision as to where to commence proceedings in such cases will be dictated by factors such as the importance of the case, whether the case is likely to raise difficult questions of law or fact, and the convenience of the court building to the parties and lawyers involved in the case. Generally, it is most apt to commence proceedings in the court where the case is likely to be tried (see **1.3.9**).

There are a number of rules restricting the choice between the High Court and County Courts. The most important are:

(a) Personal injuries claims *must* be brought in a County Court if the value of the claim does not exceed £50,000. This is discussed further at **1.3.6**.

(b) Consumer credit cases (based on hire purchase and related forms of agreement) *must* be brought in a County Court if the upper credit limit (broadly, the amount borrowed) does not exceed £25,000.

(c) Other money claims *may* be brought in the High Court provided the value of the claim exceeds £15,000. The result is that below £15,000 the claim must be brought in the County Court, and above that figure there is a choice.

(d) As an exception to paragraph (c) above, High Court proceedings can always be justified if they are suitable for inclusion in one of the specialist lists, such as commercial, patent and company court matters.

(e) Equity proceedings, contentious probate proceedings, and proceedings under the Law of Property Act 1925 (LPA 1925) can be brought in the County Court *only* if the amount of the fund or the value of the land does not exceed £30,000. If it exceeds £30,000 it must be brought in the High Court.

(f) Judicial review and defamation proceedings can *only* be commenced in the High Court.

1.3.3   THE COUNTY COURT

There are about 240 County Courts, with the country being divided into districts each being served by one or more County Courts (County Courts Act 1984 (CCA 1984), s. 1).

1.3.4   THE HIGH COURT

The High Court, together with the Crown Court and the Court of Appeal, forms part of the Supreme Court of Judicature of England and Wales. It is divided into three divisions:

(a)   The Chancery Division (Ch.D.).

(b)   The Queen's Bench Division (QBD).

(c)   The Family Division.

Business is allocated between the Divisions in accordance with the Supreme Court Act 1981 (SCA 1981), s. 61, and sch. 1. Broadly:

(a)   The Ch.D. deals with land, mortgages, trusts, administration of estates, probate, bankruptcy, intellectual property and company matters.

(b)   The QBD deals with judicial review, admiralty and commercial matters.

(c)   The Family Division is assigned all matrimonial and related matters.

Family law and procedure are dealt with in the *Family Law in Practice Manual*, so this Manual will concentrate on procedure in the QBD and Ch.D. Where the subject matter is not specifically provided for, the litigant has the choice of which Division to use. In practice, most actions in tort and contract are commenced in the QBD.

1.3.5   SPECIALIST COURTS

In addition, there are a number of specialised courts, most of which are part of either the QBD or Ch.D., although some are also part of the County Courts. Apart from the brief descriptions below, they will not be considered more than in passing elsewhere in this Manual. The main specialist courts are:

(a)   The Commercial Court, which is part of the QBD. It has its own special Practice Direction (PD 49D), and its procedures are governed by the CPR as extensively modified by the Commercial Court Guide. Its administrative office at the Royal Courts of Justice is called the Admiralty and Commercial Registry.

(b)   The Admiralty Court, which is part of the QBD. It has its own special Practice Direction (PD 49F); it shares its administrative office with the Commercial Court; and its practice follows that set out in the Commercial Court Guide.

(c)   Mercantile Courts have been established as part of the High Court sitting in a number of District Registries and in a number of County Courts, so that commercial claims commenced in these courts can be dealt with by specialist judges with procedural rules tailored for litigation of this nature. There is a special Mercantile Court Practice Direction (PD 49H), and a Mercantile Court Guide (which is far less detailed than the Commercial Court Guide).

(d)   Commercial arbitration matters are dealt with by the Commercial Court and Mercantile Courts, and have their own Practice Direction, PD 49G.

(e)   The Technology and Construction Court ('TCC'). This is primarily part of the QBD, but some TCC claims may be started in the Central London County Court and High Court District Registries. It has its own building in Fetter Lane, near the Royal Courts of Justice. The TCC deals primarily with complex building disputes and with complex engineering and technology cases. It has its own special Practice Direction, PD 49C.

(f) The Companies Court is part of the Ch.D., and deals mainly with applications under the Companies Act 1985, and with company insolvency matters. It has its own special Practice Direction, PD 49B, and, in relation to insolvency matters, PD Insolvency Proceedings.

(g) Whereas the Companies Court deals with the winding up of insolvent companies, insolvent individuals are dealt with through bankruptcy. Bankruptcy matters (like corporate insolvency) mostly fall outside the scope of the CPR, being governed instead by the Insolvency Rules 1986. Bankruptcy petitions must generally be brought in the County Court having bankruptcy jurisdiction (not all County Courts do) serving the district where the debtor lives, leaving the Ch.D. of the High Court to deal with debtors living (broadly) in Greater London and abroad (insofar as the courts of England and Wales are able to exercise jurisdiction over such people). Bankruptcy matters will be governed by PD Insolvency Proceedings.

(h) The Patents Court is mainly part of the Ch.D., but also manifests itself as the Patents County Court, which is part of the Central London County Court. It has its own Practice Direction (PD 49E), and its own court guide.

1.3.6   PERSONAL INJURIES CASES

Claims for damages in respect of personal injuries where the claimant does not reasonably expect to recover more than £50,000 must be commenced in a County Court: High Court and County Courts Jurisdiction Order 1991, art. 5. The term 'personal injuries' includes disease, impairment of physical or mental condition, and death. The value of the claim is determined as at the date the claim is commenced, and:

(a) claims for interest and costs are disregarded;

(b) contributory negligence is disregarded, unless such negligence is admitted;

(c) if provisional damages (see **13.7**) are claimed, any possible future application for further damages is disregarded; and

(d) sums required to be paid to the Secretary of State by virtue of the Social Security (Recovery of Benefits) Act 1997 (see *Remedies Manual*) are part of the claim.

Quantification of damages for personal injuries is dealt with in *Remedies Manual*. The great majority of claims are for less than £50,000. Note that the £50,000 provided by the Order is the sum of the claim for:

(a) special damages for actual financial losses incurred before trial or settlement;

(b) general damages for pain, suffering and loss of amenity relating to the injury itself; and

(c) future losses, such as future loss of earnings and the cost of future medical care.

Head (c) is calculated by multiplying the claimant's annual loss by a number of years purchase, calculated by reference to the claimant's age, occupation, etc. Losses where damages under heads (a) and (b) exceed £50,000 are comparatively rare, but where the injury results in the claimant being unable to work or only capable of low-paid work, the total award is likely to justify commencing proceedings in the High Court.

1.3.7 COST IMPLICATIONS OF COMMENCING IN THE HIGH COURT

The normal rule is that loser pays the successful party's costs. Unless there are sufficient reasons (such as complexity) for bringing an action in the High Court, a claimant who brings proceedings in the High Court which should have been commenced in the County Court is likely to be penalised in costs, even if successful. The usual penalty is that the successful claimant's award for costs is reduced by up to 25 per cent. See SCA 1981, s. 51(8), (9).

1.3.8 DELIBERATE FLOUTING

Where proceedings are commenced in the wrong court and the court is satisfied the claimant knew or ought to have known of any relevant provision allocating jurisdiction, the court may order the proceedings to be struck out: CCA 1984, ss. 40(1)(b) and 42(1)(b). It was held in *Restick* v *Crickmore* [1994] 1 WLR 420 CA that where the claimant knew or ought to have known that the action should have been started in one court, but started it in the other, the court has a discretion whether to strike the action out or to transfer it to the correct court. Normally the court will simply order a transfer and penalise the claimant in costs under SCA 1981, s. 51 (see **1.3.7**). Striking out is a draconian punishment, and should only be used where it was plain that the action was being started in the wrong court, and the claimant chose to do so in an attempt to harass the defendant, or deliberately run up unnecessary costs, or ignored a clear warning from the defendant as to the correct court, or had persistently started actions in the wrong court.

1.3.9 TRIAL ALLOCATION

Generally, an action is likely to be tried in the same court as the one in which it was commenced. However, the greater standing and experience of High Court judges makes High Court trial more appropriate for the more weighty types of cases. To this end, the courts may, either of their own motion or on application by any party, transfer proceedings either up to the High Court or down to an appropriate County Court: CCA 1984, ss. 40 and 42. The main rules for ordering such transfers are laid down in the High Court and County Courts Jurisdiction Order 1991, art. 7:

(a) equity and contentious probate proceedings involving no more than £30,000 which are commenced in a County Court (see **1.3.2**) will also be tried there;

(b) where at least one of the claims in the action seeks relief having no quantifiable financial value (such as many injunctions), the place of trial is determined according to the criteria set out below;

(c) subject to the criteria set out below, claims for less than £25,000 (valued when the proposed transfer is considered) should be tried in a County Court;

(d) claims between £25,000 and £50,000 are flexibly allocated between the High Court and County Courts using the criteria set out below; and

(e) subject to the following criteria set out below, claims over £50,000 are tried in the High Court.

The criteria are:

(i) the financial substance of the action, including the value of any counter-claim;

(ii) the importance of the case, and whether it involves questions of general public interest;

(iii) the complexity of the facts, law, remedies and procedure involved; and

(iv)   (although not sufficient on its own) whether transferring the action is likely to result in a more speedy trial.

1.4   General Principles

1.4.1   THE OVERRIDING OBJECTIVE

The CPR, r. 1.1, provides:

> *(1)   These Rules are a new procedural code with the overriding objective of enabling the court to deal with cases justly.*
> *(2)   Dealing with a case justly includes, so far as is practicable—*
>   *(a)   ensuring that the parties are on an equal footing;*
>   *(b)   saving expense;*
>   *(c)   dealing with the case in ways which are proportionate—*
>   *(i)   to the amount of money involved,*
>   *(ii)   to the importance of the case;*
>   *(iii) to the complexity of the issues; and*
>   *(iv)   to the financial position of each party;*
>   *(d)   ensuring that it is dealt with expeditiously and fairly; and*
>   *(e)   allotting to it an appropriate share of the court's resources, while taking into account the need to allot resources to other cases.*

By CPR, r. 1.2, the court has to give effect to the overriding objective when making decisions, and the parties are by r. 1.3 expected to help the court to further the overriding objective. By r. 1.4 the court must further the overriding objective by actively managing cases, which by r. 1.4(2) includes:

> *(a)   encouraging the parties to co-operate with each other in the conduct of the proceedings;*
> *(b)   identifying the issues at an early stage;*
> *(c)   deciding promptly which issues need full investigation and trial and accordingly disposing summarily of the others;*
> *(d)   deciding the order in which issues are to be resolved,*
> *(e)   encouraging the parties to use an alternative dispute resolution procedure if the court considers that appropriate and facilitating the use of such procedure;*
> *(f)   helping the parties to settle the whole or part of the case;*
> *(g)   fixing timetables or otherwise controlling the progress of the case;*
> *(h)   considering whether the likely benefits of taking a particular step justify the cost of taking it;*
> *(i)   dealing with as many aspects of the case as it can on the same occasion;*
> *(j)   dealing with the case without the parties needing to attend at court;*
> *(k)   making use of technology; and*
> *(l)   giving directions to ensure that the trial of a case proceeds quickly and efficiently.*

1.4.1.1   Dealing with cases justly

The main concept in CPR, r. 1.1, means that the primary concern of the court is doing justice. Shutting a litigant out through a technical breach of the rules will not often be consistent with this, because the primary purpose of the civil courts is to decide cases on their merits, not in rejecting them through procedural default. An example of this is *Jones v Telford and Wrekin District Council, The Times*, 29 July 1999, where service had been delayed beyond the period of validity because the claimant's solicitors had problems in obtaining psychiatric reports for service with the particulars of claim. The Court of Appeal upheld an extension of time largely because there were no previous authorities dealing with this situation, the Master of the Rolls commenting that the court must not lose sight of the fact its primary concern was doing justice. Another example is *Chilton v Surrey County Council* (24 June 1999, unreported), where the Court of Appeal indicated that dealing with a claim justly involved dealing with the real claim, and allowed the claimant to rely on a revised statement of past and future loss and expense quantifying the claim at about £400,000 rather than the original statement, which indicated a claim value of about £5,000.

1.4.1.2 Equal footing

In *Maltez* v *Lewis*, *The Times*, 4 May 1999, the concept of dealing with the parties on an equal footing was held not to extend to the court being able to prevent a party from instructing the lawyers of its choice, even if one side could not afford lawyers as expensive as those being used by the other. In *McPhilemy* v *Times Newspapers Ltd* [1999] 3 All ER 775 the Master of the Rolls said that if a party wanted the court to restrain the activities of another party with the object of achieving greater equality, the party making the application had to demonstrate they were themselves conducting the proceedings with a desire to limit expense so far as practical. However, the powers of the court to restrain excess did not extend to preventing a party from putting forward allegations which were central to their case. That said, it was open to the court to attempt to control how those allegations were litigated with a view to limiting costs.

1.4.1.3 Dealing with cases expeditiously, fairly and saving expense

In *Cadogan Properties Ltd* v *Mount Eden Land Ltd* (29 June 1999, unreported) the court at first instance had made an order for service by an alternative method in circumstances where there were no grounds for doing so. That order was set aside on appeal, with the result that proceedings had not been served and the period of validity had expired. The Court of Appeal relied on CPR, r. 1.1(2)(d), and the need to deal with cases fairly and expeditiously, and also on the need for proportionality (r. 1.1(2)(c)), to justify making an order extending the validity of the originating process. The defendant was aware of the proceedings, and suffered no significant prejudice by the course adopted by the court. In *Keene* v *Martin*, *The Times*, 11 November 1999, it was held that, on the facts, the case was not an appropriate one for using the Part 8 procedure (see **3.13**). Instead of striking out the proceedings (see **28.2**), the Court of Appeal allowed the claim to continue as an ordinary chancery action, as that was more cost-effective than forcing the claimant to start again by issuing fresh proceedings.

1.4.1.4 Allotting an appropriate share of the court's resources

In *Stephenson (SBJ) Ltd* v *Mandy*, *The Times*, 21 July 1999, the defendant appealed against an interim order restraining him from breaching a restrictive covenant in his contract of employment. The appeal came before the Court of Appeal on 30 June, and the trial had been fixed for 20 July. Given the short period before the start and the fact the claimant had given the usual undertaking in damages (see **14.5.2**), the court decided that considering the merits of the appeal would not be in accordance with the overriding objective. Expense would not be saved by hearing the appeal, and given the short time to trial hearing the appeal would not be a good use of the court's resources. An appeal was also dismissed (with costs on the indemnity basis) in *Adoko* v *Jemal*, *The Times*, 8 July 1999, in very different circumstances, on the ground of allotting to it no more than an appropriate share of the court's resources. In this case the appellant had failed to correct the notice of appeal despite a warning from the respondent that it was seriously defective, and had failed to comply with the directions relating to appeal bundles. The Court of Appeal spent over an hour trying to sort out the mess, and then decided it was inappropriate that any further share of the court's resources should be allocated to the appeal.

1.4.1.5 Cooperating

In *Chilton* v *Surrey County Council* (24 June 1999, unreported), the Court of Appeal decided against the defendant partly because it seemed that the defendant was attempting to take tactical advantage of a mistake by the claimant's solicitors in overlooking to serve the revised statement of past and future loss and expense rather than cooperating with the claimant's solicitors to put matters right.

1.4.2 COMPUTATION OF TIME

The CPR, r. 2.8 and r. 2.9, lay down a number of rules for computing periods of time fixed by the Rules and by court orders and judgments.

1.4.2.1 'Month'

'Month' means calendar month (not lunar month). Thus, if an act is required to be done within a month after 31 October, the period begins on 1 November and the last day for doing the act is 30 November.

1.4.2.2 'Clear days'

A period of time expressed as a number of days is computed as 'clear days'. This means that if an act is required to be done (say) three clear days before or after a specified date, at least that number of days must intervene between the two dates.

1.4.2.3 Short periods

When computing periods of time of 5 days or less, Saturdays, Sundays and bank holidays are excluded. For example, an application must be served three clear days before the return date (when the application will be heard by the Master). If the return date is Tuesday 12 October, the three 'clear days' would be Thursday 7 October, Friday 8 October and Monday 11 October, and the last day for service would be Wednesday 6 October.

1.4.2.4 Court office closed

When time expires on a day on which the court office is closed, and for that reason the act cannot be done on that day, the act will be in time if done on the next day that the court office is open.

1.4.2.5 Time applications

The CPR, r. 3.1(1)(a), provides that the court may extend or shorten any time period laid down by the rules or any court order. An extension may be granted after the initial period has expired. The procedure is considered further in **Chapter 10**. The costs of the application will usually be borne by the party applying for the order.

In practice, many time limits are extended by consent between the parties' solicitors. Such agreements should be in writing (usually by letter), and do not require an order being made by the court. However, the parties cannot agree to extend time if the agreement will impinge on certain 'key' dates. These include the dates set by the court for any case management conference, pre-trial review, for filing listing questionnaires, or for the trial. Further, the parties cannot agree to extend time in relation to any step carrying a sanction in default: see CPR, r. 3.9(3).

1.4.3 ERRORS OF PROCEDURE

The CPR, r. 3.10, provides:

> *Where there has been an error of procedure such as a failure to comply with a rule or practice direction—*
> *(a) the error does not invalidate any step taken in the proceedings unless the court so orders; and*
> *(b) the court may make an order to remedy the error.*

The rule is worded very widely, and consequently most procedural failures will be treated as irregularities. The rule confirms the removal of an old (pre-1964) distinction between failures rendering the proceedings or step in the proceedings a nullity (and hence incapable of cure), and failures which are mere irregularities.

However, some procedural failings are not failures 'to comply with the requirements of these rules.' For example, in *Dubai Bank Ltd* v *Galadari (No. 4), The Times*, 23 February 1990, it was assumed that the plaintiff (now called a claimant) had ceased to exist as a corporate body when the writ (the predecessor of the claim form) was issued through failing to comply with Dubai company law. Morritt J held that the requirement for a plaintiff was a basic principle of law, and if the plaintiff did not exist when the writ was issued the proceedings were a nullity and were not saved by the predecessor to r. 3.10. Another example is provided by *Bank of America National Trust and Savings Association* v *Chrismas* [1994] 1 All ER 401, where it was held that the rule is subordinate to the Limitation Act 1980, s. 35(3), which prevents certain amendments after the expiry of the limitation period. Purported service of an amended claim in breach of s. 35(3) therefore could not be cured under this rule (see **24.7.3.5**).

On an application to remedy an error, it must be kept in mind that some errors are worse than others. Using an out-of-date form or returning an acknowledgment of service form to the wrong court office are clearly less serious than serving a claim form which is no longer valid for service or serving a claim form abroad without first seeking permission where that is required. In the latter two cases, it is highly unlikely that the court would exercise its discretion in favour of the application.

1.4.4 DISCRETION

An applicant for most forms of interim order will have to establish a number of basic conditions, which will be prescribed by either the SCA 1981, CCA 1984 or rules of court. Once these conditions have been satisfied, the court will then exercise its discretion whether to grant the order applied for.

At one extreme are applications where the court is given a broad, general discretion. An example is *Corfu Navigation Co.* v *Mobil Shipping Co. Ltd* [1991] 2 Lloyd's Rep 52, CA, dealing with an application for security for costs (see **Chapter 26**). Once the basic conditions in such a case have been established, counsel's arguments should be addressed to the basic principle underlying the application, and it is inappropriate to subject the judicial reasoning in previous cases to detailed and semantic analysis.

At the other extreme are applications where, once the basic conditions are satisfied, the order follows almost as of course with little scope for any residual judicial discretion. An example is an application for summary judgment where the court finds there is no real prospect of defending the claim (see **Chapter 12**, especially **12.7.1**). In such a case the court has little if any discretion, and should make the order. Of course, establishing these conditions may be far from easy, and, in the context of summary judgment, if the conditions are not satisfied the court has a very wide discretion regarding the other forms of order it may make (see **12.7.2** to **12.7.5**).

1.4.5 CARDS ON THE TABLE

In the past, litigation was usually conducted with both sides keeping their preparations for trial as secret as possible. Keeping one's cards close to one's chest was regarded as good tactics, and was protected by legal professional privilege. The only exception was that each party had to disclose all relevant documents in their possession, custody or power to the other side. This obligation to give disclosue (see **Chapter 20**) still exists.

Although legal professional privilege remains, the position has now almost been reversed. Over the last 30 years, the following inroads have been made into secret preparation:

(a) sharing evidence in compliance with pre-action protocols (**Chapter 2**);

(b) various forms of pre-action disclosure against non-parties (**Chapter 21**);

(c) service of hearsay statements (**Chapter 31**);

(d) mutual exchange of experts' reports (**Chapter 29**);

(e) exchange of witnesses' statements (**Chapter 30**);

(f) agreement of photographs, etc.

TWO

PRE-ACTION CONDUCT OF LITIGATION

2.1　Introduction

This chapter deals primarily with the requirements of the pre-action protocol governing fast track personal injuries cases. This protocol should be seen as a pattern for other types of cases, and a similar approach will be expected even where the protocol does not strictly apply. The chapter also mentions some other topics relevant in the pre-issue period, such as sending notices and pre-action applications.

2.2　Pre-action Protocols

The intention eventually is that there will be pre-action protocols covering all the main categories of litigation. At the moment the only published protocols are for personal injury claims and medical negligence claims (also known as clinical disputes). Compliance with preaction protocols is intended to break down the old, pre-CPR, adversarial and secretive approach to case preparation. Compliance is also intended to promote the prospects of achieving settlements as early as possible and on an informed basis. Compliance with any relevant protocol will be regarded as the normal reasonable approach for solicitors to take, with failure to adhere to a relevant protocol being punished by a harsher response to applications for extensions of time later on, and possible costs penalties and other sanctions.

Litigation should be seen as a last resort. The steps required to be taken by pre-action protocols are intended to ensure that other means of resolving disputes are attempted before proceedings are issued.

2.3　Cases not Covered by Pre-action Protocols

In cases not covered by an approved protocol, the court will expect the parties, in accordance with the overriding objective, to act reasonably in exchanging information and documents relevant to the claim and generally in trying to avoid the necessity for the start of proceedings.

2.4　Personal Injury Protocol

The personal injury protocol is designed primarily for personal injuries claims worth up to £15,000, or in other words, cases likely to be allocated to the fast track if proceedings are commenced. The spirit of the protocol should be followed in larger cases. The parties can depart from the detail in the protocol, but the court will want an explanation of the reasons for departing from it if proceedings are subsequently issued. The protocol says that before issuing proceedings the following matters should be dealt with in the following order:

(a) The claimant may choose to send an informal letter to the defendant or the defendant's insurer at an early stage intimating the claim. Doing so will not start the protocol timetable.

(b) Two copies of a letter of claim should be sent to the defendant immediately sufficient information is available to substantiate a realistic claim. One copy is for the defendant and the other for his insurer. If the insurer is known, the letters should be sent separately. Also,

    (i) The letter should contain a clear summary of the facts, the nature of the injuries and details of the financial losses claimed. An example of such a letter is illustrated as **Figure 2.1**.

    (ii) If possible the letter of claim should indicate which documents should be disclosed by the defendant at this stage. Detailed lists of the types of documents that should be disclosed for different types of personal injuries cases are set out in annexes to the protocol. By way of example, the list for road traffic accident cases is set out as **Figure 2.2**. There are even more detailed lists for accidents at work, especially in cases where specific statutory provisions apply. The level of disclosure required by these lists is substantially greater than that habitually given by defendants and their insurers.

(c) The defendant must reply in 21 days naming any insurer. A failure to reply within this time justifies the issue of proceedings without further compliance with the protocol.

(d) The defendant, or the defendant's insurer, has a maximum of three months from acknowledging the letter of claim to investigate the claim and state whether liability is denied, and if so, on what grounds.

(e) In cases where the defendant disputes liability there is a requirement that the defendant must disclose documents relevant to liability (these should be in the categories identified by the claimant in the letter of claim), which must be enclosed with the denial letter.

(f) If contributory negligence is alleged, the claimant should respond to the allegations raised before proceedings are issued.

(g) A Schedule of Special Damages, together with supporting documents, must be sent as soon as possible thereafter. This is a formal document which sets out the various categories of past and future financial losses that are claimed. In difficult cases this document may be drafted by counsel.

(h) The next step will be to obtain medical evidence dealing with the client's injuries. The protocol encourages the use of a jointly selected and jointly instructed medical expert. This is an important topic, and will be considered more fully at **2.5** below.

(i) Once these steps have been taken the parties are encouraged to consider negotiating with each other, and possibly Alternative Dispute Resolution ('ADR') or mediation, before starting proceedings.

(j) Before issuing proceedings it might be sensible for the parties to carry out a joint 'stock take' of the issues in dispute and the evidence likely to be required.

(k) If proceedings are imminent, any insurer acting for the defendant should be invited to nominate solicitors and do so within 7–14 days of the intended date of issue.

Figure 2.1   Letter of claim

To: D. Stokes (Haulage) Limited, Defendant
Dear Sirs,

Re: Our client: Eleanor Jane Weldon
      Our client's address: 47 Forest Road, London N10 4RS
      Our client's employer: Ellis Cuthbert Limited, Research Department,
                             Manor Road, London N23 7PD

We are instructed by Eleanor Weldon to claim damages in connection with a road traffic accident on 26th November 1999 at the junction of Newlands Road and Waterfall Road, London N10.

Please confirm the identity of your insurers. Please note that the insurers will need to see this letter as soon as possible and it may affect your insurance cover and/or conduct of any subsequent proceedings if you do not send this letter to them.

The circumstances of the accident were that our client's car registration number S865 PGE was stationary in Newlands Road waiting at its junction with Waterfall Road in order to turn right. Her right indicator was showing. Your van registration number M633 YSJ driven by James Williams failed to stop as he approached the junction, and collided with the rear of our client's car.

The reasons why we are alleging fault are that it was negligent not to slow down in time, or to see or take account of the presence of our client's car, and to collide with the rear of her stationary vehicle. You are vicariously liable for the negligence of your driver, Mr Williams.

A description of our client's injuries is as follows:

   (a)   whiplash injury to her cervical spine; and

   (b)   nervous reaction involving disturbance of sleep, flashbacks and panic
         attacks, particularly when travelling by car.

Our client received treatment for her injuries at the North London Hospital (hospital reference EJW 7469).

Our client is employed as a research assistant by Ellis Cuthbert Limited, Research Department, Manor Road, London N23 7PD, and had two weeks off work immediately following the accident. Her approximate net weekly income is £357.

We are obtaining a police report and will let you have a copy of the same upon you undertaking to meet half the fee.

We have also sent a letter of claim to Mr Williams, and a copy of that letter is attached.

At this stage of our enquiries we would expect the documents contained in Sections A and B of the RTA standard disclosure lists to be relevant to this claim.

A copy of this letter is attached for you to send to your insurers. Finally we expect an acknowledgement of this letter within 21 days by yourselves or your insurers.

Yours faithfully,

Buchanan & Co.

Figure 2.2 Standard disclosure list for road traffic accidents

Section A   In all cases where liability is at issue—

(i)   Documents identifying the nature, extent and location of damage to the defendant's vehicle where there is any dispute about the point of impact.

(ii)   MOT certificate where relevant.

(iii)   Maintenance records where a vehicle defect is alleged or if it is alleged by the defendant that there was an unforeseen defect which caused or contributed to the accident.

Section B   Accident involving commercial vehicle as potential defendant—

(i)   Tachograph charts or entry from individual control book.

(ii)   Maintenance and repair records required for operator's licence where vehicle defect is alleged or it is alleged by defendants that there was an unforeseen defect which caused or contributed to the accident.

Section C   Cases against local authorities where highway design defect is alleged—

(i)   Documents produced to comply with s. 39 of the Road Traffic Act 1988 in respect of the duty designed to promote road safety to include studies into road accidents in the relevant area and documents relating to measures recommended to prevent accidents in the relevant area.

2.5 Selection of Experts under the Protocol

The personal injuries protocol regards the joint instruction of a single expert to be the norm. It therefore provides that before the claimant (or any other party) instructs an expert he or she should give the other party a list of the name(s) of one or more experts in the relevant speciality who are considered suitable to instruct. Within 14 days the defendant may indicate an objection to one or more of the listed experts. Provided the defendant does not object to all the proposed experts, the claimant should then instruct a mutually acceptable expert from those remaining from the original list.

If the defendant objects to all the listed experts, the parties may instruct experts of their own choice. It would be for the court to decide subsequently, if proceedings are issued, whether either party had acted unreasonably. This might be because all the claimant's listed experts are known to produce reports slanted in favour of the claimant, or it might be that the defendant does not have sustainable rational reasons for having objected to all the experts proposed by the claimant.

Some solicitors choose to obtain medical reports through medical agencies, rather than directly from a specific doctor or hospital. The defendant's prior consent to this being done should be sought, and if the defendant so requests, the agency should be asked to provide in advance the names of the doctor(s) whom they are considering instructing.

Where a medical expert is to be instructed the claimant's solicitor will organise access to the relevant medical records. A model form of letter of instruction can be seen in **Figure 2.3**. This is adapted slightly from the model letter contained in the pre-action protocol, which is in one respect inconsistent with the CPR. The cost of a report from an agreed expert will usually be paid by the claimant. Any medical report obtained by agreement under the protocol should be disclosed to the other party. The claimant should delay issuing proceedings for 21 days from disclosure of the report, to enable the parties to consider whether the claim is capable of settlement.

Either party may send to the expert written questions on the report via the claimant's solicitors. The expert should send answers to the questions separately and directly to each party. The costs of the expert replying to questions will usually be borne by the party asking the questions.

Figure 2.3 Model letter of instruction to medical expert

Dear Sir,

Re: Our client: Eleanor Jane Weldon
     Our client's address: 47 Forest Road, London N10 4RS
     Our client's DoB: 14th July 1964
     Telephone No.:   0181 764 9933
     Date of accident: 26th November 1999

We are acting for Eleanor Weldon in connection with injuries received in a road traffic accident on 26th November 1999. The main injuries appear to have been a whiplash injury to her cervical spine and a nervous reaction involving disturbance of sleep, flashbacks and panic attacks, particularly when travelling by car.

We should be obliged if you would examine our client and let us have a full and detailed report dealing with any relevant pre-accident medical history, the injuries sustained, treatment received and present condition, dealing in particular with the capacity for work and giving a prognosis.

It is central to our assessment of the extent of our client's injuries to establish the extent and duration of any continuing disability. Accordingly, in the prognosis section we would ask you specifically to comment on any areas of continuing complaint or disability or impact on daily living. If there is such continuing disability you should comment upon the level of suffering or inconvenience caused and, if you are able, give your view as to when or if the complaint or disability is likely to resolve.

Please send our client an appointment direct for this purpose. Should you be able to offer a cancellation appointment please contact our client direct. We confirm we will be responsible for your reasonable fees.

We are obtaining the notes and records from our client's GP and hospitals attended, and will forward them to you when they are to hand.

In order to comply with Court Rules we would be grateful if you would address your report to 'The Court'. The report must refer to this letter and to any other written or oral instructions given, it must give details of your qualifications and of any literature or other materials used in compiling the report, and where there is a range of opinion it must summarise the range of opinion and give reasons for your opinion. At the end of the report you will need to include a statement that you understand your duty to the Court and have complied with it. Above your signature please include a statement in the following terms: 'I believe that the facts I have stated in this report are true and that the opinions I have expressed are correct.'

In order to avoid further correspondence we can confirm that on the evidence we have there is no reason to suspect we may be pursuing a claim against the hospital or its staff.

We look forward to receiving your report within six weeks. If you will not be able to prepare your report within this period please telephone us upon receipt of these instructions.

When acknowledging these instructions it would assist if you could give an estimate as to the likely time scale for the provision of your report and also an indication as to your fee.

Yours faithfully,

Buchanan & Co.

2.6 Compliance with the Protocol with Limitation Approaching

If the claimant consults a solicitor close to the end of the limitation period, the solicitor should give as much notice to the defendant of the intention to commence proceedings as is practicable. The parties may invite the court to extend the time for service of supporting documents and/or service of the defence, alternatively, for a stay of proceedings pending completion of the steps required by the protocol. However, solicitors must ensure they issue proceedings before limitation expires.

2.7 Failure to Comply

Obviously, there will be cases where either or both parties fail to comply with the requirements of a protocol. There may be a rational justification for doing so, and if this is accepted by the court there will be no adverse consequences. Where a failure to comply arises through slackness or deliberate flouting, a claimant may be justified in commencing proceedings without going through the rest of the procedures laid down in the protocol, and either party may find they are penalised by the court at a later stage.

If, in the opinion of the court, non-compliance has led to the commencement of proceedings which might otherwise not have needed to be commenced, or has led to costs being incurred in the proceedings that might otherwise not have been incurred, by virtue of the *Pre-Action Protocols Practice Direction*, para. 2.3, the orders that court may make include:

(a) an order that the party at fault pay the costs of the proceedings, or part of those costs, of the other party or parties.

(b) an order that the party at fault pay those costs on an indemnity basis;

(c) if the party at fault is a claimant in whose favour an order for the payment of damages or some specified sum is subsequently made, an order depriving that party of interest on such sum and in respect of such period as may be specified, and/or awarding interest at a lower rate than that at which interest would otherwise have been awarded;

(d) if the party at fault is a defendant and an order for the payment of damages or some specified sum is subsequently made in favour of the claimant, an order awarding interest on such sum and in respect of such period as may be specified at a higher rate, not exceeding 10% above base rate, rather than the rate at which interest would otherwise have been awarded.

The powers set out in (a) to (d) above are to be used to place the innocent party in no worse a position than he would have been in had the protocol been complied with.

Further, the court may make an order that the defaulting party should pay a sum of money into court if the default was without good reason (CPR, r. 3.1(5)).

It is expressly provided that if the court has to consider the question of compliance, it will not be concerned with minor infringements, such as the failure by a short period to provide relevant information. A single minor breach will not exempt the 'innocent' party from complying with the protocol.

Figure 2.4 Checklist for information to be obtained from clients in personal injuries claims

(1) Circumstances of the accident, to include:

   (a) Date of accident.

   (b) Where?

   (c) Who was involved?

   (d) Who is (are) the likely defendant(s)?

   (e) What happened?

   (f) Names and addresses of all witness known to the client.

(2) Did the police attend?

(3) Was there any other accident investigation?

(4) Were criminal proceedings brought as a result of the accident? If so, what was the result, and is a certificate of conviction available? Are notes of the hearing available?

(5) Nature of the injuries and treatment.

(6) Financial losses:

   (a) Employment.

   (b) Accident related damage to car, clothes etc.

   (c) Out of pocket expenses to date, including prescriptions, travel costs, physiotherapy, medical appliances.

   (d) Nursing care (including from family): how many hours per week, did it vary over time?

   (e) DIY loss? Gardening loss? Decorating loss? Car maintenance loss?

(7) Have the documents in support of the financial losses been preserved? These should include:

   (a) Pay slips, preferably from about six months before the accident to date.

   (b) P60s and P45s.

   (c) Any employment contract or service contract or letter of appointment.

   (d) Any correspondence about job applications since the injury, and any advertisements for jobs applied for.

   (e) Receipts for out of pocket expenses.

   (f) Correspondence about matters such as pension rights, early retirement etc.

(8) The client's GP and hospital notes and records will need to be obtained.

(9) You will need the client's date of birth for the Particulars of Claim (this is often in the medical notes).

(10) The client's National Insurance number will be needed for the Compensation Recovery Unit certificate of recoupable benefits.

Figure 2.5 Table showing timetable laid down by the personal injury pre-action protocol

Time	Comments
Soon after being retained	Solicitor should consider whether an informal notification of the possible claim should be made to the defendant. This will not start the protocol timetable.
Letter of claim	This should be sent at least six months before the expiry of limitation to give time for compliance before limitation expires. Two copies of the letter should be sent to the defendant, or one to the defendant and one to the insurer.
Twenty-one days	Defendant should reply with name of insurer, or the insurer should acknowledge.
Three months from acknowledging letter of claim	Defendant should have completed investigations. If liability is denied or if contributory negligence is alleged the defendant should provide documents on liability and reasons for the denial.
(Say) one month after denial	If contributory negligence has been alleged, the claimant should respond to these allegations.
(Say) one month after defendant's letter	Claimant sends defendant a Schedule of Special Damages and documents in support. This is particularly important where liability has been admitted.
At same time	Claimant sends defendant a list of suggested experts for each field of expertise. The letter should also state the basis of the proposed joint instructing of the necessary experts: that the expert will be sent a letter of instruction in accordance with the protocol, and that a copy of the report when obtained will be immediately sent to the other side.
Fourteen days thereafter	Defendant has this time to raise any objections to the suggested experts.
Defendant objects to all suggested experts	Both parties are free to instruct their own experts. This may be penalised in costs later if either side has acted unreasonably.
Defendant does not object	Claimant selects an expert from those left, and sends a letter of instruction in accordance with the standard letter.
Receipt of report	Claimant's solicitor sends copies to client and defendant's insurer/solicitor.
Ditto	Parties consider sending questions to clarify the report to the expert. The defendant should send its questions via the claimant's solicitors.
Ditto	Parties should consider sending Part 36 offers to the other side.
Ditto	Parties should consider whether mediation or ADR might be appropriate.
Fourteen days before issue	Claimant should ask the defendant's insurers to nominate solicitors.
Fourteen days	Issue proceedings.

2.8 Notice of Proceedings

Drivers are compulsorily required by the Road Traffic Act 1988 (RTA 1988) to be insured against liability for personal injuries and death in road accidents. Three matters connected with this are discussed below.

2.8.1 RECOVERY AGAINST INSURER

A person injured in a road accident has no cause of action against a negligent driver's insurer. However, a claimant may recover damages direct from the driver's insurer, once a judgment has been obtained against the driver, provided the claimant gives the insurer notice of the proceedings against the defendant driver before or within seven days after proceedings are commenced: RTA 1988, s. 152. With regard to the form of notice, see *Desouza* v *Waterlow*, *The Independent*, 27 October 1997, CA.

2.8.2 UNINSURED DRIVERS

The Motor Insurer's Bureau has been set up by the insurance industry to provide compensation to victims of road accidents who cannot bring effective proceedings in the usual way. To this end, two agreements have been made between the Motor Insurers' Bureau and the Minister for Transport.

Under the first agreement, provided the victim satisfies a number of conditions (including giving the Motor Insurers' Bureau notice of proceedings against the negligent driver within seven days of commencement), the Bureau will pay any award of damages against an uninsured driver in respect of compulsorily insurable risks if the judgment is not paid within seven days.

2.8.3 UNTRACED DRIVERS

Under the second agreement, the Motor Insurers' Bureau will pay damages to road accident victims where the driver responsible is unidentified (e.g. a 'hit and run' driver). As there is no known defendant in such cases, claims are dealt with administratively. The Bureau considers the victim's injuries and the blame for the accident, reducing the compensation payable accordingly. The claimant can appeal from the assessment to an arbitrator, who is often a Q.C.

2.9 Other Pre-action Notices

For other types of proceedings notices of various sorts have to be sent before proceedings are issued. Examples are default notices in consumer credit cases, notice to quit and other statutory notices in landlord and tenant cases, demands in cases where money is payable on demand, and notice of assignment. These types of notices are laid down in the substantive law dealing with various different causes of action.

2.10 Pre-action Relief

The CPR allow parties to make applications before commencing the main proceedings in certain situations. The main ones are when the need for a court order arises in urgent circumstances such that there is no time to issue a claim form before having to go before the judge (a situation most frequently encountered when applying for injunctions), and in cases where it would be helpful to obtain evidence before commencing proceedings to check whether there is a good case against the proposed defendants. These situations will be considered further in **Chapters 10, 14–16** and **21**.

THREE

COMMENCEMENT OF PROCEEDINGS

3.1 Introduction

Proceedings are commenced usually by issuing a claim form. There is a prescribed form for this document. There are some other methods of commencing proceedings, and they will be considered at the end of this chapter. Issuing involves the court sealing the form with its official seal. This is an important event, because it stops time running for limitation purposes, and starts time running for service. Generally, a claim form must be served within four months of being issued. In certain circumstances the four month period may be extended, which is a subject considered in **Chapter 25**. The main topics that will be considered in this chapter will be issuing and serving proceedings.

3.2 Which Court?

Before issuing proceedings it is necessary to decide whether to use the High Court or the County Court. The High Court can generally be used in money claims with a value exceeding £15,000. A major exception is personal injuries cases, which may only be started in the High Court if they have a value exceeding £50,000. In claims where money is not the remedy being sought, it is a matter of professional judgement whether the importance and complexity of the case justifies using the High Court. These questions were considered in more detail at **1.3.2** above.

The second question is to decide on the location of the court to use. The High Court sits not only in London but also in a number of regional District Registries. There are also County Courts throughout the country. Essentially this is a question of convenience. Generally the claimant's solicitor is given the choice as to which local court to use, and as a practical matter will probably have the convenience of the claimant primarily in mind. However, if the case is defended the court will give primary consideration to the convenience of the defendant. A claimant wishing to avoid delay through the case being transferred may well decide to use the court most local to the defendant. Sometimes there is no choice. Proceedings seeking possession of residential property have to be commenced in the County Court serving the district where the property is situated.

3.3 The Claim Form

It is the responsibility of the claimant's solicitors to prepare the claim form before issue. For most proceedings there is a general purpose claim form (Form N1, see **Figure 3.1**) that should be used. To commence specialist proceedings, special claim forms as approved by any relevant Practice Direction should be used. A completed claim form will:

(a) set out the names and addresses of the respective parties;

(b) Give a concise statement of the nature of the claim;

(c) State the remedy sought; and

(d) Contain a statement of value where the claim is for money. This will be the amount sought if the claim can be specified, or, if not, whether it is expected the amount that will be recovered is no more than £5,000; between £5,000 and £15,000; or more than £15,000. In some cases all that can be said is that the amount cannot be stated. In personal injuries claims the amount expected for pain, suffering and loss of amenity must be stated as being either below or above £1,000.

Figure 3.1   Claim Form

Royal Arms *Claim Form*	In the High Court of Justice Queen's Bench Division Manchester District Registry
	Claim No. 2000 S No. 98744
Claimant Shilton Machine Tools Limited 18 Rotherham Road, Manchester M36 3BJ	SEAL
Defendant Banks Plastic Mouldings Limited	
Brief details of claim Price of goods sold and delivered, plus interest.	
Value £70,500.00	
Defendant's name and address	£

		£
	Amount claimed	70,500.00
Banks Plastic Mouldings Limited	Court fee	400.00
Registered office:	Solicitor's costs	
Unit 6,	Issue date	5.10.2000
Elland Trading Estate,		
Leeds LS8 3AN		

The court office at The Courts of Justice, Crown Square, Manchester M60 9DJ is open between 10 am and 4 pm Monday to Friday. When corresponding with the court, please address forms and letters to the Court Manager and quote the claim number,

---

Claim No. 2000 S No. 98744

Particulars of claim (attached) (to follow)

1.   By a contract contained in or evidenced by the Defendant's Order dated the 10th March 2000 the Claimant agreed to sell and deliver four plastic moulding machines to the Defendant for the sum of £60,000 plus VAT.

2.   Despite delivering the machine tools to the Defendant and rendering an invoice number ST9922 dated the 8th May 2000 the Defendant has failed to pay all or any of the price of the machines.

PARTICULARS

Price of the machine tools	£60,000.00
VAT at 17.5%	£10,500.00
Total	£70,500.00

3.   Payment was due 30 days after invoice. The Claimant is entitled to interest at the rate of 8% per annum pursuant to the Supreme Court Act 1981, section 35A on the sum of £70,500 from the 7th June 2000 to the 22nd September 2000 amounting to £1,653.36, and continuing from the 23rd September 2000 to judgment or earlier payment at the daily rate of £15.45.

AND the claimant claims:

1.   The sum of £70,500.00.

2.   Interest on the sum of £70,500 pursuant to the Supreme Court Act 1981, section 35A amounting to £1,653.36 to the 22nd September 2000, and continuing at the daily rate of £15.45.

Statement of Truth

(I believe) (The Claimant believes) that the facts stated in these particulars of claim are true.

I am duly authorised by the Claimant to sign this statement.

Full name Name of claimants' solicitor's firm	Boardman, Phipps & Co.
signed (Claimant) (Litigation friend) (Claimant's solicitor)	position or office held (if signing on behalf of firm or company)
delete as appropriate	
20 High Street, Manchester M15 9CZ	Claimant's or Claimant's solicitor's address to which documents should be sent if different from overleaf. If you are prepared to accept service by DX, fax or e-mail, please add details

3.4   **Jurisdictional Indorsements**

In cases that are to be issued in the High Court the claim form must, unless the claim is for a specified amount, be indorsed with either:

(a)   a statement that the claimant expects to recover more than £15,000 (or more than £50,000 in personal injuries claims); or

(b)   a statement that a named enactment provides that the claim may only be commenced in the High Court; or

(c)   a statement that the claim is for a named specialist High Court list, or the claim form must comply with the requirements laid down in a Practice Direction for one of the specialist lists.

Examples are:

(a) 'I expect to recover more than £15,000.'

(b) 'My claim includes a claim for personal injuries and the value of the claim is £50,000 or more.'

3.5 Particulars of Claim

Particulars of claim is the term used to describe the formal written statement setting out the nature of the claimant's case together with the nature of the relief or remedy sought from the defendant. It can be included in the claim form (on the reverse of the form), or be set out in a separate document. An example of a short form of particulars of claim in a debt recovery action can be seen on the claim form shown in **Figure 3.1**. If a separate document is used it must be served either with the claim form, or within 14 days after service of the claim form (CPR, r. 7.4(1)), and in any event within the period of validity of the claim form (usually four months from issue, see CPR, r. 7.4(2)). If contained in a separate document the claim form must state that the particulars are either attached or will follow (by deleting words at the top of the second page of the form). Further information regarding the contents of particulars of claim can be found in **Chapter 5**.

3.6 Issuing the Claim Form

The claimant's solicitors will make sufficient copies of the claim form for themselves, the court and each defendant. They retain one, and send the others to the court office, together with the prescribed fee under cover of a letter asking for the claim to be issued. Alternatively, the claimant's solicitors may attend personally at the court office to ensure the claim is issued, which may be sensible if time is short. If the documents are sent by post, the court office stamps the covering letter when it is received. In such a case time stops running for limitation period purposes on the date the covering letter is date stamped by the court rather than the date (if later) the claim form is issued (PD 7, paras 5.1, 5.2). The court issues the claim by sealing the claim forms, and enters details of the claim in its records. On issuing the claim the court will allocate a claim number to the case, which it endorses on the claim forms. The court then sends a form called a notice of issue to the claimant's solicitors that tells them the claim number, date of issue, confirms receipt of the issue fee, and, if service is effected by the court, also confirms the date of service.

3.7 Service

Service on a defendant in England and Wales must be effected within four months of issue. The period of validity for service is six months if the defendant is to be served outside the jurisdiction (CPR, r. 7.5(3)). Under the Civil Procedure Rules 1998 (unlike previous versions of the rules of court) there is a single system dealing with service, whether the document to be served is the originating process (primarily this is the claim form, but also the other types of process described at **3.12** and **3.13**), or of other documents during the course of proceedings (such as statements of case, lists of documents, and application notices). It is worth noting that 'service' deals with providing documents to the other side, and the related concept of 'filing' deals with providing documents to the court.

3.7.1 ADDRESS FOR SERVICE

The CPR, r. 6.5, sets out in tabular form the appropriate places of service for different types of party. For individuals it is their usual or last known residence. For limited liability companies it is their principal office or any place of business having a real connection with the dispute (CPR, r. 6.5) or registered office (Companies Act 1985,

s. 725). For the purposes of service of a claim form, if the defendant's solicitor is authorised to accept service for the defendant, service must be effected at the defendant's solicitor's office (CPR, r. 6.13(2)). More generally, when any party is acting by a solicitor all documents must be served at the address of the party's solicitor (CPR, r. 6.5(5)).

Figure 3.2   Addresses for service for different kinds of party

Nature of party to be served	Place of service
Individual	Usual or last known residence
Proprietor of business	Usual or last known residence, or place of business or last known place of business
Individual who is suing or being sued in the name of a firm	Usual or last known residence, or principal or last known place of business of the firm
Corporation incorporated in England and Wales other than a company	Principal office of the corporation, or any place within in the jurisdiction where the corporation carries on its activities and which has a real connection with the claim
Company registered in England and Wales	Principal office of the company, or any place of business of the company within the jurisdiction which has a real connection with the claim. Note, a company may also be served at its registered office
Any other company or corporation	Any place within the jurisdiction where the corporation carries on its activities, or any place of business of the company within the jurisdiction

3.7.2   DOCUMENTS TO BE SERVED

The documents to be served comprise the sealed claim form, the particulars of claim (although these may follow), and a 'response pack'. The response pack consists of practice forms of acknowledgment of service, admission, defence and counterclaim. Form N9 is a combined cover sheet for the response pack and tear off acknowledgment of service form. The defence and counterclaim is also a combined form. There are two types of admission form and also two types of defence and counterclaim form. Forms N9A and N9B are for use in claims for specified amounts of money. Forms N9C and N9D are for use in claims for unspecified sums of money and in non-money claims.

In personal injuries claims the particulars of claim will have to be accompanied by a medical report and schedule of loss and expense, and these must be served with the claim form if the particulars of claim are served at the same time. In legal aid cases a notice of issue of legal aid had to be served with the claim form and it is anticipated there will be a similar requirement for parties assisted by the Community Legal Service.

3.7.3   METHODS OF SERVICE

Permissible methods of service are set out in CPR, r. 6.2:

(1)   A document may be served by any of the following methods—

> (a)   personal service, in accordance with r. 6.4;
> (b)   first class post;
> (c)   leaving the document at a place specified in r. 6.5 [the address for service];
> (d)   through a document exchange in accordance with the relevant practice direction; or
> (e)   by fax or other means of electronic communication in accordance with the relevant practice direction.

3.7.3.1   Personal service

Personal service of a document is effected by leaving a copy of the document with the person to be served. If a person (whom it is intended to serve) has knowledge of the nature of the document and has been given a sufficient opportunity of possession to enable that person to exercise dominion over it for any period of time, however short, it will amount to 'leaving' for the purpose of this rule: *Nottingham Building Society* v *Peter Bennett & Co. (a firm)*, *The Times*, 26 February 1997, CA.

Personal service on a company means service on a person in a senior position, which in turn means a director, treasurer, secretary, chief executive, manager or other officer (PD 6, para. 6.2).

Personal service on partners sued in the name of the partnership is effected by leaving the claim form with a partner or a person having the control or management of the partnership business at its principal place of business (CPR, r. 6.4(5)). When effecting service in this way, at the same time it is necessary to serve a notice stating whether the person being served is served as a partner, or as having control or management, or both (PD 6, para. 4.2).

3.7.3.2   Document exchange (DX)

This is a system used by the great majority of solicitors and chambers, and a number of other businesses, for transporting documents between their offices. It only works between offices using the system. Members pay periodic lumps sums for the service. Generally documents put into the document exchange system arrive the next business day, although there are occasional delays. It is only a permissible method of service if the other side's solicitors are users of the document exchange system and have indicated a willingness to accept service through the DX system. Such a willingness may be evidenced by including a DX number on the solicitor's usual headed letter paper (PD 6, para. 2.1).

3.7.3.3   Electronic methods of service

As to fax and e-mail, PD 6, para. 3, requires the recipient to have previously indicated in writing a willingness for service to be accepted in this way. Where the recipient is acting in person, the willingness to accept service by fax must be stated in writing (para. 3.1(3)(a)). Where the recipient is acting by a solicitor, such a willingness may be shown by including a fax or e-mail number in the solicitor's printed stationery. There is no need to confirm service by fax or e-mail by sending a second copy by post or DX (PD 6, para. 3.4), but there may be later problems if there is a dispute about non-receipt.

3.7.3.4   Usual method of service

Generally service will be by the court (CPR, r. 6.3), but there are exceptions, the main one being where the party notifies the court he wishes to do it himself. Court service will generally be by first class post (PD 6, para. 8.1).

3.8   Deemed Date of Service

By CPR, r. 6.7, documents are deemed to be served on the day shown in **Figure 3.3**.

Figure 3.3   Deemed dates of service

Method of service	Deemed day of service
First class post	The second day after it was posted
Document exchange	The second day after it was left at the document exchange
Delivering the document or leaving it at a permitted address	The day after it was delivered or left at the permitted address
Fax	If it is transmitted on a business day before 4 pm, on that day, or in any other case, on the business day after the day on which it is transmitted
Other electronic method	The second day after the day on which it is transmitted
Personal service before 5 pm on a business day	Day of delivery
Personal service after 5 pm or on a non-business day	The following business day

These periods are calculated by excluding Saturdays, Sundays, bank holidays, Christmas Day and Good Friday, as they are periods less than five days (CPR, r. 2.8(4)). However, they are not periods of 'a number of days', so they are not computed as clear days (see r. 2.8(2)). A claimant effecting service must file a certificate of service within seven days of service (CPR, r. 6.14). An example is shown in **Figure 3.4**.

Figure 3.4   Certificate of service

Certificate of service	
	In the High Court of Justice Queen's Bench Division Manchester District Registry **Claim No.** 2000 S No. 98744 **Claimant** Shilton Machine Tools Limited **Defendant** Banks Plastic Mouldings Limited
On the 12th October 2000 the claim form and response pack a copy of which is attached to this notice was served on Banks Plastic Mouldings Limited	
☐ by first class post ☐ by delivering to or leaving ☐ by fax machine (.......... time sent) *(you may want to enclose a copy of the transmission sheet)*	☐ by Document Exchange ☐ by handling it to or leaving it with
☐ by other means (please specify)	
at (*insert address where service effected, including fax of DX number or e-mail address*)	Unit 6, Elland Trading Estate, Leeds LS8 3AN

being the Defendant's:
☐ residence   ☐ registered office
☐ place of business   ☐ other *(please specify)*

The date of service is therefore deemed to be 16th October 2000 *(insert date — see over for guidance)*
I confirm that at the time of signing this Certificate the document has not been returned to me as undelivered.

Signed: Position or
          Claimant's Solicitor   office held
Date: 18th October   *(if signing on behalf of firm or company)*

The deeming provisions regarding the date of service ought almost certainly to be read as being subject to the contrary being shown. Words to the effect 'unless the contrary is shown' do not appear in CPR, r. 6.7, which is the rule setting out the periods after which service is deemed to be effected. The words 'unless the contrary is proved' do, however, appear in PD 6, para. 2.2, which deals with service by DX. It will also be noticed that the certificate of service in **Figure 3.4** expressly has a declaration that the document served has not been returned undelivered. Further, it has to be contrary to the overriding objective of dealing with cases justly if the presumptions as to the date of service in r. 6.7 were irrebuttable. The result has to be that if a party can show they did not in fact receive the document in question, then they have not been served (or not effectively served).

If this is right, then the position is not very different than the position under the old rules. In *Forward* v *West Sussex County Council* [1995] 4 All ER 207 the Court of Appeal said that service by post in accordance with the old rules created a good working presumption of due service, but it was a rebuttable presumption. Whether there had been actual service depended on whether the document had come to the notice of the defendant. In this case the defendant had moved away from the address last known to the claimant five months before posting, so the writ (which was the document being served) had not come to his notice despite being sent to his 'last known address', and a declaration was made that the writ had not been served.

In *Barclays Bank of Swaziland Ltd* v *Hahn* [1989] 1 WLR 506, HL, the Bank inserted an envelope containing the writ through the letter-box of the defendant's flat in England at 3.30 p.m. on 14 April 1987. The defendant was then *en route* from South Africa, and landed at Heathrow at 5.30 p.m. The defendant was met at the airport by his caretaker, who warned him about the envelope. Instead of going home, the defendant stayed overnight in a hotel, then flew out of the country the next day. The House of Lords held that under the old rule the defendant must be within the jurisdiction at the time when the writ is served, which the defendant was not. Lord Brightman, with whom the other members of the House agreed, went on to point out that the purpose of serving a writ is to give the defendant knowledge of the existence of the proceedings, and therefore a claimant could displace the deemed date of service by proving the defendant acquired knowledge of the writ at some other date. On the facts, the Bank could 'show the contrary' because the defendant's conduct made it transparently clear that he knew of the writ in the evening of 14 April 1987.

3.9   Consensual Service

Service in accordance with an *ad hoc* agreement between the parties as to the mode of service reached just before service was effected was held to be valid under the old system even though it was strictly outside the rules regulating service: *Kenneth Allison Ltd* v *A. E. Limehouse & Co. (a firm)* [1992] 2 AC 105, HL.

It is possible that the same result would be achieved under the present rules. At one time it was suggested that the new rules should simply say that service could be effected by bringing the document to the notice of the other party without specifying approved methods of doing so. That suggestion has not been incorporated into the CPR, but an agreement such as that in *Kenneth Allison* does bring the proceedings to the notice of the defendant, and as the method is one agreed to by the defendant it is difficult to see why the power to remedy errors of procedure (see **1.4.3**) should not be used if need be.

3.10 Alternative Service

Sometimes it is not possible to effect service using the various methods set out above. The defendant may be evading service, or prove difficult to find. In such cases it is sometimes possible to persuade the court to allow service by an alternative method. An application for such an order needs to be supported by written evidence which must:

(a) state the reason alternative service is sought; and

(b) describe the steps taken to attempt service by the permitted means.

Examples of possible methods of alternative service are by advertisement in a newspaper; by affixing a copy to the door of the defendant's house where the defendant is 'keeping house' and has no letter-box; and service on the defendant at the address of his or her insurer. In *Abbey National Plc* v *Frost; Solicitors' Indemnity Fund Intervening* [1999] 1 WLR 1080, which involved a claim against a solicitor, it was held that an order to effect alternative service of proceedings upon the Solicitors' Indemnity Fund would be allowed.

3.11 Objecting to Jurisdiction

A defendant who wishes to object to the court having jurisdiction over a claim should make an application pursuant to CPR, Part 11. The main provisions of Part 11 are as follows:

> *(1)   A defendant who wishes to—*
> *(a)   dispute the court's jurisdiction to try the claim; or*
> *(b)   argue that the court should not exercise its jurisdiction,*
> *may apply to the court for an order declaring that it has no such jurisdiction or should not exercise any jurisdiction which it may have.*
> *(2)   A defendant who wishes to make such an application must first file an acknowledgment of service in accordance with Part 10.*
> *(3)   A defendant who files an acknowledgment of service does not, by doing so, lose any right he may have to dispute the court's jurisdiction.*
> *(4)   An application under this rule must—*
> *(a)   be made within the period for filing a defence and*
> *(b)   be supported by evidence.*
> *(5)   If the defendant–*
> *(a)   files an acknowledgment of service; and*
> *(b)   does not make such an application within the period for filing a defence,*
> *he is to be treated as having accepted that the court has jurisdiction to try the claim.*
> *. . .*
> *(9)   Where a defendant makes an application under this rule he need not file a defence before the hearing of the application.*

In the pre-CPR case of *Patel* v *Patel* [1999] 3 WLR 322, it was held that merely applying to set aside a default judgment did not amount to taking a step in the proceedings, and did not prevent the defendant from disputing the court's jurisdiction.

3.12   Other Types of Originating Process

There are a number of other forms used for commencing proceedings (these are called forms of originating process), two of the most common alternatives being:

(a)   Part 8 claim forms, which are used in cases where there is no dispute of fact. These are discussed further at **3.13**; and

(b)   Petitions, which are used in divorce proceedings, bankruptcy and winding up. The matrimonial and insolvency fields have their own detailed procedural rules, and will not be considered further in this Manual. They are considered in the *Family Law in Practice* and *Company Law in Practice Manuals*.

In addition, there are a number of miscellaneous forms of originating process referred to in various of the old RSC and CCR provisions preserved in schs 1 and 2 to the CPR. These are mostly highly specialised, and again will not be considered further here.

3.13   Part 8 Claims

The main type of originating process under the CPR is the claim form previously discussed, and it is used for almost all types of proceedings where there is likely to be dispute of fact. As will be seen in **Chapter 5**, the issues raised in such claims are defined in written statements of case that have to be served and filed by each party. An alternative procedure for bringing a claim is that laid down in CPR, Part 8. A claim brought under Part 8 has its own 'Part 8 claim form'. Part 8 claims are for use where there is no substantial dispute of fact (CPR, r. 8.1(2)(a)). They perform a similar function to what used to be called a construction summons under the old rules, which was a type of originating process technically called an originating summons, often brought by a trustee or executor, seeking the court's ruling on the true meaning of a clause in a trust deed or will. In such cases the court is simply being asked to construe a document, and there should be no dispute of fact. Also like the old originating summons, a Part 8 claim can be used for some applications pursuant to statute/statutory instrument. For example, Part 8 claims are used for approval of children's settlements where proceedings have not been commenced (CPR, r. 21.10(2)).

A Part 8 claim form must state that Part 8 applies, and must set out the question the claimant wants the court to decide or the remedy sought. If the claim is brought pursuant to statute the relevant statute must be stated (CPR, r. 8.2). Otherwise, a Part 8 claim form looks very much like an ordinary claim form. Note, however, that under r. 8.2A a Practice Direction may set out circumstances in which a Part 8 claim form may be used without naming a defendant.

Any evidence the claimant relies upon must be filed and served with the claim form (CPR, r. 8.5(1), (2)). After the claim form has been issued and served, any defendants have 14 days to acknowledge service (r. 8.3(1)). An acknowledgment will usually be on the official form, Form N210, but may be given informally by letter (PD 8, para. 3.2). Defendants must file their evidence when they acknowledge service. The claimant may file and serve evidence in reply within 14 days thereafter (r. 8.5(5), (6)).

Part 8 claims are treated as allocated to the multi-track (CPR, r. 8.9(c)).

3.14   Specialist Proceedings

The Practice Directions governing specialist proceedings (PD 49 to PD 49G) often lay down different requirements for things such as acknowledging service (sometimes with acknowledgment being required after service of the claim form but before service of the claimant's statement of case), track allocation and directions.

3.15 Filing

Documents are filed by being delivered to the court. A court manager has no jurisdiction to refuse to accept a document (for example) on the ground it should have been filed in another County Court (*Gwynedd County Council* v *Grunshaw* (1999) 149 NLJ 1286). If the court is closed on the final day for filing a document, filing will be in time if effected on the next day the court is open (*Aadan* v *Brent London Borough Council, The Times*, 5 November 1999).

FOUR

RESPONDING TO A CLAIM

4.1   Introduction

Time only starts running against a defendant from service of the particulars of claim. A defendant served with a claim form without particulars of claim need do nothing, although once a claim form has been served it is fairly predictable that particulars of claim will follow in the near future. As mentioned earlier, in fact the particulars of claim should be served within 14 days of service of the claim form. Once the particulars of claim have been served the defendant has a limited time to decide what to do and to do it. Essentially the time available is 14 days from the date of service of the particulars of claim.

After service of the particulars of claim the defendant has a choice of:

(a)   filing an admission;

(b)   filing a defence, which may be combined with making a counterclaim; or

(c)   filing an acknowledgment of service.

4.2   Admissions

A defendant who admits the claim is normally best advised to complete the admission form (N9A or N9C depending on whether the claim is for a specified sum of money) included in the response pack. The response pack form is illustrated at **Figure 4.1**, and the admission form N9A is illustrated at **Figure 4.2**. The admission form allows the defendant to admit either the whole claim or just a part. If the whole claim is admitted, the defendant needs to decide about payment. If the whole sum is paid within 14 days of service of the claim form, the defendant's liability for the claimant's costs will be limited to certain fixed sums laid down in the rules. This assists the defendant, because fixed costs are considerably lower than the sums recoverable in contested litigation. The admission form also allows a defendant who wants time to pay to make an offer to pay by instalments. If this is done the defendant must also complete a large number of questions set out in the form dealing with the defendant's personal and financial circumstances. The form will be returned to the court, and a copy provided to the claimant. The claimant will then consider the offer, and if it is acceptable will notify the court and a judgment will be entered for payment by the instalments offered by the defendant. If the claimant does not agree to the offer to pay by instalments, the rules make provision for the rate of payment to be determined by the court.

A defendant can also use the admission form to make a partial admission, denying the rest of the claim. The part that is denied has to be dealt with in a defence, which should be filed at court together with the admission form. Again, if this happens the claimant is asked whether the partial admission is acceptable, and if so a judgment will be entered in that sum.

Figure 4.1

Response Pack

You should read the 'notes for defendant' attached to the claim form which will tell you when and where to send the forms

Included in this pack are:

- either **Admission Form N9A** (if the claim is for a specified amount) or **Admission Form N9C** (if the claim is for an unspecified amount or is not a claim for money)
- either **Defence and Counterclaim Form N9B** (if the claim is for a specified amount) or **Defence and Counterclaim Form N9D** (if the claim is for an unspecified amount or is not a claim for money)
- **Acknowledgment of service** (see below)

Complete

If you admit the claim or the amount claimed and/or you want time to pay ►	the admission form
If you admit part of the claim ►	the admission form and the defence form
If you dispute the whole claim or wish to make a claim (a counterclaim) against the claimant ►	the defence form
If you need 28 days (rather than 14) from the date of service to prepare your defence, or wish to contest the court's jurisdiction ►	the acknowledgment of service
If you do nothing, judgment may be entered against you	

Acknowledgment of Service

Defendant's full name if different from the name given on the claim form

In the	High Court of Justice Queen's Bench Division Manchester District Registry
Claim No.	
Claimant (including ref.)	Shilton Machine Tools Limited
Defendant	Banks Plastic Mouldings Limited

Address to which documents about this claim should be sent (including reference if appropriate)

	if applicable
fax no.	
DX no.	
e-mail	

Tel. no.   Postcode

Tick the appropriate box

1. I intend to defend all of this claim ☐

2. I intend to defend part of this claim ☐

3. I intend to contest jurisdiction ☐

If you file an acknowledgment of service but do not file a defence within 28 days of the date of service of the claim form, or particulars of claim if served separately, judgment may be entered against you.

If you do not file an application within 28 days of the date of service of the claim form, or particulars of claim if served separately, it will be assumed that you accept the court's jurisdiction and judgment may be entered against you.

Signed

(Defendant)(Defendant's solicitor) (Litigation friend)

Position or office held
(if signing on behalf of firm or company)

Date

The court office at The Courts of Justice, Crown Square, Manchester M60 9DJ

is open between 10 am and 4 pm Monday to Friday. When corresponding with the court, please address forms or letters to the Court Manager and quote the claim number.

N9 m3 Response Pack (4.99)   Produced on behalf of The Court Service

Figure 4.2

Admission (specified amount)

- You have a limited number of days to complete and return this form
- Before completing this form, please read the notes for guidance attached to the claim form

When to fill in this form
- Only fill in this form if you are admitting all or some of the claim **and** you are asking for time to pay

How to fill in this form
- Tick the correct boxes and give as much information as you can. **Then sign and date the form.** If necessary provide details on a separate sheet, add the claim number and attach it to this form.
- Make your offer of payment in box 11 on the back of this form. **If you make no offer the claimant will decide how much and when you should pay.**
- If you are not an individual, you should ensure that you provide sufficient details about the assets and liabilities of your firm, company or corporation to support any offer of payment made in box 11.
- You can get help to complete this form at **any** county court office or Citizens Advice Bureau.

Where to send this form
- **If you admit the claim in full**
  Send the completed form to the address shown on the claim form as one to which documents should be sent.
- **If you admit only part of the claim**
  Send the form **to the court** at the address given on the claim form, together with the defence form (N9B).

How much of the claim do you admit?

- I admit the full amount claimed as shown on the claim form   **or**
- I admit the amount of   £ _____

1   Personal details

Surname _____

Forename _____

☐ Mr ☐ Mrs ☐ Miss ☐ Ms

☐ Married ☐ Single ☐ Other *(specify)* _____

Age _____

Address _____

Postcode _____

Tel. no. _____

In the	
Claim No.	
Claimant (including ref.)	
Defendant	

2   Dependants   *(people you look after financially)*

Number of children in each age group

under 11 ☐   11-15 ☐   16-17 ☐   18 & over ☐

Other dependants *(give details)* _____

3   Employment

☐ **I am employed as a** _____
My employer is _____

Jobs other than
main job *(give details)* _____

☐ **I am self employed as a** _____

Annual turnover is........................... £ _____

☐ **I am not** in arrears with my national insurance contributions, income tax and VAT

☐ **I am** in arrears and I owe........... £ _____

Give details of:
(a) contracts and other work in hand _____
(b) any sums due for work done _____

☐ **I have been unemployed for** ___ years ___ months

☐ **I am a pensioner**

4   Bank account and savings

☐ **I have a bank account**
☐ The account is in credit by........ £ _____
☐ The account is overdrawn by.... £ _____

☐ **I have a savings or building society account**
The amount in the account is......... £ _____

5   Residence

I live in ☐ my own house   ☐ lodgings
☐ my jointly owned house   ☐ council accommodation
☐ rented accommodation

N9A -w3- Form of admission (specified amount) (4.99)   Produced on behalf of The Court Service

6 Income

My usual take home pay *(including overtime, commission, bonuses etc)*	£	per
Income support	£	per
Child benefit(s)	£	per
Other state benefit(s)	£	per
My pension(s)	£	per
Others living in my home give me	£	per
Other income *(give details below)*		
	£	per
	£	per
	£	per
Total income	**£**	**per**

8 Priority debts *(This section is for arrears only. Do not include regular expenses listed in box 7.)*

Rent arrears	£	per
Mortgage arrears	£	per
Council tax/Community Charge arrears	£	per
Water charges arrears	£	per
Fuel debts: Gas	£	per
Electricity	£	per
Other	£	per
Maintenance arrears	£	per
Others *(give details below)*		
	£	per
	£	per
Total priority debts	**£**	**per**

7 Expenses

(Do not include any payments made by other members of the household out of their own income)

I have regular expenses as follows:

Mortgage *(including second mortgage)*	£	per
Rent	£	per
Council tax	£	per
Gas	£	per
Electricity	£	per
Water charges	£	per
TV rental and licence	£	per
HP repayments	£	per
Mail order	£	per
Housekeeping, food, school meals	£	per
Travelling expenses	£	per
Children's clothing	£	per
Maintenance payments	£	per
Others *(not court orders or credit debts listed in boxes 9 and 10)*		
	£	per
	£	per
	£	per
Total expenses	**£**	**per**

9 Court orders

Court	Claim No.	£	per

Total court order instalments	**£**	**per**

Of the payments above, I am behind with payments to *(please list)*

10 Credit debts

Loans and credit card debts *(please list)*

	£	per
	£	per
	£	per

Of the payments above, I am behind with payments to *(please list)*

11 Offer of payment

☐ I can pay the amount admitted on

or

☐ I can pay by monthly instalments of £

If you cannot pay immediately, please give brief reasons below

12 Declaration

I declare that the details I have given above are true to the best of my knowledge

Signed

Date

Position or office held *(if signing on behalf of firm or company)*

Figure 4.3

Defence and Counterclaim (specified amount)

In the	High Court of Justice Queen's Bench Division Manchester District Registry

Claim No.	
Claimant (including ref.)	Shilton Machine Tools Limited
Defendant	Banks Plastic Mouldings Limited

- Fill in this form if you wish to dispute all or part of the claim and/or make a claim against the claimant (counterclaim).
- You have a limited number of days to complete and return this form to the court.
- Before completing this form, please read the notes for guidance attached to the claim form.
- Please ensure that all boxes at the top right of this form are completed. You can obtain the correct names and number from the claim form. The court cannot trace your case without this information.

How to fill in this form
- Complete sections 1 and 2. Tick the correct boxes and give the other details asked for.
- Set out your defence in section 3. If necessary continue on a separate piece of paper making sure that the claim number is clearly shown on it. In your defence you must state which allegations in the particulars of claim you deny and your reasons for doing so. **If you fail to deny an allegation it may be taken that you admit it.**
- If you dispute only some of the allegations you must
  - specify which you admit and which you deny; and
  - give your own version of events if different from the claimant's.

- If you wish to make a claim against the claimant (a counterclaim) complete section 4.
- Complete and sign section 5 before sending this form to the court. Keep a copy of the claim form and this form.

Legal Aid
- You may be entitled to legal aid. Ask about the legal aid scheme at any county court office, Citizens Advice Bureau, legal advice centre or firm of solicitors displaying the legal aid sign.

1. How much of the claim do you dispute?

☐ I dispute the full amount claimed as shown on the claim form

or

☐ I admit the amount of £ _____

If you dispute only part of the claim you must **either**:

- pay the amount admitted to the person named at the address for payment on the claim form (see How to Pay in the notes on the back of, or attached to, the claim form). Then send this defence to the court

  or

- complete the admission form **and** this defence form and send them to the court.

  ☐ I paid the amount admitted on (*date*) _____
  or
  ☐ I enclose the completed form of admission
  (go to section 2)

2. Do you dispute this claim because you have already paid it? *Tick whichever applies*

☐ **No** *(go to section 3)*

☐ **Yes**   I paid £ _____ to the claimant

on _____ *(before the claim form was issued)*

Give details of where and how you paid it in the box below *(then go to section 5)*

3. Defence

Defence (continued)   Claim No. [   ]

4. If you wish to make a claim against the claimant (a counterclaim)

If your claim is for a specific sum of money, how much are you claiming? £ [   ]

• To start your counterclaim, you will have to pay a fee. Court staff will tell you how much you have to pay

My claim is for *(please specify nature of claim)*

[   ]

• You may not be able to make a counterclaim where the claimant is the Crown (e.g. a Government Department). Ask at your local county court office for further information.

What are your reasons for making the counterclaim?
If you need to continue on a separate sheet put the claim number in the top right hand corner

[   ]

5. Signed

(To be signed by you or by your solicitor or litigation friend)

*(I believe)(The defendant believes) that the facts stated in this form are true. *I am duly authorised by the defendant to sign this statement

*delete as appropriate

Position or office held
(if signing on behalf of firm or company)

[   ]

Date [   ]

Give an address to which notices about this case can be sent to you

[   ] Postcode

Tel. no. [   ]

if applicable

fax no. [   ]

DX no. [   ]

e-mail [   ]

4.3 Defences

A defendant disputing a claim must file a defence. Among the forms included in the response pack is a form of defence and counterclaim (N9B or N9D depending on whether the claim is for a specified sum of money), which has spaces where the defendant can set out the reasons why the claim is disputed, and also for details of any counterclaim. The defence and counterclaim form, N9B, is shown in **Figure 4.3**. Claims usually seen by counsel are sufficiently complicated to merit drafting a detailed defence which simply will not fit in the limited space available on the form in the response pack. This is recognised in the rules, which merely provide that a defence 'may' be set out in the response pack form (PD 15, para. 1.3). A defence drafted by counsel will be properly laid out, with the full title to the claim including the claim number, court and parties' names, underneath which the word 'defence' appears in capitals and in tramlines, followed by the text of the defence. The contents of defences will be considered further in **Chapter 5**.

4.4 Acknowledgment of Service

Acknowledgments of service are used if the defendant is unable to file a defence in the time limited, or if the defendant intends to dispute the court's jurisdiction. Acknowledging service delays the time within which the defence must be filed by an extra 14 days, so that the defence need not be served until 28 days after service of the particulars of claim (CPR, r. 15.4(1)(b)).

As mentioned earlier, the acknowledgment of service form is combined with the cover sheet of the response pack (Form N9). It has a heading setting out the details of the court, parties and claim number. The defendants should write in their full names if they have been misnamed in the claim form. Defendants should also insert their address for service, which must be within the jurisdiction. If they are acting by a solicitor it will be their solicitor's address. They then have to tick a single box saying whether they intend to defend the whole or part of the claim, or to contest the court's jurisdiction. The form is then signed and dated, and filed with the court. If two or more defendants acknowledge service through the same solicitors only a single acknowledgment of service need be used (PD 10, para. 5.3).

Once an acknowledgment of service is received by the court it must notify the claimant in writing (CPR, r. 10.4). This is normally done by sending a copy of the acknowledgment of service to the claimant.

4.5 Agreed Extensions

The parties may agree to extend the time for serving a defence, but any agreement can only be for a maximum of a further 28 days (CPR, r. 15.5(1)). The defendant has to notify the court in writing of the agreed extension.

4.6 Transfer

Defended claims for specified sums of money against individuals are automatically transferred to the defendant's home court on receipt by the court of a defence (CPR, r. 26.2). Transfers in other cases are governed by r. 30.3(2), with criteria for deciding whether to transfer. These criteria include the financial value of the claim, and whether it would be more convenient to try the case in another court.

4.7 Questions

Objectives

By the conclusion of this section you should have a sound understanding of:

(a) the organisation of the High Court;

(b) the organisation of the County Courts;

(c) the allocation of business between the High Court and County Courts;

(d) pre-action conduct of litigation and pre-action protocols;

(e) how proceedings are commenced;

(f) the documents required on commencing a claim;

(g) how court documents are brought to the notice of other parties;

(h) responding to claims; and

(i) the overriding objective.

RESEARCH

Read the materials contained in **Chapters 1** to **4** of this Manual.

LARGE GROUP SESSION 1

You will need to have read questions 1–3 in advance of Large Group Session 1, but there is no need to produce answers to these questions in advance of the large group class as the background material will be explained in the class.

QUESTION 1

Harold bought a rowing machine for £495 from Fitness First two weeks ago in a bid to keep fit. The third time he used it the pulley system of the machine snapped, and the force buckled the machine beyond repair. Harold went back to the shop and asked for his money back. They refused, and said it was Harold's fault the machine had broken. Harold believes that the machine was defective, and has asked for your advice on how he can sue for the return of his money.

QUESTION 2

Emily hurt her back when she landed heavily after tripping over a box at the factory of Henderson & Henderson Ltd in Birmingham two years ago. At the time she was cleaning the top of a machine. She says she did not see the box before the accident, and believes it was left there by another employee while she was in the middle of cleaning the machine. Emily was off work for six weeks. She still has pain and discomfort in her back today. You have been asked to advise Emily:

(a) on liability;

(b) on the options for funding her claim for compensation;

(c) on whether proceedings should be commenced at this stage; and

(d) on where proceedings should be commenced.

QUESTION 3

Gordon Engineering Ltd entered into a contract governed by English law and containing an English jurisdiction clause for the purchase of a consignment of steel manufactured in Poland from Better Imports Ltd, an English company, for £230,000. The steel has been paid for, but was lost in transit. There is a dispute between Gordon Engineering Ltd and Better Imports Ltd as to whether risk had passed before the goods were lost. Advise Gordon Engineering Ltd on which is the most appropriate court for bringing its claim.

SMALL GROUP SESSION 1

Questions 4 to 13 are for Small Group Session 1, and you will need to have notes on each of these questions in advance of the small group class.

QUESTION 4

 (a)   What is meant by the phrase 'the overriding objective'?

 (b)   What is 'active case management'?

 (c)   Are civil proceedings in England and Wales adversarial?

QUESTION 5

One month ago Mary was injured as a result of an accident whilst a passenger in a car driven by John. She consults solicitors, Smith & Co., who now instruct you to advise them on how to deal with her claim before proceedings are issued.

Advise Mary on the following matters:

 (a)   the procedure that should be followed if expert medical opinion is needed on the seriousness and prognosis of Mary's injuries;

 (b)   any information that should be provided to John;

 (c)   the documents that should be disclosed;

 (d)   whether ADR should be considered; and

 (e)   what Mary should do if John does not respond to Mary's correspondence.

QUESTION 6

Michael wishes to claim damages for personal injuries sustained at work when he was aged 27. As a result of his accident he sustained severe comminuted fractures of his left radius and ulna. He is right-handed. He was off work for 12 months, having accepted a job with his former employer as a weighbridge attendant. Previously he had been a machine operator, and now his gross earnings are £40 per week less than before the accident. His net loss of earnings for the year he was off work amounts to £10,600. Part of his treatment was paid for privately, the cost being £4,300. There is a real likelihood of a finding of about 20 per cent contributory negligence. Michael received State benefits amounting to £3,700 during the time he was off work.

Pre-action communications between the parties have not resulted in settlement. You have been instructed to start proceedings:

What statement of value should be put on the claim form and where should the action be commenced?

QUESTION 7

Joan has a claim for breach of contract against Steven. The claim is worth £35,000. Which court should the claim be started in?

QUESTION 8

Clare is knocked down on a pedestrian crossing in the centre of a town when Patrick, who is driving at excessive speed, is unable to stop in time. She instructs solicitors who believe medical evidence is needed on the severity and prognosis of her injuries. On the basis that the Personal Injury Pre-action Protocol applies to Clare's case, which one of the following statements about the instruction of an expert is correct?

[A] Before Clare's solicitors instruct a medical expert they should give Patrick's solicitors a list of the names of one or more medical experts who they consider are suitable to instruct.

[B] Clare should instruct her own expert for an opinion on the severity and prognosis of her injuries at this stage, but aim to jointly instruct an expert if Patrick indicates he does not agree with her chosen expert's opinion.

[C] Clare should send a list of court approved experts to Patrick and try to agree to jointly instruct one from the list.

[D] Clare must make an application to court for an order that expert evidence is necessary before instructing an expert whether jointly or otherwise.

QUESTION 9

What are the permissible methods of service of documents used in court proceedings?

QUESTION 10

Four months ago Gail issued a claim form against Jeremy, her financial advisor, claiming damages for negligent advice. Jeremy is in business on his own account. On the last day for service of the claim form Gail visited his office in order to serve the claim form. Jeremy was out interviewing a client, so Gail spoke to his personal assistant. Jeremy's personal assistant agreed to accept service on Jeremy's behalf. Jeremy returned later the same day and his personal assistant handed him the claim form. Jeremy now seeks your advice on the validity of service. In your advice consider how the court may seek to give effect to the overriding objective when dealing with any application he may make.

QUESTION 11

Jill was severely injured in a road accident as a result of David's negligent driving. After the accident, David told Jill that he was insured with Omega Insurance plc. Jill's solicitors communicated with Omega. After investigating the claim, Omega replied, 'We have made full enquiries into the facts of this accident. In our view our insured was not negligent. Any proceedings by your client should be served on our insured.' Jill's solicitors cannot now trace David to effect service of the claim form. Advise Jill.

QUESTION 12

Sam has issued a claim form against Rachel claiming damages for breach of contract. The claim form, which is accompanied by particulars of claim, is served by the court, by first class post, at Rachel's home address. Rachel has received the claim form, particulars of claim and response pack through the post and asks you what she should do.

QUESTION 13

What are the consequences, once proceedings have been issued, of an unreasonable failure to comply with a relevant pre-action protocol?

FIVE

STATEMENTS OF CASE

5.1   Introduction

Statements of case are formal documents used in litigation to define what each party says about the case. The term 'statement of case' is defined by the CPR to include all the following documents:

(a)   the claim form;

(b)   particulars of claim where these are not included in a claim form;

(c)   defence;

(d)   counterclaim;

(e)   Part 20 claims (these will be considered further in **Chapter 9**);

(e)   reply to defence; and

(f)   any further information given in relation to the above whether voluntarily or by court order.

Statements of case are usually the first documents that are served between the parties, other than the claim form and any acknowledgment of service. They are served in sequence, with the claimant serving particulars of claim first, followed by a defence from the defendant, then possibly a reply from the claimant. They are also often the first documents the judge will read when looking at the trial bundles, so the importance of having the client's case set out in a well-drafted document cannot be over emphasised.

The nature and content of statements of case are closely examined in the *Drafting Manual* and what follows is a basic outline.

5.2   The Purpose of Statements of Case

Statements of case serve two main purposes:

(a)   To inform the other side of the case they will have to meet to ensure that they are not taken by surprise at the trial.

(b)   To provide an outline of the contentions that will be put forward by the parties so that the trial judge can readily see what is in issue between the parties.

5.3   Particulars of Claim

Particulars of claim will set out the facts that the claimant needs to prove in order to establish the cause of action. In short, the particulars of claim sets out the material facts of the claim.

This means the document must set out the facts giving rise to the dispute, and must cover the facts which are the essential elements as a matter of law for the cause of action on which the case is based. For certain categories of action (such as personal injuries claims, fatal accidents and claims for the recovery of land) PD 16 sets out details that need to be included in the particulars of claim. If the claim is based on a written contract the contractual documents must be attached to or served with the particulars of claim. In addition to setting out the cause of action relied upon, particulars of claim must include details of the remedies being claimed. Thus they must contain details of any claim for aggravated or exemplary damages; any claim for provisional damages; and any other remedy sought. They must also give full details of any interest claimed, including the rate, period covered, and the authority for claiming it. Often this will be the County Courts Act 1984, s. 69 or the Supreme Court Act 1981, s. 35A.

For some classes of residential possession proceedings there are prescribed forms for particulars of claim, see PD 4 and, for example, N119, which is the form used for possession proceedings in respect of rented property.

The claim form or particulars of claim must contain a signed statement of truth. This is a statement that its contents are believed to be true (CPR, r. 22.1), and takes the form: 'I believe [the claimant believes] that the facts stated in these particulars of claim are true.' Any failure to include a statement of truth may result in an application for an unless order, with striking out as the sanction (PD 22, para. 4.2).

Particulars of claim must be served within 14 days of service of the claim form. Additionally, service of the particulars of claim must be within the period of validity of the claim form (CPR, r. 7.4(2)). If served separately from the claim form the claimant must file a copy together with a certificate of service within seven days of service (CPR, r. 7.4(3)).

In personal injuries cases, the claimant must serve a medical report and statement of loss and expense with the particulars of claim.

5.4   The Defence

The defence answers the particulars of claim. It must state which of the allegations in the particulars of claim:

(a)   are admitted, in which event it will no longer be in issue, or

(b)   the defendant is unable to admit or deny, in which event the claimant will be put to strict proof, or

(c)   denied, in which event the defendant must state reasons for the denial, and must state any alternative version of events asserted by the defendant.

Any specific allegation that is not answered will be taken to be put in issue if the general nature of the defence on the issue appears from what is said in the defence. Otherwise the issue is deemed to be admitted (CPR, r. 16.5(3), (5)). The amount of any money claim is deemed to be in dispute unless expressly admitted. If the claimant's statement of value is disputed, the defendant must say why and, if able to, give a counter-estimate.

A defence may be set out on one of the forms included in the response pack, but it is usual for defences drafted by counsel to be typed on blank A4 paper. Like all other statements of case a defence must contain a statement of truth. It must be filed at court (CPR, r. 15.2) and served on every other party (CPR, r. 15.6) within 14 days of service of the particulars of claim, or 28 days if the defendant has acknowledged service.

5.5 The Counterclaim

If the defendant has a cause of action against the claimant, this can be raised either by bringing separate proceedings or by way of counterclaim in the existing action. Assuming there is a defence, it is known as the defence and counterclaim.

It can be made using the one of the forms included in the response pack. It must be verified by a statement of truth.

A counterclaim is treated as if it were a claim. A counterclaim may be made without permission if filed with the defence (CPR, r. 20.4(2)(a)). An issue fee based on the full value of the counterclaim is payable.

5.6 Reply or Defence to Counterclaim

If the claimant wishes to deal with new matters raised in the defence, this is done in the reply. In a case where the defendant has counterclaimed, the claimant answers the counterclaim in the defence to counterclaim. Often, these are amalgamated into a reply and defence to counterclaim.

Replies must be filed within the time limited for filing allocation questionnaires, which is stated in the form and happens shortly after filing the defence. Like other statements of case the reply must be verified by a statement of truth.

5.7 Request for Further Information

Sometimes a party will take the view that the statement of case provided by the other side is not as clear as it should be, or fails to set out the other side's case with the precision that would be expected. In such cases a request may be made for further information. Generally it is to be expected that such requests should be made shortly after the relevant statement of case is served.

The procedure for requesting further information is not limited to deficiencies in the other side's statement of case. It can also be used to seek clarification of any matter in dispute, or to seek information about any such matter, even though the point in question is not contained in or referred to in a statement of case (CPR, r. 18.1). The procedure can therefore be used to try to find out about facts that might be expected to be contained in the witness statements (in which case the application would normally be expected to be made after the exchange of witness statements). The procedure can also be used by the court of its own initiative for a variety of purposes, including finding out information for case management purposes.

A party seeking clarification or information (the first party) should first serve on the party from whom it is sought (the second party) a written request for that clarification or information stating a date by which the response to the request should be served. The date must allow the second party a reasonable time to respond. A request should be concise and strictly confined to matters which are reasonably necessary and proportionate to enable the first party to prepare its own case or to understand the case that has to be met. A request may be made by letter if the text of the request is brief and the reply is likely to be brief, otherwise the request should be made in a separate document.

A request which is not in the form of a letter may, if convenient, be prepared in such a way that the response may be given on the same document. To do this the numbered paragraphs of the request should appear on the left-hand half of each sheet so that the paragraphs of the response may then appear on the right.

Unless the request is in the format described in the previous paragraph and the second party uses the document supplied for the purpose, a response must:

(a) be headed with the name of the court and the title and number of the claim;

(b) in its heading identify itself as a response to that request;

(c) repeat the text of each separate paragraph of the request and set out under each paragraph the response to it; and

(d) refer to and have attached to it a copy of any document not already in the possession of the first party which forms part of the response.

The second party must serve the response on the first party, and must file at court and serve on every other party a copy of the request and of the response. The response should be verified by a statement of truth.

If the second party objects to answering a request, or if the second party considers the time given by the first party to be too short, the second party should inform the first party of the objection promptly and within the time stated for the answers by the first party. Objections could include the disproportionate nature of the request, or that it infringes privilege, or otherwise infringes the overriding objective.

If a request for further information is not responded to, the first party is entitled to apply to the court for an order requiring the second party to reply in a stated period of time. There is no need to inform the second party of the application for such an order if the second party failed to make any response as set out in the previous paragraph within the time stated by the first party, and provided at least 14 days have passed since the request was served (PD 18, para. 5.5(1)).

5.8   False Statement of Truth

Proceedings for contempt of court may be brought by the Attorney-General (or by a party with the permission of the court) if a person makes, or causes to be made, a false statement in a document verified by a statement of truth without an honest belief in its truth (CPR, r. 32.14). Permission to bring contempt proceedings is granted in flagrant cases where there has been an attempt to interfere with the course of justice (*Malgar Ltd* v *R E Leach Engineering Ltd*, *The Times*, 17 February 2000).

Although it is to be expected that such sanctions against solicitors signing statements of truth on behalf of their clients will be very rare, it is clearly important for solicitors to have statements of case approved by their clients before they are served. Counsel drafting statements of case should obviously bear this in mind, as a solicitor is unlikely to be very impressed if drafts settled by counsel result in difficulties over false statements of truth.

5.9   Striking Out Statements of Case

The CPR, r. 3.4, provides:

> (2)   *The court may strike out a statement of case if it appears to the court—*
> (a)   *that the statement of case discloses no reasonable grounds for bringing or defending the claim;*
> (b)   *that the statement of case is an abuse of the court's process or is otherwise likely to obstruct the just disposal of the proceedings; or*
> (c)   *that there has been a failure to comply with a rule, practice direction or a court order.*

A Practice Direction supporting this rule provides that a claim may be struck out if it is incoherent or makes no sense, or if, even if the facts stated are true, they disclose no legally recognisable claim. It will also be struck out if it is vexatious, scurrilous or obviously ill-founded. Further, a defence may be struck out if it is a bare denial or otherwise fails to set out a coherent statement of facts amounting to a defence in law.

The same Practice Direction also refers to the power of the court to use this rule to strike out a claim or defence which is bound to fail, or to stay a claim which cannot proceed on the basis in which it is framed, and goes on to say the court may consider giving a party an opportunity of saving its statement of case by providing further information or documents. Even if a judge does not strike out under this power, the opposite party may still apply to strike out under r. 3.4.

5.10   Interrelation with Case Management

Filing of the defence triggers the start of standard case management intervention by the court in the form of sending out of allocation questionnaires. This is the first step in the track allocation process, and leads also to the court making case management directions. These topics will be considered further in **Chapter 7**.

Figure 5.1   Flow diagram illustrating early stages in litigation

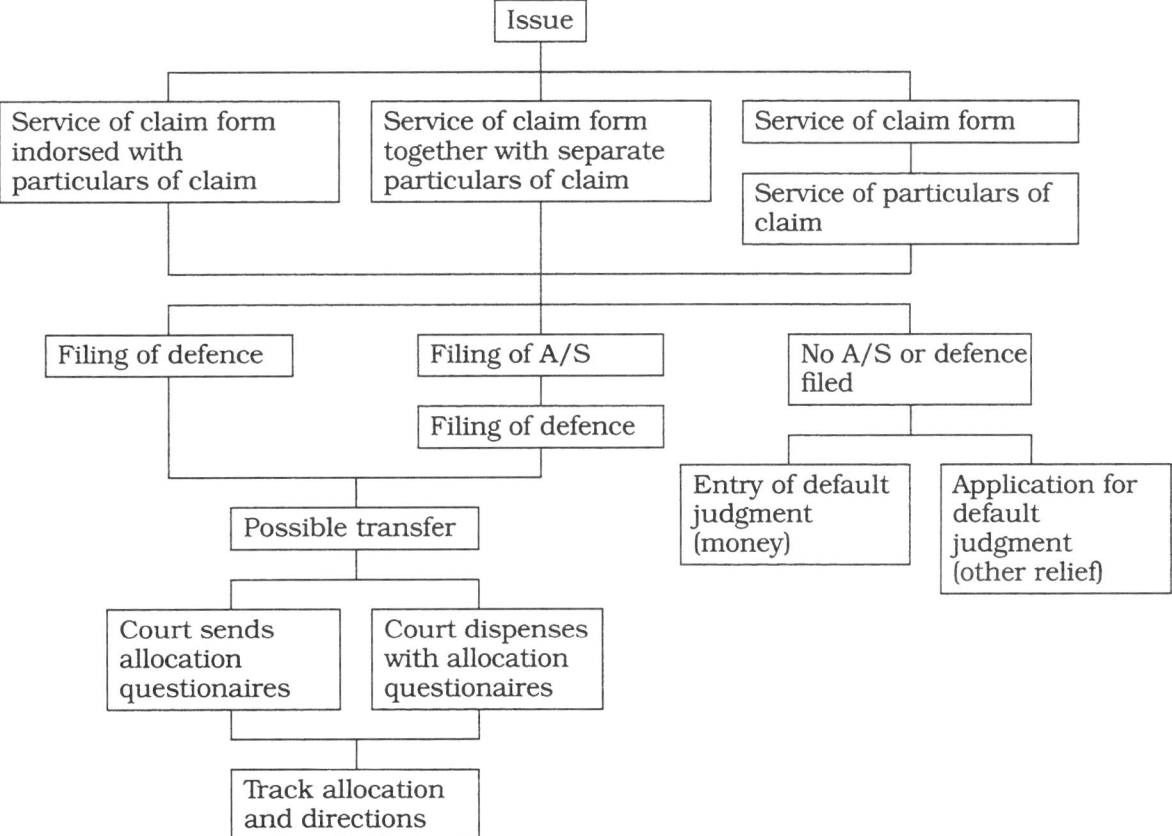

SIX

JUDGMENT IN DEFAULT

6.1 Introduction

Where the defendant does not intend to contest the proceedings, it would be a waste of time and money, and very hard on the claimant, to proceed as if the claim were defended. Therefore, the Rules of Court allow a claimant to obtain early judgment against a defendant who fails to defend the action. Usually, this does not even involve a hearing. In such cases, obtaining judgment is a purely administrative act, which is why one refers to 'signing' or 'entering' judgment.

6.2 What Constitutes Default?

A defendant who has been served with the particulars of claim has 14 days to make a response to a claim. Consequently, a defendant cannot be in default until that time has elapsed. Note that a defendant cannot be in default if a claim form is served without particulars of claim.

The CPR, r. 12.3, allows a claimant to enter a default judgment in the following circumstances:

(a) If the defendant has not filed an acknowledgment of service or a defence to the claim (or any part of the claim) and 14 days has expired since service of the particulars of claim; or

(b) If the defendant has filed an acknowledgment of service but has not filed a defence, and 28 days has expired since service of the particulars of claim.

The CPR, r. 12.3, provides:

> *(1) The claimant may obtain judgment in default of an acknowledgment of service only if—*
> *(a) the defendant has not filed an acknowledgment of service or a defence to the claim (or any part of the claim); and*
> *(b) the relevant time for doing so has expired.*
> *(2) Judgment in default of defence may be obtained only—*
> *(a) where an acknowledgment of service has been filed but a defence has not filed;*
> *(b) in a counterclaim made under rule 20.4, where a defence has not been filed,*
> *and, in either case, the relevant time limit for doing so has expired.*

6.3 Excluded Cases

Default judgments are not available in a number of cases even if the defendant fails to respond to the claim. Excluded cases fall into two categories. In the first, the nature of the proceedings is a bar to obtaining a default judgment, and in the second some step taken by the defendant prevents the claimant entering judgment in default. Cases in the first category are summarised in PD 12, para. 1.2, as follows:

(a) claims which are brought using the alternative procedure in Part 8;

(b) claims for the delivery of goods subject to an agreement regulated by the Consumer Credit Act 1974;

(c) mortgage claims;

(d) claims governed by certain specialised procedures as set out in CPR, Part 49 and the Practice Directions supplementing Part 49 where the special rules lay down procedures which do not include a requirement to file a defence or acknowledgment of service, or which provide special rules for obtaining default judgments. Cases falling into this sub-category are:

   (i) admiralty proceedings;

   (ii) arbitration proceedings;

   (iii) contentious probate proceedings; and

   (iv) claims for provisional damages.

Cases in the second category are set out in CPR, r. 12.3(3), which provides:

> (3) The claimant may not obtain a default judgment if—
> (a) the defendant has applied—
>   (i)   to have the claimant's statement of case struck out under rule 3.4; or
>   (ii) for summary judgment under Part 24,
> and in either case that application has not been disposed of;
> (b) the defendant has satisfied the whole claim (including any claim for costs) on which the claimant is seeking judgment; or
> (c) (i)   the claimant is seeking judgment on a claim for money; and
>   (ii) the defendant has filed or served on the claimant an admission under rule 14.4 or 14.7 (admission of liability to pay all of the money claimed) together with a request for time to pay.

6.4 Entering Default Judgment

6.4.1 BY FILING A REQUEST FOR JUDGMENT

In claims seeking to recover money and/or the delivery of goods, which are by far the most common types of cases, default judgments are available simply by filing a standard form request. In other words, entering judgment in undefended money claims is simply an administrative matter of posting forms to the court office, and a member of the court staff entering the judgment. There is no hearing, and no question of trying to persuade the court to enter judgment.

When proceedings are issued the court will send the claimant a notice of issue. There are three different forms of notice of issue, one for specified money claims, another for unspecified money claims, and the third for non-money claims. The two money claim notices include a tear-off section for the request for judgment. In the top part of the form the court staff enter the claim number, the date of issue, and the dates when the claim form was posted to the defendant, the deemed date of service, and the date by when the defendant has to respond. All the claimant has to do is wait until the time for responding has elapsed, then, if the claim is for a specified sum of money, tick a box saying the defendant has failed to respond, and enter details of the judgment sought. This involves calculating the amount owed together with interest and fixed costs (as set out in the CPR), and deciding whether to ask for the whole sum to be paid immediately or by stated instalments. The request form is then signed, dated and returned to the court. In claims for unspecified sums, all the claimant has to do, once the time for responding has elapsed, is to sign and date the request form, and return it to the court.

If the particulars of claim were served by the claimant, judgment in default cannot be obtained unless a certificate of service (see **Figure 3.4**) has been filed. The rule dealing with this, CPR, r. 6.14(2)(b), in fact provides that if the *claim form* is served by the claimant, judgment in default cannot be obtained unless a certificate of service has been filed. It should refer to the particulars of claim rather than the claim form in order to be consistent with the rules on responding to claims and default judgments set out in Parts 9, 10 and 12. There is no need for such a certificate if service is effected by the court and the proceedings have not been returned undelivered.

6.4.2   BY APPLYING FOR JUDGMENT IN DEFAULT

In a number of cases, even though the defendant has failed to respond to the claim within time, a default judgment can only be obtained by making an application to the court. **Chapter 10** below describes how to make applications. Generally, the application will be made by issuing an application notice and must be supported by written evidence. The evidence should include a certificate of service if the particulars of claim were served by the claimant. There is no need to serve the evidence in support on any defendant who did not acknowledge service (CPR, r. 12.11(2)). This means that a defendant who acknowledged service but failed to file a defence has to be served with the evidence in support. Although the evidence in support in many cases does not need to be served on the defendant, the defendant should in all cases (other than service outside the jurisdiction, category (a) below) be given notice of the application itself by being served with the application notice (PD 12, para. 5.1).

Default judgments in non-money and non-recovery of goods claims (principally these will be cases where some form of equitable relief is sought, such as injunctions) have to be applied for. In other words, where equitable relief is sought and the defendant does not defend the claim, a judgment can only be obtained at a hearing before a District Judge or judge who will decide whether to exercise the court's discretion to grant the relief sought.

Within the context of claims seeking money or recovery of goods, there are a number of exceptional cases where default judgments cannot be entered by filing a request, but only by obtaining permission by making an application. These are:

(a) Where the claim form was served out of the jurisdiction without permission under the Brussels and Lugano Conventions on a defendant domiciled in a contracting State (essentially these are most countries in western Europe) (see CPR, r. 12.10(b)). Service outside the jurisdiction is considered further in **Chapter 11**. In these cases the Conventions prohibit the entry of judgment in default without the court checking that service complied with the relevant Convention. The claimant's evidence in support of the application for judgment must establish that the claim is one that the English court has power to hear and decide, that no other court has exclusive jurisdiction, and that the claim form has been properly served in accordance with the Convention (PD 12, para. 4.3). The evidence in this particular case must be on affidavit (rather than the usual witness statement format) (PD 12, para. 4.5).

(b) Where the defendant is a child or patient (CPR, r. 12.10(a)(i)). Before applying for judgment the claimant must apply for the appointment of a litigation friend to represent the person under disability. On the application for judgment the evidence must satisfy the court that the claimant is entitled to the judgment sought (PD 12, para. 4.2).

(c) Where the claim is for or includes costs other than fixed costs (CPR, r. 12.9).

(d) Where the claim is brought by one spouse against the other on a claim in tort (CPR, r. 12.10(a)(ii)).

(e) Where the claim seeks delivery up of goods where the defendant is not to be allowed the alternative of paying their value. Relief in this form, as opposed to other types of delivery orders relating to claims relating to goods, is discretionary (see the Torts (Interference with Goods) Act 1977), which is why an application must be made. The evidence in support must identify the goods and say where the goods are believed to be kept and why the claimant says an order for specific delivery should be granted (PD 12, para. 4.6). Usually this will have to be because of the rare or irreplaceable nature of the goods concerned.

6.5 Final Judgment and Judgment for an Amount to be Decided

There are two main types of judgment obtainable in money claims. The best type is a final judgment, which will require the defendant to pay a set amount of money usually within 14 days. Apart from giving the defendant a limited amount of time to raise the money, this type of judgment allows the claimant to recover the whole sum straight away, or to apply to enforce if the defendant does not pay.

The other type is a judgment for damages to be decided by the court. There are variations on this form of judgment, such as judgments for the value of goods to be decided by the court and judgment for the amount of interest to be decided by the court. This type of judgment is sometimes called an 'interlocutory judgment', and the rules occasionally refer to this type of judgment as a 'relevant order'. This second type of judgment means that liability has been established and will not be considered any further, but all questions relating to the amount of damages or interest payable, or the value of the goods, have yet to be determined.

Final judgment will be entered in claims for specified sums (CPR, r. 12.5), whereas judgment for damages to be decided will be entered in claims for unspecified amounts. There is some doubt as to what is meant by 'specified'. Options are specified by the claimant, or the same meaning as a liquidated demand. Liquidated demands are claims such as for the repayment of a loan or bank overdraft, or for the price of goods or services, or for rent. For each of these the amount claimed is fixed by the underlying agreement between the parties. This is so even though the amount may need to be calculated, such as the interest payable on the overdraft, or the rent payable over a period of time. Liquidated demands are usually contrasted with claims for unliquidated damages, such as for personal injuries or for the unsatisfactory quality of goods sold. The value of unliquidated claims requires an exercise of judicial judgment. Consequently, one school of thought takes the view that all damages claims are unspecified, and so default judgments in these cases should be for damages to be decided. However, the other school of thought takes the view that if the claimant spells out in the particulars of claim the amount of damages claimed the claim becomes one for a specified amount, so that a final judgment can be obtained.

6.6 Procedure for Deciding the Amount of Damages

When the court enters a default judgment of the second type for damages or interest to be decided, or for the value of goods to be decided by the court, it will give any directions it considers appropriate. Further, if it thinks it appropriate it will also allocate the claim to a case management track (CPR, r. 12.7). Alternatively, the court may list the matter for a disposal hearing, or will stay the action while the parties try to settle the case using ADR or other means.

The orders being considered here are described as 'relevant orders' by PD 26, para. 12. In addition to being one of the possibilities on obtaining a default judgment, they may also be made on entry of judgment on an admission, on the striking out of a statement of case, on a summary judgment application, on the determination of a preliminary issue or on a split trial as to liability, or even by consent or at trial.

6.6.1 DISPOSAL HEARINGS

At a disposal hearing the court will either give directions or decide the amount payable (PD 26, para. 12.8(1)). Relevant orders made by entry of default judgment without a hearing are usually dealt with in this way.

If the case is listed for a disposal hearing and the claim is worth less than £5,000 the court will usually allocate it to the small claims track (for costs purposes) and decide the amount payable there and then (PD 26, para. 12.8(2)). If the financial value of the claim is more than £5,000 the court may still determine the amount payable at the disposal hearing, but in these cases the ordinary costs rules will apply. In cases determined at disposal hearings evidence may, unless the court otherwise directs, be adduced under CPR, r. 32.6 (see PD 26, para. 12.8(4)). This means that reliance may be placed on the matters set out in the particulars of claim (provided it is verified by a statement of truth) or by witness statement. The evidence relied upon must be served on the defendant at least three clear days before the disposal hearing.

6.6.2 ALLOCATING RELEVANT ORDER CASES TO TRACKS

Allocating a case to the fast track or multi-track after a relevant order has been made should only happen if the amount payable is genuinely disputed on grounds that appear to be substantial (PD 26, para. 12.3). This topic is considered further in **Chapter 7**.

6.6.3 HEARING TO ASSESS DAMAGES

Generally, hearings to assess damages will be listed before Masters and District Judges irrespective of the amount in issue (PD 26, para. 12.10), but the court may give directions specifying the level or type of judge who is to deal with the case (PD 26, para. 12.2(2)).

6.7 Particulars of Claim Returned Undelivered

It sometimes happens that the proceedings are served by post, no acknowledgment of service is received and default judgment is entered. The proceedings are then returned undelivered.

In such a case the claimant should take no further steps in the proceedings, and in particular no attempt should be made to enforce judgment. Rather, the claimant has two options:

(a) To get judgment set aside. This is as simple and cheap (again being purely administrative) as the entering of the judgment. Indeed it is rather like running the film in reverse, i.e. the claimant goes back to the same court office and files a request that judgment be set aside. Once this is done, the claimant is free to try again by re-serving the proceedings.

(b) Alternatively, the claimant can apply to the court for directions. Such an application is made in the usual way, with an application notice and written evidence. In practice this option would only be exercised where it is imperative to prove the validity of the original service or where the particulars of claim have been returned in circumstances indicating that the defendant has in fact been served (e.g. where the words 'not known at this address' appear on the envelope in the defendant's own handwriting!). On such an application, the court can:

(i) set the judgment aside; or

    (ii)   treat the particulars of claim as having been properly served, notwithstanding its return; or

    (iii)   make an order or give such directions it feels appropriate in the circumstances (e.g. making an order for service by an alternative method).

6.8   Setting Aside Default Judgment

Because in most cases entering default judgment is an administrative process, there is no investigation of the merits of the claim. The court, therefore, retains wide powers to set aside or vary any such judgment (see CPR, Part 13). The court may exercise the power to set aside a judgment on an application by the defendant or of its own motion.

As Lord Atkin put it in *Evans* v *Bartlam* [1937] AC 480, HL:

> The principle obviously is that unless and until the Court has pronounced a judgment upon the merits or by consent, it is to have the power to revoke the expression of its coercive power where that has only been obtained by a failure to follow any of the rules of procedure.

An application by a party is made by application notice to a Master or District Judge and must be supported by written evidence. Often a draft of the proposed defence is exhibited to the evidence in support.

6.8.1   WHEN WILL DEFAULT JUDGMENT BE SET ASIDE?

Setting aside is as of right if the default judgment was wrongly entered (CPR, r. 13.2). There is a restrictive definition for this, limited to:

(a)   situations where the essential conditions about failing to acknowledge service or defend, or the relevant time having elapsed, are not satisfied. or

(b)   the claim was satisfied before judgment was entered; or

(c)   the defendant had already applied for summary judgment; or

(d)   the defendant had already filed an admission requesting time to pay.

Otherwise, the court will only set aside or vary a default judgment if the defendant 'has real prospects of successfully defending the claim' or 'it appears . . . there is some other good reason why the defendant should . . . be allowed to defend the claim', taking into account any delay in applying (CPR, r. 13.3). In deciding whether to set aside or vary in such cases the court will take into account whether the defendant has made the application to set aside promptly.

Cases under the old rules regarded the defence on the merits as being the primary consideration, with delay being a subsidiary factor. Under the CPR delay is likely to be seen as somewhat more important. If there is a defence which carries some degree of conviction, the court will have a strong inclination to set aside a default judgment, even if strong criticism could be made of the defendant's conduct (*Citoma Trading Ltd* v *The Federal Republic of Brazil* (29 July 1999, CA, unreported), a case where judgment was set aside after seven and a half years). In *McDonald* v *Thorn plc, The Times*, 15 October 1999, the Court of Appeal approved the following principles:

(a)   while the length of any delay by the defendant had to be taken into account, any pre-action delay was irrelevant;

(b)   any failure by the defendant to provide a good explanation for the delay is a factor to be taken into account, but is not always a reason to refuse to set aside;

(c) the primary considerations are whether there is a defence with a real prospect of success, and that justice should be done; and

(d) prejudice (or the absence of it) to the claimant also has to be taken into account.

6.8.2   CONDITIONS

Note, however, that when the court sets aside a default judgment which was regularly obtained, it may impose conditions (see CPR, r. 3.1(3)). In most cases the court will order the defendant to pay the claimant's costs thrown away. In addition, the court may order the defendant to pay all or part of the disputed sum into court. Such terms will effectively amount to a precondition to allowing the defendant to contest the action, i.e., any failure to comply with the terms, and the claimant can proceed to enforce the default judgment. That being the case, the court should not impose a financial condition which the defendant cannot possibly meet, since that would be tantamount to giving judgment for the claimant. The onus, however, will be on the defendant to prove the impossibility of the condition. (See *M.V. York Motors* v *Edwards* [1982] 1 WLR 444, a case under the old rules on summary judgment, but applicable by analogy.)

6.9   Stay of Undefended Cases

If none of the defendants file admissions or defences, the claimant should generally enter judgment in default shortly after the time for doing so has elapsed, but in any event within six months of the period for filing the defence. Once the six months has elapsed, the claim is automatically stayed by virtue of CPR, r. 15.11.

Any party may apply to lift the stay. They do so by making an application in accordance with the procedure discussed in **Chapter 10**, and must give the reason for the applicant's delay in proceeding with or responding to the claim (PD 15, para. 3.4).

SEVEN

TRACK ALLOCATION

7.1   Introduction

It will be recalled from **1.4.1** above that the courts will seek to further the overriding objective of dealing with cases justly by active case management. In exercising their powers to manage cases, the courts will be seeking to ensure they are dealt with expeditiously and fairly. They will also try to allot to each case an appropriate share of the court's resources, and will endeavour to ensure they are dealt with proportionately bearing in mind factors such as the importance and complexities of the issues and the monetary value of the claim.

To assist with these aims defended actions will be assigned to one of three case management 'tracks'. This happens shortly after the defendant files a defence, which is obviously quite early on in the litigation process. By this time the issues should have been defined by the parties in their statements of case. It is intended that procedural judges will be very willing to intervene during the early stages of proceedings, particularly at the track allocation stage, so as to ensure that the issues are narrowed, that cases are prepared economically and speedily, and disposed of fairly and without undue delay or expense.

The idea behind track allocation is that cases should be dealt with procedurally on a basis that is justifiable given the overall importance of each case. Difficult and important cases will be given Rolls Royce treatment, but cases which are simple and where not a great deal is at stake will be dealt with in a far more rough and ready way.

The smallest and simplest cases will therefore be assigned to the small claims track. These cases will usually be given an immediate date for hearing, with limited preparation being required, and the strict rules of evidence do not apply. Cases with a monetary value in the range of £5,000 to £15,000 will usually be allocated to the fast track with standard directions and tight timetables of up to 30 weeks for completion of the preparatory stages before trial. Larger and more important cases will be assigned to the multi-track. The courts are given a great deal of flexibility in the way they can manage these cases, with a greater or lesser degree of intervention depending on how important the case is. Multi-track cases will mainly be dealt with at Civil Trial Centres (the larger court venues), and will usually be transferred to such locations as part of the case management process.

7.2   Allocation Questionnaires

All defended cases will be allocated by the court to an appropriate track. On the defendant filing a defence the court will usually serve allocation questionnaires on all parties, although it does have a power to dispense with these questionnaires. Questionnaires may be dispensed with if there has already been an application, such as for summary judgment, which has been treated as an allocation hearing. If there are several defendants, the questionnaires are sent out after all the defendants have filed their defences, or when the time limited for them to do so has expired. An example of an allocation questionnaire is shown in **Figure 7.1**.

Figure 7.1

Allocation questionnaire

In the

Claim No.	
Last date for filing with court office	

To

SEAL

Please read the notes on page five before completing the questionnaire.

Please note the date by which it must be returned and the name of the court it should be returned to since this may be different from the court where proceedings were issued.

If you have settled this case (or if you settle it on a future date) and do not need to have it heard or tried, you must let the court know immediately.

A Settlement

Do you wish there to be a one month stay to attempt to settle the case by alternative dispute resolution or other means?

☐ Yes ☐ No

B Track

Which track do you consider is most suitable for your case? *(Tick one box)*

☐ small claims ☐ fast track ☐ multi-track

If you think your case is suitable for a specialist list, say which:

If you have indicated a track which would not be the normal track for the case, please give brief reasons for your choice:

C Pre-action protocols

Have you complied with any pre-action protocol applicable to your claim?

☐ None applicable to this claim   ☐ Yes   ☐ No

If Yes, please say which protocol:

If No, please explain to what extent and for what reason it has not been complied with:

D Applications

If you have not already sent the court an application for summary judgment, do you intend to do so?

☐ Yes   ☐ No

If you have not already issued a claim in the case against someone not yet a party, do you intend to apply for the court's permission to do so?

☐ Yes   ☐ No

In either case, if Yes, please give details:

E Witnesses of fact

So far as you know at this stage, what witnesses of fact do you intend to call at the hearing?

Witness name	Witness to which facts

F Experts' evidence

Do you wish to use expert evidence at the hearing? ☐ Yes ☐ No

Have you already copied any experts' report(s) to the other party(ies)? ☐ None obtained as yet ☐ Yes ☐ No

Please list the experts whose evidence you think you will use:

Expert's name	Field of expertise (eg. orthopaedic surgeon, mechanical engineer)

Will you and the other party use the same expert(s)? ☐ Yes ☐ No

If No, please explain why not:

Do you want your expert(s) to give evidence orally at the hearing or trial? ☐ Yes ☐ No

If Yes, give the reasons why you think oral evidence is necessary:

G Location of trial

Is there any reason why your case needs to be heard at a particular court? ☐ Yes ☐ No

If Yes, give reasons (eg. particular facilities required, convenience of witnesses, etc.)

and specify the court:

H Representation and estimate of hearing/trial time

Do you expect to be represented by a solicitor or counsel at the hearing/trial?

☐ No ☐ Solicitor ☐ Counsel

How long do you estimate it will take to put your case to the court at the hearing/trial?

days	hours	minutes

If there are days when you, your representative, expert or an essential witness will not be able to attend court, give details:

Name	Dates not available

I Costs (only relates to costs incurred by legal representatives)

What is your estimate of costs incurred to date?

£

What do you estimate the overall costs are likely to be?

£

J Other information

Have you attached documents you wish the judge to take into account when allocating the case?

☐ Yes ☐ No

Have they been served on the other parties?

☐ Yes ☐ No

If Yes, say when

Have the other parties agreed their content?

☐ Yes ☐ No

Have you attached a list of the directions you think appropriate for the management of your case?

☐ Yes ☐ No

Are they agreed with the other parties?

☐ Yes ☐ No

Are there any other facts which might affect the timetable the court will set? If so, please state

Signed _____ Date _____

[Counsel][Solicitor][for the][Claimant][Defendant]

Notes for completing an allocation questionnaire

- If the case is not settled, a judge must allocate it to an appropriate case management track. To help the judge choose the most just and cost-effective track, you must now complete the attached questionnaire.
- If you fail to return the allocation questionnaire by the date given, the judge may make an order which leads to your claim or defence being struck out, or hold an allocation hearing. If there is an allocation hearing the judge may order any party who has not filed their questionnaire to pay, immediately, the costs of that hearing.
- If you wish to make an application, for example, for special directions, for summary judgment on the grounds that the other party has no reasonable chance of their claim or defence being successful, or for permission to add another party to the claim, you should send it and any required fee with the completed allocation questionnaire. If a hearing is fixed for your application, it may also be used as an allocation hearing.
- Any other documents you wish the judge to take into account should be filed with the questionnaire. But you must confirm that the documents have been sent to the other party, or parties, saying when they would have received them and whether they agreed their contents.
- Use a separate sheet if you need more space for your answers marking clearly which section the information refers to. Write the case number on it, sign and date it and attach it securely to the questionnaire.
- The letters below refer to the sections of the questionnaire and tell you what information is needed.

A Settlement

If you think that you and the other party may be able to negotiate a settlement you should tick the 'Yes' box. The court may order a stay, whether or not all the other parties to the case agree. You should still complete the rest of the questionnaire, even if you are requesting a stay. Where a stay is granted it will be for an initial period of one month.

B Track

The basic guide by which cases are normally allocated to a track depends on the money value of the claim, although other factors such as the complexity of the case will also be considered:

Small Claims track	Claims valued at £5,000 or less unless they include a claim for personal injuries worth over £1,000; or a claim for housing disrepair where the costs of the repairs or other work is more than £1,000 and any other claim for damages is more than £1,000
Fast track	Claims valued at more than £5,000 but not more than £15,000
Multi-track	Claims over £15,000

A leaflet available from the court office explains these limits in greater detail.

C Pre-action protocols

For certain kinds of claim, there are protocols which set out what ought to be done before court proceedings are issued. As at April 1999 there are protocols for clinical negligence and personal injury claims.

D Applications

If you intend to apply for summary judgment or for permission to add another party to the claim or make any other application you should, if you have not already done so, file the application with your completed allocation questionnaire.

E Witnesses of fact

Remember to include yourself, if you will be giving evidence; but not experts, who should be included in section F.

F Experts' evidence

Oral or written expert evidence will only be allowed at the trial with the court's permission. The judge will decide what permission it seems appropriate to give when the case is allocated to track.

G Location of trial

High Court cases are usually heard at the Royal Courts of Justice or certain Civil Trial Centres. Other multi-track cases are heard at the Civil Trial Centre for the court where they are proceeding. Fast track cases are usually heard either at the court in which they are proceeding or its Civil Trial Centre. The court office will tell you which is the Civil Trial Centre for any particular county court. Small claim cases are usually heard at the court in which they are proceeding.

H Representation and estimate of hearing/trial time

If the case is allocated to the fast track, no more than one day will be allowed for the trial of the whole case.

I Costs

Estimates should be given using Form 1 which can be found in the Schedule of Costs Forms set out in the Civil Procedure Rules. The form should be attached to and returned with your completed questionnaire.

Before sending out allocation questionnaires the court will insert the date by which the forms must be returned, and must give the parties at least 14 days to do so. The questionnaire asks for details as to whether the relevant pre-action protocol (if any) was complied with. It also asks whether a stay is sought for settlement; about possible transfer to another court; for the party's view on the appropriate track for the case; for details about expert and factual witnesses, and for details of any contemplated applications.

Parties may file additional information with their allocation questionnaires if this will assist the court in making its decisions regarding track allocation and case management. However, such additional information should only be filed if all the parties have agreed the information is correct and that it should be put before the court, or if the party intending to file the information confirms that copies have been delivered to all the other parties. The parties are encouraged to consult with one another and to co-operate in filling in their questionnaires. They are also encouraged to try to agree suggested directions, which may be sent to the court with the completed questionnaires. However, consulting between the parties should not be used as an excuse for late filing of the questionnaires.

When the parties return their completed questionnaires they should enclose a statement of their costs (an example is shown in **Figure 7.2**), and the claimant must pay a fee of £80 (unless the claim does not exceed £1,000, when no fee is payable).

When the forms are returned or the time expires the court may order parties to provide further information about their cases, and may hold an allocation hearing. An example of such an order is shown on **Figure 7.3**.

Figure 7.2   Statement of costs

IN THE HIGH COURT OF JUSTICE   Claim No. 2000 S No. 98744

QUEEN'S BENCH DIVISION

MANCHESTER DISTRICT REGISTRY

BETWEEN:

SHILTON MACHINE TOOLS LIMITED

Claimant

and

BANKS PLASTIC MOULDINGS LIMITED   Defendant

CLAIMANT'S STATEMENT OF
COSTS TO 23RD NOVEMBER 2000

Description of Fee Earners

1.   Margaret Clements (MC) Grade 1 — £135 per hour

2.   Daniel Sprake (DS) Grade 3 — £60 per hour

Attendances on client

MC: 2.25 hours @ £135 per hour   £303.75

Attendances on opponents

MC: 1.5 hours @ £135 per hour   £202.50

Attendances on others

MC: 1.75 hours @ £135 per hour   £236.25

DS: 0.75 hours @ £60 per hour   £45.00

Work done on documents

MC: 4.5 hours @ £135 per hour   £607.50

DS: 3.5 hours @ £60 per hour   £210.00

Counsel's fees

Ashley Bailey: advising in conference   £300.00

Other expenses:

Court fee   £400.00

Sub-Total   £2,001.25

VAT claimed on solicitor's and counsel's fees at 17.5%   £280.21

Total   £2,281.46

The costs estimated above do not exceed the costs which the claimant is liable to pay in respect of the work which the estimate covers.

DATED the 23rd November 2000

Signed:
    Boardman, Phipps & Co.
    Claimant's solicitors

Figure 7.3   Order for further information

Order for Further Information (allocation)	In the High Court of Justice Queen's Bench Division Manchester District Registry **Claim No.** 2000 S No. 98744
To Claimant's solicitor	**Claimant** Shilton Machine Tools Limited
Boardman Phipps & Co. 20 High Street Manchester M15 9CZ	**Defendant** Banks Plastic Mouldings Limited

SEAL

District Judge Chesterfield has considered the statements of case and allocation questionnaires filed and requires further information before making a final decision about allocation.

The District Judge orders the claimant to provide information about:

1. The attempts made (if any) to agree the joint selection of expert witnesses.

2. The reasons (if any) for needing to call expert witnesses to give oral evidence at trial.

3. On the difficulties (if any) of obtaining a signed witness statement from Mr Benetti before the 28th February 2001.

This information and any accompanying documents should be delivered to the court and copied to the other parties on or before 8th December 2000.

Note: Where an allocation hearing is necessary because a party does not provide the information ordered above, the court may order that party to pay the costs of any other party attending the hearing.

The court office at The Courts of Justice, Crown Square, Manchester M60 9DJ is open between 10 am and 4 pm Monday to Friday. Address all communications to the Court Manager quoting the claim number.

7.3   Failing to File an Allocation Questionnaire

If a party fails to file an allocation questionnaire the court may give any direction it considers appropriate (CPR, r. 26.5(5)). The court may allocate the claim if it considers it has enough information, or it may fix an allocation hearing and direct any of the parties to attend (PD 26, para. 2.5(2)). If an allocation hearing takes place because of a failure to file an allocation questionnaire, the court will usually order the defaulting party to pay the costs of the other parties on the indemnity basis (para. 6.6(2)). If the defaulting party fails to attend an allocation hearing, the court will usually make an order with sanctions (para. 6.6(3)). If all the parties are in default, the file will be referred to the judge who will usually order that allocation questionnaires are to be filed within three days from service of the order, failing which the claim and any counterclaim will be struck out (PD 26, para. 2.5(1)).

7.4   Failing to Pay the Allocation Fee

If the claimant fails to pay the allocation fee the court will serve a notice (Form N173) on the claimant requiring payment within a stated period of time, failing which the claim will be struck out. If the claim is struck out for non-payment of the fee the claimant is also required to pay the defendant's costs, unless the court otherwise orders (CPR, r. 3.7). Once the claim has been struck out the defendant is notified by the court so he or she can apply for his or her costs. Any injunction previously granted lapses after 14 days (CPR, r. 25.11). The court retains a power to reinstate it (CPR, r. 3.7(7)), and on such an application the court will apply the criteria set out in r. 3.9 relating to applications for relief from sanctions (see **28.3.6**). However, any order for reinstatement will be made conditional on the fee being paid within two days of the order.

7.5   Track Allocation

Generally, the court will allocate cases in accordance with their financial value. It may allocate a case to a higher track having regard to factors such as complexity, the value of any counterclaim, the amount of oral evidence and the importance of the case. It cannot allocate a case to a lower track than its financial value would indicate unless all the parties consent. Once it makes an allocation decision the court will send a notice of the decision to the parties, together with copies of the other parties' allocation questionnaires. An example of a notice of allocation can be seen at **Figure 7.5**. At the same time as it allocates the case to a track the court will usually also make case management directions.

Track allocation based on financial value results in the following basic position:

(a) claims with a value up to £5,000 will be allocated to the small claims track;

(b) claims between £5,000 and £15,000 will be allocated to the fast track; and

(c) claims exceeding £15,000 will be allocated to the multi-track.

However, there are some more detailed rules. For example, personal injury claims where the total claim does not exceed £5,000 will not normally be allocated to the small claims track unless the likely damages for pain, suffering and loss of amenity do not exceed £1,000 (CPR, r. 26.6(1)).

In addition to the financial value of the claim (if it has one), the court is by CPR, r. 26.8, required to have regard to the following factors when deciding which track to allocate the case to:

(a) the nature of the remedy sought;

(b) the likely complexity of the facts, law or evidence;

(c) the number of parties or likely parties;

(d) the value of any counterclaim or other Part 20 claim and the complexity of any matters relating to those claims;

(e) the amount of oral evidence which may be required;

(f) the importance of the claim to persons who are not parties to the proceedings;

(g) the views expressed by the parties — these views will be regarded as important, but the court will not be bound by any agreement or common view expressed by the parties; and

(h) the circumstances of the parties.

7.6   Case Management Directions

The court will usually give directions at the track allocation stage. The court may (and usually will) give directions of its own initiative and without holding a hearing. However, particularly in multi-track cases, the court may convene a case management conference for the purpose of giving directions.

The idea behind giving directions is to provide a timetable pursuant to which the evidence needed to prove the claim or defence must be obtained and exchanged with the other side. In most cases the court is likely to insist on the necessary steps being taken within a relatively short period of time. **Figure 7.4** sets out the usual steps that are directed in fast track cases, with the periods of time usually set for taking those steps. The times referred to in **Figure 7.4** run from the date of allocation to the fast track.

Directions are not only given as part of the track allocation procedure. The rules provide that the court will consider giving directions at the end of any hearing, such as an application for an interim injunction or for summary judgment (if the claim is to proceed). If directions have already been given at an application made in the very early stages of the proceedings there may be little or no need for the court to give further directions at the track allocation stage. Directions may also be given at later stages in the litigation, long after track allocation has been dealt with. The court may do this at a specially convened directions hearing, such as a case management conference or pre-trial review, or on an application made by one of the parties (such as an application to extend the directions timetable, or to enforce compliance with the timetable by the other side), or after any other type of interim application, such as an application for an interim payment.

Figure 7.4   Typical directions timetable for fast track cases

Step	Time from allocation
1. Disclosure of documents by serving lists of documents	4 weeks
2. Exchange of witness statements	10 weeks
3. Exchange of experts' reports	14 weeks
4. Sending listing questionnaires to the parties by the court	20 weeks
5. Returning listing questionnaires to the court	22 weeks
6. Trial	30 weeks

Figure 7.5   Notice of allocation to the multi-track

Notice of Allocation to Multi-track	In the High Court of Justice Queen's Bench Division Manchester District Registry
	Claim No. 2000 S No. 98744
To Claimant's solicitor	**Claimant** Shilton Machine Tools Limited
Boardman Phipps & Co. 20 High Street Manchester M15 9CZ	**Defendant** Banks Plastic Mouldings Limited
	SEAL

District Judge Chesterfield has considered the statements of case and allocation questionnaires filed and allocated the claim to the **multi-track**.

The District Judge has ordered that:

1. Disclosure shall take place as follows:

Each party shall give standard disclosure to every other party by list. The latest date for delivery of the lists is 10th January 2001.

The latest date for service of any request to inspect or for a copy of a document is 17th January 2001.

2. Further directions will be given at a case management conference to be heard at 10.30 am on Monday 12th February 2001.

3. Costs in the claim.

[The claim is being transferred to the [Civil Trial Centre at   County Court]
[Division of the Royal Courts of Justice] where all future applications, correspondence and so on will be dealt with]

The reason[s] the judge has given for allocation to this track [is] [are] that:

The claim has a value exceeding £15,000 and neither party has consented to it being dealt with other than on the multi-track.

Notes:

- You and the other party, or parties, may agree to extend the time periods given in the directions above provided this does not affect the date given for any case management conference, for returning the listing questionnaire, for any pre-trial review or the date of the trial or trial period.

- If you do not comply with these directions, any other party to the claim will be entitled to apply to the court for an order that your statement of case (claim or defence) be struck out.

- Leaflets explaining more about what happens when your case is allocated to the multi-track are available from the court office.

The court office at The Courts of Justice, Crown Square, Manchester M60 9DJ is open between 10 am and 4 pm Monday to Friday. Address all communications to the Court Manager quoting the claim number.

7.7 Stay for Settlement

One of the court's case management functions is to help the parties to settle the whole or part of the case (CPR, r. 1.4(2)(f)), and another is to encourage the parties to use alternative dispute resolution procedures if appropriate, and to facilitate the use of such procedures (CPR, r. 1.4(2)(e)). It is with these objectives in mind that the rules provide for a new procedure for the court ordering a stay of proceedings to allow for settlement of the case.

One of the headings in the allocation questionnaire allows a party to include a request for the proceedings to be stayed while the parties try to settle the case. If all the parties make such a request, or if the court on its own initiative considers that such a stay would be appropriate, a direction will be made staying the proceedings for one month. The court has power to extend the stay for such specified period as it thinks appropriate. Periods of extension can be sought simply by writing to the court. Extensions will not usually exceed four weeks at a time unless there are clear reasons to justify a longer time. During the period of such a stay the claimant is under a duty to inform the court if a settlement is reached (CPR, r. 26.4(4)). If, by the end of the defined period of the stay, the claimant has not told the court that the case has been settled, the court will give such directions for the management of the case as it considers appropriate, including allocating it to an appropriate track.

7.8 Trial in the Royal Courts of Justice

One of the questions that will be considered in claims brought in the High Court is whether a case should be managed and tried in the Royal Courts of Justice as opposed to another Civil Trial Centre. The idea is that only the most important cases justify use of the resources of the Royal Courts of Justice. Accordingly, generally cases with an estimated value of less than £50,000 will be transferred out of the Royal Courts of Justice to a County Court at the track allocation stage (PD 29, para. 2.2). Exceptions where claims worth less than £50,000 may be retained in the Royal Courts of Justice are:

(a) cases which are required by an enactment to be tried in the High Court;

(b)   cases falling within any of the specialist lists;

(c)   professional negligence claims;

(d)   Fatal Accident Act claims;

(e)   fraud and undue influence claims;

(f)   defamation claims;

(g)   claims for malicious prosecution and false imprisonment; and

(h)   claims against the police.

7.9   Changing Tracks

The court may make a subsequent order re-allocating a claim to a different track (CPR, r. 26.10). Where a claim was initially allocated to the small claims track, and is later re-allocated to another track, the small claims costs restrictions cease to apply from the date of reallocation (CPR, r. 27.15).

A party who is dissatisfied with an allocation decision may challenge the decision either by appealing up to the next higher court or by making an application back to the judge who made the initial decision. Applications should be used where the decision was made without a hearing of which he was given due notice or if there has been a material change of circumstances. If the party was present, represented or given due notice of the hearing where the decision was made the only appropriate route is by way of appeal (PD 26, para. 11.1(2) and 11.2).

In cases where a Part 20 claim has been issued (see **Chapter 9**) there may need to be a redetermination as to the most suitable track for the proceedings. Mere issue of a Part 20 claim will not have this effect, but where a Part 20 defence has been filed the proceedings will be reconsidered by the procedural judge to determine whether the claim should remain on its existing track (particularly in cases on the small claims and fast tracks), and whether there needs to be any adjustment to the timetable. At the same time the procedural judge will consider whether the Part 20 claim should be dealt with separately from the main action.

7.10   Allocation in Specialist Proceedings

Each specialist court has its own procedure dealing with case management at the allocation stage. Some types of specialist proceedings are automatically allocated to the multi-track (see, for example, PD 49B, para. 10, for applications under the Companies Act 1985, and PD 49C, para. 4.1, for claims in the TCC). Allocation questionnaires are not, in general, used in specialist cases automatically allocated to the multi-track. In the Commercial Court, after service of the defence, the legal representatives for each party must liaise for the purpose of preparing a short case memorandum, also, for the purpose of preparing an agreed list of important issues (with a separate section dealing with matters which are common ground between all or some of the parties), and the claimant's solicitors must prepare a case management bundle (Commercial Guide, paras D4.1, D5.1 and D6.1). There is then a mandatory case management conference which the parties must arrange to be listed for the first available date six weeks after service of the last defence (paras D7.1 and D7.2). Seven days before the case management conference each party must file a completed case management information sheet, in the form set out in the Commercial Guide, appendix 6, and it is this form that takes the place of the allocation questionnaire (para. D7.10). On the other hand, allocation questionnaires are used in Ch.D. cases despite the fact they are automatically allocated to the multi-track.

7.11 Questions

OBJECTIVES

By the conclusion of this section you should have a sound understanding of:

(a) the nature of different types of statements of case:

(b) statements of truth;

(c) the procedure followed in defended cases;

(d) the mechanics of entering default judgments in undefended cases;

(e) the nature of the judgment entered by default in different types of claim; and

(f) the allocation of claims to the three case management tracks.

RESEARCH

Read the materials contained in **Chapters 5** to **7** of this Manual and consider **19.3** to **19.3.3**.

LARGE GROUP SESSION 2

You must read the questions below in advance of Large Group Session 2. There is no need to have prepared notes in advance, as the background materials will be considered in the class. Default judgments will be considered further in Small Group Session 2, see **9.9**.

QUESTION 1

Your client, Gordon Engineering Ltd, has recently been served with a claim form, the material part of which says:

The claimant seeks the sum of £21,150 in respect of goods sold and delivered, full particulars of which have been provided to the defendant, and which, despite repeated requests, the defendant has failed to pay for:

Invoice 38724 dated 14 February 2000, comprising £18,000 and VAT of £3,150   £21,150.00

And interest on the sum of £21,150 pursuant to the County Courts Act 1984, s. 69, at 8% p.a. from 28 February 2000 to the date hereof amounting to £936.39 and continuing until trial or earlier payment at the daily rate of £4.63.

Your client agrees it has not paid this invoice, but explains that some of the goods were not delivered, and the rest had been damaged by exposure to water, and so were worth rather less than the contract price. Advise Gordon Engineering Ltd on how it should respond to this claim.

QUESTION 2

On 4 October 2000 Gregory issued a claim form in the Sheffield County Court, with particulars of claim attached, against Morgan claiming £84,000 being the price of goods sold and delivered. The claim form and particulars of claim were posted by the court by ordinary first class post on 6 October 2000. Morgan has not filed an acknowledgment of service or filed a defence. It is now 23 October 2000. Gregory seeks to enter judgment in default today for the sum of £84,000.

Which one of the following propositions is correct?

[A] Gregory may not enter judgment because the action will have to be transferred to the High Court.
[B] Gregory may enter judgment in default because the relevant time for filing an acknowledgment of service has expired.
[C] Gregory may not enter judgment in default because the relevant time for filing a defence has not yet expired.
[D] Gregory may enter judgment because at least 14 days have elapsed since particulars of claim were served.

QUESTION 3

Lynn received a claim form, with particulars of claim attached, ten days ago by which Regional Bank plc is claiming £90,000 under a contract of guarantee. The claim form was delivered by insertion through the letter box at Lynn's home. Advise Lynn, who admits liability, but wants time to pay.

QUESTION 4

Consider the three cases discussed in Questions 1 to 3 at **4.7** above. If proceedings are issued in each of these cases, and defences filed, what will happen next?

QUESTION 5

(a) What is a case management conference?

(b) What is its purpose?

(c) Who should attend?

EIGHT

PARTIES AND JOINDER

8.1   Introduction

Prior to the Judicature Acts of 1873 and 1875 any failure in bringing the correct parties before the court would have been fatal to civil proceedings. Nowadays the rules in this area are far more liberal. The general policy stated in SCA 1981, s. 49(2) is that the court

> ... shall so exercise its jurisdiction in every cause or matter before it as to secure that, as far as possible, all matters in dispute between the parties are completely and finally determined, and all multiplicity of legal proceedings with respect to any of those matters is avoided.

Nevertheless, it remains of great importance that all necessary parties, and no others, are named in proceedings when they are commenced, and that each party be correctly named. Any failure in these matters is likely to delay the ultimate resolution of the litigation and will almost certainly be penalised in costs. Any delay may prejudice the eventual resolution of the litigation either through evidence becoming stale or lost, or by the passing of a limitation period.

This chapter will first consider the rules relating to particular classes of party. It will then look at the rules governing joinder of parties and causes of action. Finally, it will consider representative proceedings, consolidation of actions, intervening and interpleading.

8.2   Parties

8.2.1   CHILDREN

8.2.1.1   General
A person attains full age at 18. Until then an individual is under disability. In the past the terms 'infant' and 'minor' were used, but the Civil Procedure Rules 1998 use the terms 'child' and 'children'.

A child must sue or be sued by his or her 'litigation friend' (CPR, r. 21.2). However, the court may make an order to permit a child to conduct proceedings without a litigation friend. It is desirable that the person appointed as the litigation friend should be someone who can fairly and competently conduct the proceedings on behalf of the child, and have no interest in the action adverse to the child. Further, where the child is a claimant (but not if a defendant), the litigation friend must undertake to pay any costs which the child may be ordered to pay, subject to any right of repayment from the child. The litigation friend must file a written certificate in the appropriate court office. An example of a certificate of suitability is shown in **Figure 8.1**.

If a child has no litigation friend, an application can be made for a suitable person to be appointed by the court.

Figure 8.1   Certificate of suitability of litigation friend

Certificate of Suitability of Litigation Friend	In the Birmingham County Court Claim No. BM00 732776 Claimant John Metcalf Defendant Alison Grainger

If you are acting:

- for a child, you must serve a copy of the completed form on a parent of guardian of the child, or if there is no parent or guardian, the carer or the person with whom the child lives

- for a patient, you must serve a copy of the completed form on the person authorised under Part VII of the Mental Health Act 1983 or, if no person is authorised, the carer or person with whom the patient lives unless you are that person. You must also complete a certificate of service (obtainable from the court office).

You should send the completed form to the court with the claim form (if acting for the claimant) or when you take the first step on the defendant's behalf in the claim together with the certificate of service (if applicable).

You do not need to complete this form if you do have an authorisation under Part VII of the Mental Health Act 1983 to conduct legal proceedings on the person's behalf.

I consent to act as litigation friend for the claimant John Metcalf

I believe that the above named person is a

☐ child   ☐ patient *(give your reasons overleaf and attach a copy of any medical evidence in support)*

I am able to conduct proceedings on behalf of the above named person competently and fairly and I have no interests adverse to those of the above named person.

* I undertake to pay any costs which the above named claimant may be ordered to pay in these proceedings subject to any right I may have to be repaid from the assets of the claimant.

* *delete if you are acting for the defendant*

Please write your name in capital letters

☐ Mr	☐ Mrs	☐ Miss	Surname	METCALF
☐ Ms	☐ Other _____		Forenames	JANET RACHEL

Address to which documents in this case are to be sent

Hutchinson & Brayhead
45 Church Street,
Birmingham   I certify that the information given in this form is correct

B3 7YS   Signed   Date 11.10.2000

The court office at 33 Bull Street, Birmingham B4 6DS is open between 10 am and 4 pm Monday to Friday. When corresponding with the court, please address forms or letters to the Court Manager and quote the claim number.

8.2.1.2 **Title**

A child acting by a litigation friend should be referred to in the title to the proceedings as, e.g., 'JANET SMITH (a child by LUCY SMITH her litigation friend)'. A child acting without a litigation friend is referred to as 'JANET SMITH (a child)'.

8.2.1.3 **Child attaining 18 years**

When a child who is a party to proceedings reaches full age he or she must serve on the other parties and file at court a notice stating that he or she is now over 18 and that the litigation friend's appointment has ceased, giving an address for service, and stating whether or not he or she intends to carry on being a party. If the child is to carry on, he or she will be described from that point on as, e.g., 'JANET SMITH (formerly a child but now of full age)'. If the child (now of full age) fails to serve such a notice, the litigation friend can serve a notice to the effect that the child has reached full age and the appointment as litigation friend has ceased. A child claimant's litigation friend's liability in costs continues until notice is given to the other parties.

8.2.1.4 **Children's settlements**

When a claim brought on behalf of a child is settled two main problems arise. First, it is necessary to protect the child, who might otherwise be pressured into accepting a disadvantageous settlement. Secondly, as a child will not be bound by an out-of-court settlement unless it is proved to have been for his or her benefit, it is necessary to find means for providing the defendant with a valid discharge for the money paid in settlement. It is to meet these two problems that Rules of Court have been made to provide for the approval by the court of children's settlements (see CPR, r. 21.10).

If a claim is settled before proceedings are commenced the parties may (and would be well advised to) make an application under Part 8 for approval of the settlement by the court. If approved, the child will be bound by the settlement. After proceedings have been commenced any settlement will only be valid if it is approved, approval being sought by making an application under Part 23 (see **Chapter 10**). CPR, r. 21.10, provides:

> (1)   Where a claim is made—
>   (a)   by or on behalf of a child or patient; or
>   (b)   against a child or patient
> no settlement, compromise or payment and no acceptance of money paid into court shall be valid, so far as it relates to the claim by, on behalf of or against the child or patient, without the approval of the court.
>   (2)   Where—
>   (a)   before proceedings in which a claim is made by or on behalf of, or against a child or patient (whether alone or with any other person) are begun, an agreement is reached for the settlement of the claim; and
>   (b)   the sole purpose of proceedings on that claim is to obtain the approval of the court to settlement or compromise of the claim,
> the claim must—
>   (i)   be made using the procedure set out in Part 8 (alternative procedure for claims); and
>   (ii)   include a request to the court for approval of the settlement or compromise.

Approval is sought from a Master or District Judge sitting in private, but the decision will be pronounced in public (in accordance with the European Convention on Human Rights, Article 6(1)). Often the court will prefer a parent to attend. In difficult cases written evidence may be required, but usually the documents required are the application and statements of case, any police reports and witness statements, both sides' medical reports, a schedule of special damages, counsel's opinion on liability and quantum, and (if in the High Court) the appropriate Court Funds office forms. If a Part 8 claim is used, the claim form must set out details of the claim and also the terms of the settlement or compromise, or must have attached to it a draft consent order. Information to be provided at the hearing includes whether and to what extent the defendant admits liability, the age and any occupation of the child, the litigation friend's approval of the proposed settlement, and details of any relevant prosecution.

If liability has not been admitted the court considers the child's prospects of success, and decides whether in the light of the medical evidence the proposed settlement is a reasonable one and for the child's benefit. If not, the Master adjourns to give the parties an opportunity to renegotiate and gives directions as to the future conduct of the litigation. If the settlement is approved, the Master gives directions as to how the money shall be dealt with.

8.2.1.5   **Investment of money recovered for persons under disability**
Money recovered for children is administered on their behalf by the High Court, whereas money recovered for patients is administered by the Court of Protection. Fees are charged by the Court of Protection, which should be included in any award of damages. If the sum is very small the court may order it to be paid to the litigation friend for it to be put into a building society account.

The courts act on the principle that money awarded to a person under disability should be applied for the purpose for which it was awarded. Decisions have to be taken as to what it should be spent on, how much should be invested for the future, and what sorts of investments should be made. From time to time, applications may be made for the release of more funds for various purchases. Money in court must be paid out to the child when he or she reaches full age.

8.2.1.6   **Limitation**
Time does not run against a child for limitation purposes until the child ceases to be under disability: see LA 1980, s. 28.

8.2.2   **PATIENTS**

Like children, persons suffering from mental disorder within the meaning of the Mental Health Act 1983 are persons under disability. Accordingly, patients must act in proceedings through a litigation friend, who may be a receiver duly appointed by the Court of Protection. In cases of conflict of interest between the patient and receiver the Official Solicitor may be appointed.

Time will not run against a patient for limitation purposes only if the patient was under disability when the cause of action accrued: LA 1980, s. 28(1). Thus, if a cause of action accrued at a time when the claimant was of full capacity, time will continue running during a subsequent period of disability through mental disorder.

8.2.3   **PARTNERS**

8.2.3.1   **General**
The RSC O. 81, r. 1 (which is preserved in CPR, sch. 1), provides:

Subject to the provisions of any enactment, any two or more persons claiming to be entitled, or alleged to be liable, as partners in respect of a cause of action and carrying on business within the jurisdiction may sue, or be sued, in the name of the firm (if any) of which they were partners at the time when the cause of action accrued.

CCR O. 5, r. 9(1) (which is preserved in CPR, sch. 2), is in very similar terms.

In most situations the partners can be named individually because their liability is in general joint or joint and several (see, e.g. Partnership Act 1890, ss. 9 and 12). Usually, however, it is more convenient to use the partnership name.

8.2.3.2   **Title**
The fact that a party is a partnership is disclosed in the title by adding the words '(a firm)' after its name.

8.2.3.3   **Service**
Service on partners was considered in **Chapter 3**. As mentioned in **Figure 3.2**, the address for service of an individual suing or being sued in the name of a firm is that person's usual or last known place of residence, or his or her place of business or last

known place of business. As mentioned at **3.7.3.1**, personal service on a partnership may be effected on the manager of its principal place of business.

8.2.3.4   Acknowledgment of Service
The RSC O. 81, r. 4 (which is preserved in CPR, sch. 1), provides:

> *(1)   Where persons are sued as partners in the name of their firm, service may not be acknowledged in the name of the firm but only by the partners thereof in their own names, but the action shall nevertheless continue in the name of the firm.*
> *(2)   Where in an action against a firm the writ by which the action is begun is served on a person as a partner, that person, if he denies that he was a partner or liable as such at any material time, may acknowledge service of the writ and state in his acknowledgment that he does so as a person served as a partner in the defendant firm but who denies that he was a partner at any material time.*
> *An acknowledgment of service given in accordance with this paragraph shall, unless and until it is set aside, be treated as an acknowledgment by the defendant firm.*

8.2.3.5   Disclosure of partners' names
A party sued by or suing a partnership may serve a notice requiring them to provide a written statement of the names and addresses of all the partners in the firm when the cause of action accrued: RSC O. 81, r. 2 and CCR O. 5, r. 9(2).

8.2.3.6   Enforcement
A judgment obtained against a partnership in the firm name may generally be enforced in the usual way against either partnership property or the property of individual partners. However, permission to enforce may be required if a partner was out of the jurisdiction when the claim was issued or if a partner did not admit to being or was not adjudged to be a partner in the course of the proceedings: RSC O. 81, r. 5, CCR O. 25, r. 9.

8.2.4   SOLE TRADERS

8.2.4.1   General
A sole trader, even if trading under an artificial trading name, must be distinguished from a partnership. Such a person must sue in his or her own name, but *may* be sued in the trading name: RSC O. 81, r. 9, CCR O. 5, r. 10 (both of which are preserved in the schedules to the CPR).

8.2.4.2   Title
If the claimant does not know the defendant's own name, the defendant may be described, e.g. 'SPEEDY MOTORS (a trading name)'. If both names are known, the description becomes, e.g., 'HENRY WILLIAMS (trading as SPEEDY MOTORS).'

8.2.5   COMPANIES

8.2.5.1   Name
Companies must sue and be sued in their full registered name. The words 'public limited company' or 'limited' are part of a limited liability company's name, and must be included. If its true legal description is not apparent from a company's name, the description should be stated in the title, e.g. 'a company limited by guarantee.'

8.2.5.2   Service
The Companies Act 1985, s. 725(1), provides 'A document may be served on a company by leaving it at, or sending it by post to the company's registered office.' Alternatives provided for by the CPR are set out in **Figure 3.2** and at **3.7.3.1** above.

Service by post on a company is deemed to be effected in the ordinary course of post, e.g. the second working day after posting (Interpretation Act 1978, s. 7).

8.2.5.3   Representation of companies
Before the introduction of the Civil Procedure Rules 1998 companies who were parties in High Court proceedings had to act through solicitors. This requirement has gone,

and directors or other duly authorised individuals can now act for their companies. Where a director or some other individual appears for a company at a hearing, a written statement must be completed giving the company's full name, its registered number, the status of the representative within the company (such as being a director), and the date and form by which the representative was authorised to act for the company. For example: '20th October 2000: Board resolution dated 20th October 2000'. See PD 39, para. 5.2.

8.2.6 UNINCORPORATED ASSOCIATIONS

These have no separate legal personality, and so generally cannot sue or be sued in their own names. There is a distinction between proprietary and members' clubs. A proprietary club may be construed as a partnership, and may be sued in accordance with RSC O. 81. If all the members of a members' club have the same interest in a dispute, one or more of their members may sue on behalf of them all in representative proceedings: CPR, r. 19.6 (see **8.4**).

8.2.7 GENDER

Where doubt may arise as to the sex or description of a party, he or she may be described by the appropriate prefix in the title of the proceedings, e.g., 'Mr', 'Miss', 'Ms' or 'Mrs' or by adding the word '(male)' or '(female)'. This can be of assistance for the purposes of service and enforcement.

Where a woman changes her name on marriage, a notice of the change must be filed in the court office and served on the other parties. The title becomes, e.g., 'ANN SMITH (formerly ANN JONES)'.

8.2.8 BANKRUPTS

Generally, when a person becomes bankrupt, all causes of action other than for personal injuries and defamation vest in the trustee in bankruptcy. A single cause of action giving rise to heads of damage in respect of loss of earnings and also for pain, suffering and loss of amenity will vest in the trustee in bankruptcy, but the trustee will be required to account as a constructive trustee to the bankrupt for the general damages: see *Ord* v *Upton* (1999) 149 NLJ 1904. The official name of the trustee is 'the trustee of the estate of JOHN JONES a Bankrupt'. The trustee need not disclose his or her own name (see Insolvency Act 1986, s. 305(4)).

If a claimant becomes bankrupt during the currency of proceedings, the trustee in bankruptcy may continue the proceedings, but must obtain an order for substitution under CPR, r. 19.2(2). If a defendant becomes bankrupt during the currency of proceedings the action may be stayed or allowed to continue on terms: Insolvency Act 1986, s. 285.

8.2.9 DEATH DURING ACTION

A claim will only abate on the death of the claimant if the cause of action is a personal one, such as a claim in libel. Otherwise, the executors or administrators of a claimant who dies during an action may obtain an order for substitution under CPR, r. 19.2(2). On the death of a defendant, a claimant may apply for an order to continue the proceedings against the defendant's personal representatives.

8.2.10 ESTATES

Where a cause of action survives for the benefit of or against the estate of a deceased person, all the deceased's executors or administrators must be named as parties to the action. If the deceased has no personal representatives, proceedings may still be commenced against the estate, describing the defendant as, e.g., 'the estate of DAVID WILLIAMS deceased'. During the four month period of validity the claimant should seek an order for the appointment of someone to represent the estate of the deceased: PD 7, para. 4.5.

If a claim is brought against someone who was in fact dead when the claim was issued, it will be treated as if it was brought against the estate of the deceased (CPR, r. 19.8(3)(b)). By way of exception to these general rules, in a claim where one of the persons having an interest in the claim has died and has no personal representatives, it is possible for any of the parties to apply to the court for an order that the claim may proceed in the absence of a person to represent the estate of the deceased (see r. 19.8(1)(a)). If such an order is made any judgment or order made in the claim will still bind the estate of the deceased (r. 19.8(5)).

8.2.11 TRUSTS

Actions in respect of trust property may be brought by or against the trustees without joining the beneficiaries, and any judgment will bind the beneficiaries unless the court orders otherwise: RSC O. 15, r. 14 (preserved in CPR, sch. 1).

8.2.12 CHARITIES

In Part 8 claims where questions arise as to the validity of charitable bequests to an established charity, the trustees are the proper parties. Where the questioned bequest could be construed as being charitable, but is not to an existing charity, the Attorney-General must be joined to represent the interests of charity.

If proceedings are brought against a charity, logic would indicate that the trustees should be named as the defendants. The practice, however, is to name an official of the charity, such as the clerk, treasurer or secretary who is sued '. . . on behalf of the [name of charity]'.

8.2.13 RELATOR ACTIONS

Actions to restrain an interference with a public right, or to abate a public nuisance, or to compel the performance of a public duty, have until May 2000 been brought in the name of the Attorney-General as he is the only person recognised by public law as entitled to represent the public in a court of law. The current position in these cases is uncertain, as the old rule dealing with this (RSC O.15, r. 11) has been revoked but not replaced.

8.2.14 THE CROWN

Proceedings by and against the Crown are governed by the Crown Proceedings Act 1947. RSC O. 77 and CCR O. 42, both of which are preserved in the schedules to the CPR, regulate proceedings involving the Crown, the basic effect of which is to give the Crown a number of privileges not enjoyed by other litigants. Periodically the Treasury publishes a list of authorised government departments and their solicitors for service. If a department does not appear on the list (e.g. Foreign and Commonwealth Office) it must sue and be sued in the name of the Attorney-General.

There are numerous quasi-governmental public bodies which are not formal departments of State. These bodies will usually have an implicit power to bring proceedings to protect their special interests in the performance of their functions (*Broadmoor Hospital Authority* v *Robinson* (9 February 2000, CA, unreported), where it was held the hospital authority had a power to bring proceedings seeking an injunction to restrain a patient from publishing a book about how he had killed someone, although the order was refused).

8.3 Joinder

The main rules dealing with joinder are:

7.3 *The claimant may use a single claim form to start all claims which can be conveniently disposed of in the same proceedings.*

19.1 *Any number of claimants or defendants may be joined as parties to a claim.*

It is therefore for the claimant to decide whether to join a number of causes of action in a single claim. For example, it may well be convenient to join causes of action where they are simply alternative ways of formulating a single claim, such as in negligence, or breach of statutory duty, or in occupier's liability. Claims joined under r. 7.3 could give rise to separate remedies, such as a creditor who joins claims for two or more separate debts in a single claim against a defendant. Regarding joinder of parties, it could be that two claimants have a joint right, such as where they are joint contractors suing the other party to the contract. Joint claimants could be suing in the alternative, such as where there may be some doubt whether a contract was entered into by one of them as an agent for the other, or as a principal. Co-defendants may be sued in a single claim where they are both liable (such as where the second defendant is alleged to be vicariously liable for the negligence of the first defendant), or where they may be liable in the alternative, such as in cases where an injured employee sues his employer, a sub-contractor and the site owner. In the last example, it is probable that different causes of action will be alleged against the different co-defendants, but joinder is still likely to be convenient.

This wide discretion given to claimants to decide what and how to include in a single claim is cut down in relation to joint (as opposed to several) rights, where CPR, r. 19.3, provides that all persons jointly entitled to the remedy must be parties, unless the court otherwise orders. If anyone does not agree to being a claimant, that person must be made a defendant, again unless the court otherwise orders.

Once causes of action or parties have been joined together in a single claim, the court retains the power to separate them if it regards the joinder as inconvenient. This may be because the joinder may make the claim unnecessarily complicated, and cause delays or an increase in costs that would be avoided if the parties had been sued or if claims had been brought separately. Case management powers available to the court to deal with this include directing separate trials, deciding on the order in which issues are to be tried, and striking out part of the claim if it is likely to obstruct the just disposal of the proceedings (see CPR, rr. 3.1(2) and 3.4(2)(b)).

8.4   Representative Actions

The CPR, r. 19.6(1), provides:

> *Where more than one person has the same interest in a claim—*
> (a)   *the claim may be begun; or*
> (b)   *the court may order that the claim be continued,*
> *by or against one or more persons who have the same interest as representatives of any other persons who have that interest.*

By CPR, r. 19.6(4), unless the court otherwise directs, any judgment or order made in representative proceedings is binding on all persons represented in the claim, but may only be enforced by or against such a person with the permission of the court.

Representative actions are comparatively rare, but contribute a convenient way of litigating a dispute where otherwise a large number of persons would have to be named in the proceedings. The rule requires the persons represented to have 'the same interest'. According to Lord Macnaghten in *Duke of Bedford* v *Ellis* [1901] AC 1, at p. 8, HL, this has three elements:

> Given a common interest and a common grievance, a representative suit is in order if the relief sought is in its nature beneficial to all whom the [claimant] proposes to represent.

An example is *Smith* v *Cardiff Corporation* [1954] QB 210. The defendants had more than 13,000 tenants. They gave notice to each tenant of a scheme to increase their rents on a differential basis according to the income of each tenant. The four claimants commenced proceedings, purporting to represent all the council's tenants, claiming a declaration that the scheme was *ultra vires*. It was held by the Court of Appeal that the tenants did not have a common grievance and that the relief claimed was not in its nature beneficial to all the tenants. Under the scheme the more affluent tenants were, in effect, to subsidise the less affluent. Therefore the tenants fell into two classes whose interests were in conflict.

8.5 Representation of Unascertained Interested Persons

In Part 8 claims to construe wills and deeds, and proceedings concerning the estates of deceased persons or trust property, the court may appoint one or more persons to represent any unascertained or unborn persons (or persons who cannot be found) who may be interested in the proceedings if it is expedient to do so: CPR, r. 19.7. Any judgment will then bind the persons represented, and the court's approval is required for any settlement. Although such an order may be made on an interim application, the order is most frequently made at the hearing.

8.6 Consolidation

The CPR, r. 3.1(2)(g), gives the court power to consolidate proceedings. This involves ordering two or more separate claims to continue together, with one of the claims being nominated as the lead claim. Nothing is said in the rule about the circumstances where this might be appropriate. It is likely to be just to make such an order, in accordance with the overriding objective, where the various claims have a strong link with each other. This may be because they all involve the same allegation of negligence against a common defendant, or the claims may all arise out of the same incident. Unless the court makes the order of its own initiative, the various claims will need to come before the same judge on a single occasion. This means that some of them may need to be transferred so they are all in the same court, and then identical applications (or a single application headed with the titles of all the claims) need to be issued, returnable on the same occasion.

An example of the operation of the rule is *Healey* v *Waddington & Sons Ltd* [1954] 1 WLR 688. An accident in a coal mine resulted in the deaths of six workmen and injuries to two others. Separate proceedings were issued by the widows of the six men killed and by the two injured. By consent, the eight actions were consolidated up to the determination of liability, and, if liability was established, hearing dates were to be fixed to determine quantum of damages for each claimant individually.

8.7 Intervening

8.7.1 JURISDICTION

By CPR, r. 19.2(2), someone who is not a party to an action as originally constituted may be ordered to be added as a party if either:

(a) the presence of the intervener is desirable to ensure the court can resolve all matters in dispute; or

(b) it would be desirable to determine a question or issue relating to the relief already claimed between the intervener and an existing party at the same time as determining the existing action.

8.7.2 WHO MAY INTERVENE?

The court has a discretion whether to allow a non-party to intervene. It may be appropriate for the court to exercise its discretion in the following situations.

(a) Where the action will directly affect the intervener's proprietary or pecuniary rights. This includes cases where the intervener will be bound to pay any damages awarded, such as the Motor Insurers Bureau where the defendant in a motor vehicle personal injuries case is uninsured: *Gurtner* v *Circuit* [1968] 2 QB 587. Another common situation is where the Legal Services Commission may be ordered to pay an unassisted defendant's costs under the Access to Justice Act 1999, s. 11(4)(d) (see **35.9.9**).

(b) Where the action involves public policy or may affect the prerogative of the Crown. In such cases the Attorney-General may intervene.

(c) Where a claimant claims to represent a class, a member of the class may be allowed to intervene to dispute the claimant's entitlement to represent the class (see CPR, r. 19.6(3)).

8.8 Interpleader

There are occasions when a person, with no personal interest in property or a debt he or she is holding, receives rival claims to that property or debt from two or more other persons. Interpleader is a procedure whereby such a stakeholder can gain protection by calling upon the rival claimants to claim against each other.

For example, Tom leaves a table with a storage company under a contract of bailment. Janet then writes to the storage company claiming the table belongs to her. Another, and more frequently recurring, situation is where the sheriff or bailiff seizes goods in execution, and subsequently some third party, such as a finance company or a member of the judgment debtor's family, claims the goods belong to them. Neither the storage company nor the sheriff or bailiff have a personal claim to the disputed property, and they can therefore interplead so that the title to the property can be decided.

Interpleader proceedings can be taken where the stakeholder either is being, or expects to be, sued by the rival claimants.

8.8.1 PROCEDURE

In the County Court, special forms of summons are prescribed (Forms N88 and N89). In the High Court, by RSC O. 17, r. 3 (preserved by CPR, sch. 1), if proceedings have not yet been commenced against the stakeholder the application is made by issuing a claim form and if proceedings have already been issued, by ordinary application notice.

In each case the application must be supported by evidence stating:

(a) that the stakeholder claims no interest in the disputed property other than for charges and costs;

(b) that the stakeholder is not colluding with any of the claimants; and

(c) that the stakeholder is willing to transfer the property as the court may direct.

8.8.2 THE HEARING

On the return day the court may:

(a) if proceedings have already been issued, order that the other claimant(s) be made defendants in substitution for or in addition to the stakeholder; or

(b) order that an issue be stated and tried, with a direction as to who should be the claimants and defendants; or

(c) if all the parties consent or the facts are not in dispute, summarily determine any question of law or the dispute; or

(d) if a claimant fails to attend, order that they be completely debarred from prosecuting their claim against the stakeholder.

8.9   Group Litigation

Where a number of claims give rise to common or related issues of fact or law, the court may make a group litigation order (a 'GLO'), see CPR, rr. 19.10 and 19.11. These orders are most likely to be made where a number of claims are made arising out of a disaster (such as a serious public transport accident) or where a number of claims are made against a manufacturer having a common cause (such as claims arising out of the side effects of a medication). If a GLO is made it will:

(a) contain directions about maintaining a group register of the claims governed by the GLO;

(b) specify the GLO issues to be dealt with under the group litigation and which will identify the claims which can be managed under the GLO;

(c) specify the court that will manage the group litigation.

Further directions made under a GLO include directing that group claims must be transferred to the management court; that certain details must be included in the particulars of claim to show that the criteria for entry of the claim on that group register have been met; that future claims raising GLO issues must be commenced in the management court; that one or more of the claims shall proceed as test cases; and that the others shall be stayed until further order. Documents disclosed (see **Chapter 20**) in a GLO claim are treated as disclosed to all the parties on the group register (CPR, r. 19.12(4)), unless the court otherwise orders. Any judgment or order made in a claim on the group register is binding on the parties to all the other claims, unless the court otherwise orders (r. 19.12(1)(a)). The court may give directions as to the extent that an order or judgment shall bind the parties to claims added to the group register after the order or judgment was made or given (r. 19.12(1)(b)).

NINE

PART 20 CLAIMS

9.1 Introduction

There are many situations where a defendant will allege that someone else is in fact responsible for the harm suffered by the claimant, or otherwise ought to be included in the action. There are three possibilities that need to be distinguished:

(a) Where the defendant alleges that the claimant has sued the wrong person, because the cause of action is against the other person and not against the defendant. Here the matter should be set out in the defence, and, if the defendant is correct, the claimant should discontinue the present action and sue the other person.

(b) Where the defendant alleges that if the claimant succeeds in the action, the other person should pay the whole amount awarded by the court (an indemnity) or a part of the amount awarded (a contribution). There are two sub-categories here:

    (i) Where the other person is not a party to the action as presently constituted, the defendant should bring them in by issuing a Part 20 claim, the other person then being known as the 'Part 20 defendant'. Instead of this inelegant phrase, this Manual will use the old fashioned term 'third party'. A third party may then consider bringing in someone else as a 'fourth party' (technically, under the Civil Procedure Rules 1998 such a party is a 'Part 20 defendant (2nd claim)') and so on, which may be necessary where, for example, a purchaser sues a retailer (the defendant) in respect of defective goods, who sues the wholesaler (the third party), who sues the importer (the fourth party), who then sues the manufacturer (the fifth party).

    (ii) Where the other party is already a defendant in the action. Typically, the other party will be a co-defendant. In this situation the claim is made by serving and filing a notice, commonly called a contribution notice, against the other party under CPR, r. 20.6.

(c) Where the defendant wants to make a claim against, or to have some legal or factual question resolved with, some person other than the claimant, where the claim or question is intimately tied in with the claim being brought by the claimant. In this situation the defendant has the option of commencing separate proceedings or seeking an order that the non-party be joined to the existing claim under CPR, r. 19.2(2)(b) on the ground that there is an issue between the defendant and the new party which is connected to the matters in dispute and it is desirable to add the new party to resolve that issue. An example would be where a claimant employer sues a defendant main contractor on a building contract. The defendant relies on frustration as a defence. If the defendant has a claim against a sub-contractor arising out of the same incident which it anticipates the subcontractor will defend by raising frustration, the defendant may want the frustration issues to be resolved simultaneously between itself, the claimant and the sub-contractor. To do so it will need to obtain an order joining the sub-contractor under r. 19.2(2)(b).

In situations (b) and (c) above the defendant almost always has the alternative option of commencing fresh proceedings against the other person. However, bringing the claim within existing proceedings usually results in a speedier determination of the claim against the other person, usually saves costs (as there will be one hearing, for example), and avoids the risk of differing results from different judges on essentially the same issues.

9.2 Scope of Part 20 Proceedings

9.2.1 WHAT TYPES OF CLAIM MAY BE MADE?

In order for a party to bring Part 20 proceedings they must ensure that their claim comes within CPR, r. 20.2. There are three types of claim which can be made under Part 20:

(a) Counterclaims (see **9.2.2**).

(b) Claims for an indemnity or a contribution (see **9.2.3**).

(c) Some other remedy (see **9.2.4**).

9.2.2 COUNTERCLAIMS

The rules on counterclaims are to be found in Part 20 of the Civil Procedure Rules 1998, but they are treated very differently from true third party claims. The straight-forward situation of a defendant counterclaiming against a claimant has already been considered at **5.5**. A rather more complex situation is where the defendant wants to make a counterclaim against someone other than the claimant (usually in addition to the claimant). Before making such a counterclaim the defendant must obtain an order from the court adding the new party to the proceedings as a defendant to the counterclaim: CPR, r. 20.5. An application for such an order may be made without notice, and a draft of the proposed statement of case must be filed with the application notice (PD 20, para. 1.2). The evidence in support of the application has to set out the stage reached in the main claim, the nature of the claim against the new party, and a summary of the facts on which that claim is based.

If an order is made adding the new party, the court will also give directions for managing the case. These are likely to include provision for service of all statements of case on the new party together with a response pack and a time for responding to the counterclaim, the role the new party can play at trial, as well as the usual matters such as disclosure of documents, witness statements etc. In the title to the proceedings the various parties are described as follows:

ALAN BEST	Claimant/Part 20 Defendant
COLIN DOWN	Defendant/Part 20 Claimant
EDNA FORBES	Part 20 Defendant

As with other counterclaims, a counterclaim against a new party needs to be issued and an issue fee must be paid (together with a fee for adding the new party).

9.2.3 INDEMNITY AND CONTRIBUTION

An indemnity is an obligation to reimburse someone. Put another way, it is a claim for the fulfilment of an obligation, not for damages for breach of one.

A right to an indemnity can arise in the following ways:

(a) Under a contractual promise to indemnify someone.

(b) Under certain relationships, e.g. between principal and agent.

(c) By statute, e.g. the LPA 1925, s. 76(1)(D) and sch. 2, Pt. IV, which implies a covenant to indemnify a mortgagee in a conveyance by way of mortgage of freehold property subject to a rent or of leasehold property.

A contribution can, broadly speaking, be defined as a partial indemnity. A right to a contribution can arise as between joint debtors or contractors, or joint wrongdoers or by statute. Under the Civil Liability (Contribution) Act 1978, where two or more persons are liable to the same claimant for the same damage, each may claim contribution towards the joint liability against the others. For example, in a two-vehicle accident the passenger in one of the vehicles may commence proceedings claiming damages for personal injuries against the driver of the other vehicle as the sole defendant. The defendant may then issue a Part 20 claim against the driver of the claimant's car seeking a contribution towards any damages the claimant might be awarded based on their relative blameworthiness for the collision. However, the defendant can only recover a contribution under the Act if the third party is liable for the 'same damage' as the defendant, which means, of course, the damage suffered by the claimant. So (altering the facts slightly for the purposes of exposition), in *Birse Construction Ltd* v *Haiste Ltd* [1996] 2 All ER 1, CA, the claimant claimed damages against the defendant for building a defective reservoir, which was settled by the defendant agreeing to build a replacement reservoir, and the defendant claimed the costs of the replacement reservoir against the third party. As the claim against the third party was not in respect of the same damage as that suffered by the claimant, the Third Party (now Part 20) claim was not for a contribution within the meaning of the Act.

9.2.4 SOME OTHER REMEDY

An example would be where a passenger involved in a two-car collision brings proceedings against one of the other drivers as a sole defendant claiming damages for personal injuries. The defendant could issue a Part 20 claim against the other driver seeking a contribution (see **9.2.2**), and also for damages for his or her own personal injuries and other damage sustained in the collision, being a claim for a remedy arising out of the same facts as the claim.

9.2.5 DISCRETION

If a Part 20 claim is technically within the grounds set out at **9.2.1**, the court still retains a discretion whether to allow the Part 20 claim to proceed. In *Chatsworth Investments Ltd* v *Amoco (UK) Ltd* [1968] 1 Ch 665 Russell LJ said that the court, in exercising its discretion under the old rules, had to take a wide approach, and ask whether the third party claim (now Part 20 claim) accorded with the general functions of third party proceedings. In *Barclays Bank Ltd* v *Tom* [1923] 1 KB 221, Scrutton LJ identified these functions as safeguarding against differing results, ensuring the third party is bound by the decision between the claimant and the defendant, ensuring the Part 20 claim is decided as close in time to the proceedings commenced by the claimant, and to save the expense of having two trials.

These ideas are largely reflected in CPR, r. 20.9(2), which provides that in deciding whether to grant permission to allow a Part 20 claim to be made (where permission is needed, see **9.5** below), or to dismiss a Part 20 claim at a later stage, the matters the court will take into account include:

(a) the degree of connection between the Part 20 claim and the main claim;

(b) whether the Part 20 claimant is seeking substantially the same remedy as is being claimed by the claimant;

(c) whether the Part 20 claim raises any question connected with the subject matter of the main claim.

9.3 Contribution Notice

A contribution notice is the old fashioned term describing a Part 20 claim made by one co-defendant against another. They are used to claim indemnities or contributions against the co-defendant (CPR, r. 20.6). However, where the defendant simply wants a contribution under the Civil Liability (Contribution) Act 1978 towards any damages that may be awarded, the accepted practice is to dispense with the service of contribution notices, and simply to ask the judge at trial to make the necessary apportionment of liability between the defendants, thereby saving the costs of the Notice.

This relaxation should not be relied on where there is some reason for having the issues between the defendant and the co-defendant defined, and so, in the following circumstances, contribution notices should be served, even though the defendant is seeking a contribution, namely where:

(a) the claim for the contribution is contractual rather than under the 1978 Act; or

(b) the defendant wants to combine the claim for a contribution with a claim for some related relief or remedy, or the determination of a related question or issue;

(c) the defendant needs to seek disclosure of documents or further information from the other party (the entitlement to which can only be decided when the issues have been defined).

9.4 The Part 20 Claim Form

An example of a Part 20 claim form appears as **Figure 9.1**. Note the following points, however:

(a) The claim against the third party should specify the different heads of claim being made — e.g. if a claim is being made for indemnity under a contract, and also for a contribution under statute, these should be separately mentioned. The same applies if there are distinct claims for debt and damages, or if different questions are to be resolved.

(b) The particulars of the Part 20 claim can be set out either in the Part 20 claim form or in a separate document attached to the claim form.

(c) It is normal to use the expression 'you' when referring to the third party in the Part 20 particulars of claim.

(d) The contents of a Part 20 claim must be verified by a statement of truth.

9.5 Issue and Service

9.5.1 WITHOUT PERMISSION

A defendant can issue a Part 20 claim form *without* seeking permission of it is issued before or at any time before filing his or her defence (CPR, r. 20.7(3)).

A third party can, in turn, issue a Part 20 claim without permission if the second Part 20 claim is issued at the same time as or before the Part 20 defence is filed.

A Part 20 claim form is issued and served in the same way as an ordinary claim form.

For limitation purposes a Part 20 claim is brought when the Part 20 claim form is issued by the court.

Service must be effected within 14 days of filing of the defence (CPR, r. 20.8(1)(b)). It must be served with a response pack of forms for acknowledging service, admitting and defending the claim. It must also be served with copies of all the statements of case already served in the proceedings (CPR, r. 20.12). A copy of the Part 20 claim form must also be served on all other existing parties.

The third party becomes a party to the proceedings once they are served with the Part 20 claim form (CPR, r. 20.10).

9.5.2 WITH PERMISSION

Permission will be required if the Part 20 claim form was not issued before filing of the defence. Permission is usually sought without giving notice to any of the existing parties or anyone else (CPR, r. 20.7(5)). The application notice has to be supported by evidence setting out the stage the main claim has reached together with a timetable of the action to date; the nature of the Part 20 claim; the facts on which it is based; and the name and address of the proposed third party (PD 20, paragraph 2.1). Where delay has been a factor an explanation for the delay should be included. If the court grants permission it will at the same time give directions as to service of the Part 20 claim form (CPR, r. 20.8(3)). Directions are likely to be similar to those mentioned above for a Part 20 claim issued without permission.

9.5.3 RESPONDING TO A PART 20 CLAIM

The time for filing a defence acknowledging service by a third party who is not already a party to the claim, is identical to that for an ordinary claim.

The general rules set out in the Civil Procedure Rules 1998 apply to Part 20 claims, and these include the provisions relating to default judgments (discussed in **Chapter 10**). If a third party fails to file a defence or acknowledge service within the 14 day period, the defendant (who will be the Part 20 claimant) may obtain a default judgment. If the Part 20 claim seeks an indemnity or a contribution, this is done simply by filing a request for judgment, and the third party will be deemed to admit the Part 20 claim and will be bound by any judgment or decision in the main proceedings which may be relevant to the Part 20 claim. If the Part 20 claim seeks some other remedy against the third party the defendant will have to make an application for judgment, although the application may be made without notice (CPR, r. 20.11).

9.6 Directions

If the third party files a defence the court must consider the future conduct of the proceedings and give appropriate directions. So far as practicable the court will seek to manage the main proceedings and the Part 20 claim together (CPR, r. 20.13).

In addition to the usual directions laying down a timetable to trial, the court may direct that 'the third party be at liberty to appear at the trial and take such part as the judge should direct', and that his liability be determined 'at the trial, but subsequent thereto'. Other orders may be made, e.g. to add or substitute a third party as a defendant.

It is important to realise that the various interim remedies available between claimant and defendant (or vice versa) are also available as between defendant and third party (or vice versa). Thus, for example, the defendant may claim summary judgment against the third party.

9.7 Interrelation with Main Action

A Part 20 claim is a separate claim, and in many ways has a life of its own independent of the main action. The fact the main claim is settled, dismissed, stayed or struck out does not necessarily terminate the defendant's Part 20 claim. If the defendant is claiming additional relief the issues it raises will still be live and the Part 20 claim will continue so that they can be determined despite the fact the main claim has been settled, dismissed, stayed or struck out.

However, if the defendant is seeking an indemnity or a contribution, the Part 20 claim is dependent on the claimant's claim as the defendant in these situations is seeking to pass on to the third party the liability to the claimant, and if the claimant's claim fails there is nothing to pass on. Therefore, in indemnity and contribution claims a distinction must be drawn between cases:

(a) where the claimant's claim is settled, because in these cases there will still be a live issue as to whether the third party should contribute towards the settlement, and if so, to what extent. In these cases the Part 20 claim will continue, see *Stott* v *West Yorkshire Road Car Co. Ltd* [1972] 2 QB 651; and

(b) where the claimant in effect loses (as when the claim is dismissed or struck out), after which there is nothing to litigate between the defendant and the third party.

9.8 The Hearing

At the beginning of the trial, the judge will usually consider the part that the third party should play. That will usually include cross-examination, and may include calling witnesses. The claimant, on the other hand, will not normally be interested in the hearing of the Part 20 claim (except possibly on the question of costs). Therefore, the judge will decide the most convenient procedure, which will depend on the facts of the particular case.

Claim Form
(Additional claims-CPR Part 20)

In the	High Court of Justice Queen`s Bench Division
Claim No.	HQ 00994485

Claimant(s)   Whiteside Properties Limited

Defendant(s)   Edmund Bailey

SEAL

Part 20 Claimant(s)   Edmund Bailey

Part 20 Defendant(s)   Fastbuck Builders Plc
Fastbuck House
Norwich
NR1 8DP

Brief details of claim

A contribution, alternatively an indemnity, against the Claimant`s claim for damages, liquidated damages and interest against the Defendant based on alleged delay in constructing works at Pembridge House, Maplethorpe Road, Peterborough PE4 9SY, and specific performance of a sub-contract between the Defendant and the Part 20 Defendant under which the Part 20 Defendant agreed to carry out works at Pembridge House, and damages and interest for breach of the sub-contract in the alternative to specific performance.

Value

More than £15,000

Defendant's name and address

Fastbuck Builders Plc
Registered office
Fastbuck House,
Norwich,
NR1 8DP

	£
Amount claimed	TBA
Court fee	400.00
Solicitors costs	
Total amount	
Issue date	

The court office at Royal Courts of Justice, Strand, London WC2A 2LL

is open between 10 am and 4 pm Monday to Friday. When corresponding with the court, please address forms or letters to the Court Manager and quote the claim number.

	Claim No.	

Particulars of Claim (attached)

1. At all material times the Defendant was an architect and you held yourself out as a builder undertaking substantial construction projects.

2. By a contract in writing dated 1st June [   ], a true copy of which is served with this claim form, the Claimant employed the Defendant to design and construct a building using the facade of Pembridge House, Maplethorpe Road, Peterborough PE4 8SY to serve as offices to be let by the Claimant on commercial leases.

[Continue as in a full Particulars of Claim].

Statement of Truth
*(I believe)(The Part 20 Claimant believes) that the facts stated in these particulars of claim are true.
* I am duly authorised by the Part 20 claimant to sign this statement

Full name   Edmund Bailey

Name of Part 20 claimant's solicitor's firm   Boardman, Phipps & Co.

signed_____ position or office held_____
*(Part 20 Claimant)('s solicitor)(Litigation friend)   (if signing on behalf of firm or company)
*delete as appropriate

Boardman, Phipps & Co.,
20 High Street,
Peterborough,
PE5 9CZ

Part 20 Claimant ('s solicitor's) address to which documents or payments should be sent if different from overleaf. If you are prepared to accept service by DX, fax or e-mail, please add details.

9.9   Questions

OBJECTIVES

This section is designed to ensure you have a sound knowledge of the rules and procedure relating to:

(a)   bringing proceedings by or against various classes of party;

(b)   multiple causes of action and multiple parties;

(c)   interpleader;

(d)   Part 20 claims; and

(e)   Part 8 claims.

RESEARCH

Read the materials contained in **Chapters 8** and **9** of this Manual, and at **3.13**.

SMALL GROUP SESSION 2

On the basis of this research, answer the following questions.

QUESTION 1

Nicholas purchased an advanced video system costing £8,000 from Jane. Jane said that she was one of six partners in a firm called Best Video Systems.

Nicholas' video has caused every possible problem and Nicholas wants his money back. If legal proceedings are necessary:

(a)   What name or names should be put in the title of the action?

(b)   Upon whom could the proceedings be served?

(c)   What steps should be taken by the defendant(s) after service?

QUESTION 2

Tom Brown aged 13 was seriously injured on 1 October 1999 when some gymnasium bars collapsed at the Dotheboys Hall School. The school is an independent charity.

(a)   If the school makes an offer of settlement of £55,000 (which you consider to be acceptable) what procedure should be followed?

(b)   If no acceptable offer of settlement is made, advise Tom of any special rules relating to starting proceedings for this type of claim.

QUESTION 3

What are the matters that the court will take into account when deciding whether it is convenient to dispose, in the same proceedings, of:

(a)   A claim brought against more than one defendant?

(b)   A claim based on a number of causes of action against the same defendant?

QUESTION 4

In March 2000, Henry, who lives in the apartment above Roland, crashed into Roland's new BMW motor car in the basement garage causing damage which cost £5,800 to repair. In June 2000, on returning from holiday, Roland found that his flat had been flooded after Henry had left a bath running overnight. The cost of the repairs and replacement furniture came to £10,000. In the course of correspondence between them Henry has failed to make any proposals as to payment. Advise Roland as to how proceedings can be started against Henry.

QUESTION 5

Solomon Carpet Cleaners have a carpet awaiting collection. Nigel has demanded the carpet back from them. So has Patrick. Advise Solomon Carpet Cleaners.

QUESTION 6

Alan visited Ben's zoo. The zoo is run by Ben as a sole trader. While Alan was watching the monkeys, Ben's elephant (which was under the control of Carol, a keeper, and which had been upset by Dennis) picked him up with his trunk and threw him into a pond. Alan swam ashore and registered a complaint with Ben which he emphasised by punching Ben in the face. Alan sued Ben and Carol as joint tortfeasors in respect of injuries he received in the pond. Ben wishes to:

(a) claim damages from Alan for assault;

(b) claim a contribution or indemnity from Carol; and

(c) claim a contribution or indemnity from Dennis.

Describe the procedural steps which you would advise Ben to take.

QUESTION 7

Robert sues Phillip in respect of a road accident. Phillip brings in Nick as a third party. Nick seeks your advice on the effect on the Part 20 proceedings of the following:

(a) the main action being settled; and/or

(b) the main action being struck out as an abuse of the process of the court.

QUESTION 8

Coral has served a claim form with particulars of claim attached on Alison claiming damages for breach of contract. You are instructed on behalf of Alison. What should Alison do if she states that she entered into the contract as an agent for Penny, an undisclosed principal?

[A] She should issue a Part 20 claim against Penny claiming an indemnity against Coral's claim.
[B] As Coral's cause of action is against Penny and not Alison, she should plead the agency in her defence.
[C] As it would be convenient to hear all the claims together, Alison may join Penny as a second defendant without permission.
[D] She should issue a contribution notice against Penny claiming a contribution in respect of Coral's claim.

QUESTION 9

Last year, Keith purchased a motor car from Len's Garages Ltd for £8,000. He has now been served with a claim form by Cutprice Finance Co. Ltd which claims to be the true owner of the vehicle which had been hired to Michael under the terms of a hire-purchase agreement. Advise Keith on how he may bring a claim against Len's Garages Ltd in case it transpires he did not acquire good title to the car when he bought it.

QUESTION 10

Mavis, in her home-made will, appointed Thomas and Edward as her executors and trustees and bequeathed them £100,000 to distribute amongst her 'friends' as they thought fit and left her residuary estate to her nephews Frederick and George. Frederick and George dispute the validity of the £100,000 gift. Advise Thomas and Edward how to bring this matter before the court so that the trust can be administered.

TEN

INTERIM APPLICATIONS

10.1 Introduction

Interim applications are made when a party to proceedings seeks an order or directions from the court prior to the substantive hearing of the claim. When the application should be made depends on the nature of the case. In urgent cases, the application may be made even before the originating process has been issued. More usually the application will be heard shortly after filing of the defence. There is a general obligation to apply early, although the court can deal with applications up to trial (and even beyond trial).

Parties seeking interim orders or directions in general have to issue an application notice on Form N244, pay the court fee, and often have to provide written evidence in support. The application must in general be served at least three clear days before the date given by the court for the hearing.

The major sub-division of interim applications is into those made in the absence of the other side ('without notice'), and those made on notice. These two categories will be considered after discussing the form of evidence used in interim applications.

10.2 Evidence

10.2.1 GENERAL

Although the court has power to hear witnesses for the purposes of interim applications (see CPR, r. 32.2), oral testimony is very much the exception to the rule. The almost universal rule is that, if evidence is required, it is given in writing. Whether or not written evidence is required depends on the nature of the application. Many of the Rules of Court governing particular kinds of interim application specifically require evidence in support. Examples are applications for summary judgment and for service by alternative methods. Further there is a general requirement for evidence in support if the application is for an interim remedy (CPR, r. 25.3(2)) as opposed to applications of a case management nature. In most other cases where the Rules are silent on the matter, evidence is still required in practice in order to establish the merits of the application. Even so, there remain a number of cases where evidence in support is unnecessary. These fall into two main categories. In the first, all the relevant matters to be considered in the application can be ascertained from the face of the statements of case, for example, on an application for security for costs on the ground that the claimant is stated in the claim form to be ordinarily resident out of the jurisdiction (see CPR, r. 25.13(2)(a)), or on an application to strike out on the ground that the statement of case discloses no reasonable cause of action. The second category covers orders and directions which are made or given almost as a matter of course. Examples would include orders for standard disclosure and directions to list for trial.

10.2.2 FORMAT OF EVIDENCE IN SUPPORT

There are four options available regarding the format of the evidence to be used in support of an interim application. They are:

(a) To provide sufficiently full factual information in support of the application in Part C of the application notice itself, and sign the statement of truth in the notice.

(b) To rely on the facts stated in a statement of case filed in the proceedings, provided it contains a statement of truth.

(c) To rely on a witness statement with a statement of truth signed by the witness, which must be served with the application. The general rule is that any fact that needs to be proved at any hearing other than the trial should be proved by the evidence of witnesses in writing, and at hearings other than the trial evidence is to be by witness statement unless the court, a Practice Direction or any other enactment requires otherwise. Consequently, evidence by witness statement is to be expected to be the primary means of adducing evidence at interim hearings.

(d) To rely on affidavit evidence. However, using affidavits may result in the loss of the additional costs over and above the cost of using an ordinary witness statement. There are some situations where affidavit evidence is required, such as in applications for search orders, freezing injunctions, applications for contempt of court, and applications for judgment in default in Brussels Convention cases.

10.2.3   FORM OF AFFIDAVITS

See generally PD32. The top right-hand corner and backsheet of the affidavit must be marked with the party on whose behalf it is filed, the initials and surname of the deponent, the number of the affidavit in relation to the deponent, the reference numbers of any exhibits, and the date it is sworn (for example: 2nd Dft: S.M. Hall: 4th: SMH3-SMH5: 10.9.00). There then follows the title of the action, then the commencement. If it is sworn, the commencement may read 'I, Sara May Hall of 2 Tower Side, London E1, state on oath as follows:—'. If the document is affirmed it is called an affirmation (rather than an affidavit), and instead of making oath the commencement will state '. . . do solemnly and sincerely affirm . . .'. The address stated may be a work address if the affidavit is sworn in the deponent's business, etc. capacity.

If the deponent is, or is employed by, a party, that must be stated. The affidavit must also state the deponent's occupation or description (e.g. 'unemployed').

The affidavit sets out the facts in numbered paragraphs, and is expressed in the first person. Dates, sums and other numbers are expressed in figures rather than in words. The text of an affidavit must indicate which of the facts stated are known to the deponent personally and those based on hearsay. Material based on information or belief must be supported by stating the sources and grounds for such belief. The source or grounds of such belief need not be an original source of evidence which would be admissible at trial, especially where the application is of an urgent nature where a deponent may not have the time to trace or identify evidence which would be admissible: *Deutsche Ruckversicherung AG* v *Walbrook Insurance Co. Ltd* [1995] 1 WLR 1017. Clearly, original sources will normally carry much more weight than intermediate sources. Where original sources *are* known they should be identified. Strict compliance with the technical rules has traditionally been required for the evidence in support of applications for summary judgment: *Barclays Bank plc* v *Piper, The Times,* 31 May 1995, CA.

Very often, documents or physical items are referred to in affidavits, and where this is so, they must be exhibited to the affidavit. This is done by identifying the exhibit in the text of the affidavit (e.g. 'SMH1', 'SMH2', etc.) and clearly marking the documents or items in the same way. Documents of a similar nature such as a series of letters and replies should be bundled together in date sequence with the earliest on top, and paginated at centre bottom. Where a number of documents are collected in one exhibit, a front page must be attached listing its contents. If copies are used, care must be taken that all the pages are clearly legible.

The affidavit itself must be written or typed leaving a 3.5 cm margin and using just one side of the paper. It must, if possible, be securely bound (traditionally with green ribbon, but not with anything, such as plastic strips, which will make it more bulky than it needs to be). If the pages are left loose, each page should bear the claim number and the initials of the deponent and the person before whom it was sworn. It must be sworn or affirmed before a proper officer, usually a solicitor or commissioner for oaths, and signed by the deponent. The jurat (stating where and before whom the affidavit was sworn) must be completed and signed by the person before whom it was sworn, who must also initial any alterations.

10.2.4 WITNESS STATEMENTS

Witness statements take much the same form as affidavits and affirmations, except they are not sworn or affirmed, and instead contain a simple statement of truth. Consequently, all the formalities required for affidavits, such as corner markings, and the rules on paragraphing, exhibits etc., have to be complied with. However, a witness statement will not have a commencement, and it will not have a jurat. Also, because it is not sworn there will be a saving of the fees payable for swearing an affidavit (£5 for the affidavit plus £2 per exhibit). The statement of truth at the end of a witness statement takes the form: 'I believe the facts stated in this witness statement are true.'

An example of a witness statement for use in an interim application is shown in **Figure 10.1**.

Figure 10.1 Witness statement seeking to set aside a judgment in default and transfer of action

	Made on behalf of the Defendant Witness: B. Parkes 1st statement of witness Exhibits: BP 1 to BP 3 Made: 15.11.2000
IN THE HIGH COURT OF JUSTICE	2000 S No. 98744
QUEEN'S BENCH DIVISION	
MANCHESTER DISTRICT REGISTRY	
BETWEEN	
SHILTON MACHINE TOOLS LIMITED	Claimant
and	
BANKS PLASTIC MOULDINGS LIMITED	Defendant

WITNESS STATEMENT OF
BRIAN PARKES

1. I am Brian Parkes, of Unit 6, Elland Trading Estate, Leeds LS8 3AN. I am a director of the Defendant company. I have full knowledge of the facts of this case and I am duly authorised to make this statement on behalf of the Defendant in support of its application to set aside a default judgment entered on 3rd November 2000. Insofar as the contents of this statement are within my personal knowledge they are true, otherwise they are true to the best of my knowledge, information and belief.

2. The Defendant has a trading account with the Claimant, and it is true that it ordered 4 moulding machines from the Claimant on 13th March 2000 at a price of £60,000 plus VAT. Although the machines were delivered, they have been the subject of repeated breakdowns and have suffered a number of faults. The main problem with 2 of the machines is that despite a number of site attendances by the Claimant's engineers they have proved incapable of producing mouldings to industry standards. I have been advised by Mr Edward Knight, a consulting engineer of 36 Harrogate Road, Leeds LS3 8DQ, that these 2 machines are so badly designed that it will be impossible to put them right.

3. As a result of the problems with all 4 machines the Defendant has suffered a substantial loss of business. In particular, it has lost a contract with United Plastic Containers Plc, under which the Defendant was producing goods valued at between £10,000 and £20,000 per month. There is now shown to me marked 'BP1' a bundle containing true copies of the Defendant's contractual documentation with United Plastic Containers Plc, monthly invoices, and recent correspondence in which the termination of the contract is explained. I have been advised by the Defendant's solicitors and believe that it has a substantial counterclaim with a value significantly above the value of the claim.

4. As soon as I received the court papers in this action I raised the matter with Mrs Elaine Stepney, the finance director of the Claimant. A true copy of my letter to her dated 18 October 2000 is at page 1 of the bundle of correspondence now shown to me marked 'BP 2'. Her reply, at page 2, says she will look into the matter. Nevertheless, judgment was entered on 3rd November 2000.

5. For the reasons set out above, I ask that this judgment be set aside on the merits. There is now shown to me marked 'BP 3' a draft defence and counterclaim which the Defendant intends to file if judgment is set aside, and I confirm the truth of the contents of the draft defence and counterclaim.

6. If judgment is set aside and the case allowed to continue, I respectfully ask that the action be transferred to the Leeds County Court, the local court of the Defendant.

Statement of truth

I believe the facts stated in this witness statement are true.

Signed:

Dated: 15th November 2000.

10.2.5   OTHER MATERIALS

In any application the court may, of course, wish to see the claim form and statements of case, and earlier orders. In addition, letters from the other side consenting to orders being made are frequently placed before the court.

10.3   Applications Without Notice

10.3.1   GENERAL

Applications made in the absence of the other side used to be called *ex parte* applications. They are exceptions to the general rule that applications must be made on notice to other parties (CPR, r. 23.4(1)). Such an application can only be made if there is some sufficient reason. Sufficient reasons are:

(a) where there is no other party on the record (for example, on an application for permission to serve process outside the jurisdiction under CPR, r. 6.20); or

(b) where no other party is affected (for example, to correct an accidental slip in a Master's order: CPR, r. 40.12); or

(c) where there is real urgency; or

(d) where secrecy prior to the application is essential for the order to be efficacious.

Applications without notice can be made either with or without an oral hearing.

10.3.2 FULL AND FRANK DISCLOSURE

It is the duty of a party seeking an order without notice to give full and frank disclosure to the court of all material facts, including those that go against the application. This is a continuing duty. Any failure in observing this duty will usually result in any order obtained being set aside as of right: *R v Kensington Income Tax Commissioners, ex parte Polignac* [1917] 1 KB 486. (See also **15.6.1.3**.)

The amount of detail required in order to discharge this duty depends on the nature of the relief sought and the conditions for granting that relief. Thus, in applications for search orders (see **Chapter 16**) it is necessary to show an extremely strong *prima facie* case on the merits. The applicant for such an order must disclose any known weaknesses in the cause of action against the defendant and any known defences, including any such matters which could have been discovered on making reasonable inquiries. When in doubt, the applicant must err on the side of excessive disclosure. To take a different example, on an application to extend the validity of a claim form (see **Chapter 25**) the main condition is that there must be a good reason for granting the extension sought. The merits of the case are not in issue, so the applicant is not required to give a detailed analysis of its strengths and weaknesses.

10.3.3 NATURE OF ORDERS MADE WITHOUT NOTICE

Generally, orders made without notice are provisional. If the other side objects to such an order, the correct procedure is to apply back to the court to set it aside (CPR, r. 23.10), and not to appeal. Where an order made without notice will affect other parties, it must contain a statement explaining that it is possible to apply to set aside or vary the order, and that such an application must be made within seven days of service of the order: CPR, r. 23.9(3).

10.3.4 PROCEDURE ON MAKING AN APPLICATION WITHOUT NOTICE

Even in applications made without notice to the other parties, the applicant must in general issue an application notice in Form N244 and pay a court fee. As explained at **10.2** above, usually the application will need to be supported by written evidence. Sometimes, a party will decide to make an application at a hearing that has already been fixed, but there is insufficient time to serve an application notice. In cases of this sort the applicant should inform the other parties and the court (preferably in writing) as soon as possible of the nature of the application, the reason for it, and then make the application orally at the hearing (PD 23, para. 2.10).

10.3.5 THE APPLICATION NOTICE AND EVIDENCE IN SUPPORT

Applications without notice should normally be made by filing an application notice (CPR, r. 23.3(1)), which must state the order being sought and the reasons for seeking the order (CPR, r. 23.6). The application notice must be signed, and include the title of the claim, its reference number and the full name of the applicant. If the applicant is not already a party it should also give his or her address for service. If the applicant wants a hearing, that too must be stated. The nature of any evidence in support must be identified in the notice. In an application made without notice, the supporting evidence must state the reasons why notice was not given, in addition to setting out the evidence in support of the relief sought (CPR, r. 25.3(3)). An example of an application notice is shown in **Figure 10.2**.

Figure 10.2   Application notice

Application Notice	In the High Court of Justice
	Queen's Bench Division
● You must complete parts A and B, and C if applicable	Manchester District Registry
	Claim No. 2000 S No. 98744
● Send any relevant fee and the completed application to the court with any draft order, witness statement or other evidence; and sufficient copies of these for service on each Respondent	Claimant Shilton Machine Tools Ltd
	Defendant Banks Plastic Mouldings Ltd

You should provide this information for listing the application

1.   Do you wish to have your application dealt with at a hearing?
Yes ☐   No ☐   If yes, please complete 2
2. Time estimate _____ (hours) 15   (mins):
Is this agreed by all parties: ☐ Yes   ☐ No
Level of judge District Judge
3.   Parties to be served: Claimant
_____
_____

Part A

I (We) Messrs. Davis, Hendry & Co. (on behalf of) (the Claimant) (the Defendant) intend to apply for an order (a draft of which is attached) that:

(1)   the judgment entered on the 4th November 2000 be set aside;

(2)   the costs of this application may be provided for,

because there is a defence on the merits of the claim, and judgment was entered while the Claimant's representative said she would look into the points raised by the Defendant as to why it was not liable on the claim.

Part B

I (We) wish to rely on: *tick one box*
    the attached (witness statement) (affidavit)   ☐
    my statement of case   ☐
    evidence in part C overleaf   ☐
in support of my application

Signed   Position or office held
    Applicant's Solicitor   (if signing on behalf of a firm or company)

Address to which documents about this claim should be sent (including reference if appropriate)

                                                              if applicable
Messrs. Davis, Hendry & Co.   fax no. 0113 365 0849
12 Market Street   DX no. 87644 Leeds 1
Leeds   e-mail
Tel no. 0113 278 3237   Postcode LS2 9JF

The court office at The Courts of Justice, Crown Square, Manchester M60 9DJ is open from 10 am to 4 pm Monday to Friday. When corresponding with the court please address forms or letters to the Court Manager and quote the claim number.

Part C   Claim No. 2000 S No. 98744

I (We) wish to rely on the following evidence in support of this application:

Statement of Truth
*(I believe) (the Applicant believes) that the facts stated in this application are true
*delete as appropriate

Signed   Position or office held
   Applicant's Solicitor   (if signing on behalf of a firm or company)
   ('s litigation friend)
                                    Date

10.3.6 URGENT APPLICATIONS

The court has a power to dispense with the need to have issued an application notice (CPR, r. 23.3), which may be appropriate if the application is sufficiently urgent. In applications arising in urgent circumstances, where there is no practical possibility of giving the required minimum of three clear days' notice to the other side, informal notification should be given to the other parties unless the circumstances require secrecy (PD 23, para. 4.2).

Generally, applications can only be brought after a claim form has been issued. However, if an application is sufficiently urgent, or if otherwise it would be in the interests of justice, the court has power to consider an application before the main proceedings have been commenced (CPR, r. 25.2). Usually, if the court entertains an application before proceedings have been issued, it will give directions requiring a claim to be issued.

10.3.7 URGENT INJUNCTION HEARINGS

Cases where injunctions are needed occasionally have to be dealt with by the court more or less straight away, or else the harm that the applicant wants to avoid will be done. Examples are where an allegedly libellous article is going to be published within the next few hours, or if a proposed defendant is about to remove assets from the jurisdiction.

If the court is approached during the working day while the court is still sitting, the hearing will take place in court as soon as the circumstances permit. This means that generally such applications are heard before any other matters already listed as soon as the court sits in the morning, or immediately after lunch. The necessary arrangements must be made with the court staff, who will invariably do all they can to ensure urgent applications are dealt with at the first available opportunity. Solicitors should therefore contact the court by telephone as soon as they know they will need to make an urgent application so as to allow the court time to make the necessary arrangements. Sometimes urgent applications arise during the course of the morning or afternoon in circumstances where it is not possible to wait for the beginning of the next session. If the case is sufficiently urgent the court will interrupt whatever it is doing at a convenient moment so that it can hear the urgent application.

On other occasions the need for a pre-action interim injunction arises at a time when it is not possible to wait until the next occasion when the court will be sitting. If the application is of extreme urgency it may be dealt with by telephone (PD 25 Interim

Injunctions, para. 4.2). Telephone hearings, however, are only available if the applicant is acting by solicitors or counsel (PD 25 Interim Injunctions, para. 4.5(5)). If the problem has arisen during business hours, but in circumstances where it will not be possible to go before a judge before the close of business, initially it is necessary to telephone the court (either the High Court on 0171 936 6000 or the appropriate County Court) asking to be put in touch with a High Court judge of the appropriate Division or County Court judge available to deal with an emergency application (PD 25 Interim Injunctions, para. 4.5(1)).

If the problem has arisen outside office hours the applicant should telephone either the High Court (on the same number as above) asking to be put in touch with the clerk to the appropriate duty judge (or the appropriate area Circuit judge where known), or should telephone the urgent court business officer of the appropriate Circuit, who will contact the local duty judge.

If the facilities are available a draft of the order sought will usually be required to be sent by fax to the duty judge who will be dealing with the application.

10.4 Applications on Notice

As mentioned above, the general rule is that applications must be made on notice (see CPR, r. 23.4(1)), and should normally be made by filing an application notice stating the order being sought and the reasons for seeking the order: CPR, r. 23.3(1) and r. 23.6 (see **10.3.5** above). On receipt of the application notice the court may either notify the parties of the time and date of the hearing, or may notify them that it proposes to consider the application without a hearing (PD 23, para. 2.4).

Unless the applicant notifies the court to the contrary, the normal rule is that the court will serve the application notice and documents in support by first class post. Alternatively, the applicant may notify the court that he or she wishes to effect service himself or herself. When the court is to effect service, the applicant must file with the court copies of the evidence in support for service on the respondents and a copy of any draft order prepared on behalf of the applicant.

Service must be effected as soon as possible after the application is issued, and in any event not less than three days before it is to be heard (CPR, r. 23.7(1)). In accordance with the general rules on computing time, this means clear days (excluding the date of effective service and the date of the hearing), and, because the period is less than five days, also excluding weekends, bank holidays, Christmas and Good Friday. Thus, take for example a hearing which is listed for Wednesday 18 October 2000. Assume the solicitor for the applicant decides to serve the application and evidence in support by document exchange. The three clear days before the hearing are 13 (Friday), 16 (Monday) and 17 October 2000 (Tuesday). The documents must arrive on Thursday 12 October, and given the deeming provision in CPR, r. 6.7 that documents transmitted by DX are deemed to be served on the second day after being left at the document exchange, the latest the documents could be left at the document exchange would be Tuesday 10 October 2000.

10.5 Disposal Without a Hearing

One of the ways stated for furthering the overriding objective is that the court may save costs by dealing with cases without the parties needing to attend court (CPR, r. 1.4(2)(j)). As part of this objective the CPR, r. 23.8, says the court may deal with an interim application without a hearing if either:

(a) the parties agree that the court should dispose of the application without a hearing. The applicant's view on whether there should be a hearing should be stated in the application notice; or

(b) the court does not consider that a hearing would be appropriate.

A party dissatisfied with any order or direction made without a hearing is able to apply to have it set aside, varied or stayed (CPR, r. 3.3(5)(a)). Such an application must be made within seven days after service of the order, and the right to make such an application must be stated in the order (CPR, rr. 3.3(5)(b) and 3.3(6)).

10.6 Hearing by Telephone

Active case management in accordance with the overriding objective includes dealing with cases without the parties needing to attend court, and by making use of technology (CPR, r. 1.4(2)(j) and (k)). Both may be achieved by dealing with some applications by telephone conference calls, which is specifically provided for by CPR, r. 3.1(2)(d). The rule enables the court to hold a hearing by telephone or any other method of direct oral communication, so other means of electronic communication may be used as technology develops. Telephone hearings will normally only be held if all parties consent, and if all the parties are legally represented (or, if acting in person, if they are assisted by a responsible person, such as a doctor, clergyman or police officer).

10.7 Orders Made on the Court's Own Initiative

As part of the new ethos of active case management, the courts can exercise their powers on their own initiative where this is appropriate. This power is intended to be exercised for the purpose of managing the case and furthering the overriding objective. Orders made in this way must, by virtue of CPR, rr. 3.3(5)(b) and (6), include a statement that parties who are affected may apply within seven days (or such other period as the court may specify) after service for the order to be set aside, varied or stayed.

There is a related power enabling the court to make orders on its own initiative after giving the parties an opportunity of making representations on the matter. Where the court proposes to make such an order it will specify a time within which the representations must be made (CPR, r. 3.3(2)).

10.8 Court Hearing

The general rule is that hearings on interim applications will be in public (CPR, r. 39.2). There are exceptions, including hearings where publicity would defeat their object, and in matters involving national security.

At the hearing the applicant should bring a draft order, unless the application is particularly simple. If the order is unusually long or complex the draft should be supplied on disk as well as on hard copy (PD 23, para. 12). In addition to dealing with the specific application that has been made, the court may wish to review the conduct of the case as a whole and give any necessary case management directions. The parties will therefore have to be prepared for this and be able to answer any questions the court may ask (PD 23, para. 2.9). The procedural judge will keep, either by way of a note or a tape recording, brief details of all proceedings before him or her, including a short statement of the decision taken at each hearing (PD 23, para. 8).

10.9 Summary Determination of Interim Costs

Where an interim application is disposed of in less than a day (which will cover the vast majority of such applications), the court may well make a summary assessment of the costs of the application immediately after making its order: PD 44, para. 4.4(1)(b). To assist the judge in assessing costs the parties are required to file and serve not less than 24 hours before the interim hearing signed statements of their costs for the interim hearing (**Figure 7.2**). The court must not, however, make a summary assessment of the costs of a legally assisted party (para. 4.9(1)), or of a party under a disability unless the solicitor waives the right to further costs (para. 4.9(3)). However, the court can make a summary assessment of the costs payable by an assisted party (para. 4.9(2)) or by a person under a disability (para. 4.9(4)).

Any failure to file or serve a statement of costs, without reasonable excuse, will be taken into account in deciding the costs order to be made on the application. A failure to comply might be taken as indicating that the party in default would not be seeking an order for costs.

Immediate summary assessment of costs will only be appropriate where the court decides to order costs in any event. Where the interim costs are to be in the case, assessment of the costs will almost certainly be left to the conclusion of the case (PD 44, para. 4.4(3)). In cases where costs are awarded in any event, the court should make a summary assessment there and then, but may decide to give directions for a further hearing to deal with the costs (PD 44, para. 4.4(1) and 4.8). Summary assessment will be unnecessary in cases where the parties have agreed the amount of costs (PD 44, para. 4.4(4)).

10.10 General Powers regarding Interim Relief and Orders

The CPR, r. 3.1(2), sets out a non-exhaustive list of orders that may be made for the purpose of managing cases, and CPR, r. 25.1(1), sets out a non-exhaustive list of interim remedies that may be granted by the court. These various powers include:

(a) extending or shortening time for compliance with rules and orders, see **1.4.25** and **28.3**;

(b) adjourning or bringing forward hearing dates, see **33.10**;

(c) requiring a party or a legal representative to attend court;

(d) dealing with part of a case as a preliminary issue, see **33.3**;

(e) consolidating two or more actions, see **8.6**;

(f) deciding the order in which issues are to be tried;

(g) excluding an issue from consideration;

(h) granting interim injunctions, see **Chapter 14**;

(i) making freezing injunctions (*Marevas*) and search orders (*Anton Pillers*), see **Chapters 15** and **16**; and

(j) granting interim payments, see **Chapter 13**.

ELEVEN

SERVICE OUTSIDE THE JURISDICTION

11.1 Introduction

11.1.1 PROBLEMS THAT ARISE

When intending litigants live in different countries, a number of problems arise. These include:

(a) In which country should proceedings be commenced?

(b) Which system of law should govern the dispute?

(c) If proceedings are commenced in one country, how can documents be served in another?

(d) If proceedings are commenced over the same dispute in different countries, which takes precedence, or will they be permitted to proceed in competition with each other?

(e) If proceedings are issued in one country and served in another, how can the defendant contest the jurisdiction of the issuing courts to determine the dispute?

Item (b) above is resolved by the principles pertaining to the conflict of laws, and is outside the scope of this Manual. Answers to the other questions will be attempted in this chapter.

11.1.2 DEFENDANTS OUTSIDE THE JURISDICTION

Usually proceedings in England and Wales must be served on a defendant within the jurisdiction. If the defendant is outside the jurisdiction it is sometimes possible to obtain permission under CPR, r. 6.20, to serve proceedings outside the jurisdiction (see **11.3**). Where the proposed litigation has a European flavour, it may, however, be possible to issue proceedings in England and Wales for service abroad without the permission of the court, and this will be considered at **11.2**.

11.2 Service Without Permission

11.2.1 INTRODUCTION

Three conditions must be satisfied for service of proceedings out of the jurisdiction without permission (CPR, r. 6.19), the third being capable of being fulfilled in three alternative ways:

(a) the court must be given power to determine each claim by virtue of the Civil Jurisdiction and Judgments Act 1982 (see **11.2.3** and **11.2.5**); and

(b) there are no other pending proceedings concerning the same claim in the UK or any other Convention territory (see **11.2.6**); and

(c) either

   (i) the defendant is domiciled in a Convention territory (see **11.2.4**); or

   (ii) art. 16 confers exclusive jurisdiction to the courts of England and Wales (see **11.2.7.1**); or

   (iii) one of the parties is domiciled in a Convention territory and they have conferred jurisdiction on the courts of England and Wales by agreement (art. 17) (see **11.2.7.2**).

11.2.2 CONVENTIONS AND CIVIL JURISDICTION AND JUDGMENTS ACTS

In cases governed by the Brussels Convention 1968 on jurisdiction and the enforcement of judgments in civil and commercial matters (the 'Brussels Convention') permission is not required to serve originating process outside the jurisdiction. The Brussels Convention has had the force of law in the UK since 1 January 1987 by virtue of the Civil Jurisdiction and Judgments Act 1982 (CJJA 1982), s. 2(1). The Brussels Convention is set out in CJJA 1982, sch. 1. The provisions of the Brussels Convention apply to proceedings in Contracting States. These are Austria, Belgium, Denmark, Finland, France, Germany, Greece, Holland, Italy, Luxembourg, Portugal, Republic of Ireland, Spain, Sweden and the UK.

A 'parallel convention' was signed by the member states of the EC and the European Free Trade Association (comprising Iceland, Norway and Switzerland), in Lugano in 1988. The Lugano Convention is in similar terms to the Brussels Convention, and has the force of law in this country by virtue of the CJJA 1991.

The UK itself is divided into 'Parts' (England and Wales; Scotland and Northern Ireland), and a separate Modified Convention (set out in CJJA 1982, sch. 4) allocates jurisdiction between the courts of each part. The Modified Convention broadly follows the scheme of the Brussels Convention, and is not considered further. The Brussels Convention does not apply to the Channel Islands, etc. (art. 60), and these too will not be considered further.

The Brussels and Lugano Conventions apply to civil and commercial actions, with a number of exceptions. Exceptions include revenue, administrative, matrimonial, insolvency, social security and arbitration matters.

11.2.3 THE GENERAL RULE

Article 2 provides:

> *Subject to the provisions of this Convention, persons domiciled in a Contracting State shall, whatever their nationality, be sued in the courts of that State.*

By art. 3, jurisdiction can no longer be founded on service on the defendant while temporarily present in the UK in respect of defendants domiciled in other Contracting States.

11.2.4 DOMICILE

By art. 52, domicile is determined by the law of the courts seised of the matter. The CJJA 1982, ss. 41–46, define domicile in terms approximating to genuine residence. By s. 41(2):

an individual is domiciled in the UK if and only if—
    (a) he is resident in the United Kingdom; and
    (b) the nature and circumstances of his residence indicate that he has a substantial connection with the United Kingdom.

By s. 41(6), 'substantial connection' is presumed by three months' residence, unless the contrary is proved.

By s. 42, a corporation has its 'seat' either in the country:

(a) where it was incorporated and has its registered office; or

(b) where its central management and control is exercised.

11.2.5   SPECIAL JURISDICTION

11.2.5.1 Special jurisdiction
Article 5 specifies seven types of claim where a person domiciled in one Contracting State may be sued in another. The most important are:

    (1) in matters relating to a contract, in the courts for the place of performance of the obligation in question;
    (3) in matters relating to tort, in the courts for the place where the harmful event occurred;
    (6) in his capacity as settlor, trustee or beneficiary of a trust created by the operation of a statute, or by a written instrument, or created orally and evidenced in writing, in the courts of the Contracting State in which the trust is domiciled.

11.2.5.2 Contract
A dispute as to the existence of a contract does not deprive a national court of the jurisdiction it would otherwise have under art. 5(1): *Effer Spa v Kantner* [1982] ECR 825 (ECJ). However, the bare assertion of the existence of a contract is not enough. If there is no serious question to be tried or good arguable case on whether there was a contract, the defendant will be entitled to apply to set aside service of the claim: *Tesam Distribution Ltd v Shuh Mode Team Gmbh* [1990] ILPr 149, CA and *Boss Group Ltd v Boss France SA* [1996] 4 All ER 970, CA. Whether art. 5(1) applies to a transaction which is void *ab initio* was referred to the ECJ: *Barclays Bank plc v Glasgow City Council* [1994] QB 404, CA. The ECJ would not make a ruling as the question arose under the Modified Convention. The case eventually went to the House of Lords where it was held that a claim to recover money paid under a contract which was *ultra vires* and void *ab initio* did not come within art. 5(1) or 5(3): *Kleinwort Benson Ltd v Glasgow City Council* [1999] 1 AC 153, HL.

Jurisdiction is given under art. 5(1), however, where the only connection with this country is an alleged non-disclosure or misrepresentation in relation to the making of a contract, these being matters 'relating to a contract': *Agnew v Länsförsäkringsbolagens AB* [2000] 1 All ER 737, HL.

Individual contracts of employment are not governed by the usual rule in art. 5(1). By virtue of the EC Contractual Obligations Convention 1980, art. 6, which was implemented in the UK by the Contracts (Applicable Law) Act 1990, proceedings should be commenced in the country where the employee habitually carries out his or her work: *Roger Ivenel v Helmut Schwab* [1982] ECR 1891 (ECJ). This exception applies only when there is a relationship of employer and employee of a personal nature. It does not apply to contracts of commercial agency: *Mercury Publicity Ltd v Wolfgang Loerke GmbH, The Times*, 21 October 1991, CA.

For most contracts the question under art. 5(1) is simply to determine where the contractual obligation giving rise to the claim was to be performed. The claimant may then bring proceedings in that country under art. 5(1), or in the country of the defendant's domicile under art. 2. Thus, in a claim based on a failure to supply goods reasonably fit for their known purpose, jurisdiction was given by art. 5(1) to the country where the goods were delivered (*Viskose Ltd* v *Paul Kiefel GmbH* [1999] 1 WLR 1305, CA).

In more complex disputes involving a number of obligations arising under a single contract, the country where the principal obligation is to be performed has jurisdiction. See *Shenevai* v *Kreischer* [1987] ECR 239, ECJ and *Union Transport Group plc* v *Continental Lines SA* [1992] 1 WLR 15, HL.

11.2.5.3 Tort

Obviously, the law of tort differs considerably between the Contracting States. In order to ensure consistency in the application of the Brussels Convention it seems the courts must give the term 'tort' an 'independent' interpretation broadly consistent with what is common between the laws of the Contracting States: see *Netherlands* v *Ruffer* [1980] ECR 3807 (ECJ).

The expression '. . . place where the harmful event occurred' in art. 5(3) gives the claimant the option of commencing proceedings either at the place where the wrongful act or omission took place or at the place where the damage occurred: *Handelskwekerij GJ Bier BV* v *Mines de Potasse d'Alsace SA* [1976] ECR 1735 (ECJ). However, the place where the damage occurred is not the place where the damage was quantified or where steps are taken to mitigate damage caused by the wrongful act or omission: *Netherlands* v *Ruffer* [1980] ECR 3807.

The claimants in *Shevill* v *Presse Alliance SA* [1995] 2 AC 18, ECJ, [1996] AC 959, HL, complained of a libel in a French newspaper. The newspaper had a daily circulation of 200,000 copies in France, and about 250 in England. The amended statement of claim relied solely on publication in England. It was held that English proceedings had been validly served without permission. The claimants could rely on the common law presumption of damage to show that the 'harmful event' in art. 5(3) occurred in England provided they restricted their claim to the harm caused in England, even if the substance of their original complaint was the publication in France.

In the case of a negligent misstatement, the harmful event takes place where the misstatement is made rather than where it is received: see *Domicrest Ltd* v *Swiss Bank Corporation* [1999] 2 WLR 364.

11.2.5.4 Jurisdiction in insurance and consumer contracts

Special rules allocate jurisdiction in insurance matters (arts 7–12A) and proceedings concerning consumer contracts (arts 13–15). Broadly,

(a) insurers may be sued in their own country or in the policyholder's country (art. 8);

(b) insurers may only sue in the defendant's country (art. 11);

(c) consumers (non-traders who buy goods on credit or who contract for goods or services in response to advertising or specific invitations) may be sued only in their own country (arts 13,14);

(d) suppliers to consumers may be sued in their own country or in the consumer's country (arts 13,14).

11.2.5.5 Multiple parties and cross-claims

Article 6 provides:

> A person domiciled in a Contracting State may also be sued:
> 1. Where he is one of a number of defendants, in the courts for the place where any one of them is domiciled;
> 2. As a third party . . . in the court seised of the original proceedings, unless these were instituted solely with the object of removing him from the jurisdiction of the court which would be competent in his case;

3. On a counterclaim arising from the same contract or facts on which the original claim was based, in the court in which the original claim is pending . . .

These exceptions must not be extended beyond their proper limits so as to derogate from the general requirement in art. 2 that defendants should be sued in the courts of the country where they are domiciled: *Gascoine v Pyrah, The Times*, 26 November 1991. The ECJ in *Kalfelis v Bankhaus Schröder, Münchmeyer, Hengst und Co.* [1988] ECR 5565 decided that for art. 6(1) to apply there must exist a connection between the claims against the various defendants of such a kind that it is expedient for those claims to be tried together to avoid the risk of irreconcilable judgments resulting from separate proceedings.

In *Kinnear v Falconfilms NV* [1994] 3 All ER 42, an action was brought in England by the administrators of an actor's estate against a film company claiming damages arising out of an incident when the actor fell from a horse while shooting a film in Spain. The defendant issued a third party notice (now called a Part 20 claim) claiming an indemnity or a contribution against the Spanish hospital that treated the actor, alleging that the actor's death was caused by the negligence of the hospital. The hospital's application to strike out the third party proceedings was dismissed, because the nexus required for bringing third party claims under the former provisions of the rules of court was in practical terms sufficient to satisfy the special jurisdiction granted by art. 6(2) and to confer jurisdiction on the English Court.

11.2.6   NO OTHER PENDING PROCEEDINGS

The second condition in CPR, r. 6.19(1), is that there must be no proceedings concerning the same claim pending in another Convention country. There are a number of procedural safeguards to ensure such a conflict does not arise.

11.2.6.1   Indorsement of claim form

The PD 7 para. 3.5, provides in part that a claim which is to be served out of the jurisdiction without permission must be indorsed before it is issued with a statement that the Court has power under the CJJA 1982 to hear and determine the claim, and that no proceedings involving the same cause of action are pending between the parties in Scotland, Northern Ireland or another Convention territory. Further, CPR, r. 6.19(3), provides that the claim form must state the grounds on which the claimant is entitled to serve it out of its jurisdiction.

11.2.6.2   Conflicting proceedings

If for any reason proceedings involving the same cause of action are pending in more than one country, any court other than the court first seised must decline jurisdiction of its own motion (arts 21 and 23). If actions are related rather than involving the same cause of action, the later actions may be stayed rather than jurisdiction being declined (art. 22). For the purposes of art. 22, actions are deemed to be related where they are so closely connected that it is expedient to hear and determine them together to avoid the risk of irreconcilable judgments resulting from separate proceedings.

The Courts in England and Wales become 'seised' of the proceedings for the purposes of these Articles when the defendant is served with the originating process: *Dresser UK Ltd v Falcongate Freight Management Ltd* [1992] QB 502, CA. In *Neste Chemicals SA v DK Line SA* [1994] 3 All ER 180, the Court of Appeal held there are no exceptions to this simple rule, not even when there has been some actual exercise of jurisdiction, such as the granting of a freezing injunction or the making of a search order. Contrast the domestic rule that proceedings are 'pending' after issue of process. If it is not clear, as a matter of the foreign law, whether foreign proceedings involving the same cause of action became definitively pending before service of an English claim, it may be appropriate to adjourn the English proceedings until after a ruling by the foreign court as to the date the foreign proceedings became definitively pending: *Polly Peck International Ltd v Citibank NA, The Times*, 20 October 1993.

A defendant to proceedings in one Contracting State is not permitted to bring proceedings in another Contracting State to challenge the jurisdiction of the courts of the first Contracting State: *Overseas Union Insurance Ltd* v *New Hampshire Insurance Co.* [1992] 1 QB 434, ECJ.

11.2.6.3 *Forum non conveniens*

CJJA 1982, s. 49 provides that nothing in the Act prevents the court from staying proceedings on the ground of *forum non conveniens* (see **11.3.2.2** and **11.3.2.3**), 'where to do so is not inconsistent with the 1968 Convention'. It is implicit in this that the court cannot stay proceedings on this ground where to do so would be inconsistent with the Convention: *In re Harrods (Buenos Aires) Ltd* [1992] Ch 72, CA per Dillion LJ.

11.2.7 DEFENDANT DOMICILED, ETC.

The usual way of fulfilling the third condition in CPR, r. 6.19(1), is by the proposed defendant being domiciled in another Contracting State. However, art. 16 gives certain courts exclusive jurisdiction over certain matters, and art. 17 gives effect to jurisdiction agreements.

11.2.7.1 Exclusive jurisdiction

Article 16 gives exclusive jurisdiction to the courts of the State where the relevant land or register is situated in the following cases:

(a) rights in and tenancies of land;

(b) the validity of various company matters;

(c) the validity of entries in public registers; and

(d) the registration or validity of patents and other registrable industrial property rights.

Exclusive jurisdiction is only conferred by art. 16 if the relevant matter is the principal subject-matter of the action.

11.2.7.2 Jurisdiction agreements

By art. 17, provided one of the parties, whether the claimant or defendant, is domiciled in a Contracting State, they may by agreement in writing confer jurisdiction on the courts of their choice. Such an agreement will not displace:

(a) art. 16 cases; or

(b) insurance contracts being enforced by the insured or consumer contracts being enforced by the consumer (arts 12 and 15).

However, exclusive jurisdiction given under art. 17 takes precedence over the rules on conflicting proceedings in arts 21 and 22 (see **11.2.6.2**): *Continental Bank NA* v *Aeokos Compania Naviera SA* [1994] 1 WLR 588, CA and over the rules in art. 6(2) (see **11.2.5.5**): *Hough* v *P&O Containers Ltd, The Times*, 6 April 1998.

In *Kurz* v *Stella Musical Veranstaltungs GmbH* [1992] Ch 196 Hoffmann J held that art. 17 is to be interpreted so as to allow the parties to confer jurisdiction on the courts of more than one country, thereby giving themselves a choice of venue.

Also by art. 17, if a jurisdiction agreement is concluded by parties neither of whom is domiciled in a Contracting State, the rule is that the courts of other States shall have no jurisdiction unless the chosen courts decline jurisdiction.

11.3 Service with Permission

11.3.1 INTRODUCTION

This section considers the more traditional jurisdiction of the courts in England and Wales to grant permission to serve proceedings abroad, which still governs cases where the defendant is abroad in a non-EC country.

11.3.2 WHEN WILL PERMISSION BE GRANTED?

The principles to be applied when the court is considering an application for permission to allow service out of the jurisdiction were restated by the House of Lords in *Seaconsar Far East Ltd* v *Bank Markazi Jomhouri Islami Iran* [1994] 1 AC 438 as altered by the CPR, r. 6.21. There are three matters that the intending claimant must establish:

(a) There must be a good arguable case that the court has jurisdiction within one of the 17 grounds set out in CPR, r. 6.20: see **11.3.2.1**.

(b) There must be a reasonable prospect of success on the merits. This formulation was introduced on 2 May 2000 by amendment of the CPR. Since *Seaconsar*, this second limb had been satisfied by showing a 'serious issue to be tried', which was the same test as that applied in applications for interim injunctions under the *American Cyanamid* principles (for which, see **14.3.1.1**). Before *Seaconsar*, the accepted test had been one of showing a 'good arguable case' on the merits.

(c) The court must be satisfied that England and Wales is the proper place in which to bring the claim (CPR, r. 6.21(2A)). This requirement is considered further at **11.3.2.2** and **11.3.2.3**.

11.3.2.1 What are the grounds for granting permission?

The CPR, r. 6.20, lists 17 grounds on which service out of the jurisdiction is permissible. These grounds include cases where:

> *(3) a claim is made against someone on whom the claim form has been or will be served and—*
> *(a) there is between the claimant and that person a real issue which it is reasonable for the court to try; and*
> *(b) the claimant wishes to serve the claim form on another person who is a necessary or proper party to that claim;*
> *(4) a claim is made for an interim remedy under section 25(1) of the 1982 Act;*
> *(5) a claim is made in respect of a contract where the contract—*
> *(a) was made within the jurisdiction;*
> *(b) was made by or through an agent trading or residing within the jurisdiction;*
> *(c) is governed by English law; or*
> *(d) contains a term to the effect that the court shall have jurisdiction to determine any claim in respect of the contract;*
> *(6) a claim is made in respect of a breach of contract committed within the jurisdiction;*
> *(7) a claim is made for a declaration that no contract exists where, if the contract was found to exist, it would comply with the conditions set out in paragraph (5);*
> *(8) a claim is made in tort where—*
> *(a) damage was sustained within the jurisdiction; or*
> *(b) the damage sustained resulted from an act committed within the jurisdiction;*
> . . .

It has been held that the intending claimant may choose which ground to rely on. Generally, the grounds are to be read disjunctively. However, the case must fall within the spirit, as well as the letter, of the rule (*Johnson* v *Taylor Bros* [1920] AC 144). There is a large body of case law dealing in detail with the various paragraphs of this rule, but which is beyond the scope of the civil litigation component of this course.

11.3.2.2 What is a 'proper case'? The doctrine of *forum conveniens*
The third requirement from *Seaconsar* (see **11.3.2**) gives the court an overriding discretion to refuse permission. The court applies what is often called 'the doctrine of *forum conveniens*' and will grant permission only if satisfied that England is the most appropriate forum for the trial of the claim. This means that England must be the place where the case can be tried most suitably for the interests of all parties and the ends of justice. The tag of *forum conveniens* is somewhat inapt, in that the question is not one of convenience but of appropriateness.

The intending claimant has the burden of proving that England is clearly the appropriate forum for the trial.

11.3.2.3 Factors which the court will take into consideration in determining the appropriate forum
The court will consider any factors which point towards another forum being more appropriate than England. These include the availability of witnesses (including experts), local knowledge, the places where the parties reside and carry on business, the law governing the relevant transaction, and whether justice can only be obtained elsewhere at excessive cost, delay or inconvenience.

Sometimes the intending claimant will have some legitimate personal or juridical advantage in bringing proceedings in England. Recurring examples relate to disclosure, limitation periods, and damages. Usually this should not be a factor in considering permission: the claimant's advantage will ordinarily be the defendant's disadvantage. However, there may be cases where, provided the claimant has not acted unreasonably, it may be appropriate in order to secure the ends of justice to allow the claimant to take advantage of, for example, a longer limitation period in England.

In *Spiliada Maritime v Cansulex Ltd* [1986] AC 460, Lord Templeman said:

> The factors which the court is entitled to take into account in considering whether one forum is more appropriate are legion. The authorities do not, perhaps cannot, give any clear guidance as to how these factors are to be weighed in any particular case.

Lord Goff, in the same case, said:

> It is also significant to observe that the circumstances specified in [what is now CPR, r. 6.20], as those in which the court may exercise its discretion to grant leave to serve proceedings on the defendant outside the jurisdiction, are of great variety, ranging from cases where, one would have thought, the discretion would normally be exercised in favour of granting leave (e.g. where the relief sought is an injunction ordering the defendant to do or refrain from doing something within the jurisdiction) to cases where the grant of leave is far more problematical. In addition, the importance to be attached to any particular ground invoked by the plaintiff may vary from case to case.

11.3.3 PROCEDURE

Permission is sought by issuing an application notice supported by written evidence, and is dealt with by a Master or District Judge without a hearing and without giving notice.

CPR, r. 6.21(1) and (2) provide:

> *(1) An application for permission under rule 6.20 must be supported by written evidence stating—*
> *(a) the grounds on which the application is made and the paragraph or paragraphs of rule 6.20 relied on;*
> *(b) that the claimant believes that his claim has a reasonable prospect of success; and*

(c)   the defendant's address or, if not known, in what place or country the defendant is, or likely, to be found.
(2)   Where the application is made in respect of a claim referred to in rule 6.20(3), the written evidence must also state the grounds on which the witness believes that there is between the claimant and the person on whom a claim form has been, or will be served, a real issue which it is reasonable for the court to try.

The application is made without notice so the claimant has the usual duty of giving full and frank disclosure in the evidence in support.

11.4   Submission to the Jurisdiction

Even in cases outside the scope of CPR, rr. 6.19 and 6.20, the defendant may submit to the jurisdiction of the courts of England and Wales. This may be by agreement after the dispute has arisen, or by a failure to dispute the jurisdiction after acknowledging service. However, in cases governed by the CJJA 1982, a defendant cannot submit to the jurisdiction where exclusive jurisdiction is given to another court by art. 16: see art. 18.

11.5   Service Abroad

11.5.1   ACKNOWLEDGMENT OF SERVICE

The claim form and acknowledgment of service forms must be amended to give the defendant an enhanced period to acknowledge. For Contracting States to the Brussels and Lugano Conventions the period is 21 days. The periods for other countries are set out in a table to the service out PD, e.g. USA is 22 days, India 23 days, Vanuatu 29 days.

11.5.2   EFFECTING SERVICE

The general rule is that service must be in accordance with the law of the country where the defendant is to be served. Depending on the status of the country where the defendant resides, and on whether that country is a member of the Hague Convention 1965 or any other Civil Procedure Convention, one or other of the following methods of service should be used:

(a)   the government of the defendant's country;

(b)   the British consular authority;

(c)   the judicial authorities of the defendant's country;

(d)   the authority designated under the Hague Convention; and

(e)   by instructing local agents to effect service according to local law.

11.6   Period of Validity

Where a claim form is to be served within the jurisdiction, it is initially valid for four months. If the claim form is to be served out of the jurisdiction it is valid initially for six months: CPR, r. 7.5(3).

11.7   Objecting to Service Abroad

A defendant who wishes to dispute the jurisdiction of the court after being served abroad must first acknowledge service, then apply to set aside service or discharge the order giving permission.

11.8 Judgment in Default

By CPR, r. 12.10(b)(i), judgment cannot be entered in default of giving notice of intention to defend (see **Chapter 6**) without permission where the claim form was served abroad without permission under the CJJA 1982. Applications for permission under CPR, r. 12.10(b)(i), are made without notice by an affidavit stating that the deponent believes each claim made by the claim form is one which, by virtue of the CJJA 1982, the court has power to hear and determine, that no other court has exclusive jurisdiction under art. 16, and that service satisfied the relevant rules.

TWELVE

SUMMARY JUDGMENT

12.1　Introduction

In cases where the defendant fails to defend it is usually possible to enter a default judgment (see **Chapter 6**). Where there is no real defence, it is possible for a defendant to go through the motions of defending in order to delay the time when judgment may be entered. It is possible for defendants to put up the pretence of having a real defence to such an extent that some cases run all the way through to trial before judgment can be entered. There are a number of ways that the Civil Procedure Rules 1998 use to try to avoid this happening. The court can use its power to strike out (see **Chapter 28**) to knock out hopeless defences, such as those that simply do not amount to a legal defence to a claim. Entering summary judgment is a related procedure, and is used where it is felt that a purported defence filed by a defendant can be shown to have no real prospects of success.

The procedure is not limited to use by claimants against defendants. It can also be used by defendants to attack weak claims brought by claimants. Further, it is envisaged by the Civil Procedure Rules 1998 that summary judgment can be used by the court of its own initiative to perform the important function of stopping weak cases from proceeding. The procedure can also be used to attack the weaker parts of cases, thereby reducing complexity and costs. It should be noted:

(a)　that the procedure is available not only to claimants against defendants, but also to defendants who can use it to knock out the whole or part of the claim;

(b)　the procedure supplements the power to strike out, and allows the court summarily to dispose of cases on points of law;

(c)　that the procedure may be invoked by the court of its own initiative; and

(d)　that the main test is whether the claim or defence has a real prospect of success. This makes it rather easier to obtain summary judgment under the Civil Procedure Rules 1998 than it was under the pre-1999 system, where the defendant could escape a summary judgment application merely by showing a triable issue.

Summary judgment is closely related to the power to strike out under CPR, r. 3.4 (discussed at **5.9** and **28.2**). Both powers are used to achieve the active case management aim of summarily disposing of issues that do not need full investigation at trial (CPR, r. 1.4(2)(c)). It is very common for parties to make applications in suitable cases for striking out and summary judgment in the alternative. Striking out under r. 3.4 is primarily aimed at cases and issues that are weak in the way in which they are set out in the relevant statement of case, whereas summary judgment is primarily aimed at cases that are weak on the facts, so that they can be said to have no real prospect of success (see CPR, r. 24.2(a)). There is an inevitable overlap between the two concepts.

121

12.2   Time at which the Application May Be Made

A claimant may only apply for summary judgment after the defendant has filed either an acknowledgment of service or a defence, unless the court gives permission (CPR, r. 24.4(1)). If the defendant fails to do either of these within the time limited by the Civil Procedure Rules 1998, the claimant may enter a default judgment, either with or without the court's permission, depending on the nature of the claim. By analogy with CPR, r. 25.2(2)(c), a defendant likewise can only apply for summary judgment after either filing an acknowledgment of service or a defence.

It is normally appropriate to make the application early on in the litigation process, if possible very shortly after the acknowledgment or defence, because if the other side have no realistic prospects of success entering summary judgment early prevents unnecessary costs being incurred. Under the old Rules there was nothing to prevent a late application for summary judgment (see, for example, *Brinks Ltd v Abu-Saleh (No. 1)* [1995] 1 WLR 1478), but as a practical matter the judge dealing with a late application might well have felt there was a lack of conviction on the part of the applicant if the application was significantly delayed. Under the Civil Procedure Rules 1998 the application should be made before or when the applicant files the Allocation Questionnaire (PD 26, para. 5.3(1)). PD 26, para. 5.3, provides:

(1)   A party intending to make [an application for summary judgment] should do so before or when filing his allocation questionnaire.
(2)   Where a party makes an application for such an order before a claim has been allocated to a track the court will not allocate the claim before the hearing of the application.
(3)   Where a party files an allocation questionnaire stating that he intends to make such an application but has not done so, the judge will usually direct that an allocation hearing is listed.
(4)   The application may be heard at that allocation hearing if the application notice has been issued and served in sufficient time.

Figure 12.1   Flow diagram showing stages for applying for default and summary judgments

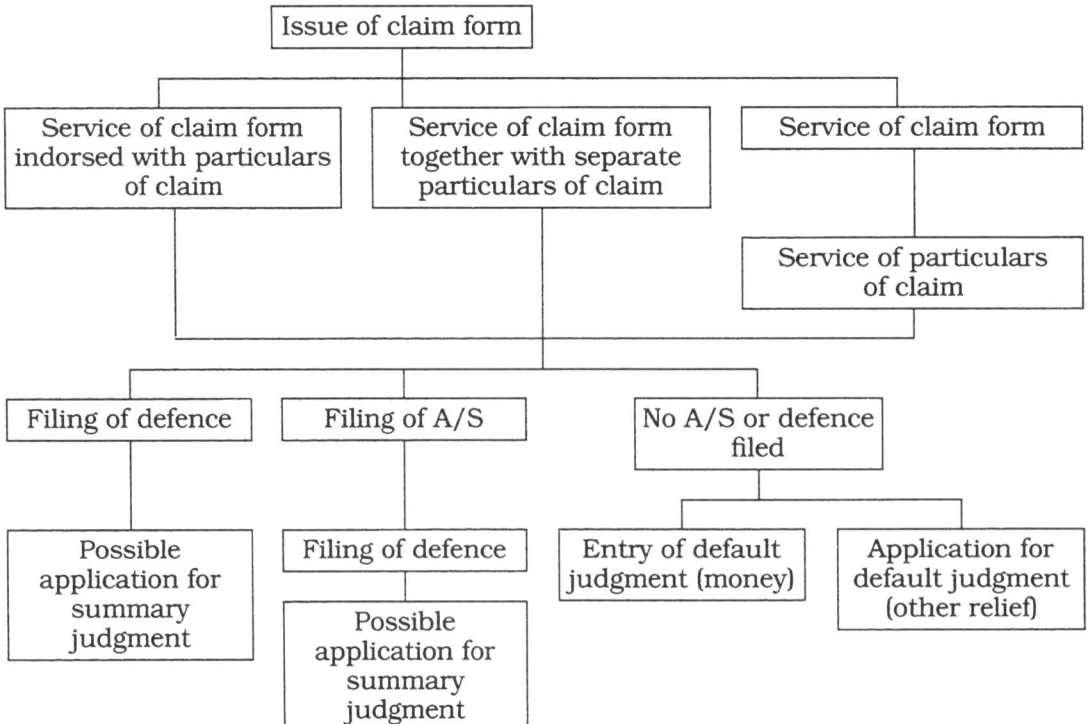

12.3   Excluded Proceedings

Under CPR, r. 24.3(2), the only excluded proceedings in cases where the application is brought by the claimant are residential possession proceedings (whether brought against a tenant, mortgagee or a person holding over at the end of a tenancy), admiralty claims *in rem* and contentious probate proceedings. In applications against claimants there are no excluded types of proceedings (CPR, r. 24.3(1)).

Actions against the Crown are also excluded by virtue of RSC O. 77 and CCR O. 42, both of which are preserved in the schedules to the Civil Procedure Rules 1998.

12.4   Effect of Making an Application for Summary Judgment

There are three procedural effects of having a pending application for summary judgment:

(a)   If the application is made after filing an acknowledgment of service but before filing of the defence, there is no need to file a defence before the hearing (CPR, r. 24.4(2)). At that stage the court will give directions, which will include providing a date for filing the defence. The permissive wording of the rule confirms *Natural Resources Inc* v *Origin Clothing Ltd* [1995] FSR 280, which held that there is nothing to prevent a defendant from serving a defence in the period before the hearing if the defendant chooses to do so.

(b)   Where a party makes a summary judgment application before a claim has been allocated to a case management track, the court will not allocate the claim before hearing the summary judgment application. See PD 26, para. 5.3(2) and **12.3**.

(c)   Where a defendant has applied for summary judgment against a claimant, the claimant cannot obtain a default judgment until the summary judgment application has been disposed of: CPR, r. 12.3(3)(a).

12.5   Procedure

The general rules on making interim applications (see **Chapter 10**) apply on making an application for summary judgment, with certain refinements. The application is made by application notice, which must be supported by evidence (CPR, r. 25.3(2)). The evidence in support is most likely to be contained either in Part C of the application notice, or in a separate witness statement. The facts supporting the claim will have been verified by a statement of truth included in the particulars of claim. The evidence in support of an application by a claimant will have to state a belief that there is no defence with a reasonable prospect of success. It may be prudent to go further and to give details of the background facts and to exhibit relevant documentation to show there is no reasonable defence. On an application by the defendant there may or may not be a filed defence. If not, clearly the evidence will have to explain why the claim is unlikely to succeed, and will probably have to go into the background in some detail.

The rules specifically mention that the court may fix a summary judgment hearing of its own initiative: CPR, r. 24.4(3). If the court is minded to make use of this power, it is most likely to do so on the initial scrutiny at the track allocation stage shortly after filing of the defence. If the court uses the power it will not allocate the case to a track, but instead it will fix a hearing, giving the parties 14 days' notice and informing them of the issues it proposes to decide: PD 26, para. 5.4.

Instead of the usual notice period of three clear days which applies to most types of interim application, the notice period in applications for summary judgment is 14 clear days: CPR, r. 24.4(3). The 14 day period of notice may be varied by Practice Directions (r. 24.4(4)), and has been shortened for specific performance claims (see **12.9**).

The respondent must file and serve any evidence in reply at least seven clear days before the hearing: CPR, r. 24.5(1). The application notice must inform the respondent of this time limit: PD 24, para. 2(5). If the applicant wishes to respond to the respondent's evidence, the further evidence must be served and filed at least three clear days before the hearing of the application: CPR, r. 24.5(2).

In cases where the hearing is fixed by the court on its own initiative, all parties must file and serve their evidence at least seven clear days before the return day, and if they want to respond to their opponents' evidence, that must be done at least three clear days before the return day: CPR, r. 24.5(3).

In the time-honoured phrase, the evidence in reply must 'condescend to particulars'. For example, it should deal with the specific allegations in the particulars of claim, and state the nature of and facts in support of the defence.

12.6   The Hearing

12.6.1   DEFENDANT FAILS TO ATTEND

In such cases the Master is almost bound to make the order, unless the particulars of claim for some reason give cause for concern. By CPR, r. 23.11 and PD 24, para. 8, 'judgment given against a party who does not attend may be set aside or varied'. On such an application, the onus on the defendant is to satisfy the court as to:

(a)   the merits of the defence; and

(b)   the reasons for the non-attendance.

12.6.2   NO NOTICE OF DEFENDANT'S EVIDENCE IN RESPONSE

Sometimes, the defendant attends on the return day with written evidence in support of a defence, having failed to give the claimant the necessary seven days' notice. In such cases, the Master usually adjourns to give the claimant time to serve evidence in reply. The costs thrown away are usually ordered against the defendant.

12.6.3   EFFECTIVE RETURN DAY

Where both parties attend, the claimant mentions the nature of the application and refers to the evidence in support. The defendant refers the Master to his or her evidence setting out the reasons against entering summary judgment. The claimant then argues that there is no defence to the action, referring to the evidence in reply, if any. The defendant then argues that there is a defence or some other reason for a trial, and that the application should be dismissed. (See the **Advocacy Manual**.)

12.6.4   GOING BEHIND THE WRITTEN EVIDENCE

An application for summary judgment is not a trial of the veracity of the written evidence. Generally, the court must act on the defendant's evidence, and *per* Lord Lindley in *Codd* v *Delap* (1905) 92 LT 810, HL, the defendant's evidence should only be rejected 'if it is obviously frivolous and practically moonshine'.

In *Banque de Paris et des Pays-Bos (Swisse SA)* v *de Naray* [1984] 1 Lloyd's Rep 21, Ackner LJ said:

It is of course trite law that [summary judgment] proceedings are not decided by weighing the two affidavits. It is also trite that the mere assertion in an affidavit of a given situation which is to be the basis of a defence does not, *ipso facto*, provide leave to defend; the court must look at the whole situation and ask itself whether the defendant has satisfied the court that there is a fair or reasonable probability of the defendants' having a real or *bona fide* defence.

A slightly different formulation, approved in *National Westminster Bank plc* v *Daniel* [1993] 1 WLR 1, CA, was: 'Is what the defendant says credible?' If it is not, there is no fair or reasonable probability of the defendant being able to set up a defence. The rigid formulation of categories where it is appropriate to go behind the defendant's evidence, as attempted by Webster J in *Paclantic Financing Co. Inc.* v *Moscow Narodny Bank Ltd* [1983] 1 WLR 1063, was deprecated in *National Westminster Bank plc* v *Daniel* as too narrow. However, Webster J's categories are still useful examples. They are where:

(a) the defendant's evidence is inherently unreliable through being self-contradictory; or

(b) the defendant's evidence is inadmissible; or

(c) the defendant's evidence is irrelevant; or

(d) there is affirmative evidence which is either admitted or unchallengeable by the defendant which is unequivocally inconsistent with the written evidence, there being no plausible explanation for the inconsistency.

12.7 Possible Orders

The orders available to the court are:

(a) judgment on the claim;

(b) striking out or dismissal of the claim;

(c) dismissal of the application; and

(d) a conditional order.

It is possible to combine these orders. Thus, if the claimant claims £50,000, and there is a reasonable defence in the sum of £30,000, the order should be judgment in favour of the claimant in the sum of £20,000, with the application dismissed as to the balance.

12.7.1 ENTERING SUMMARY JUDGMENT

The CPR, r. 24.2, provides:

> *The court may give summary judgment against a claimant or defendant on the whole of a claim or on a particular issue if—*
> *(a) it considers that—*
> *(i) that claimant has no real prospect of succeeding on the claim or issue; or*
> *(ii) that defendant has no real prospect of successfully defending the claim or issue; and*
> *(b) there is no other compelling reason why the case or issue should be disposed of at a trial.*

Under the old rules the defendant had merely to point to a triable issue. Under the Civil Procedure Rules 1998 the respondent has to show a case with real prospects of success. This means that the well known 'shadowy' defence, which under the old rules would have resulted in conditional leave to defend, will now be regarded as one that does not have a 'real prospect of success' so that summary judgment will be entered under the new rules. The 'real prospect of success' formula is the same as that applied on an application to set aside a judgment in default. In *Swain* v *Hillman, The Times*, 4 November 1999, Lord Woolf MR said that 'real prospect of success' did not need any amplification as the words spoke for themselves. The word 'real' directed the court to the need to see whether there was a realistic, as opposed to a fanciful, prospect of success. The phrase does not mean 'real and substantial' prospects of success. Nor does it mean that summary judgment will only be granted if the claim or defence is 'bound to be dismissed at trial'. The Master of the Rolls went on to say that summary judgment applications have to be kept within their proper role. They are not meant to dispense with the need for a trial where there are issues which should be considered at trial. Further, summary judgment hearings should not be mini-trials. They are simply summary hearings to dispose of cases where there is no real prospect of success.

In *United Bank Ltd* v *Asif* (11 February 2000, CA, unreported), the court considered the defence put forward, and decided it was fanciful and no more than a sham, and so summary judgment was entered. In *Penningtons* v *Abedi* (30 July 1999, unreported), there had been ongoing litigation in which the defendant had advanced a series of defences which had each been shown to be false. An application was made for summary judgment, and it was held that the defendant's conduct of the litigation was such that there was no realistic prospect of her successfully defending the claim. In *Public Trustee (as executor of the estate of Priscilla Gordon deceased)* v *Williams* (27 January 2000, unreported), the estate sought to recover the sum of £74,000 which was received by one of the defendants and used by her to buy a house. The evidence of the recipient filed in response to an application for summary judgment was at its best unclear and at its worst confusing as to where she thought the money had come from. However, there was no clear evidence that the money had come from the estate, and it was held that it was not a suitable case for summary judgment.

The claimant is entitled to judgment where the respondent's only suggested claim or defence is a point of law which is clearly misconceived, or which can be shown to be unsustainable after relatively short argument. Where a case raises difficult questions of law which call for detailed argument and mature consideration, there is a real prospect of success, and summary judgment is inappropriate: *Home and Overseas Insurance Co. Ltd* v *Mentor Insurance Co. (UK) Ltd* [1990] 1 WLR 153, CA.

A dispute of facts will usually produce a real prospect of success. For this reason it is unusual to obtain summary judgment in personal injuries cases, which often turn on disputed facts. However, there is no rule to this effect, and in *Dummer* v *Brown* [1953] 1 QB 710 summary judgment was given in a personal injuries case in favour of a passenger in a coach where the coach driver had previously pleaded guilty to dangerous driving. Even if there is a conviction, summary judgment may be refused if there are good reasons for believing the conviction was erroneous: *McCauley* v *Vine* [1999] 1 WLR 1977, CA.

12.7.2 CONDITIONAL ORDERS

PD 24, para. 4.3, provides:

> *Where it appears to the court possible that a claim or defence may succeed but improbable that it will do so, the court may make a conditional order . . .*

PD 24, para. 5.2, provides:

> *A conditional order is an order which requires a party:*
> *(1) to pay a sum of money into court, or*
> *(2) to take a specified step in relation to his claim or defence, as the case may be, and provides that that that party's claim will be dismissed or his statement of case will be struck out if he does not comply.*
> *(Note — the court will not follow its former practice of granting leave to a defendant to defend a claim, whether conditionally or unconditionally.)*

Conditional orders are similar to the old conditional leave to defend. They are appropriate for cases in the grey area between granting judgment and dismissing the application. PD 24, para. 4, says that conditional orders should be made where it appears to be possible but improbable that the respondent will succeed.

If money is paid into court pursuant to a conditional order, the claimant is protected against the defendant's bankruptcy. The claim must still be proved in the insolvency, but the claimant has security for the sum paid into court: *Re Ford* [1900] 2 QB 211.

In *Yorke (MV) Motors* v *Edwards* [1982] 1 WLR 444, HL, Lord Diplock said that in his experience, extending over 50 years, conditional orders are now made more frequently than they were formerly. A condition of payment of £12,000 into court within 28 days had been ordered by the judge, who was 'sceptical' about Mr Edwards' defence to the £23,000 claim. He appealed to the Court of Appeal and House of Lords against the condition. He was unemployed, living with his father, and had legal aid with a nil contribution. Lord Diplock endorsed the following principles:

(a) A defendant seeking to limit a financial condition must make full and frank disclosure and must put sufficient and proper evidence of his or her impecuniosity before the court.

(b) Reliance on a legal aid certificate is not sufficient.

(c) The test as to the appropriateness or otherwise of the condition is whether it will be impossible for the defendant to fulfil it, as this would be equivalent to giving judgment. However, merely finding the condition difficult to fulfil is no ground for complaint.

On the facts the House of Lords substituted a condition for bringing £3,000 into court.

12.7.3 SET-OFF

If a cross-claim is for a sum of money and it amounts to a defence it is called a set-off. (A set-off is pleaded in any defence and is usually also pleaded as a counterclaim.) As a set-off is a defence it will justify dismissing the application up to the amount of the set-off claimed. The following are established set-off situations:

(a) Mutual debts. Under statute, if the claimant and defendant both owe each other liquidated sums, even if unconnected, the defendant's debt should be set-off against the debt to the claimant.

(b) Sale of Goods Act 1979, s. 53(1). Where the seller sues for the price of goods sold and delivered the buyer can set-off a claim for damages for breach of the statutory implied terms (such as the goods being not of satisfactory quality, not fit for their purpose, or not corresponding to description).

(c) On a claim for the price of services, the defendant can set-off a counterclaim for damages for poor workmanship: *Basten* v *Butler* (1806) 7 East 4710.

(d) Equitable set-off. Although it is clear that an equitable set-off is a defence, the ambit of the doctrine is less certain. Lord Wilberforce in *The Aries* [1977] 1 WLR 185, HL, at 405 said 'One thing is clear — there must be some equity, some ground for equitable intervention, beyond the mere existence of a cross-claim.' In *Hanak* v *Green* [1958] 2 QB 9, CA the claimant sued her builder for breach of contract for failing to complete, or complete properly, certain building works on her house. The defendant counterclaimed by way of set-off:

(i) a quantum meruit for extra work done outside the contract;

(ii) losses sustained by the claimant's refusal to admit his workmen; and

(iii) damages for trespass to his tools.

It was held that all three heads were equitable set-offs, because a court of equity before the Judicature Acts would have required that either side should take the other side's claims into account before insisting on its own claims.

It is clear that the mere existence of a cross-claim is not enough. Even where the claim and cross-claim arose out of the same contract or transaction, there would only be a set-off if the two claims were so inseparably connected that the one ought not to be enforced without taking the other into account: *Dole Dried Fruit and Nut Company* v *Trustin Kerwood Ltd* [1990] 2 Lloyd's Rep 309, CA. Putting the matter slightly differently, it must be manifestly unjust to allow one party to enforce payment without taking into account the cross-claim: *Insituform (Ireland) Ltd* v *Insituform Group Ltd, The Times*, 27 November 1990, CA.

A classic example of an equitable set-off is that a tenant is allowed to set-off a counterclaim for damages for breach of covenant in the lease in respect of which the landlord is claiming arrears of rent: *British Anzani (Felixstowe) Ltd* v *International Marine Management (UK) Ltd* [1980] QB 137 (QBD).

12.7.4 THE CHEQUE RULE

It is an old rule that a cheque, bill of exchange or promissory note is given and taken as so much cash: *Jackson* v *Murphy* (1887) 4 TLR 92. The so-called 'cheque rule' is that where *inter alia* goods or services are paid for by a cheque which is subsequently dishonoured, the payee is entitled to summary judgment on the cheque and the defendant cannot set-off against that claim any cross-claim for damages allegedly due under the contract of sale or services. The doctrine goes as far as laying down that the defendant will not even get a stay of execution pending resolution of a counterclaim. It was held in *Esso Petroleum Co. Ltd* v *Milton* [1997] 1 WLR 938, CA, that the same rule applies to payments by direct debit.

There is both a commercial and a legal justification for the rule. Commercial people regard cheques as almost equivalent to cash, and expect payment at the end of the usual clearing period. In legal terms there are two contracts: the underlying contract of sale or services; and the independent contract on the bill of exchange itself. It is because the plaintiff is suing on the independent cheque contract that cross-claims on the sale contract will not be entertained.

A number of limited defences have been recognised to cheque actions, namely:

(a) fraud;

(b) invalidity;

(c) illegality;

(d) duress;

(e) total failure of consideration;

(f) as a partial defence, ascertained and liquidated partial failure of consideration; and

(g) rather doubtfully, misrepresentation.

12.7.5 SOME OTHER REASON FOR A TRIAL

Even if there is no claim or defence with a real prospect of success, summary judgment should not be given if there ought for some other reason be a trial. Other reasons include:

(a) Where the defendant has been unable to contact an important witness who may provide material for a defence.

(b) Where the applicant has acted harshly or unconscionably, so it would be desirable to ensure that judgment is obtained only in the full light of publicity.

12.8   Summary Proceedings for the Possession of Land

12.8.1   INTRODUCTION

The RSC O. 113 and CCR O. 24 (both preserved in the schedules to the Civil Procedure Rules 1998) provide similar procedures for obtaining speedy possession orders against trespassers and squatters. The High Court and County Courts have concurrent jurisdiction over these cases. For ease of exposition, only the County Court rules are cited in **12.8.2** to **12.8.4**. Note also that it is an offence for any person who is on premises as a trespasser to fail to leave on being required to do so by the residential occupier or a protected intended occupier: Criminal Law Act 1977, s. 7, as substituted by the Criminal Justice and Public Order Act 1994, s. 73. A constable in uniform may arrest such a person without a warrant.

Under RSC O. 113 and CCR O. 24 there is no conventional trial. This procedure is therefore appropriate only in cases where the defendants have no real defence. In *Filemart Ltd* v *Avery* [1989] 2 EGLR 177, CA the defendants had put forward a defence raising a triable issue, but the County Court judge did not believe their evidence and attached no weight to what they said. Given that the defendants' evidence was rejected, it was appropriate for the case to be dealt with summarily. Had that not been so, ordinary possession proceedings would have been necessary.

12.8.2   CASES WHERE SUMMARY POSSESSION PROCEEDINGS MAY BE BROUGHT

The CCR O. 24, r. 1, provides:

> *Where a person claims possession of land which he alleges is occupied solely by a person or persons (not being a tenant or tenants holding over after the termination of the tenancy) who entered into or remained in occupation without his licence or consent or that of any predecessor in title of his, the proceedings may be brought by claim form in accordance with the provisions of this Order.*

12.8.3   PROCEDURE

A witness statement or affidavit has to be filed when the claim is issued, stating the applicant's interest in the land, the circumstances in which the land became occupied, and that all the occupants whose names are known to the claimant have been made parties. Named respondents may be served personally, by post or by leaving the papers at the premises. If there are persons whose names are not known to the claimant in the premises they may be made parties, being sued as 'persons unknown'. In such a case the proceedings must be served by affixing a copy to the front door or other conspicuous place, with an additional copy being inserted through the letter box (or, in the case of open land, by affixing copies to stakes in the ground) in transparent envelopes addressed to 'the occupiers'. Unless the case is one of urgency, the hearing must be not less than five days (residential premises) or two days (other land) after service.

If made, the order for possession may be with immediate effect, or may order possession to be given on a specified date. Any warrant of possession to enforce the order for possession must generally be issued within three months of the date of the order.

12.8.4   INTERIM POSSESSION ORDERS

If the applicant cannot wait for a possession order in the usual way, an application may be made for an interim possession order under CCR O. 24, rr. 8 to 15. This is only possible where the only claim in the proceedings is for possession (so there can be no claim for damages); it is in respect of premises (not open land); and the application must be made within 28 days of the applicant knowing of the wrongful occupation. There are prescribed forms of claim form, evidence in support and notice of application, which must be used. Once issued, the court must fix a date for consideration of the application, which must be not less than three days after proceedings are issued. The applicant must effect service within 24 hours after issue (in a similar fashion to that discussed at **12.8.3**). The respondent is permitted to file evidence in response, and again a prescribed form must be used. At the hearing no oral evidence is adduced other than that in response to questions from the court. If the court decides to make an interim order for possession, the applicant is required to give a number of undertakings, including one to reinstate the respondent if the court later holds that the interim order should not have been made, and to pay damages if, again it is later held that the interim order should not have been made. An interim order requires the respondent to vacate the premises within 24 hours. If the respondent does not vacate the premises within 24 hours, he or she will commit an offence under the Criminal Justice and Public Order Act 1994, s. 76 and, therefore, the applicant should ask the police to intervene. There is then a second return date, when the court will consider whether to make a final order for possession, or to dismiss the claim for possession.

12.9 Specific Performance, Rescission and Forfeiture in Property Cases

An even speedier process for obtaining summary judgment is available by virtue of PD 24, para. 7, in claims for specific performance and similar claims arising out of mortgage and tenancy agreements. Summary judgment in these cases can be sought at any time after the claim is served, rather than having to wait until after acknowledgment or defence, and the application can be made even in the absence of particulars of claim. The application notice, evidence in support and a draft order must be served no less than four clear days before the hearing.

THIRTEEN

INTERIM PAYMENTS AND PROVISIONAL DAMAGES

13.1 Interim Payments

13.1.1 THE PROBLEM BEHIND THE INTRODUCTION OF INTERIM PAYMENTS

Regrettably but inevitably, the administration of justice takes time. There are often occasions when it is clear for one reason or another that the claimant will recover damages at the end of the day, even though the exact amount may be uncertain. In such cases, the system of interim payments has been devised to prevent the claimant from being 'kept out of his money' for an indecently long period.

13.1.2 INTERIM PAYMENTS IN GENERAL

Interim payments can be defined as payments on account of any damages, debt or other sum which a party to an action may be held liable to pay to another party if a final judgment is given in favour of that party. An interim payment will be ordered where it is clear that the claimant will be at least partially successful and it would be unjust to delay immediate payment of that entitlement.

Interest, but not costs, may be included in an interim payment.

Interim payments may be ordered in respect of counterclaims and in Part 20 claims.

13.2 Qualification for an Interim Payment

13.2.1 JURISDICTION

The circumstances in which an interim payment may be ordered are set out in CPR, r. 25.7, which provides:

> (1) The court may make an order for an interim payment only if—
> (a) the defendant against whom the order is sought has admitted liability to pay damages or some other sum of money to the claimant;
> (b) the claimant has obtained judgment against that defendant for damages to be assessed or for a sum of money (other than costs) to be assessed.
> (c) except where paragraph (3) applies, it is satisfied that, if the claim went to trial, the claimant would obtain judgment for a substantial amount of money (other than costs) against the defendant from whom he is seeking an order for an interim payment; or
> (d) the following conditions are satisfied—
> (i) the claimant is seeking an order for possession of land (whether or not any other order is also sought); and

> (ii) the court is satisfied that, if the case went to trial, the defendant would be held liable (even if the claim for possession fails) to pay the claimant a sum of money for the defendant's occupation and use of the land while the claim for possession was pending.

13.2.2 PERSONAL INJURY CASES

The general rule, cited above, is subject to paragraph (2). This provides that in personal injuries cases an interim payment order can be made only if:

(a) the defendant is insured in respect of the claim; or

(b) the defendant's liability will be met by—

    (i) an insurer under the Road Traffic Act 1988; or

    (ii) an insurer acting under the MIB Agreement, or the MIB where it is acting itself (this formulation reflects the decision in *Sharp* v *Pereira* [1999] 1 WLR 195, where it was held that interim payments should be available in MIB cases both where the driver had an invalid insurance policy and where the driver was completely uninsured); or

(c) the defendant is a public body.

13.2.3 STANDARD OF PROOF

The CPR, r. 25.7(1)(c) and (d), provide that the court must be 'satisfied' the defendant 'would be held liable' if the claim went to trial before ordering an interim payment. This means that the claimant must satisfy the court on a balance of probabilities, but to a high standard within the range: *Shearson Lehman Bros Inc.* v *Maclaine Watson & Co. Ltd* [1987] 1 WLR 480, CA.

13.2.4 CROSS-CLAIMS AND DEFENCES

Where the application is under ground (c), obviously any defence available to the defendant has to be fully taken into account before the court can be satisfied that the claimant will obtain judgment at any trial. Where a cross-claim amounts to a set-off (and hence a defence), it must be taken into account both in considering whether the claimant would obtain judgment and in deciding whether to make an order and its amount: *Shanning International Ltd* v *George Wimpey International Ltd* [1989] 1 WLR 981, CA. General cross-claims or counterclaims not amounting to defences must be taken into account in all cases at the second stage of the court's determination, namely in deciding whether to make an order, and in what amount.

13.2.5 MULTIPLE DEFENDANTS

The Court of Appeal in *Ricci Burns Ltd* v *Toole* [1989] 1 WLR 993, following *Breeze* v *R. McKennon & Sons Ltd* (1985) 32 Build LR 41, CA, held that where there were two or more defendants, the claimant could only obtain an interim payment if it could be shown, to the necessary standard, that judgment would be obtained against a particular defendant. If the court is satisfied, to this standard, in respect of more than one defendant it can make an order for interim payments against those defendants.

The decision in *Ricci Burns* v *Toole* [1989] 1 WLR 993 is confirmed by the wording of CPR, r. 25.7(1)(c) (see above), which says that an interim payment may be made if it is shown that the claimant will obtain judgment '. . . against the defendant from whom . . .' the interim payment is sought. However, a special exception has been provided for personal injuries cases by r. 25.7(3), which provides:

> (3) In a claim for personal injuries where there are two or more defendants, the court may make an order for the interim payment of damages against any defendant if—

> (a) it is satisfied that, if the claim went to trial, the claimant would obtain judgment for substantial damages against at least one of the defendants (even if the court has not yet determined which of them is liable); and
>
> (b) paragraph (2) [status of the defendants] is satisfied in relation to each of the defendants.

13.2.6 RELATIONSHIP WITH SUMMARY JUDGMENT

It is quite common to combine applications for summary judgment with applications for interim payments. Summary judgment is available where the defence has no real prospect of success, and interim payments are available where the claimant can show liability will be established. Obviously these are similar concepts. Further, on the summary judgment application the court may make a 'relevant order' entering judgment for damages to be assessed, which would itself provide grounds for making an order for an interim payment. Another possibility is that the court may make a conditional order on the summary judgment application, and the court may be invited to make an interim payment order as the condition. Under the old rules there were a number of reported cases that considered the question of whether it was possible to make an interim payment order if a summary judgment application was unsuccessful. The better view under the old rules was that an interim payment order should not be made in such cases, although it was possible to make an interim payment order if conditional leave to defend (the old equivalent to a conditional order) was granted. With the increased availability of summary judgment under the new rules, there can be no doubt that if summary judgment is refused it would be inconsistent for the court to then decide that the claimant 'would' succeed so as to give grounds for an interim payment. There may even be a little doubt about whether making an interim payment order can be consistent with making a conditional order, again because of the change in the test for summary judgment. If the defence is on the border of having a real prospect of success (the situation where conditional orders are appropriate), how can the court simultaneously find that the claimant will win for the purposes of making an interim payment order?

13.3 Restrictions on Awards of Interim Payments

13.3.1 THE AMOUNT

13.3.1.1 General factors
It is important that the court should not order an interim payment greater than the amount ultimately awarded at the trial, since there may be difficulty in recovering an overpayment. In other words, the court will wish to be fairly certain that the amount ultimately awarded will exceed the interim payment it is preparing to award.

An interim payment must not exceed 'a reasonable proportion' of the likely damages, taking into account any contributory negligence, set-off or counterclaim.

There is no requirement to show a need for the money: *Schott Kem Ltd* v *Bentley* [1991] 1 QB 61, CA, unless this has been changed by PD 25 (Interim Payments), para. 2.1(2) (see **13.4.1**(b)).

Smith v *Glennon, The Times*, 26 June 1990, CA, is of interest in that the judge awarded an interim payment of, in effect, £190,000 in a personal injuries case out of the minimum £280,000 he considered would be awarded at trial.

13.3.1.2 Personal injury claims
Although the courts are quite ready to award interim payments to cover the claimant's loss of earnings, costs of treatment, and expenses necessary to help the claimant cope with the injury sustained, the courts are very reluctant to award significant sums out of the claim for general damages. The court may be prepared to order even a substantial interim payment out of general damages where the amount asked for is clearly below the amount the claimant will recover. It used to be thought (see, for

example, *Schott Kem Ltd* v *Bentley* [1991] 1 QB 61, CA) that in personal injury claims the claimant was required to establish some need for the money. This was rejected in *Stringman* v *McArdle* [1994] 1 WLR 1653, where the Court of Appeal held that even in personal injuries cases once the conditions have been made out the court's duty was to order an interim payment in such amount it thought just not exceeding a reasonable proportion of the damages. Objections that the claimant may use the interim payment for wrong or extravagant purposes were irrelevant.

13.3.1.3 Defendant's resources

In personal injuries claims, there is no jurisdiction to make an interim payment if the defendant is impecunious: CPR, r. 25.7(2) and **13.2.2**. In other cases, the defendant's lack of resources is a very relevant factor to be taken into account when fixing the amount of any interim payment; *British & Commonwealth Holdings plc* v *Quadrex Holdings Inc.* [1989] QB 842, CA.

13.4 How to Apply for an Interim Payment

13.4.1 THE PROCEDURE

Applications for interim payments are made on notice, and must be served at least 14 clear days before the hearing of the application. The evidence in support should set out all relevant matters including:

(a) the amount sought by way of interim payment;

(b) what the money will be used for;

(c) the likely amount of money that will be awarded;

(d) the reasons for believing a relevant ground (see above) is satisfied;

(e) in a personal injuries claim, details of special damages and past and future loss; and

(f) in a claim under the Fatal Accidents Act 1976, details of the persons on whose behalf the claim is made and the nature of the claim.

All relevant documents in support should be exhibited. In personal injuries claims these will include the medical reports.

Respondents wishing to rely on evidence in reply must file and serve their witness statements at least seven clear days before the hearing. If the applicant wants to respond to the respondent's evidence, any further evidence must be filed and served at least three clear days before the hearing. In personal injuries claims the defendant will need to obtain a certificate of recoverable benefits from the Secretary of State under the Social Security (Recovery of Benefits) Act 1997. A copy of the certificate should be filed at the hearing, and any order made must set out the amount by which the payment to be made to the claimant has been reduced in accordance with the Act and the Social Security (Recovery of Benefits) Regulations 1997.

13.4.2 SECOND OR FURTHER APPLICATIONS

Second or further applications may be made upon cause being shown. This might be, for example, because the proceedings have been delayed longer than originally envisaged by the parties, or if, in the case of an action for damages for personal injury, the claimant has had to undergo additional private treatment, or has suffered additional hardship.

13.5   The Main Trial

As with Part 36 payments (see **27.12**), an interim payment must not be disclosed to the court until all issues of liability and quantum have been decided, unless the defendant agrees. There may be occasions, however, where the public interest requires that an interim payment should be ordered in open court rather than in private, for example, where the amount is large and two public companies are involved, to ensure that a false market is not created (*British & Commonwealth Holdings plc* v *Quadrex Holdings Inc. (No. 2), The Times*, 8 December 1988, CA).

13.6   Adjustments after Judgment

On making its final order the court will, upon the interim payment being revealed, make whatever consequential adjustments are necessary. In particular, the court may order repayment by the claimant and adjustments between defendants: CPR, r. 25.8. Any repayment may be ordered with interest. There are detailed provisions about how the judgment drawn up by the court should be formulated where there has been an interim payment in PD 25 Interim Payments, paras 5.1 to 5.6.

13.7   Provisional Damages

Under general principles, an award of damages in a personal injuries case is a once-and-for-all payment. This is far from ideal where there is a danger of the claimant's condition deteriorating some time in the future. It was to remedy this situation that the courts were given power to make awards of provisional damages.

13.7.1   JURISDICTION

The SCA 1981, s. 32A, applies to personal injuries cases where there '. . . is proved or admitted to be a chance that at some definite or indefinite time in the future the [plaintiff] will . . . develop some serious disease or suffer some serious deterioration in his physical or mental condition.'

In such cases the section empowers the court to make an award of provisional damages, namely:

(a)   immediate damages, which are assessed on the assumption that the claimant will not develop the disease or suffer the deterioration; and

(b)   an entitlement to apply for further damages in the future if the disease develops or deterioration is suffered.

The section contemplates such an order being made in favour of a living claimant. There is jurisdiction, however, where a claimant has been awarded provisional damages, for the claimant's dependants, in the event of later injury-related death, to recover further damages under the FAA 1976: Damages Act 1996, s. 3.

The County Court has a similar power under CCA 1984, s. 51.

13.7.2   CONDITIONS

There are three conditions:

(a)   the claim for provisional damages must be set out in the particulars of claim;

(b)   the possible future disease or deterioration must be 'serious' in nature; and

(c)   it must be 'proved or admitted' that there is a 'chance' of the future development or deterioration.

13.7.2.1 'Serious' disease or deterioration

According to Scott Baker J in *Willson* v *MoD* [1991] 1 All ER 638, 'serious' means something beyond ordinary deterioration. The effect on the particular claimant, e.g. a hand injury on a concert pianist, is one of the relevant factors. Osteoarthritis is a commonly occurring sequela in personal injuries cases. Scott Baker J took the view that arthritic deterioration to the point that it required surgery or a change in the claimant's employment would not qualify as being serious. This view is consistent with that of Michael Davies J in *Allott* v *Central Electricity Generating Board* (19 December 1988, unreported).

13.7.2.2 A 'chance' of future deterioration

This is rather easier to establish. It must be measurable rather than fanciful: *Willson* v *MoD* [1991] 1 All ER 638. In *Patterson* v *MoD* [1987] CLY 1194, Simon Brown J assessed the claimant's chances of developing further pleural thickening in the region of 5 per cent, but regarded the chance of this occurring as 'plain'.

13.7.2.3 Subsequent injury

It seems to have been held in *Hughes* v *Cheshire County Council* (2 March 1989, unreported) that a subsequent injury caused as a result of the injury for which the defendant is responsible may be a 'deterioration' within SCA 1981, s. 32A. This appears to have been doubted in *Willson* v *MoD* [1991] 1 All ER 638.

13.7.2.4 Discretion

Where the basic conditions are satisfied, the court retains a discretion whether to make a provisional damages award rather than a conventional damages award. The following factors were identified by Scott Baker J in *Willson* v *MoD*:

(a) Diseases which by their nature follow a developing pattern are not suitable for provisional damages awards.

(b) If the claimant can point to some clear-cut future event, provisional damages may be appropriate.

(c) The greater the degree of risk of future deterioration the more likely an award will be made.

(d) The possibility of doing better justice by reserving the claimant's right to return to court.

13.7.3 PROCEDURE

Whether provisional damages are agreed or ordered after trial, PD 41 sets out the form of order and for the lodgement in court of a case file of relevant documents. These include the order or judgment, medical reports, statements of case, and any transcript of the judgment and of the claimant's evidence as the judge may consider necessary.

Hurditch v *Sheffield Health Authority* [1989] QB 562, CA was an asbestosis case. The parties agreed to a provisional damages award. However, there was some conflict between the two sides' medical reports on the question of future deterioration, and some dispute on the drafted statement of facts. The defendants resiled from the agreement. The Court of Appeal held that the presence of a few 'loose ends' did not prevent the court making a provisional damages order. The purpose of the case file is to provide material to assist the court in the event of the claimant applying for further damages in the future. If the disputes over the documents were limited, the papers filed could be restricted to what was agreed. If the disputes were more serious, the Master could order a trial of the outstanding issues.

13.7.4 THE ORDER

By CPR, r. 41.2, the order must specify the disease or diseases or type of deterioration which will entitle the claimant to apply for further damages, and will specify the period (or an indefinite period) within which the application may be made. The period may be extended, but only one application for further damages may be made in respect of each disease or type of deterioation specified in the order. An application to extend the period for making an application for further damages is made by application notice supported by evidence which should include a current medical report.

An application for further damages is made after giving the defendant and the defendant's insurers 28 days' notice of the intention to make the application. This is necessary because it may be several years since the case was last considered, and the defendant will need to retrieve its file from storage. The subsequent procedure is the same as that for applying for an interim payment, with the application being made on notice, and being served at least 14 clear days before the hearing of the application. The defendant must file and serve any evidence in reply at least seven clear days before the hearing. If the claimant wants to respond to the respondent's evidence, any further evidence must be filed and served at least three clear days before the hearing. Causation of any further damages within the scope of the provisional damages order is determined when the application for further damages is made.

13.8 Questions

OBJECTIVES

This section is designed to ensure that you have a sound working knowledge of the procedure and principles relating to:

(a) the nature of the judgment entered in default in different types of claim;

(b) whether judgment can be maintained after problems in effecting service;

(c) the practice and procedure on applications to set aside default judgments;

(d) making interim applications;

(e) summary judgment;

(f) summary proceedings for possession of land;

(g) interim payments; and

(h) provisional damages claims.

RESEARCH

Read the materials contained in **Chapters 10** to **13** of this Manual.

LARGE GROUP SESSION 3

You need to read questions 1 to 3 in advance of Large Group Session 3. There is no need to prepare notes.

QUESTION 1

In which of the following situations can the application described be made without notice?

(a) Amanda wishes to obtain an interim injunction to restrain a television company from naming her in a programme due to be broadcast this evening.

(b) Brian wishes to obtain permission to extend the period of validity of his claim form in which he is seeking damages for personal injuries against his former employer.

(c) Catherine wishes to amend her claim form and particulars of claim, which were served on Dennis six months ago, to name Elizabeth as a second defendant.

(d) Fred wishes to obtain a freezing injunction against Gerald.

(e) Hannah's lawyers wish to obtain the approval of the court for a settlement of her claim for damages which has been agreed with the insurers for Ian. Hannah is 12 years old.

QUESTION 2

Which one of the following statements about summary judgment under CPR, Part 24 is INCORRECT?

[A] A defendant is able to bring an application for summary judgment.
[B] If the defendant can show that there is a serious issue to be tried he will be entitled to an order for unconditional leave to defend.
[C] The procedure can be invoked by the court of its own initiative.
[D] Summary judgment will usually be entered if the respondent has no real prospect of success in the whole case or on a particular issue.

QUESTION 3

Gordon Engineering Ltd brought a claim against Better Imports Ltd claiming damages for non-delivery of goods pursuant to a contract for the sale of goods. Better Imports Ltd failed to respond to the claim and judgment was entered for Gordon Engineering Ltd.

(a) What form of judgment should have been entered?

(b) Gordon Engineering Ltd have medium term cash flow problems. When can they expect to be paid?

SMALL GROUP SESSION 3

On the basis of your research, answer questions 4 to 14 in advance of Small Group Session 3.

QUESTION 4

Sophie has issued and served proceedings on Deborah claiming damages and an injunction to restrain Deborah from obstructing Sophie's right of way over Blackacre.

Deborah has failed to acknowledge service of the claim form. Advise Sophie.

QUESTION 5

Penny started proceedings against Don claiming £65,000. Don failed to reply to the claim form. Penny entered judgment in default.

The claim form has now been returned through the post marked 'Gone away'. Advise Penny.

QUESTION 6

On 8 September 2000 Trilby Hats Ltd ('Trilby') issued a claim form, with particulars of claim attached, against Martin claiming £7,300 being monies paid under a mistake of fact. The claim form was personally served on Martin at 6 pm on 21 September 2000. On 16 October 2000, in the absence of any acknowledgment of service notifying an intention to defend, Trilby entered judgment for the whole of their claim. It is now 6 November 2000. Martin states that his failure to acknowledge service was an oversight and that he has a good defence to the claim.

Your best advice to Martin would be that:

[A] He should make an application to the District Judge for permission to acknowledge service out of time supported by a witness statement stating his explanation for failing to acknowledge service in time.
[B] He should make an application to the District Judge for judgment to be set aside, supported by a witness statement stating his defence on the merits and his explanation for failing to acknowledge service in time.
[C] He should pay the whole sum into court before the court will have jurisdiction to consider any application he may make.
[D] He should appeal against the judgment to a judge in private.

QUESTION 7

Janet recently served a claim form on Kevin claiming 'the sum of £36,000 being the cost of repairing damage to 47 Selvage Street, Lincoln and interest thereon pursuant to s. 35A of the Supreme Court Act 1981 occasioned by a lorry negligently driven by the defendant on 7 March 1999'. Kevin forgot to instruct solicitors and has now received a judgment for £36,000 and interest of £4,800 signed by Janet in default of acknowledgment of service.

You have been instructed to advise Kevin, who wishes to defend the claim on the basis of inevitable accident, saying he skidded on black ice despite driving with due caution.

QUESTION 8

You are instructed by Easy Rider Garages who have sold a second-hand motor car to Stephen for £15,000. Stephen paid by cheque but on presentation it was returned 'orders not to pay'. Inquiries have shown that his account is in fact substantially in credit. The garage have received a letter of complaint from Stephen saying that the car has numerous defects and that he has already put it into his local garage for these to be rectified, and that this will cost him at least £4,000.

Advise Easy Rider Garages as to the procedures they should follow in order to obtain judgment.

QUESTION 9

Edward has sued Frederick in the County Court for £3,250 being the price of a consignment of radios sold two years ago. Frederick has delivered a defence claiming the goods were of poor quality. This is the first time Edward has heard of this complaint and believes it to be a sham. You are briefed on behalf of Edward, who has applied for summary judgment. Frederick has filed a witness statement which states in para. 3 that Frederick found the radios to be faulty when they were unpacked, and that he complained to Edward on the telephone later the same day; in para. 4 that Edward refused to take the radios back; and in para. 5 that the radios were unsaleable, and were disposed of at the city dump. Edward has filed a witness statement in reply stating in para. 2 that Frederick did not telephone at any time complaining about the radios or asking for Edward to take them back; in para. 6 that Frederick bought further consignments of the same brand of radio from Edward three and seven months after the consignment in question, exhibiting the relevant purchase orders and copy invoices; and in para. 7 that further orders were refused through Frederick's unexplained (at the time) failure to pay for the consignment in question.

How will the court deal with the conflicting witness statement evidence in this case, and what order is the court likely to make?

QUESTION 10

Michael returns from holiday in Portugal to find that his small terraced house in Manchester is occupied by squatters. They refuse either to open the door or to give their names.

Advise Michael who wishes to recover possession of his house.

QUESTION 11

John sues his employer, Brickbuilding Ltd, for damages for personal injuries sustained in an accident at work. Liability it admitted, and John obtains judgment for damages to be assessed. He also makes an application for an interim payment. Which one of the following tests should the District Judge apply in determining the amount of any such interim payment?

[A] It should be a sum not exceeding the total sum John is claiming by way of special damages.
[B] It should be a sum not exceeding a reasonable proportion of the total sum John is claiming by way of special damages.
[C] It should be a sum not exceeding a reasonable proportion of the total damages which John is likely to recover.
[D] It should be a sum not exceeding one third of the total damages which John is likely to recover.

QUESTION 12

Keith was seriously injured when travelling as the front seat passenger in a car driven by Sally which was involved in a head-on collision with a car driven by Rodney. Proceedings have been issued against both drivers. In her defence, Sally denies liability and blames Rodney. In his defence Rodney denies liability alleging his vehicle skidded on black ice, and further alleges that Keith was contributorily negligent in not wearing a seat belt. Keith is in the process of giving disclosure.

Keith has already lost earnings of £14,000 over the last 15 months, and is unlikely to return to work for at least another six months. He has used up all his savings, and is rapidly sinking into debt.

Advise Keith as to whether any interim relief can be obtained, and the principles that will be applied by the court.

QUESTION 13

In a claim for personal injuries, Miranda wishes to make an application for an interim payment against William.

(a) What does Miranda's evidence in support need to cover?

(b) If Miranda is successful in obtaining an order for an interim payment, can she use this fact at any subsequent trial to prove that she has a strong case against William?

QUESTION 14

Neil suffered head injuries and a fractured shoulder when he was struck by a falling object while working on a building site 18 months ago. He was employed on a casual basis at the time of the accident, and his employment was terminated with immediate effect. He was off work for five months. The wounds to Neil's head cleared up, leaving minor scarring, after three months, but he has been left with a continuing slight loss of movement in his shoulder. Further, the medical reports that have been obtained state there is a 20% risk of the onset of severe epilepsy over the next ten years. Neil's employer has recently made an offer to settle in the sum of £25,000. Proceedings have not yet been issued. Advise Neil:

(a) on whether the £25,000 should be accepted; and

(b) on any procedural points that apply specifically to Neil's claim.

FOURTEEN

INTERIM INJUNCTIONS

14.1   Introduction

If a defendant's alleged wrongdoing will cause the claimant irreparable continuing damage pending trial, or if the damage may have already been done by the time the case comes on for trial, it is appropriate for the courts to have power to make orders to avoid the potential injustice that would otherwise arise. To meet this need the courts have jurisdiction to grant interim injunctions to regulate the position between the parties pending the trial. A number of special terms are used in this area, and the following definitions may be of assistance:

Perpetual injunction	Final judgment for an injunction normally granted at trial.
Interim injunction	Provisional order made before trial.
Mandatory injunction	Order requiring specific acts to be done. It is the substance of the order that makes it mandatory, not its positive wording.
Prohibitory injunction	Order to refrain from doing specific acts.
Quia timet injunction	Order to prevent an apprehended legal wrong, where none has been committed at the date of the application.

14.2   Jurisdiction

14.2.1   HIGH COURT

Jurisdiction to grant interim injunctions in the High Court derives from the SCA 1981, s. 37, which provides:

> *(1)   The High Court may by order (whether interlocutory or final) grant an injunction or appoint a receiver in all cases in which it appears to the court to be just and convenient to do so.*
> *(2)   Any such order may be made either unconditionally or on such terms and conditions as the court thinks just.*

14.2.2   COUNTY COURT

County Court jurisdiction to grant interim injunctions derives from the CCA 1984, s. 38(1), which allows the court to make any order which could be made by the High Court if the proceedings were in the High Court. The only restrictions are in relation to search orders and freezing injunctions, see **1.2.1.3**.

14.2.3   CAUSE OF ACTION

In *The Siskina* [1979] AC 210 at 256, Lord Diplock said:

> A right to obtain an interlocutory injunction is not a cause of action. It cannot stand on its own. It is dependent on there being a pre-existing cause of action against the

defendant arising out of the invasion, actual or threatened, by him of a legal or equitable right of the plaintiff for the enforcement of which the defendant is amenable to the jurisdiction of the Court. The right to obtain an injunction is merely ancillary and incidental to the pre-existing cause of action.

In this particular case, a *Mareva* (freezing) injunction was refused because there was no dispute justiciable in the courts of England and Wales at all. In other cases, injunctions have been refused because the claimant's allegations do not amount to a cause of action.

The correctness of *The Siskina* was confirmed by the Privy Council in *Mercedes-Benz AG* v *Leiduck* [1996] 1 AC 284. However, in *Morris* v *Murjani* [1996] 2 All ER 384, the Court of Appeal while not disputing that *The Siskina* and *Mercedes-Benz* v *Leiduck* correctly stated the position regarding litigation affecting the private rights of litigants distinguished the position in respect of cases where a public duty was involved. In such circumstances even though there may be no pre-existing cause of action there was still a 'substantive right' which could be protected by an interim injunction.

The case involved the Insolvency Act 1986, s. 333, which imposed a public duty on a bankrupt which was owed to the trustee in bankruptcy. The trustee tried to enforce this duty under s. 333 by commencing committal proceedings for contempt of court against the bankrupt. The trustee applied without notice for an interim injunction restraining the bankrupt from leaving the country pending the application for committal. The injunction was granted, and upheld by the Court of Appeal.

Therefore, in most ordinary disputes which will relate to private rights, a pre-existing cause of action is necessary, but in cases involving public duties the court may not insist on a pre-existing cause of action as a prerequisite to the granting of an interim injunction.

14.3 Principles

14.3.1 THE *AMERICAN CYANAMID* GUIDELINES

Interim injunctive relief is both temporary and discretionary. Guidelines on how that discretion should be exercised were laid down by the House of Lords in the leading case of *American Cyanamid Co.* v *Ethicon Ltd* [1975] AC 396. The facts were that Ethicon, the defendants, manufactured absorbable catgut sutures. Cyanamid patented a synthetic absorbable suture, and started eating into Ethicon's market. Ethicon then produced its own synthetic suture with a slightly different chemical composition from Cyanamid's. Cyanamid issued proceedings, and applied for an interim injunction to restrain Ethicon's sales. Ethicon said their suture was different from that patented by Cyanamid, or alternatively that the patent was invalid. Voluminous affidavits and exhibits were filed by both parties on the interim application. The following paragraphs set out the principles stated by Lord Diplock.

14.3.1.1 Serious question to be tried

It is no part of the court's function at this stage of the litigation to try to resolve conflicts of evidence on affidavits as to facts on which the claims of either party may ultimately depend nor to decide difficult questions of law which call for detailed argument and mature consideration. (p. 407H)

The purpose sought to be achieved by giving the court discretion to grant such injunctions would be stultified if the discretion were clogged by a technical rule forbidding its exercise if upon that incomplete untested evidence the court evaluated the chances of the plaintiff's ultimate success in the action at 50 per cent or less, but permitting its exercise if the court evaluated his chances at more than 50 per cent. (p. 406G)

The court no doubt must be satisfied that the claim is not frivolous or vexatious; in other words, that there is a serious question to be tried. (p. 407G)

This initial hurdle is fairly easily satisfied. However, the condition will not be satisfied where the claimant relies on a cause of action unknown to the law, or if the cause of action is unarguable on the facts. Seriously flawed evidence as to the likelihood of customers being deceived by a rival product in a passing off action was not regarded as being so weak that there was no serious issue to be tried in *Dalgety Spillers Foods Ltd v Food Brokers Ltd* [1994] FSR 504. Weakness on the facts was the problem in *Morning Star Co-operative Society Ltd v Express Newspapers Ltd* [1979] FSR 113 where the claimants alleged the defendants were proposing to pass off the soon to be released '*Daily Star*' as the '*Morning Star*'. Given the differences between the publications, Foster J was inclined to the view that there was no serious question to be tried, as 'Only a moron in a hurry would be misled.'

Unless the material available to the court fails to disclose that the plaintiff has any real prospect of succeeding in his claim at trial, the court should go on to consider the balance of convenience. (p. 408B)

Therefore, if a serious issue is disclosed the court will proceed to consider the balance of convenience in its wide sense (see **14.3.1.2** to **14.3.1.7**).

14.3.1.2 Adequacy of damages to the claimant

. . . the court should first consider whether, if the plaintiff were to succeed at the trial in establishing his right to a permanent injunction, he would be adequately compensated by an award of damages for the loss he would have sustained as a result of the defendant's continuing to do what was sought to be enjoined between the time of the application and the time of the trial. If damages in the measure recoverable at common law would be an adequate remedy and the defendant would be in a financial position to pay them, no interlocutory injunction should normally be granted, however strong the plaintiff's claim appeared to be at that stage. (p. 408C)

Damages will not be adequate if:

(a) the defendant is or is likely to be unable to pay;

(b) the wrong is irreparable, e.g. loss of the right to vote;

(c) the damage is not pecuniary, e.g. many nuisances;

(d) damages would be difficult to assess, e.g. loss of business reputation, disruption to business.

14.3.1.3 Adequacy of the undertaking in damages as protection for the defendant

If . . . damages would not provide an adequate remedy for the plaintiff in the event of his succeeding at the trial, the court should then consider whether, on the contrary hypothesis that the defendant were to succeed at the trial in establishing his right to do that which was sought to be enjoined, he would be adequately compensated under the plaintiff's undertaking as to damages for the loss he would have sustained by being prevented from doing so between the time of the application and the time of the trial. If damages in the measure recoverable under such an undertaking would be an adequate remedy and the plaintiff would be in a position to pay them, there would be no reason upon this ground to refuse an interlocutory injunction. (p. 408D, E)

Undertakings given by claimants on the grant of interim injunctions to pay damages to defendants who may suffer unjustifiable loss where it transpires the injunction should not have been granted are considered at **14.5**. One of the reasons for introducing such undertakings was that '. . . it aided the court in doing that which was its great object, viz. abstaining from expressing any opinion on the merits of the case until the hearing': *Wakefield* v *Duke of Buccleugh* (1865) 12 LT 628.

If the undertaking does adequately protect the defendant, there is 'no reason' for refusing the injunction at this stage, and the court should consider the balance of convenience (narrow sense). If the claimant is not in a financial position to honour the undertaking and appreciable damage to the defendant is likely, it was said, *obiter*, in *Morning Star Co-operative Society Ltd* v *Express Newspapers Ltd* [1979] FSR 113 that the injunction should be refused. In this case the likely damage to the defendants if the launch of their newspaper was restrained was unquantifiable, and the financial evidence showed that the claimant was unlikely to be able to pay on the undertaking. In *Merrell Dow Pharmaceuticals Inc* v *HN Norton & Co. Ltd* [1994] RPC 1 a patentee would probably have had to make a permanent reduction in its prices as a result of an alleged infringement, which was an ascertainable loss, whereas the defendant had an unascertainable loss in the possible market share it would not achieve if an injunction were granted. The application for an interim injunction was refused.

14.3.1.4 Narrow balance of convenience

> It is where there is doubt as to the adequacy of the respective remedies in damages available to either party or to both, that the question of balance of convenience arises. It would be unwise to attempt even to list all the various matters which may need to be taken into consideration in deciding where the balance lies, let alone to suggest the relative weight to be attached to them. These will vary from case to case. (p. 408F)

> The extent to which the disadvantages to each party would be incapable of being compensated in damages in the event of his succeeding at the trial is always a significant factor in assessing where the balance of convenience lies. (p. 409B)

On the facts in *American Cyanamid*, the balance of convenience tended to favour the claimants. Ethicon's new sutures were not at that time on the market. Granting the injunction would not close factories or cause unemployment. If refused, Cyanamid may have failed to increase its growing market and effectively lost the benefit of its patent.

The following cases are other examples of the operation of the balance of convenience.

Fellowes & Son v *Fisher* [1976] QB 122, CA. Solicitors sued their former clerk for breach of a covenant in restraint of trade. The interim injunction was refused because the defendant would otherwise have been deprived of his job, and that was likely to be more serious to him than the harm to the claimants through his continuing to work for a rival firm.

Hubbard v *Pitt* [1976] QB 142, CA. An interim injunction was granted to the claimant estate agents to restrain the defendants picketing their office. The claimant was likely to suffer irreparable damage, whereas the defendants could press their views elsewhere.

Potters-Ballotini Ltd v *Weston-Baker* [1977] RPC 202, CA. An interim injunction to prevent the defendants manufacturing products allegedly in breach of covenant was refused, because it would have been catastrophic to compel the defendants to close their factory.

Roussel-Uclaf v *G.D. Searle & Co.* [1977] FSR 125. An interim injunction to restrain the sale of a drug with life-saving qualities, which was alleged to infringe the claimant's patent, was refused, because it was in the public interest to keep the drug on the market.

Dalgety Spillers Foods Ltd v *Food Brokers Ltd* [1994] FSR 504. Factors influencing the court in refusing an interim injunction in a passing off action were that the defendant had undertaken to maintain accurate records of sales of the products in question, and the fact the claimant had not responded to a letter from the defendant frankly stating its plans for its new product and enclosing sample containers.

14.3.1.5 Status quo
As part of the balance of convenience,

> Where other factors appear to be evenly balanced it is a counsel of prudence to take such measures as are calculated to preserve the status quo. (p. 408G)

In *Garden Cottage Foods Ltd* v *Milk Marketing Board* [1984] AC 130, HL, it was held that the status quo means the state of affairs immediately before the issue of the claim form, ignoring minimal periods of time, unless the claimant is guilty of unreasonable delay. If the claimant has delayed, the status quo will be the state of affairs immediately before the application. Delay, therefore, tends to benefit the defendant.

14.3.1.6 Special factors
Also as part of the balance of convenience,

> . . . there may be many other special factors to be taken into consideration in the particular circumstances of individual cases. (p. 409D)

A special factor identified in *American Cyanamid* was that, once doctors and patients had got used to Ethicon's suture in the period prior to trial, it might well have become commercially impracticable for Cyanamid to insist after trial that it be withdrawn. Therefore, the interim injunction was granted.

14.3.1.7 The merits of the case
If other factors do not differ widely,

> . . . it may not be improper to take into account in tipping the balance the relative strength of each party's case as revealed by the affidavit evidence adduced on the hearing of the application. This, however, should be done only where it is apparent upon the facts disclosed by evidence as to which there is no credible dispute that the strength of one party's case is disproportionate to that of the other party. The court is not justified in embarking upon anything resembling a trial of the action upon conflicting affidavits in order to evaluate the strength of either party's case. (p. 409B, C)

14.3.2 *AMERICAN CYANAMID* IN PRACTICE

The impact of *American Cyanamid* was to remove the need to show a *prima facie* case on the merits before an interim injunction would be granted. The extent to which the merits of the case could be looked at were considered by Lord Diplock in his comments at **14.3.1.1** and **14.3.1.7**. It was generally thought that this meant that once a serious issue had been shown the court should not embark further upon an examination of the claimant's prospects of success (unless **14.3.1.7** was relevant).

In *Series 5 Software Ltd* v *Clarke* [1996] 1 All ER 853, a decision at first instance, Laddie J, considered whether the comments by Lord Diplock in *American Cyanamid* meant, if there was a dispute on the evidence, that the court could not take into account its view on the strength of each party's case. He held that Lord Diplock did not intend to exclude consideration of the strength of the case in most applications for interim relief but intended that the court should not attempt to resolve difficult issues of fact or law. If, however, the court was able to come to a clear view as to the strength of each party's case on credible evidence, then it could do so, and it would be a factor the court could bear in mind when deciding whether or nor to grant an interim injunction.

This appears to be a radical departure from the traditional interpretation of the *American Cyanamid* decision but it may well reflect what is actually happening in practice.

It is clear, however, that the principles stated by Lord Diplock must not be read as if they were statutory provisions. The remedy is always discretionary, and the *American Cyanamid* principles are applied with some degree of flexibility.

14.3.3 EXCEPTIONAL CASES

In a number of fairly well-defined areas, the courts do not adopt a strict *American Cyanamid* approach to the granting of interim injunctions. It is sometimes said that these cases can be explained by the 'special factors' referred to by Lord Diplock (**14.3.1.6**). It is also said that *American Cyanamid* is restricted to '. . . cases where the legal rights of the parties depend upon facts that are in dispute . . .' (p. 406H). In other cases it is said that *American Cyanamid* was decided on the assumption there would be a trial (e.g. 'these are matters to be dealt with at the trial', p. 407H), and, if there will be no trial, Lord Diplock's principles do not apply. Whether these are strictly exceptions to, or particular applications of, the *American Cyanamid* principles has little practical importance.

14.3.3.1 Interim injunction would finally dispose of the action

In *NWL Ltd* v *Woods* [1979] 1 WLR 1294, 1306, Lord Diplock said '*American Cyanamid* v *Ethicon Ltd* . . . was not dealing with a case in which the grant or refusal of an injunction at that stage would, in effect, dispose of the action finally in favour of whichever party was successful in the application, because there would be nothing left on which it was in the unsuccessful party's interest to proceed to trial.' In such cases, Lord Diplock said, '. . . the degree of likelihood that the plaintiff would have succeeded in establishing his right to an injunction if the action had gone to trial is a factor to be brought into the balance by the judge in weighing the risks that injustice may result from his deciding the application one way rather than the other.'

In *Cayne* v *Global Natural Resources plc* [1984] 1 All ER 225, CA the claimants, who were shareholders in the defendant company, sought interim injunctions to restrain the company from:

(a) implementing a merger transaction; and

(b) issuing or allotting any shares to one of the parties to the proposed merger,

without first obtaining the approval of the company in general meeting. The alleged purpose of the deals was to maintain the directors in office. The claimants' evidence supported the case they presented. The company's evidence, if true, completely destroyed the claimants' case. If the relief claimed by the claimants were to be granted, the injunction would have lasted until the next annual general meeting of the company. By the time of trial, that meeting would already have taken place. If the injunction was refused, the deals would have been implemented and there would be no point in seeking an injunction. Therefore there was no realistic prospect of a trial.

It was held that the *American Cyanamid* principles on balance of convenience did not apply. The court was to apply the broad principle of doing its best to avoid injustice. An interim injunction could only properly be granted if the claimants' case on the merits was overwhelming. Here it was not, and the injunction was accordingly refused. As Eveleigh LJ said, '. . . it would be wrong to run the risk of causing an injustice to a defendant who is being denied the right to trial where the defence put forward has been substantiated by affidavits and a number of exhibits.'

In *Lansing Linde Ltd* v *Kerr* [1991] 1 All ER 418, CA, however, a restraint of trade case where the court considered the merits as the granting or refusal of an interim injunction may have finally determined the issue, Staughton LJ said that in the circumstances of the case justice simply required '. . . some assessment of the merits . . . more than merely a serious issue to be tried'.

It was also made clear in *Lansing* that, the claimant's assertion that it would in any event wish to proceed to trial to recover damages could in appropriate circumstances be disregarded as unlikely.

14.3.3.2 Negative covenants
Where the defendant is in breach of a valid express negative covenant a perpetual injunction has been held to issue 'as of course': *Doherty* v *Allman* (1878) 3 App Cas 709, HL. The same principle applies to interim injunctions: *A-G* v *Barker* [1990] 3 All ER 257, CA.

14.3.3.3 No defence
In *Official Custodian for Charities* v *Mackay* [1985] Ch 168, Scott J said 'I do not . . . think that this is a case to which the *Cyanamid* principles can be applied. Those principles are not, in my view, applicable to a case where there is no arguable defence to the plaintiff's claim.'

The effect, in such cases, is that *prima facie* the claimant is entitled to interim relief. As James LJ said in *Stocker* v *Planet Building Society* (1879) 27 WR 877, CA, 'Balance of convenience has nothing to do with a case of this kind; it can only be considered where there is some question which must be decided at the hearing.' Alternatively, it may be appropriate in such cases to apply immediately for final relief by way of summary judgment: *Cadogen* v *Muscatt, The Times*, 15 May 1990, CA.

14.3.3.4 Defamation actions
Since the nineteenth century (*Bonnard* v *Perryman* [1891] 2 Ch 269) it has been held that, generally, interim injunctions will not be granted in defamation actions, or will be discharged if granted without notice, if the defendant intends to plead justification. In *Bestobell Paints Ltd* v *Bigg* [1975] FSR 421 it was held that this rule is unaltered by *American Cyanamid*, because of the overriding public interest in protecting the right to free speech. There are two conditions:

(a) the defendant must state in his or her witness statement an intention to set up justification; and

(b) the alleged libel must not be obviously untruthful.

In *Holley* v *Smyth* [1998] 2 WLR 742, CA, it was held that the defendant's motive in seeking to publish material, alleged to be defamatory by the claimant, was irrelevant in deciding whether the threatened publication ought to be restrained.

Woodward v *Hutchins* [1977] 1 WLR 760 extended the rule in that the claimants claimed articles in a national newspaper were libellous and also written in breach of confidence. The defendants intended to justify, and it was held that the added possible breach of confidence made no difference, and the injunction was refused.

It has been suggested that *Woodward* v *Hutchins* would now be decided differently in the light of the *Spycatcher* case (*A-G* v *Guardian Newspapers Ltd* [1987] 1 WLR 1248, HL): *Cambridge Nutrition Ltd* v *BBC* [1990] 3 All ER 523 at first instance (see the judgment of Kerr LJ at p. 534).

14.3.3.5 Actions against public authorities
Generally, public authorities should not be restrained from exercising their statutory powers, such as implementing the change-over from grammar to comprehensive education, unless the claimant has an extremely strong case on the merits. In such cases, the public interest is an important factor in considering the balance of convenience: *Smith* v *Inner London Education Authority* [1978] 1 All ER 411, CA.

14.3.3.6 Industrial disputes
By the Trade Union and Labour Relations (Consolidation) Act 1992, s. 221(2), where an interim injunction is sought against a union which claims it

> . . . *acted in contemplation of a trade dispute, the court shall, in exercising its discretion whether or not to grant the injunction, have regard to the likelihood of that party's succeeding at the trial of the action in establishing any matter which would afford a defence to the action under [sections 219 or 220].*

Although views differ as to the precise effect of this section, it seems that there are three matters the court must consider (*NWL Ltd* v *Woods* [1979] 1 WLR 1294, HL, per Lord Scarman):

(a) whether there is a serious question to be tried;

(b) the balance of convenience; and

(c) the likelihood of establishing the statutory defence.

14.3.4 COVENANTS IN RESTRAINT OF TRADE

Care needs to be taken in deciding the appropriate principles to be applied in applications for interim injunctions in cases involving covenants in restraint of trade.

In *Office Overload Ltd* v *Gunn* [1977] FSR 39, CA, the defendant was the claimant's branch manager at its Croydon agency. In his contract of employment he covenanted that he would not work for or set up a competing business in the Croydon area for one year after ceasing to work for the claimant. The defendant gave notice and immediately started competing. The claimant applied for an interim injunction. Lord Denning MR said 'Covenants in restraint of trade are in a special category . . . if they are *prima facie* valid and there is an infringement the courts will grant the injunction.' Bridge LJ pointed out that often the trial would be some years after issuing the claim form. If the merits of the case were not considered, and the injunction refused, the effect would be to deprive the claimant completely of the benefit of his covenant. Therefore, if:

(a) all the facts are before the court; and

(b) there is no substantial question of law, i.e. the covenant is *prima facie* reasonable in duration, area and ambit of business;

the injunction should be granted in the usual case unless there are good reasons for not doing so in any individual case.

In *Lawrence David Ltd* v *Ashton* [1991] 1 All ER 385, CA, however, Balcombe LJ stated at p. 393 'it should now be firmly stated that the principles of the *American Cyanamid* case apply as well in cases in interim injunctions in restraint of trade as in other cases'. The Court of Appeal made it clear in that case, however, that if there is no serious issue to be tried because the case is an open and shut one then it is a case where an interim injunction should be granted without further consideration of the balance of convenience.

Office Overload Ltd v *Gunn* can, therefore, be explained as a case where there was no serious issue to be tried as the covenant was clearly valid and is thus akin to the general category of cases where there is no defence (see **14.3.3.3**). *Lawrence David* itself was not an open and shut case. The claimants had dismissed the defendant from their employment, and it was in issue whether this amounted to a repudiatory breach. Regarding the covenant, Balcombe LJ described it as impossible to say it was obviously bad. In those circumstances it was entirely appropriate to apply *American Cyanamid*.

If the action in respect of the covenant in restraint of trade cannot be tried before the period of restraint has expired or has run a large part of its course, so that the grant of an interim injunction would effectively dispose of the action, the case will fall within the exception to the rule in *American Cyanamid* considered in *NWL Ltd* v *Woods* (see **14.3.3.1**); *Lawrence David Ltd* v *Ashton*; *Lansing Linde Ltd* v *Kerr*.

Applications for interim injunctions to prevent the misuse of confidential information when employees leave the claimant's employment and join a competing business, where there is no covenant in restraint of trade, are governed by the principles in *American Cyanamid Co.* v *Ethicon Ltd* [1975] AC 396, HL: see *Lock International plc* v *Beswick* [1989] 1 WLR 1268, Hoffmann J.

14.3.5 MANDATORY INTERIM INJUNCTIONS

The court is far more reluctant to grant an interim mandatory injunction than to grant an equivalent prohibitory injunction. In *Shepherd Homes Ltd* v *Sandham* [1971] Ch 340, 351 Megarry J said that 'In a normal case' the court must feel a 'high degree of assurance' that at trial an injunction would be granted. This formulation was approved by the Court of Appeal in *Locabail International Finance Ltd* v *Agroexport* [1986] 1 WLR 657 in refusing a mandatory injunction for the payment of money.

14.3.6 DEFENCES

Any of the following matters may be raised in defence to an application for an interim injunction:

(a) Delay or laches. There is authority for saying that the court will more readily refuse an interim injunction on the ground of delay than a perpetual injunction: *Johnson* v *Wyatt* (1863) 2 De GJ & S 18.

(b) Acquiescence. Again, acquiescence is more readily established as a defence at the interim stage. Further, a failure to apply for an interim injunction may be a factor in establishing acquiescence at trial: *Shaw* v *Applegate* [1977] 1 WLR 970.

(c) Hardship. An injunction may be refused if granting it would inflict a hardship on the defendant: *Shell UK Ltd* v *Lostock Garage Ltd* [1976] 1 WLR 1187, 1202 per Ormrod LJ. At the interim stage this will usually be considered as part of the balance of convenience.

(d) Inequitable conduct by the claimant. 'He who comes to equity must come with clean hands' in relation to the subject-matter of the dispute.

(e) Incapable of being effectively enforced.

14.4 Procedure

14.4.1 GENERAL

An application for an interim injunction may be made by any party to an action or matter, and whether or not a claim for the injunction was included in the originating process. Such applications must generally be made to a Judge, and not a District Judge or Master. Exceptional cases where a County Court District Judge can grant interim injunctions include actions with a value below £15,000; and where the determination is by permission of the Circuit Judge and with the consent of the parties. Exceptional cases where a Master can grant interim injunctions include where it is by consent in the terms agreed by the parties or it is ancillary or incidental to a charging order or the appointment of a receiver by way of equitable execution.

14.4.2 URGENT CASES

Applications for interim injunctions can be made before the issue of the originating process in urgent cases or where it is otherwise in the interests of justice. The test on whether notice should be given to the other side is whether there has been a true impossibility in giving notice to the other side: *Bates* v *Lord Hailsham of St. Marylebone* [1972] 1 WLR 1373. If the impossibility in giving the three clear days' notice has arisen through delay on the part of the claimant, or is otherwise insufficiently explained, the application may be refused (unless, perhaps, the case is overwhelming on the merits) on this ground alone (see **10.3.7** for further information on urgent applications).

14.4.3 PAPERWORK

In County Court cases there is a prescribed form of application for interim injunctions (Form N16A), which, among other things, requires the applicant to set out the terms of the injunctions sought. Evidence in support is required, usually by witness statement.

The documents required in High Court cases are:

(a) an application notice;

(b) the claim form and any statements of case;

(c) copies of the witness statements and exhibits in support of the application;

(d) draft order;

(e) skeleton argument (in all but the simplest cases).

The draft order should, in the absence of good reason to the contrary, be in the standard form originally laid down by *Practice Direction* [1996] 1 WLR 1551. A computer disk containing the draft order should also be made available to the court.

The evidence in support of an application for an interim injunction should contain a clear and concise statement of the following matters (see PD 25 Interim Injunctions):

(a) the facts giving rise to the cause of action against the defendant;

(b) the facts giving rise to the claim for injunctive relief;

(c) the precise relief sought.

Further, if the application is made without notice:

(d) the facts relied on as justifying the application being made without notice, including details of any notice given to the defendant, or, if none has been given, the reasons for giving none;

(e) any answer asserted by the defendant, or which it is thought is likely to be asserted, either to the claim or to the interim relief; and

(f) any facts known to the claimant which might lead the court to refuse the interim relief.

14.5 Undertakings

14.5.1 UNDERTAKINGS ON APPLICATIONS WITHOUT NOTICE

As appropriate, the claimant may be required to undertake to issue and/or serve proceedings, serve and file the evidence in support, and to serve the order, usually 'on the same or the next working day'. The undertakings are incorporated into the order when it is drawn up.

14.5.2 UNDERTAKING IN DAMAGES

If an interim injunction is granted against a defendant, but no perpetual order is obtained at trial, in effect the defendant will have been unjustifiably restrained from doing whatever the injunction prohibited while it was in force. To safeguard the defendant against such an eventuality, the claimant is invariably required to give an undertaking in damages on being granted an interim injunction. The undertaking is to pay compensation to the defendant for any loss in fact incurred as a result of the injunction. The court may even require the claimant to fortify such an undertaking.

The court may dispense with an undertaking in favour of a government department or a local authority seeking to enforce the general law: *Hoffmann-La Roche* v *Secretary of State for Trade and Industry* [1975] AC 295; *Kirklees Borough Council* v *Wickes Building Supplies Ltd* [1993] AC 227, HL.

Where the claimant is of limited means, so that the undertaking is of little value, the injunction may still be granted in a proper case: *Allen* v *Jambo Holdings Ltd* [1980] 1 WLR 1252, CA. In such cases the undertaking may be dispensed with. An impecunious claimant may be required to fortify the undertaking by providing security or paying money into court.

14.5.3 INQUIRY AS TO DAMAGES

Where, after the grant of an interim injunction, the claimant fails to obtain a perpetual injunction at trial, or it is established before trial that the injunction should not have been granted, the defendant may apply for an order for an inquiry as to damages. The application is made to the trial judge or to the judge dealing with the interim application during which it becomes clear that the injunction should not have been granted.

When an interim injunction is discharged before trial the court has four options (see *Cheltenham and Gloucester Building Society* v *Ricketts* [1993] 1 WLR 1545, CA):

(a) to order that the undertaking in damages shall be enforced, and to assess the damages immediately. This is only appropriate if all the relevant evidence on damage is available;

(b) to direct an inquiry as to damages. The inquiry is usually conducted by a Master, who will determine all issues of causation and quantum;

(c) to adjourn the application until trial; and

(d) to refuse the application for an inquiry as to damages.

The order is not penal; it is simply to compensate the defendant for damage suffered during the currency of the injunction. If it is likely that the defendant has suffered no provable damage, the inquiry may be refused: *McDonald's Hamburgers Ltd* v *Burger King UK Ltd* [1987] FSR 112.

Ordinary principles of the law of contract are applied both as to causation and quantum: *Hoffmann-La Roche (F) & Co. AG* v *Secretary of State for Trade and Industry* [1975] AC 295, HL.

14.5.4 DEFENDANTS' UNDERTAKINGS IN LIEU OF AN INJUNCTION

Instead of contesting an application for an interim injunction, the defendant may give undertakings in terms similar to the injunction sought by the claimant. The defendant will then be bound in the same way as if an injunction had been granted, and the claimant will be required to enter into a cross undertaking in damages to safeguard the defendant.

14.5.5 CONSEQUENCES OF NOT APPLYING FOR INTERIM RELIEF

Sometimes a claimant may commence proceedings but avoid making an application for an interim injunction where one might be obtained, simply to avoid the potential liability under the undertaking in damages. This occurred in two recent cases, with conflicting results. In *Blue Town Investments Ltd* v *Higgs & Hill plc* [1990] 1 WLR 696 the Vice-Chancellor ordered that the claimant's action be struck out unless it applied for an interim injunction accompanied by an undertaking in damages. In *Oxy Electric Ltd* v *Zainuddin* [1991] 1 WLR 115, Hoffmann J, also at first instance, doubted the decision in *Blue Town* and said there was no jurisdiction either under what is now CPR, r. 3.4 or in the court's inherent jurisdiction to strike out in such circumstances.

Failing to apply for an interim injunction may provide grounds for awarding damages in lieu of a final injunction at trial: *Jaggard* v *Sawyer* [1995] 1 WLR 269.

14.6 Discharge

Interim injunctions are invariably granted subject to later discharge. For example, injunctions made on notice are usually granted 'until trial or further order.' A defendant seeking discharge of an interim injunction will often find that the application is heard by the same judge who granted the initial injunction. Grounds for discharge include:

(a) Material non-disclosure on an application made without notice.

(b) Failure by the claimant to comply with the terms on which the injunction was granted.

(c) That the facts do not justify interim injunctive relief.

(d) The oppressive effect of the injunction (though this may justify a variation of its terms).

(e) A material change in the circumstances of the parties or in the law since the injunction was granted.

(f) Failure by the claimant to prosecute the substantive claim with due speed.

(g) That the injunction interferes with the rights of innocent third parties.

14.7 Breach of an Injunction

Disobedience of the terms of an injunction is a contempt of court. When the injunction is drawn up it will contain a penal notice warning the defendant of this fact. The serious consequences of breach are such that the terms of the order should be sufficiently precise so the defendant knows exactly what it is that must or must not be done. Sequestration of assets and committal to prison for up to two years are possible sanctions if contempt proceedings are brought. See **38.12**.

FIFTEEN

FREEZING INJUNCTIONS

15.1 Introduction

In certain circumstances, a claimant, who has a very strong case against a defendant, may feel that there is a serious risk that the defendant will dispose of his or her assets before the case proceeds to trial, thereby preventing the claimant, if successful at the trial, from being able to execute judgment, as there may no longer be any assets available which would realise the value of the judgment debt.

The freezing injunction is a form of interim injunction designed to guard against this, and has the effect of restraining defendants from disposing of, or dissipating, their assets so as to frustrate any judgment which the claimant may obtain against them.

Freezing injunctions have for many years been called '*Mareva*' injunctions. This name stems from the decision of the Court of Appeal in *Mareva Compania Naviera SA* v *International Bulk Carriers SA* [1980] 1 All ER 213. In this case the claimants were shipowners and the defendants voyage charterers. The defendants failed to pay the hire charges due to the claimants. The defendants had received money from their sub-charterers, which had been paid into a bank account in London. The court refused to consider itself bound by *Lister & Co.* v *Stubbs* (1890) 45 Ch D 1, CA, which had held that a defendant could not be compelled to give security before judgment, relying on the wide discretion conferred by what is now SCA 1981, s. 37. This was held to be a proper case for granting an injunction restraining the defendants from removing or disposing out of the jurisdiction the moneys in the London bank.

15.2 Jurisdiction

We have already seen that SCA 1981, s. 37(1), which is extracted at **14.2.1**, enables the High Court to grant interim injunctions if it is 'just and convenient to do so'. Specific statutory confirmation of the *Mareva* jurisdiction is contained in s. 37(3), which provides:

> *The power of the High Court . . . to grant an interlocutory injunction restraining a party to any proceedings from removing from the jurisdiction of the High Court, or otherwise dealing with, assets located within that jurisdiction shall be exercisable in cases where that party is, as well as in cases where he is not, domiciled, resident or present within that jurisdiction.*

As we have seen at **1.2.1.3**, the powers of the County Courts to grant freezing injunctions are in general limited.

15.3 Principles

There are four requirements:

(a) A cause of action justiciable in England and Wales.

(b)   A good arguable case.

(c)   The defendant having assets within the jurisdiction.

(d)   A real risk that the defendant may dispose of or dissipate those assets before judgment can be enforced.

These four requirements will now be considered, together with the exception to requirement (c) in the case of so-called 'worldwide' freezing injunctions.

15.3.1   JUSTICIABLE IN ENGLAND AND WALES

The claimant's claim must be justiciable in England and Wales: *Siskina* v *Distos Compania Naviera* [1979] AC 210, HL. The claim may be justiciable here if the defendant can be served with process within the jurisdiction. Note that a defendant who is abroad may nevertheless submit to the jurisdiction. Alternatively, the case may fall within CPR, r. 6.19 or 6.20, see **Chapter 11**. Furthermore, the Civil Jurisdiction and Judgments Act 1982, s. 25 empowers the English courts to grant interim relief, including freezing injunctions, where proceedings between the same parties are pending in the courts of another Convention State.

15.3.2   GOOD ARGUABLE CASE

The claimant's affidavit must disclose a good arguable case as regards the merits of the substantive claim against the defendant, see *The Niedersachsen* [1983] 2 Lloyd's Rep 600, 605. Anticipation that the defendant will in the future be in breach of contract is insufficient: *Veracruz Transportation Inc.* v *V.C. Shipping Co. Inc.* [1992] 1 Lloyd's Rep 353, CA; *Zucker* v *Tyndall Holdings plc* [1993] 1 All ER 124, CA.

15.3.3   ASSETS

15.3.3.1   General

It is usually the case that the claimant has to show that the defendant has some assets within the jurisdiction. 'Assets' for this purpose is given a wide meaning, and includes chattels such as motor vehicles, jewellery, *objets d'art* and choses in action (*CBS UK Ltd* v *Lambert* [1983] Ch 37, 42 per Lawton LJ) as well as money. The assets must be owned in the same capacity as that in which the defendant is being sued. Assets held by a defendant as a bare trustee will not be covered by the order: *Federal Bank of the Middle East* v *Hadkinson* [2000] 2 All ER 395, CA.

15.3.3.2   Bank accounts

If the defendant has a bank account in England, the court is likely to infer the presence of assets within the jurisdiction even if that account is in fact overdrawn.

If the defendant holds a bank account jointly with someone who is not a party to the action, that account may none the less be frozen by a *Mareva*: *SFC Finance* v *Masri* [1985] 1 WLR 876.

If the order is to be made against a bank account, the claimant must give the best possible particulars of that account (e.g. branch and account number, if known).

15.3.3.3   Land

Land can be the subject of a freezing injunction. However, the order is not 'made for the purpose of enforcing a judgment' and so cannot be registered as a land charge under Land Charges Act 1972, s. 6(1)(a): *Stockler* v *Fourways Estates Ltd* [1984] 1 WLR 25 (Kilner Brown J). Nevertheless, it can be registered as a caution.

15.3.3.4   Related companies

In two decisions, *Atlas Maritime Co. SA* v *Avalon Maritime Ltd (No. 3)* [1991] 1 WLR 917, CA, and *TSB Private Bank International SA* v *Chabra* [1992] 1 WLR 231, the courts were prepared to look beyond the corporate structure adopted by the defendants in order to give the claimants *Mareva* relief. In the *TSB* case it was clear the claimant had a good cause of action against Mr Chabra, the first defendant, and equally clear that there was no independent cause of action against the second defendant, a company owned by Mr Chabra and/or his wife. A freezing injunction was unlikely to be effective against Mr Chabra. As there was credible evidence that assets apparently owned by the second defendant in fact belonged to Mr Chabra, Mummery J granted a freezing injunction against the second defendant on the ground that it was ancillary and incidental to the claim against Mr Chabra.

15.3.3.5 Worldwide freezing injunctions

A freezing injunction will not normally extend to assets outside the jurisdiction. However, in an exceptional case, the court may make an order affecting assets both here and abroad. Moreover, in *Derby* v *Weldon (No. 2)* [1989] 1 All ER 1002, CA, it was held that the court may make an order affecting assets abroad even if there are no assets in England.

Such an order will be rare. It will certainly not be made where there are sufficient assets within the jurisdiction to satisfy any judgment which the claimant may obtain: *Derby* v *Weldon (No. 1)* [1990] Ch 48, CA.

To avoid the problem of the court trying to assume an exorbitant jurisdiction over third parties outside the jurisdiction, the terms of the order should state that it shall not affect third parties unless, and to the extent that, it may be enforced by the courts of the State where the assets are located: *Derby* v *Weldon (No. 2)* [1989] 1 All ER 1002, CA; *Babanaft International Co. SA* v *Bassatne* [1990] Ch 13, CA.

15.3.4 RISK OF DISPOSAL

In order to obtain a freezing injunction, the claimant must show that there is a risk that the defendant will remove assets from the jurisdiction, or dispose of them, or dissipate them, or hide them. The SCA 1981, s. 37(3), which is extracted at **15.2**, makes it clear that a freezing injunction may be granted whether the defendant is or is not resident within the jurisdiction. However, the court is likely to infer the risk of disposal of assets more readily if the defendant is resident overseas, or is a company based overseas. However, as Kerr LJ said in *Z* v *A-Z* [1982] 1 QB 558, at 585, an order should not be made against someone who has substantial links with England, such as persons who are 'established within the jurisdiction in the sense of having assets here which they could not, or would not wish to, dissipate merely to avoid some judgment which seems likely to be given against them'.

In *Montecchi* v *Shimco Ltd* [1979] 1 WLR 1180, CA it was held that the fact that the judgment of the English court is enforceable overseas by virtue of reciprocal enforcement provisions is a relevant factor to take into account in deciding whether or not to grant a freezing injunction. An order will only be made in such a case if there is good reason to apprehend that without an order, the judgment creditor would not be able to enforce any judgment that is obtained. So the claimant will have to show grounds for believing that, despite the reciprocal enforcement provisions, the defendant will be able to evade satisfying the judgment. This will of course be particularly relevant in the case of EC defendants, by virtue of the Civil Jurisdiction and Judgments Act 1982.

In *Customs & Excise Commissioners* v *Anchor Foods Ltd* [1999] 1 WLR 1139, it was said that the court would be slow to prevent a bona fide transaction in the ordinary course of business by granting a freezing injunction, especially where the price payable accorded with a professional valuation. However, in this case there was conflicting valuation evidence provided by the claimant's experts, and a freezing injunction was continued (but with additional safeguards for the defendants).

15.3.5 DISCRETION

Under SCA 1981, s. 37(1), the court has a power to grant freezing injunctions where it is 'just and convenient'. In deciding whether or not to grant a *Mareva*, a factor the court will consider is the value of the defendant's assets from the claimant's point of view, namely their resale value in the light of the amount which the claimant is claiming in the action. In other words, would these assets in fact assist the claimant in a material way to satisfy any judgment that may be obtained?

For example, in *Rasu Maritima* v *Perusahaan Pertambangan* [1978] QB 644, CA, the claimant was a Liberian company and the defendant an Indonesian state-owned company. The claim was for very substantial damages for a breach of charterparty. The assets in respect of which the claimant sought a freezing injunction comprised part of a fertiliser plant to be built in Indonesia. Its value as such was some $12 million; but its scrap value was only about $350,000. Lord Denning MR described that (at p. 663) as a 'drop in the ocean' compared to the immense claim which was being made. His Lordship said that 'this amount is so trifling in the circumstances that it does not seem proper to interfere with the construction work on this fertiliser plant to secure it'.

15.4 Procedure

As it would defeat the purpose of the order if the defendant were to be warned of the application, applications for freezing injunctions are made without notice to the defendant. The application is heard by a judge, and may be made at any stage in the proceedings, even before a claim form has been issued, (if the application is urgent), or after judgment in aid of execution.

The applicant will need to issue an application notice setting out the nature of the order sought. The application needs to be supported by evidence, and this is one of the rare occasions where the evidence must be in the form of affidavits (PD 25 Interim Injunctions, para. 3.1).Whenever possible a draft of the order sought should be filed with the application notice, together with a disc containing the draft in Wordperfect 5.1 (para. 2.4).

15.5 The Order

15.5.1 FORM OF THE ORDER

Standard forms of worldwide and domestic freezing injunctions are laid down in PD 25 Interim Injunctions. These should be used save to the extent that the judge considers there is a good reason for adopting a different form. A standard domestic freezing injunction is illustrated in **Figure 15.1**.

15.5.2 UNDERTAKINGS

The claimant has to give the following undertakings, which are incorporated into the order:

(a) The usual undertaking as to damages. This should normally be supported by a bank guarantee, for a fixed amount, which the claimant undertakes to obtain within a certain period of time.

(b) Because the application is without notice, to notify the defendant forthwith of the order and to serve on the defendant a copy of the affidavit used in support of the application, together with the claim form (unless it has already been served) and the order.

(c) To inform affected third parties of their right to apply to the court for directions or for variation of the order.

(d) To indemnify any third party in respect of expenses incurred in complying with the order. For example, where the claimant seeks an order which affects the defendant's bank account, an undertaking is required to indemnify the bank against any costs which it reasonably incurs in complying with the order: *Searose* v *Seatrain* [1981] 1 Lloyd's Rep 556.

15.5.3   PUBLICLY FUNDED CLAIMANT

In *Allen* v *Jambo Holdings Ltd* [1980] 2 All ER 502 the claimant, who was legally aided, made a claim under the Fatal Accidents Acts in respect of the death of her husband. She obtained a freezing injunction preventing the defendant from removing a propeller engined aeroplane from the jurisdiction. The Court of Appeal continued the injunction despite the fact Mrs Allen could not give a valuable undertaking in damages. The defendants had sworn incredible evidence on the application to discharge, and could obtain a release of their aeroplane if they provided security. It was therefore just and convenient to continue the order.

15.5.4   TERMS OF THE ORDER

The amount frozen by the order should not exceed the maximum amount of the claimant's claim against the defendant (taking account of interest and costs), leaving the defendant free to deal with the balance as desired.

If, at the time the order is granted, the defendant does not have sufficient assets to meet the claimant's claim, the order need not state a maximum sum: *Z* v *A-Z* [1982] 1 QB 558 at 576, per Lord Denning MR. The order will then cover assets which are acquired by the defendant between the granting of the injunction and the execution of any judgment obtained in the action: *TDK* v *Video Choice Ltd* [1986] 1 WLR 141, 145 (Skinner J).

15.5.5   PURPOSE OF THE ORDER

There are two points:

(a)   The object of a freezing injunction is not to give the claimant priority over the defendant's other creditors.

(b)   The effect of the freezing injunction should not be such as to place undue pressure on the defendant to settle the action on terms unduly favourable to the claimant.

To ensure the just operation of the *Mareva* jurisdiction, certain provisos must be incorporated into each freezing injunction order.

15.5.6   PROVISOS

15.5.6.1   Banks

'To safeguard the bank, the order will expressly state that it does not prevent the bank from exercising any right of set-off it may have in respect of facilities afforded by it to the defendant before the date of the order. Once the order has been served, the bank should recall any cheque card previously issued to the defendant': *Z* v *A-Z* [1982] 1 QB 558 at 591 per Kerr LJ.

15.5.6.2   Living/business expenses

The order should make provision for the defendant's ordinary living expenses if the defendant is an individual. In assessing what constitutes ordinary living expenses, the court takes account of the defendant's lifestyle: *PCW* v *Dixon* [1983] 2 All ER 697, CA. The order often allows the defendant to pay the ordinary costs of the present litigation if no other funds are available.

It is a breach of the order to spend sums allocated to ordinary living expenses under the order for extraordinary purposes, such as the payment of Queen's Counsel's fees in unrelated litigation or the purchase of an expensive motor car, even if there are unused 'living expenses' funds in the defendant's account: *TDK* v *Video Choice Ltd* [1986] 1 WLR 141 (Skinner J).

If the defendant is a trader or company, the order should make provision for the defendant's ordinary and proper business expenses.

15.5.6.3 Trade debts

If the defendant is a trader or a company, the order should make provision for legitimate dealing or disposal of assets in the ordinary course of trading (even if the defendant has to use assets within those otherwise frozen by the court). Trade debts may be defined as payments which are made in good faith in the ordinary course of business: *Iraqi Ministry of Defence* v *Arcepy Shipping Co. SA* [1981] QB 65.

15.5.7 ANCILLARY ORDERS

The court has power to order disclosure of documents and/or administration of requests for further information designed to enable the claimant to ascertain the whereabouts of the defendant's assets. Similar problems arise as with search orders regarding the privilege against self-incrimination, see **16.5.4**. For the problems that can arise in relation to ancillary disclosure orders in cases where the defendant may be involved in money laundering, sec *C* v *S (Money Laundering: Discovery of Documents)* [1999] 1 WLR 1551, CA.

Even if the defendant swears an affidavit as to his or her assets, it may be that the claimant feels that the information given is evasive or incomplete. In such a case the claimant may apply for an order for cross-examination on the affidavit. Such an order would be an exceptional measure: *Yukong Line Ltd of Korea* v *Rendsburg Investments Corp. of Liberia, The Times*, 22 October 1996. If an order is made, the cross-examination is generally to be conducted before a Master.

15.5.8 DURATION

A freezing injunction granted without notice will either remain in force until judgment or further order or for a limited period (often about five days) until a 'return date', which will be fixed by the judge when granting the order. If a return date has been specified then so far as practicable, any application for the discharge or variation of the order should be dealt with effectively on the return date. However, the standard forms of freezing injunction order also contain a clause enabling the defendant or anyone else notified of the order to apply to the court at any time to vary or discharge the order on first informing the claimant's solicitors. This enables the defendant to apply back to the judge (usually the judge who granted the original order) on short notice.

15.5.9 EFFECT OF THE ORDER

The order is addressed to the defendant, but it also binds third parties with knowledge of it. A person with knowledge of the order who assists in the disposal of enjoined assets is therefore in contempt of court: *Z* v *A-Z* [1982] 1 QB 558, 572 per Lord Denning MR.

If an order is made against a bank account, it operates to freeze the account up to the amount of the order as soon as the bank has notice of the grant of the order. The bank would be in contempt of court if it subsequently honoured cheques drawn on the account. The order should therefore be served on the bank and then on the defendant.

15.6 Discharge or Variation

15.6.1 GROUNDS FOR DISCHARGE

15.6.1.1 Not an appropriate case

An application to discharge the order may be made where the defendant can show that the claimant does not have a good arguable case on the merits or by showing that there is insufficient risk that the assets will be dissipated.

15.6.1.2 Defendant providing security

The defendant may also obtain discharge of the order by offering security for the claimant's claim instead. This may take the form of creating a charge over the defendant's property, paying money into a bank account in the joint names of the solicitors acting for the claimant and the defendant, or even paying the sum claimed into court.

15.6.1.3 Claimant guilty of material non-disclosure

The claimant is under a strict duty to make full and frank disclosure in the affidavit of all facts and matters which are or which reasonably should be within his or her knowledge. This means that as well as stating what is in fact known, the claimant is also under a duty to make reasonable inquiries. The claimant's duty of disclosure includes fairly stating any points which could be made against the claim. The judge should be informed of any counterclaim or defence which the defendant may have to the substantive claim and any facts known to the claimant as regards the defendant's financial standing, see *Third Chandris Shipping Corp.* v *Unimarine SA* [1979] QB 645, 688 (Lord Denning MR). Material facts must appear in the affidavit in support itself. It is not sufficient if they appear in exhibited documents: *National Bank of Sharjah* v *Dellborg, The Times*, 24 December 1992, CA. Nor is it enough for counsel to refer to an affidavit prepared earlier in the action which sets out the defendant's answer to the claim: it is part of counsel's duty to the court to attempt to persuade the judge to read it (*Art Corporation* v *Schuppan, The Times*, 20 January 1994). Any shortcomings in the claimant's own financial standing, which is relevant to the adequacy of the undertaking in damages, must also be disclosed. A breach of an advocate's duty to the court may result in sanctions being imposed against the client: *Memory Corporation* v *Sidhu, The Times*, 15 February 2000, CA.

In *Dormeuil Frères SA* v *Nicolian International (Textiles) Ltd* [1988] 1 WLR 1362, Ch.D. (as subsequently interpreted in *Tate Access Floors* v *Boswell* [1991] Ch 512) the Vice-Chancellor said that where an alleged material non-disclosure could only be established by combing through large volumes of disputed evidence, it would be appropriate for the matter to be left for investigation at trial. In more straightforward cases, the courts must investigate alleged non-disclosures at the interim stage, and determine whether there has been any failure by the claimant, and whether such failure was innocent or deliberate: *Behbehani* v *Salem* [1989] 1 WLR 723, CA.

In deciding what should be the consequences of any breach of duty, it is necessary to take into account all the relevant circumstances, including the gravity of the breach, the excuse or explanation offered, the severity and duration of any prejudice occasioned, and whether the consequences of the breach were remediable and had been remedied. The court must also apply the overriding objective and the need for proportionality: *Memory Corporation* v *Sidhu*. It is important that the rule against material non-disclosure does not itself become an instrument of injustice: *Brink's Mat* v *Elcombe* [1988] 1 WLR 1350.

When the injunction has been set aside for material non-disclosure, the question then arises as to whether, on the full facts, a second injunction should be granted in its place. A fresh order will only be granted if:

(a) the non-disclosure was innocent (i.e. there was no deliberate attempt to mislead the court); and

(b) on the whole of the facts, including the fact of the original non-disclosure, a freezing injunction could properly be granted.

See *Lloyds Bowmaker* v *Britannia Arrow* [1988] 1 WLR 1337, CA and *Brink's Mat* v *Elcombe* [1988] 1 WLR 1350, CA.

Note, however, that the court will do its best to do justice between the parties. For example, in *Behbehani* v *Salem* [1989] 1 WLR 723, CA, discharge was upheld upon the defendant giving an undertaking not to dispose of property within the jurisdiction without giving reasonable notice to the claimant.

15.6.2   GROUNDS FOR VARIATION

If the order does not make provision for ordinary living expenses or legitimate trade debts, or freezes an amount in excess of the claimant's claim against the defendant, the defendant may apply for the order to be varied so as to remedy these defects.

Where the application is for living expenses or trade debts, the defendant has to show that there are no other assets out of which payment could reasonably be made: *A v C (No. 2)* [1981] QB 961.

A change in the management of a company defendant, e.g. by the appointment of an administrative receiver by a debenture holder (see *Company Law in Practice Manual*) may remove the risk of dissipation of the company's assets and give grounds for varying or even discharging a freezing injunction: *Capital Cameras Ltd* v *Harold Lines Ltd* [1991] 1 WLR 54.

15.7   Change of Circumstances

In *Commercial Bank of the Near East* v *P* [1989] 2 Lloyd's Rep 319, Saville J said that in the period up to the first hearing on notice, it is the claimant's duty to bring to the attention of the court any material changes in the circumstances which occur after the freezing injunction is granted.

Figure 15.1   Freezing injunction

IN THE HIGH COURT OF JUSTICE — Freezing Injunction

QUEEN'S BENCH DIVISION

Before the Honourable Mr Justice HARDY — Claim No.

BETWEEN

MYSTERY CRUISES — Applicant

and

AJAY LTD — Respondent

SEAL

Name, address and reference of Respondent
Ajay Limited,
21 Smart's Road,
London WC1 2A

PENAL NOTICE

IF YOU THE WITHIN NAMED AJAY LIMITED DISOBEY THIS ORDER YOU MAY BE HELD TO BE IN CONTEMPT OF COURT AND LIABLE TO IMPRISONMENT OR FINED OR YOUR ASSETS SEIZED

IMPORTANT:

NOTICE TO THE RESPONDENT

You should read the terms of the Order and the Guidance Notes very carefully. You are advised to consult a solicitor as soon as possible.

Figure 15.1 Freezing injunction continued

This Order prohibits you, the Respondent, from dealing with your assets up to the amount stated in the Order, but subject to any exceptions set out at the end of the Order. You have a right to ask the Court to vary or discharge this Order.

If you disobey this Order you may be found guilty of Contempt of Court and in the case of a corporate respondent, it may be fined, its directors may be sent to prison or fined, or its assets may be seized.

THE ORDER

An Application was made today the 3rd November 2000 by Counsel for the Applicant to Mr Justice Hardy who heard the application. The judge read the affidavits listed in Schedule A and accepted the undertakings set out in Schedule B at the end of this Order.

As a result of the application IT IS ORDERED that until the 10th November 2000 ('the return date') [or further Order of the Court]:

1. The Respondent must not remove from England and Wales or in any way dispose of or deal with or diminish the value of any of his assets which are in England and Wales whether in his own name or not and whether solely or jointly owned up to the value of £1.7 million. This prohibition includes the following assets in particular:

    (a) the property known as Ajay House, 21 Smart's Road, London WC1 2AP or the net sale money after payment of any mortgages if it has been sold;
    (b) the property and assets of the Defendant's business carried on at Ajay House, 21 Smart's Road, London WC1 2AP or the sale money if any of them have been sold; and
    (c) any money in the accounts numbered 9318214 at Kingsway, London, WC1 branch of Zampac Bank.

2. If the total unincumbered value of the Respondent's assets in England and Wales exceeds £1.7 million, the Respondent may remove any of those assets from England and Wales or may dispose of or deal with them so long as the total unincumbered value of his assets still in England and Wales remains above £1.7 million.

3. Exceptions to this Order:

    (1) This Order does not prohibit the Respondent from spending £2,000 a week towards his ordinary and proper business expenses and also a reasonable sum on legal advice and representation. But before spending any money the Respondent must tell the Applicant's legal representatives where the money is to come from.

    (2) This Order does not prohibit the Respondent from dealing with or disposing of any of his assets in the ordinary and proper course of business.

    (3) The Respondent may agree with the Applicant's legal representatives that the above spending limits should be increased or that this Order should be varied in any other respect, but any such agreement must be in writing.

    (4) The Respondent may cause this Order to cease to have effect if the Respondent provides security by paying the sum of £1.7 million into court or makes provision for security in that sum by some other method agreed with the Applicant's legal representatives.

Figure 15.1   Freezing injunction continued

4.   The Respondent must:

(1)   Inform the Applicant in writing at once of all his assets in England and Wales and whether in his own name or not and whether solely or jointly owned, giving the value, location and details of all such assets.

The Respondent may be entitled to refuse to provide some or all of this information on the grounds that it may incriminate him.

(2)   Confirm the information in an affidavit which must be served on the Applicant's legal representatives within 10 days after this Order has been served on the Respondent.

GUIDANCE NOTES

EFFECT OF THIS ORDER

(1)   A Respondent who is an individual who is ordered not to do something must not do it himself or in any other way. He must not do it through others acting on his behalf or on his instructions or with his encouragement.

(2)   A Respondent which is a corporation and which is ordered not to do something must not do it itself or by its directors, officers, employees or agents or in any other way.

VARIATION OR DISCHARGE OF THIS ORDER

The Respondent (or anyone notified of this Order) may apply to the Court at any time to vary or discharge this Order (or so much of it as affects that person), but anyone wishing to do so must first inform the Applicant's legal representatives.

PARTIES OTHER THAN THE APPLICANT AND RESPONDENT

(1)   Effect of this Order. It is a Contempt of Court for any person notified of this Order knowingly to assist in or permit a breach of the Order. Any person doing so may be sent to prison, fined, or have his assets seized.

(2)   Set off by Banks. This injunction does not prevent any bank from exercising any right of set off it may have in respect of any facility which it gave to the Respondent before it was notified of the Order.

(3)   Withdrawals by the Respondent. No bank need enquire as to the application or proposed application of any money withdrawn by the Respondent if the withdrawal appears to be permitted by this Order.

INTERPRETATION OF THIS ORDER

(1)   In this Order, where there is more than one Respondent (unless otherwise stated), references to 'the Respondent' means both or all of them.

(2)   A requirement to serve on 'the Respondent' means on each of them.

However, the Order is effective against any Respondent on whom it is served.

(3)   An Order requiring 'the Respondent' to do or not to do anything applies to all Respondents.

Figure 15.1 Freezing injunction continued

COMMUNICATIONS WITH THE COURT

All communications to the court about this Order should be sent, where the Order is made in the Chancery Division, to Room TM510, Royal Courts of Justice, Strand, London WC2A 2LL quoting the claim number. The telephone number is 0171 936 6827; and where the order is made in the Queen's Bench Division, to Room W11 (0171 936 6009). The offices are open between 10 am and 4.30 pm Monday to Friday.

SCHEDULE A

Affidavits

The Applicant relied on the following draft affidavit:

Sophia Elizabeth Potts, 1st affidavit, sworn on 2nd November 2000 on behalf of the Applicant

SCHEDULE B

Undertakings given to the Court by the Applicant

(1) If the Court later finds that this Order has caused loss to the Respondent, and decides that the Respondent should be compensated for that loss, the Applicant will comply with any Order the Court may make.

(2) The Applicant will on or before the 6th day of November 2000 cause a written guarantee in the sum of £75,000 to be issued from a bank having a place of business within England or Wales, such guarantee being in respect of any Order the Court may make pursuant to paragraph (1) above. The Applicant will further, forthwith upon issue of the guarantee, cause a copy of it to be served on the Respondent.

(3) As soon as practicable the Applicant will issue and serve on the Respondent a claim form in the form of the draft produced to the Court claiming the appropriate relief together with this Order.

(4) The Applicant will cause an affidavit to be sworn and filed substantially in the terms of the draft affidavit produced to the Court.

(5) As soon as practicable the Applicant will serve on the Respondent an Application for the return date together with a copy of the affidavits and exhibits containing the evidence relied upon by the Applicant.

(6) Anyone notified of this Order will be given a copy of it by the Applicant's legal representatives.

(7) The Applicant will pay the reasonable costs of anyone other than the Respondent which have been incurred as a result of this Order including the costs of ascertaining whether that person holds any of the Respondent's assets and if the Court later finds that this Order has caused such person loss, and decides that such person should be compensated for that loss, the Applicant will comply with any Order the Court may make.

(8) If for any reason this Order ceases to have effect (including in particular where the Respondent provides security as provided for above or the Applicant does not provide a bank guarantee as provided for above), the Applicant will forthwith take all reasonable steps to inform, in writing, any person or company to whom he has given notice of this Order, or who he has reasonable grounds for supposing may act upon this Order, that it has ceased to have effect.

Figure 15.1   Freezing injunction continued

NAME AND ADDRESS OF THE APPLICANT'S LEGAL REPRESENTATIVES

The Applicant's Legal Representatives are:
Dean & Co.,
41 Sparrow Walk,
London
WC1 3ST
Tel: 0171 523 1729 (office hours)
08311 291 0548 (out of office hours)
Fax: 0171 523 4000
Reference: MAF/8774R

SIXTEEN

SEARCH ORDERS

16.1 Introduction

Search orders are a form of interim injunctive relief that until recently were known as the *Anton Piller* orders. This name came from *Anton Piller KG* v *Manufacturing Processes Ltd* [1976] Ch 55, CA. The claimants were German manufacturers of electric motors and generators. One of their products was a frequency converter for use in computers. The defendants were the claimants' UK agents. Two 'defectors' employed by the defendants flew to Germany and informed the claimants that the defendants had been secretly negotiating with the claimants' competitors with the object of supplying the competitors with manuals, drawings and other confidential information which would allow the competitors to copy the claimants' products and ruin their market. The 'defectors' had documentary evidence in support of their claims.

The claimants were worried that if the defendants were given notice of court proceedings they would destroy or remove any incriminating evidence. So, before they had time even to issue the contemplated proceedings, their solicitors applied without notice and obtained an order requiring the defendants to permit them to enter their premises for the purposes of searching for and seizing relevant documents and other evidence.

The jurisdiction of the courts to grant search orders has now been placed on a statutory basis by virtue of the Civil Procedure Act 1997, s. 7.

16.2 Relief of Last Resort

The search order, involving the violation of the defendant's home and business premises, is recognised as a draconian measure. The reason, according to Dillon LJ in *Booker McConnell plc* v *Plascow* [1985] RPC 425, CA, is that '... the courts have always proceeded ... on the basis that the overwhelming majority of people in this country will comply with the court's order.' The fact that someone is a tortfeasor or is in breach of contract, and hence can be sued, does not necessarily mean they will disobey an order of the court. In many cases it may be enough to apply for some less drastic form of interlocutory relief. Examples are:

(a) An application on notice under CPR, r. 25.1, to enter the defendant's premises and inspect property.

(b) An application on notice for negative injunctions with orders to deliver up documents or material belonging to the claimant.

(c) An order on notice that the defendant delivers up documents to his or her own solicitor.

(d) An order on notice that the defendant allows the claimant's solicitor to make copies of documents.

(e) Awaiting disclosure of documents in the usual way.

16.3 Principles

In *Anton Piller KG* v *Manufacturing Processes Ltd* [1976] Ch 55, Ormrod LJ identified three basic requirements that must be satisfied before the court may grant a search order (although it could be said that the third requirement can be subdivided in two). Each of the requirements must be substantiated in the affidavit in support. Note that even if the three requirements are made out, the granting of a search order remains in the discretion of the court. The three requirements are:

(a) There must be an extremely strong *prima facie* case on the merits.

(b) The defendant's activities must cause very serious potential or actual harm to the claimant's interests.

(c) There must be clear evidence that incriminating documents or things are in the defendant's possession and that there is a real possibility that such material may be destroyed before any application on notice can be made.

For a period in the 1980s it was thought that the conditions for the grant of *Anton Piller* orders had been relaxed by two Court of Appeal decisions, *Yousif* v *Salama* [1980] 1 WLR 1540 and *Dunlop Holdings Ltd* v *Staravia Ltd* [1982] Com LR 3.

However, since *Booker McConnell plc* v *Plascow* [1985] RPC 425, CA the courts have insisted on the strict observance of the conditions laid down by Ormrod LJ in *Anton Piller KG* v *Manufacturing Processes Ltd* [1976] Ch 55. The importance of strict compliance with the conditions was emphasised in *Columbia Picture Industries Inc.* v *Robinson* [1987] Ch 38 by Scott J, who said the effect of a search order is often to close down the defendant's business. The defendant's business records and, in many cases, the whole stock-in-trade will be removed. If the order is combined with a freezing injunction it will be served on the defendant's bankers who will almost certainly decline any further credit. Even if the defendant's business is not closed down, a search order plainly carries the suggestion that the defendant is not to be trusted, and may result in people being reluctant to carry on business with the defendant in the ordinary way.

An example of the present practice is *Lock International plc* v *Beswick* [1989] 1 WLR 1268. The defendants had held key posts with the claimant, which manufactured metal detectors. They became dissatisfied with the management of the company, and joined a new company which was intended to compete in the metal detector business. The claimant apprehended that the defendants were making use of its trade secrets and confidential information, and obtained and executed a search order. On the defendants' application to discharge the order, Hoffmann J said:

> The evidence [on the application without notice] came nowhere near disclosing an 'extremely strong *prima facie* case' or 'clear evidence that the defendants [had] in their possession incriminating documents or things' or that there was a 'grave danger' or 'real possibility' that the defendants might destroy evidence. The lack of specificity in the [claimant's] affidavit was such that I have some doubt whether it could be said to have raised a triable issue. Furthermore, these defendants were no fly-by-night video pirates. They were former long-service employees with families and mortgages, who had openly said that they were entering into competition and whom the [claimant] knew to be financed by highly respectable institutions.

16.4 Procedure on Application for Search Order

Applications for search orders are made by issuing an application notice with a draft order (and a copy on disc), supported by evidence on affidavit (rather than witness statement).

Secrecy is essential if the order is to be effective. The application is therefore made without notice, and in Ch.D. cases the court sits in private rather than in open court. Usually the application is made after issue but before service of the claim form, although in urgent cases the application can be made before issue.

As the application is made without notice, the claimant has the usual duty of swearing an affidavit giving full and frank disclosure of all material facts. This is especially important in applications for search orders, and the claimant should err on the side of excessive disclosure.

16.5 Form of the Order

A standard form of search order was laid down by PD 25 Interim Injunctions. This standard form should be used save in so far as the judge considers there are good reasons for adopting a different form.

16.5.1 CLAIMANT'S UNDERTAKINGS

The claimant is required to provide certain safeguards for the defendant in the form of undertakings incorporated into the search order. The undertakings are divided into two categories: those entered into by the claimant personally; and those entered into by the claimant's solicitors. Commonly, the claimant will personally undertake:

(a) If the application was of an urgent nature, to issue process, and to swear and file affidavits forthwith as appropriate.

(b) To serve the search order by a solicitor together with copies of the affidavits, photocopiable exhibits in support, and an application for a hearing a few days after service.

(c) To serve the defendant with a written report on the carrying out of the order to be prepared by the supervising solicitor. This will be considered by the court on the return day.

(d) To abide by any order as to damages.

(e) Not to inform any third party of the proceedings until the return day.

(f) Not to use items seized other than for the purposes of the claim without the court's leave.

(g) To insure items removed from the defendant's premises.

The claimant's solicitors will normally undertake:

(h) To retain all documents and articles seized in safe custody.

(i) Within two working days, to deliver the originals of the documents and articles seized, to the defendant or defendant's solicitors except original documents belonging to the claimant.

16.5.2 IMPLIED UNDERTAKING

An undertaking not to use items seized for collateral purposes will also be implied against the claimant: *Crest Homes plc* v *Marks* [1987] AC 829, HL. The reason is that a search order operates as an order for disclosure in advance of the usual directions given as part of judicial case management. In proper cases permission can be given to use the material disclosed in related civil proceedings (*Crest Homes* v *Marks*) or criminal prosecutions (*A-G for Gibraltar* v *May* [1999] 1 WLR 998, CA).

16.5.3 THE ORDER

16.5.3.1 The operative provision

The order is that the defendant 'must allow' the supervising solicitor and the claimant's solicitor together with a limited number of other persons to enter his or her premises. An order that the claimant's representatives 'be entitled to enter' is defective: *Manor Electronics Ltd* v *Dickson* [1988] RPC 618, Scott J. The order is not a civil search warrant, and reasonable force may not be used to gain entry. The wording of the standard order is as follows:

(1) The Respondent must allow Mr/Mrs/Miss _____ ('the Supervising Solicitor'), together with _____ a solicitor of the Supreme Court, and a partner in the firm of _____ the Applicant's solicitors _____ and up to ____ other persons being employees of __ _____ accompanying them, to enter the premises mentioned in Schedule A to this Order and any other premises of the Respondent disclosed under paragraph 4(1) below and any vehicles under the Respondent's control on or around the premises so that they can search for, inspect, photograph or photocopy, and deliver into the safekeeping of the Applicant's solicitors all the documents and articles which are listed in Schedule B to this Order ('the listed items') or which _____ believes to be listed items.

(2) The Respondent must allow those persons to remain on the premises until the search is complete, and to re-enter the premises on the same or the following day in order to complete the search.

16.5.3.2 Safeguards for the defendant

The Courts are anxious to prevent the oppressive use of the *Anton Piller* jurisdiction. A number of safeguards must therefore be incorporated into the terms of the order. These include:

(a) That the order must be served, and its execution must be supervised, by a named solicitor other than a member of the firm acting for the claimant. The supervising solicitor must be an experienced solicitor with familiarity with the workings of search orders. The affidavit in support of the application for the order must give details of the proposed supervising solicitor's experience.

(b) That the order must be served on a weekday between 9.30 am and 5.30 pm. This is to give the defendant a realistic prospect of seeking legal advice (see (g) below).

(c) That if the defendant is a woman living alone, that a woman must accompany those executing the order.

(d) That, even in the case of business premises, the order must only be executed in the presence of a responsible representative of the defendant.

(e) Restricting the number of people who may seek entry under the order.

(f) That the supervising solicitor must explain the meaning and effect of the order to the defendant in everyday language.

(g) That the supervising solicitor must advise the defendant of the right to seek legal advice before complying with the order, provided such advice is sought at once.

(h) That, unless it is impracticable to do so, e.g. if the defendant may get violent, a list of the items removed must be prepared on the premises before they are removed, and the defendant must be given an opportunity to check it. This is intended to reduce the risk of disputes as to what has been removed.

It is most important that the order is drawn so as to extend no further than the minimum extent necessary to preserve the documents or articles which may otherwise be destroyed or concealed: *Columbia Picture Industries Inc.* v *Robinson* [1987] Ch 38,

Scott J. The order will expressly give the defendant liberty to apply to discharge or vary the order on short notice and will provide in the order for a return date for a hearing on notice.

16.5.3.3 Provisions to assist execution

The defendant will commonly be ordered to do a number of things to facilitate the execution of the order. These include:

(a) Where it is anticipated that evidence is stored on computer, an order that the defendant print out material in legible or computer readable form.

(b) An order that the defendant open locked drawers, safes, etc. on the premises.

(c) An order that the defendant provide washing and toilet facilities for the claimant's representatives.

16.5.3.4 Ancillary orders

It is common to augment the main search order with a number of ancillary orders. Examples are:

(a) To deliver to the claimant any documents or articles covered by the search order but which are at addresses other than those stated in the order.

(b) To deliver within, say, 48 hours to the claimant any relevant documents coming into the defendant's possession after service of the order.

(c) To swear an affidavit verifying that all relevant documents have been delivered up to the claimant.

(d) To disclose addresses not covered by the order where relevant documents are stored.

(e) To restrain the defendant from warning other persons of the existence of the proceedings.

(f) To disclose, and verify on affidavit, the names and addresses of persons who have been involved in the defendant's activities.

16.5.4 PRIVILEGE AGAINST SELF-INCRIMINATION

The last of the ancillary orders in **16.5.3.4**, for the disclosure of other persons against whom the claimant may have causes of action, is especially useful in cassette and video pirating cases. The decision of the House of Lords in *Rank Film Distributors Ltd v Video Information Centre* [1982] AC 380 threatened to destroy its utility by holding that where a criminal charge was more than a contrived, fanciful or remote possibility the defendant could refuse to provide the information, relying on the privilege against self-incrimination. In pirating cases, conspiracy to defraud was an appropriate description of the defendant's activities.

Parliament immediately intervened by enacting SCA 1981, s. 72, which removed the privilege in intellectual property and passing off cases, subject to the defendant's answers being inadmissible in subsequent criminal proceedings. A similar position has been reached where the defendant alleges that disclosure may lead to a prosecution for a substantive crime under the Theft Act; see Theft Act 1968, s. 31(1).

Privilege against self-incrimination can still be raised in cases not covered by SCA 1981, s. 72 or Theft Act 1968, s. 31(1), e.g. in non-intellectual property etc. cases where, for example, there is a serious risk of prosecution for conspiracy to defraud. In relation to search orders, it was held in *Tate Access Floors* v *Boswell* [1991] Ch 512 that where the privilege is available it covers both:

(a) those parts of the order which require the defendant to produce and verify documents and information; and

(b) the part of the order which requires the defendant to permit the claimant to enter the defendant's premises and to search for and seize relevant documents. (The new standard form search order makes it clear, however, that the supervising solicitor (but not the claimant or the claimant's solicitor) should be allowed to enter the premises even if privilege is raised).

If the risk of the information obtained under the search order being used against the defendant in subsequent criminal proceedings can be removed then the right of the defendant to avoid the impact of a search order by raising the privilege against self-incrimination can be avoided. This can be achieved by securing the written agreement of the Crown Prosecution Service that they do not wish to make use of such information, and by inserting a suitable clause in the search order itself: *AT & T Istel Ltd* v *Tulley* [1993] AC 45, HL. The clause approved in *AT & T Istel* was to the effect that no disclosure made in compliance with the order shall be used as evidence in the prosecution of any offence alleged to have been committed by the defendant or the defendant's spouse. Unless the prosecuting authorities do agree in writing, an *AT & T Istel* clause will not be included in an order: *United Norwest Co-Operatives Ltd* v *Johnstone, The Times*, 24 February 1994, CA.

When such a clause cannot be used, the search order should not be executed until after the defendant has had his right to claim privilege explained to him in everyday language, and has expressly declined to claim privilege: *IBM United Kingdom Ltd* v *Prima Data International Ltd* [1994] 4 All ER 748.

It is not permissible to include in a search order a requirement that the defendant must hand potentially self-incriminating material to the supervising solicitor, even simply for safekeeping: *Den Norsk Bank ASA* v *Antonatos* [1999] QB 271, CA.

16.6 Execution of the Order

The concept of having a supervising solicitor to serve and execute *Anton Piller* orders was introduced by Sir Donald Nicholls V-C in *Universal Thermosensors Ltd* v *Hibben* [1992] 1 WLR 840. Before then the practice was for the claimant's own solicitor to serve the order on the defendant. Decisions before 1992 must therefore be read with this change of practice in mind.

In *Manor Electronics Ltd* v *Dickson* [1988] RPC 618 one of the reasons for discharging the search order was that the claimant's solicitor was a daughter of the claimant's chief executive, it being inappropriate that the person supervising execution of the order had a personal connection with the claimant.

Execution of the order needs to be properly planned. If there are several addresses covered by the order, it is important that execution is simultaneous. The police are often informed beforehand if there is any anticipation of a breach of the peace.

The order is not a search warrant, and the solicitors cannot use force to gain entry. There is a heavy duty on the solicitors to comply strictly with the terms as to the addresses covered and the goods and documents to be seized. The claimant's solicitor retains the articles seized, not the claimant, and must comply with the undertakings as to listing items removed and duly returning them to the defendant after they are copied. It is important that neither the claimant nor the claimant's employees be allowed to conduct searches of documents belonging to a trade competitor, even if the competitor is the defendant to the action.

16.7 Non-compliance by the Defendant

There are two sanctions:

(a) The claimant can bring contempt proceedings, which may result in the defendant being committed to prison.

(b) 'The refusal to comply may be the most damning evidence against the defendant at the subsequent trial,' *per* Ormrod LJ in *Anton Piller KG v Manufacturing Processes Ltd* [1976] Ch 55, CA.

The standard search order requires the supervising solicitor to inform the defendants that they are not obliged to comply with the order until they have sought legal advice, which must be sought within two hours. While the defendant is seeking legal advice the supervising solicitor must be admitted to the premises. Other people named in the order may be excluded in this period. Although the supervising solicitor may be inside the premises, the search will not be started until the defendant has obtained legal advice (or the two hours has elapsed). Once that time has expired, the defendant will be at risk of committal proceedings. While it stands, an order must be obeyed. That is so even if an application is successfully made shortly thereafter for the order to be discharged or varied: *Wardle Fabrics Ltd v G. Myristis Ltd* [1984] FSR 263. However, the bare fact of a refusal of entry, and hence breach of the order, does not mean that the breach was contumacious or that it requires punishment. Important factors are whether the application to discharge is merely a device to postpone the search and whether there is evidence of impropriety in respect of any relevant materials during the period of the delay: *Bhimji v Chatwani* [1991] 1 WLR 989.

16.8 Material Changes Before Execution

If a material change takes place between the granting of a search order and its execution, it is the claimant's duty to return to the court so that the court can reconsider the application in the light of the new facts: *O'Regan v Iambic Productions Ltd* (1989) 139 NLJ 1378, Sir Peter Pain.

16.9 Application to Discharge

16.9.1 THE APPLICATION

The order itself will contain express liberty for the defendant to apply to vary or discharge on short notice. The application to discharge or vary is made on notice usually to the judge who granted the original order. Evidence in support will be given on affidavit.

16.9.2 GROUNDS FOR DISCHARGE

Grounds upon which a search order may be discharged include:

(a) One or more of the basic conditions not being satisfied.

(b) Material non-disclosure on the application without notice.

Misstatements as to the claimant's means have occurred in several cases. This is usually material because it affects the value of the claimant's undertaking in damages. The usual penalty for any material non-disclosure is the discharge of the order. However, if the non-disclosure is inadvertent and no injustice is caused to the defendants, the court has a discretion to maintain the order.

16.9.3 ORDER FOR DISCHARGE

Once a search order has been executed there is a strong argument that it should not be discharged, even if there are grounds for doing so. Discharging the order is always a matter in the court's discretion, and discharge can be little more than an empty gesture, enforcing the undertaking in damages being a matter which can wait until trial.

However, there are cases where justice requires the immediate discharge of an executed search order:

(a) If the ground is material non-disclosure, the argument in favour of immediate discharge is stronger (and, usually irresistible) if the non-disclosure is not concerned with the merits of the cause of action, because such a question would not usually be investigated at trial.

(b) If the ground is material non-disclosure as to the claimant's solvency, the justice of the case may point towards the defendant being able to recover on the claimant's undertaking in damages immediately rather than being on risk pending trial.

(c) The continuing stigma of having a search order hanging over the defendant may be interfering with the defendant's business.

See *Dormeuil Frères SA* v *Nicolian International (Textiles) Ltd* [1988] 1 WLR 1362, as interpreted by *Tate Access Floors* v *Boswell* [1991] Ch 512.

16.9.4 VARIATION

The usual ground for varying a search order is that it has been drawn too widely. The safeguards established by the courts may not have been incorporated into the order, for example, the plaintiff may have been allowed to retain the defendant's documents for more than a reasonable period, or the classes of documents covered by the order may be wider than necessary.

16.10 Misconduct by the Claimant

The solicitor executing a search order in *VDU Installations Ltd* v *Integrated Computer Systems & Cybernetics Ltd, The Times*, 13 August 1988, negligently failed to explain the effect of the order to the defendant in a fair and accurate manner. Knox J held the solicitor to be in contempt of court.

If the order is executed in an excessive or oppressive manner, the claimant may become liable under the undertaking in damages. 'Excessive' means simply beyond the terms of the order, such as by seizing more documents than those listed in the order. In such circumstances the defendant may be entitled to aggravated and, perhaps, exemplary damages: *Columbia Picture Industries Inc.* v *Robinson* [1987] Ch 38.

It is incumbent on a claimant who has obtained and executed a search order to press on with the main action without delay. In *Hytrac Conveyors Ltd* v *Conveyors International Ltd* [1982] 1 WLR 44, CA a search order was executed on 30 April 1982. Over ten weeks after the defendants had given notice of intention to defend the claimant had still not served the Statement of Claim. Lawton LJ said that claimants 'must not use *Anton Piller* orders as a means of finding out what sort of charges they can make,' and refused the claimant's application for permission to appeal against the judge's order dismissing the action.

16.11 Questions

OBJECTIVES

By the conclusion of this section you should:

(a) have a sound understanding of the procedure for applying for an interim injunction;

(b) be able to state the principles that apply in applications for interim injunctions;

(c)   be able to give reasons why those principles apply, and to apply them to the facts of individual cases;

(d)   understand the meaning and effect of the usual undertakings and cross-undertakings given in interim injunction cases;

(e)   have a sound understanding of freezing injunctions, including—

   (i)   the procedure for obtaining such an injunction,

   (ii)   the terms to be incorporated in drafting such an injunction, and

   (iii)   the grounds upon which an application may be made to vary or discharge such an injunction;

(f)   have a sound understanding of search orders, including:

   (i)   the procedure for obtaining such an order, and

   (ii)   how such orders are executed.

RESEARCH

Read the materials contained in **Chapters 14** to **16** of this Manual, and refer to **1.2.1.3**, and **Chapter 12**. Consult PD 25 (Interim Injunctions).

LARGE GROUP SESSION 4

In advance of Large Group Session 4, read questions 1 to 3, which will be dealt with in the class.

QUESTION 1

Your client owns the internationally well-known Harrogate Hotel in the West End of London. Located in the hotel is a long-established casino, unsurprisingly called the Harrogate Casino. Your client is concerned about a web site, www.harrogatecasino.uk, which is not run by your client. Inquiries have established that the web site is owned by Web Pirates Ltd. Your client is concerned that the web site will have an adverse effect on its business. What advice should you give on how to protect your client's commercial interests?

QUESTION 2

Ekron Property Co. Ltd are suing Derek for arrears of rent amounting to £60,000. The premises comprise a garage with facilities for petrol retail and motor repairs, and forecourt and showroom areas for car sales. It is clear that the rent due under the lease is far higher than the rent that could be obtained if the premises were to be relet today, and that the lease has no market value. A claim form, with particulars of claim attached was issued six weeks ago, and the next quarter's rent falls due in four weeks. You have been briefed on behalf of Ekron to appear on an application for summary judgment in seven days' time. Your instructing solicitors are now talking to you on the telephone. They say that Ekron's agent visited the garage this morning, and saw posters bearing the legend: 'Clearance Sale due to owner going to America' in the windows, and that only nine used cars were in the showrooms instead of the usual 40 or so. What advice should you give Ekron?

[A]   To make an application for summary possession under RSC O. 113.
[B]   To apply to abridge time under CPR, r. 3.1(1)(a) so as to bring forward the hearing of the application for summary judgment.
[C]   To make a further application for an interim payment under CPR, r. 25.1(1)(k) to be heard at the same time as the application for summary judgment.

[D] To apply for a freezing injunction restraining Derek from removing or dealing with his assets save in so far as they exceed £60,000.

QUESTION 3

Richard is the former chief executive of GM Foods International Plc, who are your clients. It is believed that Richard was systematically defrauding the company of large sums of money during the time he was its chief executive. There is a considerable amount of documentary evidence available to your clients concerning the relevant transactions, which points towards the alleged fraud, but all the key documents are missing. The transactions themselves were very complicated, and involved money being transferred between various accounts, making it extremely difficult to identify exactly how much was being misappropriated. Richard lives in Surrey. It is believed that his accountants, Hyde & Co. of London, were instrumental in assisting Richard with the impugned transactions. What advice would you give to GM Foods International Plc to protect their position?

SMALL GROUP SESSION 4

On the basis of your research, answer questions 4 to 12 in advance of Small Group Class 4.

QUESTION 4

You act for the claimant in an action who is making an application, without notice, for an interim injunction. Which one of the following statements about the claimant's duty to give full and frank disclosure when making the application is *incorrect*?

[A] The duty extends to material facts known to the claimant and to material facts which could reasonably have been known following proper inquiries.
[B] A deliberate failure to disclose a material fact usually entitles the defendant to have the order discharged.
[C] The claimant's solicitors are required to file at court a certificate that the duty has been fully complied with.
[D] There is a duty on the claimant to disclose any material change in circumstances while the proceedings continue on a 'without notice' basis.

QUESTION 5

Francis, an author, lives in a terraced house adjoining the factory premises of Grimby and Murdstone Ltd. They have recently installed new plant which they operate from 8 o'clock in the morning to 6 o'clock at night. Francis complains that the machinery causes excessive noise and vibration which substantially disturbs him while working in his study, and has commenced proceedings alleging nuisance in the Warrington County Court.

Describe the procedure by which Francis can apply to the court to prevent the machinery being employed pending the trial and the principles which the court will apply in determining the application.

QUESTION 6

You are instructed by the Willesden Environmental Society who are concerned at a proposed series of experiments at the University of Neasden using radioactive substances. They have obtained a scientific report which says that there is a slight risk of local contamination. The University's scientists say that this is totally incorrect, and that there is no risk; that the experiments have been commissioned by the Ministry of Defence and are of urgent public importance; and that they plan to make the first test in a fortnight.

What steps would you take to protect your client's interests pending the trial of any proceedings, and what principles will be applied by the court in dealing with an application before trial?

QUESTION 7

The *Gourmet's Guide*, an annual publication, is to be published tomorrow. An advance copy has just come into your client's possession. It describes your client's exclusive club restaurant as purveying food which 'could only be of interest to the Public Health Inspector'. What steps would you take to protect your client's reputation?

QUESTION 8

(a) Hilary is employed as the confidential secretary to the managing director of Instant Staff Co., an employment agency in Barchester. Hilary's contract of employment provided that she should not take employment with any similar concern in Barchester for a period of one year after her employment ceased. Last week she resigned and has now set up a new agency in Barchester with four other former members of staff. The senior partner of Instant Staff Co. has noticed that confidential lists of customers and budgets for the next year are missing and believes that these have been taken by Hilary. Advise Instant Staff Co.

(b) Assume Hilary attends on the interim hearing. If Instant Staff Co. accepts an undertaking by Hilary not to work in breach of its contract and to return the lists and budgets, and an order is duly made, what is the legal position?

(c) The only live issue at trial is whether the contractual provision was reasonable, and the trial judge finds in Hilary's favour. She was unable to find employment during the relevant year. What application is Hilary likely to make?

QUESTION 9

Mrs Prior's husband was killed by an aircraft propeller as he was attempting to board the aircraft at Birmingham airport. This plane is still in England for servicing. The plane is owned by a Nigerian company which employed the pilot. The Nigerian company has no other assets in this country. The plane is soon to be returned to Nigeria. Mrs Prior is legally aided.

Advise Mrs Prior as to whether there is any immediate application she should make against the Nigerian company. In particular, advise her:

(a) as to the requirements for any application;

(b) the procedure; and

(c) her chances of success and whether her chances will be prejudiced by the fact that she is legally aided.

QUESTION 10

You are instructed by Hudson's British Fashions Inc. (a well-established tailoring business in New York) who have been served with a claim form in proceedings started by their former suppliers Ramsbottom Textiles Ltd claiming £50,000 for the price of material sold and delivered. They have also been served with an injunction made without notice restraining them from using any funds held by them within the jurisdiction. They in fact have substantial funds with their bankers in London which they intended to use to discharge monthly invoices from their present suppliers in England. They intend to contest the claim for the price of the materials delivered by Ramsbottom on the grounds that the material was defective; this matter was clearly raised by them in correspondence immediately after the delivery in question.

175

Advise Hudson on any grounds they might have for applying to vary or discharge the injunction, and on the procedure to be adopted.

QUESTION 11

With regard to a search order which one of the following propositions is correct?

[A] The order must be served by a supervising solicitor on a weekday between 6 am and 7.30 pm.
[B] The order will only be granted if there is a good arguable case on the merits.
[C] The defendant may on the grounds of privilege refuse to allow entry to anyone other than the supervising solicitor in an appropriate case.
[D] The application for a search order must be made after proceedings have been issued but before they have been served.

QUESTION 12

J.K. Films Incorporated (an American film distributor) believe that unauthorised copies of their films are being produced at the studio premises of Lesley's Video Ltd in Whitechapel. They have obtained information to this effect from a member of Lesley's staff. They are anxious to ascertain the identity of the persons who are delivering the films to Lesley's studio and also the identity of the retailers to whom unauthorised copies have been sold.

Advise J.K. Films Inc.:

(a) On any application that may be made to the court.

(b) On how any order may be executed.

(c) On whether the defendants may rely on any privilege.

(d) On what should be done after the order has been executed.

SEVENTEEN

SMALL CLAIMS TRACK

17.1 Introduction

In accordance with the ideas set out in the overriding objective that cases should be dealt with proportionately to the amount at stake and to the importance of the case, the Civil Procedure Rules 1998 provide for the allocation of claims with a limited financial value to what is known as the small claims track. This is intended to provide a streamlined procedure with limited pre-trial preparation, very restricted rules on the recovery of costs from the losing party, and with the strict rules of evidence not applying to the hearing. It is appropriate for the most straightforward types of cases, such as consumer disputes, accident claims where the injuries suffered are not very serious, disputes about the ownership of goods, and landlord and tenant cases other than claims for possession.

As discussed in **Chapter 7**, track allocation is considered by the court (usually a District Judge) in defended cases after receipt of allocation questionnaires from the parties. These questionnaires are sent to the parties after receipt of the defence, so allocation occurs usually a few weeks after the proceedings were served.

17.2 Allocation to the Small Claims Track

This is the normal track for defended claims with a value not exceeding £5,000 (CPR, r. 26.6(3)). Although most claims up to £5,000 will be dealt with on the small claims track, the following types of claim will not normally be allocated there even if they have a value up to £5,000:

(a) personal injuries cases where the value of the claim for pain, suffering and loss of amenity exceeds £1,000 (CPR, rr. 26.6(1)(a) and (2));

(b) claims by tenants of residential premises seeking orders that their landlords should carry out repairs or other works to the premises where the value of the claim exceeds £1,000 (CPR, r. 26.6(1)(b));

(c) claims by residential tenants seeking damages against their landlords for harassment or unlawful eviction (CPR, r. 26.7(4)); and

(d) claims involving a disputed allegation of dishonesty.

Even if the claim is worth less than £5,000 there may be other reasons why it should not be allocated to the small claims track. One relates to expert evidence, which is not allowed in small claims track cases, either by calling an expert at the hearing or simply relying on an expert's report, unless the court gives permission: CPR, r. 27.5. Although permission may be granted, there are also severe restrictions on the costs recoverable for expert evidence in small claims track cases, including a limit of £200 for experts' fees (PD 27, para. 7.3(2)), which may make it unjust for a small case which requires expert evidence to be allocated to this track.

If the claim is worth more than £5,000 the parties may consent to it being allocated to the small claims track: CPR, r. 26.7(3). However, the court retains control, and may refuse to allocate the case in accordance with the parties wishes if it feels the case is not suitable for the small claims track. For example, it is unlikely to agree to a case being allocated to the small claims track if the hearing is likely to take more than a day. If the court agrees with the parties and allocates the case to the small claims track, the case is treated for the purposes of costs as a fast track case, except that trial costs are in the discretion of the court: CPR, r. 27.14(5).

17.3 Provisions of the Civil Procedure Rules 1998 that Do Not Apply

The idea behind having a small claims track is to provide a relatively inexpensive means of resolving disputes having a limited financial value. Some of the more sophisticated procedures available for larger claims are therefore inappropriate for cases on the small claims track, and do not apply once a case has been allocated to the small claims track. These include:

(a) most interim remedies, except interim injunctions;

(b) standard disclosure of documents (a more limited form of disclosure applies, see below);

(c) several of the rules on experts;

(d) requests for further information; and

(e) Part 36 offers and payments (because this would interfere with the no costs rule, see below).

17.4 Standard Directions

Once a case has been allocated to the small claims track the court will give directions, which are usually set out in the notice telling the parties that the case has been allocated to this track.

There are a number of options available to the court, but it is most likely that the court will give what are described as standard directions. Different forms of standard directions apply to different categories of small claims. However, the general form of standard directions provides for:

(a) the parties to serve on the other side copies of the documents they intend to rely upon no later than 14 days before the hearing;

(b) the original documents to be brought to the hearing;

(c) notice of the hearing date and the length of the hearing; and

(d) an obligation on the parties to inform the court if they settle the case by agreement.

17.5 Special Directions

A District Judge allocating a claim to the small claims track may decide that standard directions will not ensure the case is properly prepared, and may instead formulate special directions specifically for the case in hand. At the same time the District Judge may fix the date for the final hearing, or may list the matter for further directions.

Alternatively. if the District Judge takes the view that it will be necessary to have a hearing with the parties present in court to ensure they understand what they must do to prepare the case, or if the District Judge is minded to consider whether the claim should be struck out or summarily disposed of, the case will be listed for a preliminary hearing where these matters can be dealt with.

The general rule in small claims track cases is that no expert evidence is allowed, whether oral or in the form of a report. If a party regards expert evidence as necessary, a special direction will be required, and this should be mentioned in the allocation questionnaire.

17.6 Determination Without a Hearing

If all the parties agree, a small claim can be determined by the District Judge on the papers without a hearing: CPR, r. 27.10.

17.7 Final Hearings

Final hearings in small claims track cases are usually dealt with by County Court District Judges. Hearings are generally conducted in the judge's room rather than in one of the court rooms. The normal rule is that hearings will be in public, but there are several exceptions, such as the parties agreeing to the hearing being in private.

Small claims hearings are informal, and the strict rules of evidence do not apply. The informality in small claims proceedings was stressed by the Court of Appeal in *Bandegani* v *Norwich Union Fire Insurance Ltd* (20 May 1999, unreported) when allowing an appeal against a decision to dismiss a claim after a submission of no case to answer. The submission had been based on the claimant's failure to produce expert evidence for the value of his car, which had been damaged in an accident. The Court of Appeal also made the point that permission to call expert evidence in small claims cases ought not to be encouraged for reasons of proportionality.

The District Judge may proceed in any way that is considered fair. The District Judge may ask the witnesses questions before allowing the parties to do so, may refuse to allow cross-examination until all the witnesses have given evidence-in-chief, and may impose limits on the scope of cross-examination. Unless the District Judge intervenes in one of these ways, the usual sequence of events is for the claimant's representative to make a short opening (just a few sentences), and then to call their evidence. Everyone will be sitting around the District Judge's table, so no one leaves their seat when this is being done. Each witness is questioned first on behalf of the claimant, then on behalf of the defendant. The District Judge makes a note of the evidence as it is given, and will ask questions as appropriate. There may be scope for some re-examination. Once all the claimant's evidence has been introduced, the claimant's representative says that is the case for the claimant. It is then the defendant's opportunity to call its evidence. Once the defendant's evidence has been introduced, the defendant's representative will make some closing remarks. The claimant's representative's closing submissions come last.

The District Judge will usually give a short reasoned judgment there and then. The judgment is likely to be as short and simple as the nature of the case will allow. After giving judgment the form of the order to be made and costs are considered.

17.8 Costs

Claims allocated to the small claims track, are subject to severe costs restrictions. The rule is that no costs will be ordered between the parties except:

(a) the fixed costs relating to issuing the claim;

(b)   court fees;

(c)   witness expenses for travel, subsistence and loss of earnings up to £50 per day;

(d)   expert's fees, up to £200 per expert; and

(e)   in cases involving a claim for an injunction or specific performance, the cost of legal advice and assistance up to £260.

The above restrictions apply in the vast majority of small claims cases. There is however an exception if the court finds that one of the parties has behaved unreasonably. In such cases the court may make a summary assessment of costs in favour of the innocent party.

Another exception worth noting is that some cases are above the small claims financial limits, but are allocated to the small claims track by consent. In these cases the simple and speedy small claims track procedure applies, but costs are dealt with as though the case was on the fast track.

17.9   Appeals and Rehearings

A party who did not attend the final hearing may apply to set aside the order made in his or her absence and for an order that the claim be reheard. An application for a rehearing must be made within 14 days of the absent party being notified of the judgment. A rehearing will be allowed only if there is a good reason for the absence and if the absent party has a reasonable prospect of success at a reconvened hearing.

There is a restricted right of appeal from a decision in a small claims case. The only grounds permitted are that there was a serious irregularity affecting the proceedings, or the court made a mistake of law. Given the scope given by the rules to the procedure that may be adopted by the District Judge at the hearing, it is very difficult to establish a serious irregularity, and District Judges do not often make mistakes of law in small claims cases, as, apart from anything else, these are by definition generally simple cases.

EIGHTEEN

FAST TRACK

18.1 Introduction

The fast track is intended for medium sized cases that require more careful preparation than small claims track cases, but still do not justify the detailed and meticulous preparation appropriate for complex and important cases. Procedure on the fast track steers a middle course between the extremes of simple preparation on the small claims track, and the often time consuming and expensive procedures appropriate for the important cases on the multi-track. The reason it is called the fast track is that at the same time as a case is allocated to this case management track the court will give directions laying down a timetable for all the stages up to and including trial, but with the trial date or window no more than 30 weeks after the track allocation decision. It is intended that the timetable will be sufficient for the parties to undertake the work necessary for preparing the case for trial, but sufficiently tight to discourage elaboration. Discouraging elaboration is seen as important, as one of the aims is to prevent costs in fast track cases spiralling out of control.

The majority of defended actions within the £5,000 to £15,000 monetary band will be allocated to the fast track. Non-monetary claims such as injunctions, declarations and claims for specific performance which are unsuitable for the small claims track and do not require the more complex treatment of the multi-track will also be dealt with on the fast track.

The full range of interim remedies and orders are available in fast track cases. However, once a case is allocated to the fast track and directions are given there will be a limited period of up to seven months in which to prepare the case for trial. There will be limited time, therefore, for indulging in tactical procedural applications.

18.2 Allocation to the Fast Track

The fast track is the normal track for cases broadly falling into the £5,000 to £15,000 bracket, and which can be disposed of by a trial which will not exceed a day. The financial value criterion is a little more complicated than this broad position, and technically the following cases will normally be allocated to the fast track:

(a) personal injuries cases with a financial value between £5,000 and £15,000;

(b) personal injuries cases with an overall value under £5,000, but where the damages for pain, suffering and loss of amenity are likely to exceed £1,000;

(c) claims by residential tenants for orders requiring their landlords to carry out repairs or other work to the premises where the financial value of the claim is between £1,000 and £15,000;

(d) claims by residential tenants for damages against their landlords for harassment or unlawful eviction where the financial value of the claim does not exceed £15,000; and

(e) other categories of cases, where the financial value of the claim is between £5,000 and £15,000.

18.3 Directions

When it allocates a case to the fast track, the court will send an allocation notice to the parties which will include case management directions given by the District Judge which set a timetable for the steps to be taken from that point through to trial. An example of a notice of allocation (in fact to the multi-track, but the fast track form is very similar) was illustrated in **Figure 7.5**. The directions given will be designed to ensure the issues are identified and the necessary evidence is prepared and disclosed. Usually the court will give directions of its own initiative without a hearing, but will take into account the respective statements of case, the allocation questionnaires, and any further information provided by the parties. If any direction or order is required that has not been provided for, it is the duty of the parties to make an application as soon as possible so as to avoid undue interference with the overall timetable: PD 28, para. 2.8. If a directions hearing becomes necessary because of the default of any of the parties the court will usually impose a sanction: PD 28, para. 2.3.

Figure 7.4 sets out the usual main provisions of fast track directions, together with typical periods for compliance. Each direction actually made will state a date (and time) by which it must be completed. Model form directions are set out in the Appendix to the Fast Track Practice Direction (PD 28), and provide for matters such as:

(a) service and filing of further statements of case, such as replies;

(b) requests for further information arising out of the statements of case;

(c) disclosure and inspection of documents;

(d) service of witness statements from witnesses as to fact;

(e) expert evidence, including instruction of experts, exchange of reports, and whether experts will be allowed at trial or whether their evidence should be admitted simply in the form of their reports;

(f) without prejudice meetings between experts;

(g) written questions put to experts for the purpose of clarifying their reports;

(h) requests for further information arising out of disclosure of documents, and the exchange of witness statements and experts' reports;

(i) filing of listing questionnaires;

(j) trial bundles;

(k) trial.

Fast track directions will be tailored to the circumstances of each case. For example, if the parties have already given full disclosure of documents there will be no need for any directions dealing with this. It may be that the court takes the view that no expert evidence is required. Alternatively, it may be that the court decides that expert evidence is necessary, but that a single jointly instructed expert will suffice. Yet alternatively, it may decide that each party should be allowed to instruct their own experts on an issue, that there should be mutual exchange of experts' reports, and perhaps that there should be a without prejudice discussion between the experts to seek to narrow the expert issues. Further, the court may decide that the parties should be given an opportunity to put written questions to the experts in order to clarify technical points in the reports.

18.4   Time Limits Set Out in the Rules

In addition to the requirements of the express directions made by the court at the allocation stage, there are a number of time limits for taking procedural steps set out in the rules. These include time limits relating to service of hearsay notices under the Civil Evidence Act 1995, service of notices to admit, and the requirements relating to preparation of trial bundles. The result is that the specific directions given in a case are not the only time limits that have to be complied with. Details will obviously vary from case to case depending on the actual directions that have been made, but **Figure 18.1** sets out on a chronology of typical events in a fast track case from issue of proceedings through to trial. It will be seen that the process may take less than 40 weeks, or about 10 months.

Figure 18.1   Progress of fast track case to trial

Week	Step in the proceedings	Time limit
1	(a) Issue of proceedings	Usual limitation period
	(b) Service by court (takes effect on second day after posting)	4 months from issue (6 months if outside the jurisdiction)
3	Acknowledgment of service or filing of defence	14 days after deemed service of the particulars of claim
(Say) 5	(a) Service of allocation questionnaires (may be dispensed with)	Not before all defendants have filed defences, or expiry of time for filing defences
	(b) Possible transfer to defendant's home court	On filing defence
7	Return of allocation questionnaires	Not less than 14 days after service of the questionnaire
(Say 9)	Allocation decision and directions given by the procedural judge	After return of questionnaires
13	Disclosure of documents by lists	Usually 4 weeks after allocation
14	Inspection of documents	Usually 7 days after lists
19	(a) Exchange of witness statements	Usually 10 weeks after allocation
	(b) Service of hearsay notices	With witness statements
23	Experts reports'	Usually 14 weeks after allocation
29	Service of listing questionnaires (may be dispensed with)	Usually 20 weeks after allocation
31	Return of listing questionnaires	Usually 22 weeks after allocation
(Say) 33	(a) Any directions arising out of the listing questionnaires	Optional
	(b) Hearing if listing questionnaires not returned	Only if parties in default

36	(a) Confirmation of trial date	3 weeks before trial
	(b) Service of notice to admit	21 days before trial
38	Lodging trial bundle	3 to 7 days before trial
39	Service and filing of statements of costs	Not less than 24 hours before the hearing
39	Trial	30 weeks after allocation

18.5 Experts in Fast Track Claims

One of the powers available to the court is that of directing that the evidence on particular issues may be given by a single expert jointly instructed by the opposing parties: CPR, r. 35.7. In order to keep down costs and to reduce the length of fast track trials, it will be usual for the court to make directions for the joint instruction of a single expert unless there is good reason for doing something else: PD 28, para. 3.9(4). In addition, in fast track cases the court will not direct an expert to attend at trial unless it is necessary to do so in the interests of justice: CPR, r. 35.5(2).

Normally expert evidence should be prepared and be ready for exchange about 14 weeks after the order giving directions: PD 28, para. 3.12. However, there are a number of options, including:

(a) Sequential service of experts' reports. Normally it will be the claimant who will serve first.

(b) Simultaneous exchange of reports on some issues, with sequential service on the others.

(c) Holding of a discussion between experts in cases where the other side's reports cannot be agreed within a short time (usually 14 days) after service. This form of direction provides for a specified calendar date by which the discussion must take place, and the filing of a joint statement of the agreed issues and those in dispute (with reasons for the lack of agreement) by another specified date (which will often be close to the date for filing listing questionnaires).

(d) That expert evidence is not necessary and no party has permission to call or rely on expert evidence at the trial.

(e) That the parties may rely on experts' reports at trial, but cannot call oral expert evidence.

(f) That the parties may rely on expert reports, and the court will reconsider whether there is any need for experts to be called when the claim is listed for trial.

18.6 Listing Questionnaires

At least eight weeks before the trial date the parties must (unless dispensed with by the court) return listing questionnaires to the court. An example is shown in **Figure 18.2**. These forms are similar to allocation questionnaires, and are designed to check whether the parties have complied with the directions made at the allocation stage and whether the case is ready for trial. At the same time the claimant must pay the listing fee of £200. This is refundable if the court is notified at least seven days before trial that the case has settled. Further, both parties must file statements of costs (see **Figure 7.2**).

Figure 18.2

Listing questionnaire

<table>
<tr><td colspan="2">In the</td></tr>
<tr><td>Claim No.</td><td></td></tr>
<tr><td>Last date for filing
with court office</td><td></td></tr>
</table>

To

- The court will use the information which you and the other party(ies) provide to fix a date for trial (or to confirm the date and time if one has already been fixed), to confirm the estimated length of trial and to set a timetable for the trial itself. In multi-track cases the court will also decide whether to hold a pre-trial review.

- If you do not complete and return the questionnaire the procedural judge may
    - make an order which leads to your statement of case (claim or defence) being struck out.
    - decide to hold a listing hearing. You may be ordered to pay (immediately) the other parties' costs of attending.
    - if there is sufficient information, list the case for trial and give any appropriate directions.

- Separate estimates of costs incurred to date and those which will be incurred if the case proceeds to trial, should be given using Form 1 in the Schedule of Costs Forms set out in the Civil Procedure Rules. This form should be attached to and returned with your completed questionnaire. (This relates only to costs incurred by legal representatives.)

A Directions complied with

1. Have you complied with all the previous directions given by the court? ☐ Yes ☐ No

2. If no, please explain which directions are outstanding and why

Directions outstanding	Reasons directions outstanding

3. Are any further directions required to prepare the case for trial? ☐ Yes ☐ No

(If no go to section B)

4. If yes, please explain directions required and give reasons

Directions required	Reasons required

185

B Experts

1. Has the court already given permission for you to use written expert evidence? ☐ Yes ☐ No

(If no go to section B6)

2. If yes, please give name and field of expertise.

Name of expert	Whether joint expert *(please tick, if appropriate)*	Field of expertise

3. Have the expert(s') report(s) been agreed with the other parties? ☐ Yes ☐ No

4. Have the experts met to discuss their reports? ☐ Yes ☐ No

5. Has the court already given permission for the expert(s) to give oral evidence at the trial? *(If yes go to Q8)* ☐ Yes ☐ No

6. If no, are you seeking that permission? ☐ Yes ☐ No

(If yes go to Q7)   *(If no go to section C)*

7. Give your reasons for seeking permission.

8. What are the names, addresses and fields of expertise of your experts?

Expert 1	Expert 2	Expert 3	Expert 4

9. Please give details of any dates within the trial period when your expert(s) will not be available.

Name of expert	Dates not available

C Other witnesses

(If you are not calling other witnesses go to section D)

1. How many other witnesses (including yourself) will be giving evidence on your behalf at the trial? *(do not include experts - see section B above)*

(Give number)

2. What are the names and addresses of your witnesses?

Witness 1	Witness 2	Witness 3	Witness 4

3. Please give details of any dates within the trial period when you or your witnesses will not be available?

Name of witness	Dates not available

4. Are any of the witness statements agreed? ☐ Yes ☐ No
(If no go to Q6)

5. If yes, give the name of the witness and the date of his or her statement

Name of witness	Date of statement

6. Do you or any of your witnesses need any special facilities? ☐ Yes ☐ No
(If no go to Q8)

7. If yes, what are they?

8. Will any of your witnesses be provided with an interpreter? ☐ Yes ☐ No
(If no go to section D)

9. If yes, say what type of interpreter e.g. language (stating which), deaf/blind etc.

D Legal representation

1. Who will be presenting your case at the hearing or trial? ☐ You ☐ Solicitor ☐ Counsel

2. Please give details of any dates within the trial period when the person presenting your case will not be available.

Name	Dates not available

E Other matters

1. How long do you estimate the trial will take, including cross-examination and closing arguments?

Minutes	Hours	Days

If your case is allocated to the fast track the maximum time allowed for the whole case will be no more than one day.

2. What is the estimated number of pages of evidence to be included in the trial bundle?

(please give number)

Fast track cases only

3. The court will normally give you 3 weeks notice in the fast track of the date fixed for a fast track trial unless, in exceptional circumstances, the court directs that shorter notice will be given. Would you be prepared to accept shorter notice of the date fixed for trial? ☐ Yes ☐ No

Signed

Claimant/defendant or Counsel/Solicitor for the claimant/defendant

Date

188

18.7 Listing Directions

The court may hold a listing hearing, after which it will confirm the trial date and may give further directions. However, in most cases it will not feel the need to have a listing hearing, and will simply confirm or alter the trial date as appropriate, and may make further directions. The court will give the parties at least three weeks' notice of the date of the trial unless, in exceptional circumstances, the court directs that shorter notice will be given: CPR, r. 28.6(2).

18.7.1 TRIAL BUNDLES

Standard listing directions will provide that an indexed, paginated, bundle of documents contained in a ring binder must be lodged with the court not more than seven days or less than three days before the trial. Slightly inconsistently, the standard direction in the Appendix to PD 28 provides that trial bundles must be lodged at least seven days before trial. The parties must seek to agree the contents of the trial bundle a reasonable time in advance, which in practical terms means no later than 14 days before the trial. Responsibility for lodging the bundle is that of the claimant. Lodging the bundle at court is required so that the trial judge can read the case papers in advance of the trial. Judges are likely to take a very dim view if the bundle is not lodged in time. Identical bundles will be needed for each of the parties, with an additional bundle for the witness box.

18.7.2 CASE SUMMARY

Standard listing directions give the procedural judge the option of directing that a case summary should be included in the trial bundle. This document should be no more than 250 words, and should outline the matters in issue, referring where appropriate to the relevant documents in the trial bundle. Again, responsibility for this rests with the claimant and, if possible, it should be agreed with the other side.

18.7.3 TRIAL TIMETABLE

The court may, if it considers that it appropriate to do so, and in consultation with the parties, set a timetable for the trial. Setting a timetable is discretionary (CPR, r. 28.6(1)(b)), but if it decides to do so, it must consult with the parties (CPR, r. 39.4). The timetable contemplated is not the same as the directions timetable, but will define how much time the court will allow at trial for the various stages of the trial itself. A suitable direction may limit the time to be spent by each party in calling its evidence and in addressing the court in closing submissions. More sophisticated timetables will define how much time will be allowed for each witness, or even for cross-examination and re-examination.

18.8 Failing to Pay the Listing Fee

If the claimant fails to pay the listing fee the court will serve a notice (Form N173) on the claimant requiring payment within a stated period of time, failing which the claim will be struck out. If the claim is struck out for non-payment of the fee the claimant is also required to pay the defendant's costs, unless the court otherwise orders (CPR, r. 3.7). Once the claim has been struck out the court retains a power to reinstate it (CPR, r. 3.7(7)), and on such an application the court will apply the criteria set out in r. 3.9 relating to applications for relief from sanctions (see **Chapter 28**). However, any order for reinstatement will be made conditional on the fee being paid within two days of the order.

18.9 Varying the Directions Timetable

The parties may agree to vary the timetables set by the court at the allocation and listing stages (or at other times), however they cannot between themselves agree to change the date for returning listing questionnaires or the trial date: CPR, r. 28.4(2). If a party cannot complete the necessary preparation in time, or if there are other difficulties, it is possible to make an application to break the trial date.

PD 28, para. 5, makes it clear that variations involving loss of the trial date will be considered matters of last resort. However, it is recognised there will be cases where it will become necessary to vary the date for trial. Examples include cases where there are significant problems with the evidence, where there is a change of solicitor, where proceedings are issued at the very end of the limitation period, and in personal injuries cases where the prognosis is uncertain. Any necessary postponement will be for the shortest possible time, and the court will give directions for taking the necessary steps outstanding as rapidly as possible. In some of these cases the best course may be to have split trials of liability and quantum, or to proceed only on those issues that are ready. Where this happens the court may disallow the costs of the remaining issues, or order them to be paid by the party in default in any event.

18.10 Fast Track Trials

Trials will usually take place in the County Court where they are proceeding, but may take place in a Civil Trial Centre or any other court if it is appropriate because of listing difficulties, the needs of the parties, or for other reasons. The judge (who will often be a District Judge) will generally have read the trial bundle and may well dispense with opening speeches. Unless the trial judge otherwise directs, the trial will be conducted in accordance with any order previously made laying down a trial timetable (see **18.7.3** above). This means the judge is free to set a different trial timetable: PD 28, para. 8.3. Given the time constraints and the need for proportionality, it is likely the trial judge will exercise the power (see **Chapter 30**) to order witness statements to stand as their evidence in chief, and otherwise control the evidence to be presented. If a trial is not concluded on the day it is listed, the judge will normally sit on the following day to complete it: PD 28, para. 8.6.

18.11 Fast Track Costs

The normal rule is that costs in fast track cases will be dealt with by the trial judge by way of summary assessment at the end of the trial. This means that the judge will decide there and then how much the loser will have to pay towards the winner's costs of the entire action. To assist with this process, each party is required to file and serve a statement of costs (see **Figure 7.2**) at least 24 hours before the hearing.

There are also rules on fixed trial costs for fast track cases. The basic rules for trial costs (i.e. the costs of the day of the trial, which are in addition to the general costs of the action, discussed in the previous paragraph) provide that advocates' fees in fast track cases are:

Awards up to £3,000	£350
Awards between £3,000 and £10,000	£500
Claims for non-money remedies	£500
Awards over £10,000	£750
Additional fee for solicitor attending trial with counsel	£250

For the purpose of quantifying the amount of the claim, for a successful claimant it is the amount of the judgment excluding interests, costs and any reduction for contributory negligence, whereas for a successful defendant it is the amount the claimant specified on the claim form (or the maximum amount that could have been recovered on the pleaded case): CPR, r. 46.2(3). If there is a counterclaim and both parties succeed, the relevant amount is the difference (if any) between the trial costs recoverable given the value of the two claims: CPR, r. 46.3(6). If there is a counterclaim with a greater value than the claim, and the claimant succeeds on the claim and defeats the counterclaim, the relevant amount is the value of the counterclaim: CPR,

r. 46.2(6). There are detailed rules dealing with cases where there are several claimants or several defendants, including whether more than one party can be awarded fast track trial costs, which are set out in CPR, r. 46.4. For claims for non-monetary remedies the court has a discretion to make some other order, see CPR, r. 46.2(4).

The additional allowance for a solicitor attending with counsel is provided by CPR, r. 46.3. The solicitor's attendance fee will only be payable if the court awards fast track trial costs and if the court considers that it was necessary for a legal representative to attend to assist counsel: CPR, r. 46.3(2).

If a fast track claim settles before the start of the trial, costs may be allowed in respect of the advocate preparing for trial, but the amount allowed cannot be more than the above figures: CPR, r. 44.10. In deciding the amount to be allowed for the abortive preparation, the court will take into account when the claim settled and when the court was notified of that fact.

If there are split trials, such as on liability and quantum, it is possible to be awarded a second tranche of fast track trial costs, but the second award should not exceed two-thirds of the amount payable under the first award, subject to a minimum award of £350: CPR, r. 46.3(3), (4).

A successful party may by CPR, r. 46.3(7), be awarded less than the above fixed fast track trial costs for unreasonable or improper behaviour during the trial, and the losing party may be ordered to pay an additional amount if it is guilty of behaving improperly during the trial: CPR, r. 46.3(8).

NINETEEN

MULTI-TRACK

19.1 Introduction

The multi-track is intended for the more complex and important cases. However, there will be a great variety of cases on this track, and efficient case management dictates that they will have to be dealt with in different ways dependent on each case's own particular circumstances. In fact, any case not allocated to either the small claims track or fast track will be dealt with on the multi-track, and so will any case commenced using the alternative procedure in the Civil Procedure Rules 1998, Part 8 and most specialist proceedings. Cases on the multi-track will range from simple contractual disputes involving just over the £15,000 threshold, through to complex commercial cases involving difficult issues of fact and law with values of several million pounds. Case management on the multi-track is intended to reflect this. Simpler cases should be given standard directions not very different from those given in fast track cases without the need for hearings, and the parties will be expected to comply with those directions without complicating or delaying matters. At the other end of the scale, the courts will adopt a far more active approach, possibly with several directions hearings in the form of case management conferences and pre-trial reviews. The courts are expected to adopt a flexible approach to ensure that each case is dealt with in an appropriate way.

19.2 Directions on Allocation

As already mentioned earlier in the Manual, when a case is allocated to the multi-track the court will send the parties a notice telling them of the allocation decision. An example of such a notice was illustrated at **Figure 7.5**. At the same time as allocating the case the procedural judge will decide whether to give directions or to fix a case management conference or pre-trial review (or both a case management conference and a pre-trial review and such other directions as are thought fit). The court will seek to make directions suitable to the needs of the case, and the steps the parties have already taken to prepare it for trial. It will also take into account the extent to which the parties have complied with any pre-action protocol (see **Chapter 2**). The court's concern will be to ensure the issues between the parties are identified, and that the evidence required for the trial is prepared and disclosed.

Similar things will be dealt with in multi-track directions as are dealt with in fast track cases. They will deal with disclosure of documents, exchange of witness statements, expert evidence, and arrangements for trial. However, because many multi-track cases are rather complex it is recognised that the time required for each step may be considerably longer than that allowed in fast track claims. Moreover, difficulties encountered at any of the stages, such as disclosure of documents, may impact the subsequent stages. It is for this reason that allocation directions may be quite limited, and why directions hearings in the form of case management conferences and pre-trial reviews are often held in multi-track cases.

19.2.1 INADEQUATE INFORMATION

There will be cases allocated to the multi-track where the parties provide little or no information other than that contained in their statements of case. In such cases the court could call a case management conference, and it could order the parties to provide further information, with sanctions in default. However, it is perhaps more likely that it will simply impose directions giving a tight timetable for trial: PD 29, para. 4.10. Doing so will put enormous pressure on the parties. They will either have to comply, or will find themselves in considerable difficulty unless they apply promptly for tailored directions. This is because the court will assume for the purposes of any later application (in the absence of any appeal or application within 14 days to vary) that the parties were content that the directions were correct in the circumstances then existing: PD 29, para. 6.2(2).

The general approach in these cases where there is inadequate information is for directions along the following lines to be made by the court of its own initiative:

(a) filing and service of any further information required to clarify either party's case;

(b) standard disclosure (for further details on which, see **Chapter 20**) between the parties;

(c) simultaneous exchange of witness statements;

(d) for the appointment of a single expert unless there is good reason for not doing so;

(e) simultaneous exchange of experts' reports in cases or on issues where single expert directions have not been given (unless expert evidence is required on both liability and quantum, in which event the direction may be for simultaneous exchange on the liability issues, but sequential exchange on quantum issues);

(f) if experts' reports are not agreed, that there be a discussion between the experts for the purpose of identifying the expert evidence issues, and, if possible, reaching agreement between the experts, and the preparation of a statement setting out the issues on which they are agreed and a summary of their reasons on the issues where they disagree;

(g) listing a case management conference after the final date in the above directions; and

(h) specifying a trial period.

19.2.2 AGREED DIRECTIONS

If the parties in a case likely to be allocated to the multi-track agree proposals for the management of the case and the court considers that the proposals are suitable, the court may simply approve them without the need for a directions hearing: PD 29, paras 4.6, 4.7. This is encouraged by the Civil Procedure Rules 1998, as it obviously saves costs and court time. In order to obtain the court's approval the agreed directions must:

(a) if appropriate, include a direction regarding the filing of a reply;

(b) if appropriate, provide for amending any statement of case;

(c) include provision about the disclosure of documents;

(d) include provision about both factual and expert evidence (the provision about expert evidence may be to the effect that no expert evidence is required);

(e) if appropriate, include dates for service of requests for further information and/or questions to experts, and when they should be answered;

(f) include a date or a period when it is proposed the trial will take place; and

(g) if appropriate, a date for a case management conference.

It will be seen that only items (c), (d) and (f) are obligatory in all cases, although the others will frequently arise in practice. Proposed agreed directions must lay down a timetable by reference to calendar dates. The court will scrutinise the timetable carefully, with particular attention to the proposals for the trial and case management conference, and will be astute to ensure these are no later than is reasonably necessary.

The provision in any agreed directions relating to disclosure may:

(a) limit disclosure to standard disclosure, or less than that; and/or

(b) direct that disclosure will take place by the supply of copy documents without a list of documents, but if so, it must say either that the parties must serve a disclosure statement with the copies, or that they have agreed to disclose in this way without a disclosure statement.

The provision regarding factual and expert evidence should, if appropriate, deal with:

(a) whether the evidence should be disclosed simultaneously or sequentially;

(b) the use of a single expert; and

(c) without prejudice discussions between the experts if a single expert is not going to be instructed.

The court is free to reject directions that have been agreed between the parties, but will take them into account when making its own directions (either without a hearing or on a case management conference).

19.3 Case Management Conferences

Case management conferences are an integral part of the new system of active case management by the courts. They are not simply directions hearings, but are intended to ensure that the real issues between the parties are identified. Side issues will be dispensed with either by agreement between the parties with due encouragement from the judge, or by means of summary or striking out determinations at an early stage. Case management conferences may be held immediately after a case is allocated to the multi-track or at any time thereafter through to the listing stage. They can be used as the vehicle for laying down directions at the allocation stage, or may be used later in order to assess how the case is progressing when the initial directions on allocation should have been completed. Normally the court has a discretion whether to call a case management conference. However, where it is contemplated that an order may be made either for the evidence on a particular issue to be given by a single expert, or that an assessor should be appointed, PD 29, para. 4.13, provides that a case management conference must be held unless the parties have consented to the order in writing.

Case management conferences will also be called in cases where the court feels it cannot properly give directions on its own initiative, and where no agreed directions have been filed which it feels can be approved: PD 29, para. 4.12.

By encouraging the parties to settle their dispute or resolve it outside the court system, and by forcing the parties into identifying the real issues at an early stage, it is hoped that case management conferences will be a means of using court time to save more time.

19.3.1 LISTING OF CASE MANAGEMENT CONFERENCES

The minimum period of notice the court will give to the parties of the date for the case management conference is three clear days: CPR, r. 3.3(3) and PD 29, para. 3.7.

19.3.2 ATTENDANCE AT CASE MANAGEMENT CONFERENCES

If a party has a legal representative, someone familiar with the case must attend the case management conference: CPR, r. 29.3(2). The person attending will have to be the fee-earner concerned, or someone (possibly counsel) who is fully familiar with the file, the issues and the proposed evidence. They must be able to field the questions that are likely to be covered at the hearing, and have the authority to agree and/or make representations on the matters reasonably to be expected to arise. Where the inadequacy of the person attending or his instructions leads to the adjournment of the hearing, it will be normal for a wasted costs order to be made: PD 29, para. 5.2(3).

In the Ch.D., whenever possible the advocates instructed or expected to appear at trial should attend case management conference and other case management hearings: Chancery Guide, para. 5.5. In the Commercial Court, case management conferences should be attended on behalf of each party both by the fee earner with conduct of the case (Commercial Guide, para. D7.8) and by at least one of the advocates retained (para. D7.9). This is because case management conferences in the Commercial Court are regarded as particularly significant stages in the litigation, and are conducted by a judge who will usually form part of the two-judge team that will manage the case, one of whom will usually subsequently be the trial judge: paras D3.1 and D3.2.

19.3.3 ISSUES TO BE DEALT WITH AT CASE MANAGEMENT CONFERENCES

At a case management conference the court will:

(a) make a thorough review of the steps the parties have taken to date in preparing the case for trial;

(b) consider the extent to which they have complied with any previous orders and directions;

(c) decide on the directions needed to progress the action in accordance with the overriding objective;

(d) ensure that reasonable agreements are made between the parties about the matters in issue and the future conduct of the action; and

(e) record all such agreements.

To assist the court the legal representatives for all parties should ensure that all documents (and in particular witness statements and expert reports) the court is likely to ask to see are brought to court. They should also consider whether the parties themselves should attend, and consider in advance what orders and directions may be appropriate.

In the TCC, the claimant must apply within 14 days of filing the acknowledgment of service or defence for the fixing of a case management conference: PD 49C, paras 4.2 and 5.1. The court will then notify the parties of the date for the case management conference, and send them a case management questionnaire and a case management directions form: see PD 49C, para. 5.2 and apps 1 and 2. These should be completed and exchanged, and then filed by 4 pm two days before the case management conference: para. 5.3. The parties are encouraged to seek to agree directions.

In the Commercial Court, the legal representatives for each party must liaise for the purpose of preparing a short case memorandum, which will be included in the case management bundle. They must also prepare an agreed list of important issues (with a separate section dealing with matters which are common ground between all or some of the parties), and the claimant's solicitors must prepare the case management bundle: Commercial Guide, paras D4.1, D5.1 and D6.1. The case management bundle must contain the above documents, together with the claim form and statements of case (or case summaries under para. C1.3 if any of the statements of case exceed 25 pages), and any orders etc. made at that time (see para. D6.2), being careful to avoid any reference to interim payments and Part 36 offers and payments (as the case management judge could well be the trial judge). The case management bundle must be lodged with the Commercial Court Registry at least seven days before the first case management conference: para. D6.4.

19.4 Interim Applications in Multi-track Cases

In multi-track cases the appropriate time to consider most forms of interim relief, if possible, is the first case management conference. PD 29, para. 3.8, says that applications in multi-track cases must be made as early as possible so as to minimise the need to change the directions timetable, and that an application to vary a directions timetable laid down by the court (perhaps on its own initiative) must ordinarily be made within 14 days of service of the directions (para. 6.2). If at all possible any applications contemplated by the parties should be issued in time to be heard on any case management conference fixed for the case.

19.5 Case Summary

There will be occasions when the court will be assisted by a written case summary. This should be a short document not exceeding 500 words which is designed to assist the court in understanding and dealing with the issues raised in the case. It should give a brief chronology of the claim, state the factual issues that are agreed and those in dispute, and the nature of the evidence needed to decide them. Responsibility for preparing the document rests with the claimant, and if possible it should be agreed by the other parties.

19.6 Fixing the Date for Trial

The court will fix the trial date or the period in which the trial is to take place as soon as practicable: CPR, r. 29.2(2). This may be possible when it gives allocation directions, but in complex cases this may have to be delayed, perhaps for a considerable period of time. Where fixing the trial date is postponed, it may be revisited either at a later case management conference, or on the application of the parties, or after further scrutiny by the court.

19.7 Listing Questionnaires

Directions will tell the parties when they must file listing questionnaires. These may be dispensed with. The questionnaires will be sent out to the parties by the court for completion and return by the date specified in the directions given when the court fixed the date or period for trial: CPR, r. 29.6. The specified date should be not less than eight weeks before the trial date or 'window': PD 29, para. 8.1(3). The forms should be served by the court at least 14 days before they must be returned. Each party is under an obligation to return a completed questionnaire before the specified date, and the claimant is required to pay the listing fee of £300 (£400 in the High Court). The fee is payable even if questionnaires are dispensed with. It is refundable if the court is notified at least seven days before trial that the case has settled. There is a possible sanction of automatic striking out for non-payment after a reminder from the court: CPR, r. 3.7. Further, both parties must file statements of costs (see **Figure 7.2**).

19.7.1 PURPOSE OF LISTING QUESTIONNAIRES

Listing questionnaires are used to check that earlier orders and directions have been complied with, and to provide up to date information to assist the court with deciding when to hold the trial and how long it will take, and in making trial timetable directions. Once all the questionnaires have been received, or the time limit has expired, the file will be placed before the procedural judge, who will make directions for trial, or direct that there should be a listing hearing or pre-trial review.

19.7.2 EXCHANGE OF QUESTIONNAIRES

The Civil Procedure Rules 1998 do not require the parties to exchange copies of their listing questionnaires, but doing so may avoid the parties giving conflicting or incomplete information to the court: PD 29, para. 8.1(5). Getting this right may avoid the court feeling there is a need for a listing hearing or pre-trial review.

19.7.3 FAILURE TO FILE LISTING QUESTIONNAIRES

If no-one returns a listing questionnaire by the specified date the court will usually make an order that the parties must do so within three days of service of the order, failing which the claim and any counterclaim will be struck out: PD 29, para. 8.3(1). Where only some of the parties file listing questionnaires, the court will fix a listing hearing. It will also fix a listing hearing if any of the questionnaires do not provide the necessary information, or if the court considers that such a hearing is necessary to decide what further directions should be given to complete the preparations for trial: CPR, r. 29.6(3).

19.7.4 LISTING HEARINGS

Listing hearings concentrate on making the decisions relevant to fixing the date of the trial. They are fixed for dates as early as possible, and the parties are given at least three clear days' notice of the date. Even if a listing hearing is fixed because some of the parties did not file their questionnaires, the court will normally fix or confirm the trial date and make orders about the steps to prepare the case for trial: PD 29, para. 8.3(2). The court is likely to make further directions similar to those set out in **19.8.3** below.

The court is primarily concerned with whether the parties are, or soon will be, ready for trial, and with identifying the most convenient trial date or window given the constraints on court time and the availability of witnesses. It is not enough for a legal representative to attend with a list of dates to avoid: the court may question the reasons why experts and witnesses are said to be unable to attend, and if reasons are not given or are found to be inadequate, the court may proceed to fix the trial for the earliest free date: *Matthews* v *Tarmac Bricks & Tiles Ltd* (14 June 1999, CA, unreported).

19.7.5 LISTING IN THE ROYAL COURTS OF JUSTICE

In non-specialist cases in the QBD and Ch.D. proceeding in the Royal Courts of Justice in London, a direction will be given as early as possible (often the first case management conference) with a view to fixing the trial or trial window. It will often direct that the trial is not to begin before a specified date, or that it will be held within a specified period. The claimant must then, within the next seven days, take out an appointment with the Listing Officer and give notice of the appointment to the other parties. At the listing hearing the claimant must bring any case summary, the Particulars of Claim and any orders relevant to listing, and all parties must have details of the dates of availability of their witnesses, experts and counsel. The Listing Officer will try to provide the earliest firm trial date or trial window consistent with the case management directions.

19.8 Pre-trial Review

If a pre-trial review is listed it is likely to take place about 8 to 10 weeks before trial. The purpose of a pre-trial review is to settle a statement of the issues to be tried, and to set a programme and budget for the trial. The pre-trial review gives the court a further opportunity to check the parties have complied with earlier orders and directions, and may help in promoting settlement. They are not held in all cases, but only in those that merit the additional hearing. The intention is that they should be conducted by the eventual trial judge.

19.8.1 NOTICE OF PRE-TRIAL REVIEW

The fact there should be a pre-trial review may be set out in earlier directions made by the court of its own initiative or on a case management conference. The court may make the decision to hold a pre-trial review, or may actually fix the pre-trial review at a later stage, in which event it will give the parties at least seven clear days' notice of the hearing: CPR, r. 29.7.

19.8.2 ATTENDANCE

The same rules about a fully informed representative being present apply to pre-trial reviews as apply to case management conferences. However, because the court may well use the hearing to decide a trial timetable it will often be advisable for trial counsel to attend.

19.8.3 PRE-TRIAL REVIEW DIRECTIONS

The court will not readily go behind earlier directions, and will apply the same principles as are applied generally when the parties fail to comply with case management directions: PD 29, para. 9.3.

Perhaps the most important task on a pre-trial review is to determine the timetable for the trial itself. This can lay down time limits for examination and cross-examination of witnesses, and for speeches. Doing this is intended to force advocates to focus their preparation, and to produce better managed trials. Other matters to be dealt with are:

(a) Evidence, particularly expert evidence. At this stage there should have been full disclosure and perhaps also discussions between the experts. It may be possible to make more rigorous directions about which experts really do need to be called at the trial, and which experts (or which parts of the expert evidence) can be taken from the experts' reports.

(b) A time estimate for the trial.

(c) Preparation of trial bundles.

(d) Fixing a trial date or week.

(e) Fixing the place of trial. This will normally be the court where the case is being managed, but it may be transferred depending on the convenience of the parties and the availability of court resources: PD 29, para. 10.1.

19.8.4 AGREED PRE-TRIAL REVIEW DIRECTIONS

The parties are required to seek to agree the directions to be made on the pre-trial review, and may file an agreed order. The court may then make an order in the terms agreed, or make some other order, or reject the proposals and continue with the pre-trial review.

19.9 Variation of Case Management Timetable

The parties may vary the timetable by consent provided doing so does not make it necessary to vary the dates for any case management conference, pre-trial review, return of listing questionnaires or of the trial. Otherwise, any variation is only with the court's permission: CPR, r. 29.5. As in fast track cases (see **18.9**), the courts are very reluctant to vacate trial dates if the only reason is that one of the parties has failed to keep to the directions timetable.

19.10 Trial

This will be considered further in **Chapter 33**.

TWENTY

DISCLOSURE OF DOCUMENTS

20.1 Introduction

20.1.1 WHAT IS DISCLOSURE?

Disclosure is the process whereby a party to an action is obliged to disclose to the other party the existence of all documents which are or have been in his or her control which are material to the issues in the action. Initially, disclosure is given by an exchange of lists of documents, and this should take place after allocation to the fast or multi-track. The other party is then entitled to inspect and take copies of the documents disclosed, except any document which is privileged.

20.1.2 THE IMPORTANCE OF DISCLOSURE

It may appear that the preparation of lists of documents is a routine and tedious step in a claim. However, many cases are lost or won by documents which are disclosed during this process, and effective use of the entitlement to disclosure (at every stage of an action) can be one of the most powerful weapons in the litigant's armoury.

Further, failure to make full or sufficient disclosure may lead to penalties in terms of adjournments and costs; in addition a court may draw adverse inferences as to the credit of the party failing to provide proper disclosure.

The importance of disclosure and the duties of practitioners and their clients with regard to disclosure cannot be over-emphasised. Counsel should remind both solicitors and their lay clients of their duties to ensure disclosure is properly undertaken. Indeed, it is advisable for a solicitor to begin the process of disclosure as early as possible. It is the duty of a solicitor to ensure that material documents are preserved. Further, the obligation upon parties to litigation is a continuing one. Thus, documents coming into existence or which came to the party's notice after the service of a list of documents must also be disclosed: CPR, r. 31.11.

20.2 Disclosure by Lists

The parties to fast track and multi-track proceedings are obliged to disclose to each other all the documents in their control that relate to the proceedings. This obligation covers not only documents that support the party making the list, but extends to documents that adversely affect that party, and which they would prefer to keep secret. Many litigants find it hard to believe that they are obliged to let their opponents see documents of this nature. However, lawyers are under professional duties to advise their clients on the scope of their obligations regarding the disclosure of documents, and cannot continue acting for clients who refuse to comply. As we saw in **Chapter 17**, the same does not apply in small claims track cases, where the obligation is simply to disclose the documents each party intends to rely upon.

Disclosure will usually be made by serving lists of documents (see the example in **Figure 20.1**). As the name suggests, this is a document simply listing the documents that a party has relating to the case. A list must identify the documents in a convenient order and as concisely as possible. It must indicate which documents are said to be privileged (see **20.5** below), and which documents are no longer available and what has happened to them. Further, the list must contain a disclosure statement (see **20.4.5** below) unless this has been dispensed with (by the court or by agreement in writing between the parties).

However, the court may make directions requiring disclosure but dispensing with lists, or for disclosure to take place in stages, and the parties may agree to disclosure taking place in a similar informal, or staged, manner. For example, CPR, r. 31.10(8) provides:

> *The parties may agree in writing—*
> (a) *to disclose documents without making a list; and*
> (b) *to disclose documents without the disclosing party making a disclosure statement.*

20.3 Stage when Disclosure Takes Place

Generally, directions made at the allocation stage or at a case management conference will include provision for disclosure and inspection of documents. The direction will state whether lists should be provided, and whether a disclosure statement is required (see below). It will also give a calendar date for the last day for compliance. Allocation takes place within a few weeks of the filing of defences, and disclosure is normally ordered for a few weeks thereafter. The result is that disclosure is often required about two months after the defence is filed.

With the increasing use of pre-action protocols there will be increasing numbers of cases where disclosure will effectively take place before proceedings are issued. This is because proposed defendants who deny liability are required to provide copies of a wide range of documents with their letter denying liability, and proposed claimants must likewise provide a wide range of documents to support their damages claims. Consequently, a great proportion of the documents that might be disclosed during proceedings will be disclosed beforehand. If full disclosure has taken place in this way, the court should be informed with the allocation questionnaires so the directions made on allocation reflect the correct position.

20.4 Documents Required to be Disclosed

The meaning of 'documents' is not restricted to paper writings, but extends to anything upon which evidence or information is recorded: CPR, r. 31.4. Thus, tape recordings (whether audio or video) and computer disks are disclosable.

A computer 'database' (e.g. the hard disk) is, in so far as it contains information capable of being retrieved and converted into readable form, a 'document'.

20.4.1 DOCUMENTS IN A PARTY'S CONTROL

Disclosure must be made of documents which are, or have been, in a party's control. 'Control' is defined as covering documents which are or have been in a party's physical possession, and also where a party had a right to possession or to inspect or take copies: CPR, r. 31.8.

For example, a bailee or agent has physical possession of documents entrusted to him or her on behalf of the owner. An employer or principal has a right to possession of documents in the hands of an employee in the course of the employee's employment or an agent in the course of the agency. It is a question of fact whether the documents of a subsidiary are within the power of its parent company.

Documents to be disclosed are not limited to those which are within the jurisdiction (i.e. England and Wales). If a material document outside the jurisdiction is in a party's power, it must be disclosed (however, this rule does not apply to *Norwich Pharmacal* actions (**21.2**): *Mackinnon* v *Donaldson Lufkin* [1986] Ch 482).

20.4.2 STANDARD DISCLOSURE

An order to give disclosure is an order to give standard disclosure unless the court directs otherwise: CPR, r. 31.5. The court may dispense with or limit standard disclosure. Further, the parties may agree in writing to dispense with or to limit standard disclosure. The nature of the documents that must be disclosed under standard disclosure is described by CPR, r. 31.6, which provides:

> *Standard disclosure requires a party to disclose only—*
> (a) *the documents on which he relies; and*
> (b) *the documents which—*
>   (i)   *adversely affect his own case;*
>   (ii)   *adversely affect another party's case; or*
>   (iii) *support another party's case; and*
> (c) *the documents which he is required to disclose by a relevant practice direction.*

In addition to disclosing documents relied upon, it can be seen that adverse documents must also be disclosed. There is a further obligation to disclose the documents which may be specified by a relevant Practice Direction. At the moment this does not take us much further, because although it is intended that an Annex to PD 31 will be published setting out the types of documents which must always be disclosed under an order for standard disclosure, the Annex has yet to be published. In the fulness of time the Annex to PD 31 will require standard disclosure of the types of documents listed in the existing pre-action protocols, and no doubt others as well as the protocols and rules are developed.

Under the old, pre-1999, system discovery had to be given of documents falling into four categories, as explained by Brett LJ in *Compagnie Financiere* v *Peruvian Guano Co.* (1882) 11 QBD 55. These were:

(a)   documents that would be evidence upon any issue in the case;

(b)   documents that would advance the case of the party seeking discovery;

(c)   documents that would damage the case of the party giving discovery; and

(d)   documents which could fairly lead to a train of inquiry which might have either of the consequences in (b) or (c).

Standard disclosure in accordance with CPR, r. 31.6, is narrower than the old test in that it does not include train of inquiry documents.

20.4.3 EXAMPLES OF DISCLOSABLE DOCUMENTS

(a)   In an action concerning the satisfactory quality or fitness for purpose of a set of garage doors supplied by Closs Ltd, which Closs Ltd attempted to repair following their supply, the following documents, among others, would be required to be disclosed:

   (i)   All notes and plans relating to the construction of the doors.

   (ii)   All notes and reports relating to the repair of the doors.

   (iii) All communications, including notes and plans, between Closs Ltd and its sub-contractors or any independent surveyor.

(b) In an action for misrepresentation by Zipp Ltd, following its purchase of a business together with goodwill from Shady Ltd on the basis that the annual turnover was misrepresented, the following documents, amongst others, would be required to be disclosed:

(i) The past accounts of Shady Ltd for the business.

(ii) Accountant's or other reports prepared for Shady Ltd before the sale, projecting future growth.

(c) In a personal injuries action where an issue at trial would be the financial loss resulting from the claimant's injury, the claimant may be required to disclose all his past hospital records and general practitioner's notes: *Dunn v British Coal Corporation, The Times*, 5 March 1993, CA. Such documents are relevant as the level of damages may be affected by any pre-existing injury to the site of the injury complained of in the action, or by some wholly unrelated condition which might supervene to affect the claimant's earning capacity before normal retirement. Such documents are in the claimant's control by virtue of the Access to Health Records Act 1990 (see **21.3.6**) or by a simple consent to their release. However, there may be a question whether the requirement to give disclosure of this nature infringes Article 8(1) of the European Convention on Human Rights.

20.4.4 DUTY TO SEARCH

When giving standard disclosure, a party is required to make a reasonable search for documents falling within the meaning of standard disclosure. The factors relevant in deciding the reasonableness of a search include:

(a) the number of documents involved;

(b) the nature and complexity of the proceedings;

(c) the ease and expense of retrieval of any particular document; and

(d) the significance of any document which is likely to be located during the search.

The CPR, r. 31.7, provides:

(1) When giving standard disclosure, a party is required to make a reasonable search for documents falling within r. 31.6(b) or (c).
(2) The factors relevant in deciding the reasonableness of a search include the following—
(a) the number of documents involved;
(b) the nature and complexity of the proceedings;
(c) the ease and expense of retrieval of any particular document; and
(d) the significance of any document which is likely to be located during the search.
(3) Where a party has not searched for a category or class of document on the grounds that to do so would be unreasonable, he must state this in his disclosure statement and identify the category or class of document.

20.4.5 DISCLOSURE STATEMENT

A list of documents must contain a 'disclosure statement' setting out the extent of the search that has been made and certifying the party understands the duty to disclose and that to the best of the disclosing party's knowledge the duty has been carried out. Where a party has not searched for a category or class of document on the grounds that to do so would be unreasonable, this must be stated in the disclosure statement and the categories or classes of document not searched for must be identified. An example of a disclosure statement can be seen in **Figure 20.1**. Making a false disclosure statement, without an honest belief in its truth, may be punished as a contempt of court: CPR, r. 31.23.

20.4.6   THE DUTY OF THE SOLICITOR TO ENSURE FULL DISCOSURE IS MADE

It is the duty of a solicitor to ensure that the client does provide full disclosure as required by the rules. The duty is an active one. The client must be advised as to the requirements of disclosure and the solicitor must ensure (so far as possible) that the originals of all disclosable documents are preserved and made available for disclosure to the other side.

20.5   Privilege

Some classes of documents, although they must be disclosed (i.e. included in the list of documents), are nevertheless privileged from production and inspection (for further reading see **Evidence Manual**).

There are three main categories of privileged documents:

(a)   documents protected by legal professional privilege;

(b)   documents tending to criminate or expose to forfeiture the party who would disclose them; and

(c)   documents protected on the grounds of public policy.

20.5.1   LEGAL PROFESSIONAL PRIVILEGE

This category may be divided into two classes, namely:

(a)   Those that are privileged whether or not litigation was contemplated or pending.

(b)   Those that are privileged only if litigation was contemplated or pending when they were made or when they came into existence.

20.5.1.1   Privilege although no litigation pending

Communications between a party and his or her solicitors are privileged from production, provided that they are confidential and written to or by the solicitor in a professional capacity and for the purpose of getting legal advice or assistance for the client, but not otherwise. Legal advice is not confined to telling the client the law, but includes advice about what should prudently and sensibly be done in the relevant legal context.

However, the range of assistance given by solicitors, and the range of activities carried out by solicitors, has greatly broadened in recent times, e.g. many solicitors provide investment advice to clients. Although the scope of legal professional privilege has to be kept within reasonable bounds, advice from a solicitor on the commercial wisdom of entering into a particular transaction may be privileged: *Nederlande Reassurantie Groep Holding NV* v *Bacon & Woodrow* [1995] 1 All ER 976.

The same privilege also attaches to communications with a solicitor in the service of a party (e.g. a solicitor in a legal department of a commercial enterprise or government department), provided that such communication relates to legal, as distinct from administrative, matters.

Instructions and briefs to counsel, and counsel's opinions, drafts and notes are also privileged. However, counsel's indorsement on a brief of the result of a trial or the order made is not.

20.5.1.2   Privilege only when litigation is contemplated or pending

This category also falls to be considered in two parts.

Communications between a party's solicitor and a third party   Such communications, which come into existence after litigation is contemplated or commenced and are made with a view to such litigation, either for the purpose of obtaining or giving advice in regard to it, or of obtaining or collecting evidence which may be used in it, are privileged. The document in respect of which privilege is claimed must have come into existence at a time when litigation was contemplated or pending. Thus, it is not possible to attach privilege to enclosures to a letter to a solicitor simply because they were sent under cover of a letter which itself may be privileged.

Examples of documents which fall into this category and are privileged include:

(a)   Witness statements obtained by a solicitor for the purpose of a contemplated or current action.

(b)   Expert's reports, e.g. a surveyor's report, obtained by a solicitor for the purpose of a contemplated or current action.

Communications between the party personally and a third party   It is this category which presents most difficulties in practice. The general principle is that such documents are privileged if, and only if, the *dominant purpose* for which the document was prepared was for submission to a legal adviser in view of contemplated or pending litigation (see *Waugh* v *BRB* [1980] AC 521). Thus, to ascertain whether a document in this category is protected by privilege, the issues which fall to be considered are whether:

(a)   at the time when the document came into existence litigation was contemplated or pending; and

(b)   the dominant purpose for which the document was prepared was for its submission to a legal adviser in view of the litigation.

As to (a), the Court of Appeal (*Re Highgrade Traders Ltd* [1984] BCLC 151, CA; *Guinness Peat Properties Ltd* v *Fitzroy Robinson Partnership* [1987] 1 WLR 1027, CA) has held that, if litigation is *reasonably in prospect*, documents brought into existence for the purpose of enabling solicitors to advise whether a claim shall be made or resisted are protected by privilege, whether or not a decision to instruct solicitors has been made at that time, provided, of course, that such purpose is the dominant purpose of their creation.

As to (b), problems often arise where the document was prepared for a number of purposes. For example, in the case of an accident, the preparation of an accident report may be for the purpose of the avoidance of similar accidents in the future, as much as to determine blame in the individual case.

The dominant purpose of a document is not necessarily determined by reference to the intentions of its actual author. For example;

(a)   Where a report has been prepared by an employee at the request of his employer, the dominant purpose will be ascertained by looking at the intention of the *employer* or the person requesting the report.

(b)   Similarly, where a report has been prepared by an independent expert at the request of a potential party to an action, the dominant purpose will again be determined by looking at the intention of the party, and not the expert.

(c)   Also, where a document has been prepared at the request of insurers, the test will be the intention of the insurers at the time that the document was made.

In any event, the test is: What was the dominant purpose at the time when the document came into existence? The fact that the document may *subsequently* have been used by solicitors in the conduct of the litigation is irrelevant if the *original* purpose was different. The question of the dominant purpose is a matter of fact to be decided by the court in each particular case.

20.5.1.3 Extension to others providing legal services
The Courts and Legal Services Act 1990, s. 63, extends legal professional privilege to communications with persons other than barristers and solicitors who are authorised to provide advocacy, litigation, conveyancing and probate services.

20.5.1.4 Loss of legal professional privilege by reason of fraud
A party is not entitled to assert legal professional privilege as a ground for refusing to disclose communications which have been made in furtherance of a fraudulent or illegal design. A party seeking disclosure of such communications should establish a strong *prima facie* case of fraud. However the court will be very slow to deprive a party of the important protection of legal professional privilege on an interim application and will judge each case on its facts, striking a balance between the important considerations on which legal professional privilege is founded and the gravity of the charge of fraud that is made.

Communications in furtherance of fraud are not protected by legal professional privilege regardless of whether the claimant's case is founded on that particular fraud.

The privilege was lost on this ground in a case where a search order was obtained using information which had been gathered in breach of the Data Protection Act 1984: *Dubai Aluminium Co. Ltd* v *Al Alawi* [1999] 1 WLR 1964.

20.5.2 DOCUMENTS TENDING TO CRIMINATE OR EXPOSE TO A PENALTY

A party is entitled to claim privilege in respect of documents which may tend to criminate him or her (i.e. presents a risk of criminal prosecution or exposure to a penalty). It has been held that subsequent committal proceedings for contempt of court are penal for this purpose (*Memory Corporation plc* v *Sidhu*, *The Times*, 3 December 1999), but disqualification proceedings under the Company Directors Disqualification Act 1986 are regulatory rather than penal (*In re Westminster Property Management Ltd*, *The Times* 19 January 2000). The rule applies only to criminal liability or penal proceedings in the UK, and not to penal proceedings abroad. However, liability to a penalty under EC legislation forming part of the law in the UK by virtue of the European Communities Act 1972 is a penalty under the law of the UK.

By SCA 1981, s. 72, privilege in respect of compliance with orders for disclosure or the answering of questions on the grounds of self-incrimination relating to infringements of intellectual property rights has been withdrawn. The section applies to proceedings in respect of the infringement of rights pertaining to intellectual property (e.g. patent and copyright) and passing-off. This provision has particular relevance to the operation and effect of search orders (see **16.5.4**).

20.5.3 PROTECTION ON THE GROUNDS OF PUBLIC POLICY

Strictly this is not a head of privilege at all, and is often referred to as 'public interest immunity'. The rule is that if disclosure of a document would be injurious to the public interest it must be withheld. Thus, for example, diplomatic despatches, Cabinet minutes and documents dealing with matters of national defence are normally immune from disclosure. Unlike claims to privilege properly so-called, if disclosure would be injurious to the public interest there is no question of waiver of the protection, and if immunity is not raised by a party, it must be insisted on by the judge.

20.5.3.1 The test
The test is whether the production of a document would be injurious to the public interest or, in other words, whether the withholding of a document is necessary for the proper functioning of the public service. The fact that a document is a 'State Document'

or marked 'confidential', or that disclosure might invoke public discussion or criticism of a government department is not sufficient. The court should balance the public interest in concealment against the public interest that the administration of justice should not be frustrated.

20.5.3.2 The principles
The principles defining this ground of privilege and the conditions of its exercise are found in the House of Lords decisions *Burmah Oil Co. Ltd* v *Governor of the Bank of England* [1980] AC 1090 and *Conway* v *Rimmer* [1968] AC 910.

20.5.3.3 Procedure
Under CPR, r. 31.19(1), a person (who need not be a party) may apply, without notice, for an order permitting him to withhold disclosure of a document on the ground that disclosure would damage the public interest. Often the person most likely to apply will be the Secretary of State for the government department asserting public interest immunity in the document. By r. 31.19(2), unless the court otherwise orders, any order made under this rule must not be served on any other person, and must not be open to inspection by any other person. Claims for protection may alternatively be made in the list of documents served by a party (r. 31.19(4)), or may be insisted upon by the court of its own initiative.

It is questionable whether these procedures, particularly the procedure under CPR, r. 31.19(1), comply with the European Convention on Human Rights, Article 6(1). In *Rowe and Davis* v *United Kingdom, The Times*, 1 March 2000, the European Court of Human Rights considered the procedural aspects of withholding evidence in criminal trials on the grounds of public interest. It was decided that withholding evidence on the grounds of public interest had to comply with the requirements of adversarial proceedings; equality of arms; and must incorporate safeguards to protect the interests of the accused. It was found that to comply with Article 6(1) the accused had to be given information about the withheld information appropriate to the category of the evidence involved, and that it was for the trial judge (rather than a court on appeal) to decide whether the evidence should be withheld. The procedures under r. 31.19 allow orders to be made without giving any information to the parties (or to just one side if one of the parties is the government department seeking to withhold disclosure), and for decisions to be made by judges other than the trial judge, which would seem to fall short of the safeguards contemplated by the Convention. In criminal trials there are the additional minimum rights given by Article 6(3), which do not apply to civil cases, but this difference is unlikely to have a substantial effect on the implications of the decision in civil cases.

20.5.4 WAIVER OF PRIVILEGE

With the exception of public interest immunity, the privilege in all cases is that of the client and not the legal adviser. Privilege is not waived by mere reference to the document in a statement of case or in written evidence. Waiver as to one or some of several documents does not amount to waiver of the others. If part of a document is put in evidence or read in court, privilege will be waived for the whole document, unless the remaining part deals with an entirely different subject matter.

Further, if a party relies upon a document, in respect of which he could have claimed privilege in an interim application, he or she will be taken to have waived privilege in respect of that document altogether.

Where a party mistakenly includes privileged documents in the first part of his or her list, the mistake may be rectified prior to inspection by notifying the other party and stating the grounds of the objection to producing them. Where a party inadvertently allows a privileged document to be inspected (see **20.6** below), the party who has inspected the document may use it or its contents only with the permission of the court (CPR, r. 31.20).

A former client who sues its solicitors impliedly waives its privilege in all documents relevant to the suit to the extent necessary to enable the court to adjudicate the dispute fully and fairly: *Lillicrap* v *Nalder & Son (a firm)* [1993] 1 WLR 94, CA. Thus if the defendant's solicitor alleges that even if there was negligence there was no causation, because the claimant never listened to the solicitor's advice, the implied waiver of privilege will extend to other transactions undertaken by the solicitor for the claimant and not just the transaction forming the basis of the action. However, there are limits on the implied waiver of privilege in solicitors' negligence claims. In *Paragon Finance plc* v *Freshfields* [1999] 1 WLR 1183, CA, Freshfields had acted for the finance company in relation to a number of mortgage transactions. The finance company made a number of claims against insurance policies entered into in relation to the mortgages, which the insurer disputed. The finance company then retained a second firm of solicitors to pursue outstanding insurance claims, and later sued Freshfields for professional negligence. A question arose as to whether the finance company had, by suing Freshfields, impliedly waived its privilege in respect of the work done by the second firm in pursuing the insurance claims. It was held that by suing Freshfields the finance company had only put its relationship with that firm into the public domain, and had not done so in respect of the work done by the second firm, and so had not waived its privilege in respect of the work done by the second firm.

20.5.5 WITHOUT PREJUDICE COMMUNICATIONS

The purpose of 'without prejudice' privilege is to enable the parties to negotiate, without risk of their proposals being used against them if negotiations fail.

Documents which form part of 'without prejudice' negotiations between the parties, whether litigation was current or not, are privileged from production. *Depending on the circumstances this may also be the case even if the words 'without prejudice' or the equivalent were not used.* However, conversely, the words 'without prejudice' are not necessarily conclusive and do not automatically render the document privileged. If privilege is claimed, but challenged, the court has to examine the documents and decide whether they are truly without prejudice in nature.

However, as a rule of good practice, if possible, a judge (or Master) other than the trial judge should decide such a dispute. If a challenge to privilege is raised before trial this should not present difficulty. However, if a challenge to privilege is raised during a trial in the County Court, it is possible for the trial judge to adjourn that particular question to the District Judge.

'Without prejudice' material will be admissible upon the issue as to whether or not the negotiations resulted in an agreed settlement. 'Without prejudice' material in applications to dismiss for want of prosecution may also be used to explain apparent delays or to provide material about the 'innocent' party's conduct: *Family Housing Association (Manchester) Ltd* v *Michael Hyde and Partners* [1993] 1 WLR 354, CA.

The House of Lords have confirmed that a document, once privileged by reason it was 'without prejudice' will always be privileged. Thus an admission made in 'without prejudice' communications by one party will not be admissible in other proceedings against that party: *Rush & Tompkins Ltd* v *Greater London Council* [1989] AC 1280.

Not only are without prejudice documents privileged from use in the instant proceedings, they should not be used to found subsequent proceedings. If they are, the subsequent proceedings will be struck out as an abuse of process, unless the claimant in the subsequent proceedings can show that the statements relied upon were made improperly, or some other public interest reason in favour of their subsequent use: *Unilever plc* v *The Proctor & Gamble Co.* [1999] 1 WLR 1630.

20.5.6 CONFIDENTIAL MATERIAL

Documents which are regarded as confidential (and also perhaps damaging to a party's case) are often, but incorrectly, thought to be privileged. Unless a document falls within one of the above categories of privilege it is not protected by privilege, whether the document is confidential in nature or damaging to the party giving disclosure, and must therefore be disclosed. Thus, a litigant is not entitled to claim privilege in respect of a document merely by reason that it was supplied in confidence by a third party.

However, protection (not strictly by way of privilege) will be given by the court in certain cases of confidentiality. Where a party claims secrecy in relevant material (e.g. a defendant in a patent infringement action who claims that a process is secret), the governing principle is that the court should order a controlled measure of disclosure. In each case the court must decide what measure of disclosure is appropriate, to whom it should be made, and upon what terms.

20.5.7 SECONDARY EVIDENCE

A party able to rely on privilege is entitled to refuse to produce a privileged document. Privilege does not operate (apart from public interest immunity) so as to prohibit the other side from proving the facts stated in the privileged material by other means.

20.5.8 LISTING PRIVILEGED DOCUMENTS

Documents in respect of which privilege is claimed must also be contained in the list. The description to be given in the list of the document is not for the purpose of enabling the other party to learn the contents of the document but to test the claim for privilege. Accordingly, a very concise description is sufficient.

However, the party claiming privilege in respect of any document must include in the list a sufficient statement of the grounds of the privilege claimed. For example:

(a) 'Correspondence between the defendant and his solicitors for the purpose of obtaining legal advice.'

(b) 'Documents which came into existence and were made by AB Ltd [being a subsidiary of the defendant], its officers or servants, after this litigation was in contemplation and in view of such litigation for the purpose of obtaining for and furnishing to the solicitors of the defendant evidence and other information for the use of those solicitors to enable them to advise the defendant in the conduct of the defence of this action.'

20.6 Inspection

20.6.1 ENTITLEMENT TO INSPECT DOCUMENTS

A party who has served a list of documents must allow the other parties, including co-defendants, to inspect the documents referred to in the list (other than any to which there is an objection to production, i.e. those in respect of which privilege is claimed). A party wishing to inspect must send a written notice to that effect to the other side, and the other side must give their permission within the next seven days: CPR, r. 31.15(a), (b).

Normally, documents must be disclosed for inspection in their entirety, but there is scope for blanking out irrelevant passages: *GE Capital Corporate Finance Group Ltd v Bankers Trust Co.* [1995] 1 WLR 172, CA.

The court has the power to give directions as to whether the inspection of documents should be by electronic means (e.g. by CD Rom) or hard copy: see *Grupo Torras SA v Al Sabah, The Times*, 13 October 1997.

20.6.2 ENTITLEMENT TO COPIES OF DOCUMENTS

By CPR, r. 31.15(c), a party who is entitled to inspection may serve notice on the other party requiring the supply of copies of the documents upon undertaking to pay reasonable copying charges.

20.7 Orders for Disclosure

20.7.1 PARTY FAILING COMPLY WITH DISCLOSURE DIRECTION

Where a party fails to give disclosure as required by a disclosure direction, an application can be made for an order compelling this to be done. Before issuing the application the innocent party should write to the defaulting party warning that an application will be issued if the default is not remedied. The court is likely to consider making an 'unless' order with the effect that some sanction, such as striking out the claim or Defence, will take effect if disclosure is not given within a limited period of time.

20.7.2 SPECIFIC DISCLOSURE

20.7.2.1 Applying for specific disclosure

An application for specific disclosure may be used to challenge the sufficiency of a list of documents. It also has a wider use, and such an application may be made at any stage of an action, for example:

(a) In interim injunctions (particularly in freezing injunctions and search orders), an order for specific disclosure is a powerful weapon indeed, as at the time of seeking a freezing order, the claimant may apply for an order that the defendant disclose the whereabouts of any assets and give disclosure of material documents: see *A v C* [1980] 2 All ER 347; *Bankers Trust v Shapira* [1980] 1 WLR 1274.

(b) Specific disclosure may be ordered against a claimant before service of the defence where it would assist the defendant to plead a full defence rather than an initial bare denial.

The CPR, r. 31.12, provides:

> *(1) The court may make an order for specific disclosure or specific inspection.*
> *(2) An order for specific disclosure is an order that a party must do one or more of the following things—*
> *(a) disclose documents or classes of documents specified in the order;*
> *(b) carry out a search to the extent stated in the order;*
> *(c) disclose any documents located as a result of that search.*
> *(3) An order for specific inspection is an order that a party permit inspection of a document referred to in rule 31.3(2).*

If it is established that the other side have not given standard disclosure the order will usually be made (PD 31, para. 5.4). This procedure may also be used if a party wants disclosure of 'train of inquiry' documents (see *Peruvian Guano*), but on such an application the court will be particularly astute to apply the overriding objective (PD 31, para. 5.4).

20.7.2.2 Making the application

An application for specific disclosure must specify the order asked for and be supported by evidence stating that, in the belief of the deponent, the other party has or has had certain specific documents relating to a matter in question.

The evidence must show:

(a) that such documents are or were in the control of the other party; and

(b) that the specified documents are disclosable under standard disclosure, or should otherwise be disclosed in accordance with the overriding objective.

20.7.2.3 At trial

During the course of a trial, in particular as a result of cross-examination, the existence of previously undisclosed material documents is often revealed. In such a case an application for specific disclosure of the documents may be made to the judge.

20.8 Inspection of Documents Referred To

By CPR, r. 31.14, a party may at any time serve on another, whose statements of case, witness statements, affidavits or expert's reports make reference to any document, a notice requiring the other party to produce that document for inspection. The other party must permit inspection within seven days. If objection is taken to the production of any document, the notice must specify the document and state the grounds of the objection.

The documents need not be identified or particularly described in the statement of case or affidavit, etc.; it is sufficient that they are referred to generally. Thus, an incautious statement in an affidavit referring to 'documents relevant to this matter that I have seen' is likely to leave a party vulnerable to an early request for production of those documents.

20.9 Order for Inspection

If a party has difficulty in obtaining inspection of documents referred to in the other side's list of documents or any statement of case or written evidence an application can be made to the court for an order for specific inspection: CPR, r. 31.12. The application must be supported by evidence.

20.10 Misuse of Material Obtained on Disclosure

20.10.1 LIMITATION ON THE USE OF DOCUMENTS DISCLOSED

The fact that a party may be required to give disclosure and inspection of highly confidential and potentially damaging material is somewhat mitigated by the limited use which the other party may make of documents disclosed in the course of proceedings.

A party given disclosure may use the documents disclosed only for purposes connected with the proper conduct of that action: CPR, r. 31.22(1). Any misuse of the documents may be restrained by injunction or punished as a contempt of court or by striking out subsequent proceedings based on documents disclosed in the course of earlier proceedings (see *Riddick* v *Thames Board Mills Ltd* [1977] QB 881). Permission to use the materials disclosed may be sought, see **16.5.2**.

The protection against subsequent use of disclosed documents is not, however, absolute. The CPR, r. 31.22, provides:

> *(1)   A party to whom a document has been disclosed may use the document only for the purpose of the proceedings in which it is disclosed except where—*
> *(a)   the document has been read to or by the court, or referred to, at a hearing which has been held in public;*
> *(b)   the court gives permission; or*
> *(c)   the party who disclosed the document and the person to whom the document belongs agree.*
> *(2)   The court may make an order restricting or prohibiting the use of a document which has been disclosed, even where the document has been read to or by the court, or referred to, at a hearing which has been held in public.*
> *(3)   An application for such an order may be made—*

(a)   by a party; or
(b)   by any person to whom the document belongs.

The lifting on the ban against use outside the scope of the present proceedings after documents have been used in open court stems from a compromise reached arising from the proceedings in *Home Office* v *Harman* [1983] 1 AC 280, HL. It will be noticed from r. 31.22(2) that after use at trial, the court may reimpose the restrictions on subsequent use, and by r. 31.22(3)(a) such an application may be made 'by a party'. That expression was interpreted in *Singh* v *Christie*, *The Times*, 11 November 1993, as meaning a party to the original proceedings in which the documents were disclosed, and not the parties to any subsequent proceedings in which the documents may be used. There is no obvious reason why this interpretation should not be applied to the rule as it appears in the Civil Procedure Rules 1998.

Figure 20.1   Specimen list of documents

List of documents: standard disclosure

In the	High Court of Justice Queen`s Bench Division Manchester District Registry

Notes:
- The rules relating to standard disclosure are contained in Part 31 of the Civil Procedure Rules.
- Documents to be included under standard disclosure are contained in Rule 31.6
- A document has or will have been in your control if you have or have had possession, or a right of possession, of it **or** a right to inspect or take copies of it.

Claim No.	
Claimant (including ref)	Shilton Machine Tools Limited
Defendant (including ref)	Banks Plastic Mouldings Limited
Date	

Disclosure Statement

I state that I have carried out a reasonable and proportionate search to locate all the documents which I am required to disclose under the order made by the court on *(insert date)* 13th November

(I did not search for documents -

1.   pre-dating

2.   located elsewhere than
     my office and that of my solicitor
3.   in categories other than
     the contractual documents and correspondence relating to the sale of teh goods   )

I certify that I understand the duty of disclosure and to the best of my knowledge I have carried out that duty. I further certify that the list of documents set out in or attached to this form, is a complete list of all documents which are or have been in my control and which I am obliged under the order to disclose.

I understand that I must inform the court and the other parties immediately if any further document required to be disclosed by Rule 31.6 comes into my control at any time before the conclusion of the case.

(I have not permitted inspection of documents within the category or class of documents (as set out below) required to be disclosed under Rule 31(6)(b)or (c) on the grounds that to do so would be disproportionate to the issues in the case.)

N/A

Signed		**Date**	

(Claimant)(Defendant)('s litigation friend)

Position or office held *(if signing on behalf of firm or company)*
Please state why you are the appropriate person to make the disclosure statement.

List of documents:
continued overleaf

N265 - w3 standard disclosure (4.99)

Printed on behalf of The Court Service

List and number here, in a convenient order, the documents (or bundles of documents if of the same nature, e.g. invoices) in your control, which you do not object to being inspected. Give a short description of each document or bundle so that it can be identified, and say if it is kept elsewhere i.e. with a bank or solicitor

I have control of the documents numbered and listed here. I do not object to you inspecting them/producing copies.

1. Letters from Defendants to Claimants
2. Copy letter from Claimants to Defendants
3. Bundle of specifications and advertising literature for Claimants` plastic mouldings machines
4. Purchase order, ref. 8603678
5. Copy delivery note, ref XA07811
6. Copy invoice, ref ST9922
7. Copy letters from Claimants` solicitiors to Defendants` solicitors
8. Letters from Defendants` solicitors to Claimants` solicitors
9. Statements of case, questionnaires and orders common to both parties

---

List and number here, as above, the documents in your control which you object to being inspected. (Rule 31.19)

I have control of the documents numbered and listed here, but I object to you inspecting them:

1. Communications between the Claimants and their solicitor in his professional capacity for the purpose of obtaining or giving legal advice.
2. Instructions to, opinions of and statements of case settled by Counsel in this claim.
3. Communications between the Claimants` officers, servants or agents when litigation was pending for the purpose of obtaining information or evidence for use in this claim.

Say what your objections are

I object to you inspecting these documents because:

They are protected from inspection by legal professional privilege.

List and number here, the documents you once had in your control, but which you no longer have. For each document listed, say when it was last in your control and where it is now.

I have had the documents numbered and listed below, but they are no longer in my control.

The original copies of the copy documents numbered 2, 5, 6 and 7 in the first section of this list.

TWENTY ONE

SPECIAL DISCLOSURE ORDERS

21.1 Introduction

This chapter deals with a number of special rules, most of comparatively recent origin, that supplement the general rules governing disclosure. Search orders, which are a special form of disclosure, have already been dealt with in **Chapter 16**. Disclosure of documents has been considered in **Chapter 20**, and requests for further information are discussed at **5.7** and **Chapter 22**.

21.2 *Norwich Pharmacal* Orders

21.2.1 THE PRINCIPLE

A *Norwich Pharmacal* order is a procedure whereby it is possible to find out the identity of an alleged wrongdoer.

The classic statement of the principle is by Lord Reid in *Norwich Pharmacal Co. v Customs and Excise Commissioners* [1974] AC 133, 175, HL:

> [The authorities] seem to me to point to a very reasonable principle that if through no fault of his own a person gets mixed up in the tortious acts of others so as to facilitate their wrongdoing he may incur no personal liability but he comes under a duty to assist the person who has been wronged by giving him full information and disclosing the identity of the wrongdoers. I do not think that it matters whether he became so mixed up by voluntary action on his part or because it was his duty to do what he did. It may be that if this causes him expense the person seeking the information ought to reimburse him. But justice requires that he should co-operate in righting the wrong if he unwittingly facilitated its perpetration.

The facts were that Norwich owned the patent to a chemical used for immunising poultry. Statistics published by the Commissioners revealed that the number of importations of the chemical was higher than those brought in by Norwich. Norwich were unable to take direct steps to protect their patent, so they brought proceedings against the Commissioners to compel them to disclose the identities of the other importers. It was held that although Norwich had no substantive cause of action against the Commissioners, the Commissioners had facilitated the wrongdoing of the importers and were ordered to disclose their identities.

The key factor, therefore, is that the person against whom the order is sought has facilitated the wrongdoing.

In *P v T Ltd* [1997] 4 All ER 200 the court extended the principle by holding that an order could be obtained for disclosure to assist a prospective claimant to obtain the information and documents necessary to bring a possible action in tort even though it could not be ascertained (without the information sought by the order) whether the person to be identified had actually committed a tort against the prospective claimant.

The principle was further extended by *Murphy* v *Murphy* [1999] 1 WLR 282, where an order was made against a settlor to disclose to a potential beneficiary the names and addresses of the trustees under a settlement, to enable the potential beneficiary to communicate with the trustees with a view to being considered for the distribution of trust property held on discretionary trusts. Obviously, the trustees were not accused of any wrongdoing.

Norwich Pharmacal orders are principally used as a procedure to identify an alleged wrongdoer. In *Mercantile Group (Europe) AG* v *Aiyela* [1994] QB 366, CA, however, the order related to more extensive information. In that case judgment was entered against the defendant, and a *Mareva* (freezing) injunction was subsequently granted in aid of execution. There was *prima facie* evidence that the defendant's wife was mixed up in the defendant's attempts to frustrate the judgment, and she was ordered, under the *Norwich Pharmacal* principle, to disclose financial information about herself and the defendant.

21.2.2   MERE WITNESS RULE

Someone who observes the facts giving rise to a cause of action between two other people can be called as a witness at trial. A witness can be compelled to attend to give oral evidence or to produce documents by serving a witness summons (**33.12.6**). But, until trial, the witness can refuse to answer questions and to disclose documents. Subject to the procedure discussed at **21.4** below, a witness must not be joined as a party for the sole purpose of obtaining disclosure.

In *Norwich Pharmacal* situations one of the most difficult questions is as to whether the respondent is a mere witness or is someone who has got mixed up with and facilitated another's wrongdoing. A case falling on the wrong side of the line was *Ricci* v *Chow* [1987] 1 WLR 1658, CA. The claimant alleged that the journal published by the Seychellois National Movement defamed him. The defendant was the Secretary General of the Movement, but had nothing to do with the printing and publication of the article, and had in no way facilitated its preparation. The fact that he was aware of the identities of the alleged tortfeasors did not justify making a *Norwich Pharmacal* order against him.

21.2.3   DEFENDANT A TORTFEASOR

In *X Ltd* v *Morgan-Grampian (Publishers) Ltd* [1991] 1 AC 1, HL, it was held that where the claimant had a cause of action against the defendant (against whom the claimant sought disclosure of the identity of an unknown tortfeasor) connected with the cause of action against the unknown tortfeasor, the defendant was amenable to the full scope of the court's wide power to order disclosure on notice, irrespective of the *Norwich Pharmacal* jurisdiction. In most such cases this will include disclosure of the identity of the unknown tortfeasor.

Once the identity of the unknown tortfeasor is known they can be made a party to the action against the existing defendant (who is also a tortfeasor) or separate proceedings can be commenced against them.

21.2.4   OF GENERAL APPLICATION

British Steel Corporation v *Granada Television Ltd* [1981] AC 1096, HL, is authority for the proposition that *Norwich Pharmacal* orders are not restricted to any particular categories of cases.

The Contempt of Court Act 1981, s. 10, does, however, provide a statutory privilege against the disclosure of journalist's sources in certain defined circumstances: see *X Ltd* v *Morgan-Grampian (Publishers) Ltd*; *Goodwin* v *United Kingdom* (1996) 22 EHRR 123, and *Camelot Group plc* v *Centaur Communications Ltd* [1998] 2 WLR 379, CA.

21.2.5　REAL INTEREST IN SUING

A *Norwich Pharmacal* order will not be made for the mere gratification of curiosity. The claimant must have a real and unsatisfied claim against the unknown wrongdoer which cannot be brought unless the facilitator reveals the wrongdoer's identity: *British Steel Corporation* v *Granada Television Ltd.* This is best fulfilled if the wrongdoer's name is sought for the purpose of bringing proceedings against him or her. In *British Steel* Lord Wilberforce said he would have been prepared, if necessary, to hold that, given a cause of action, '. . . an intention to seek redress, by court action or otherwise, would be enough'. Other methods of redress could include dismissal or deprivation of pension. This fairly wide approach has been confirmed in *X Ltd* v *Morgan-Grampian (Publishers) Ltd* [1991] 1 AC 1, HL.

21.2.6　REMEDY IS DISCRETIONARY

The remedy (being equitable) is discretionary. Therefore, even if the basic conditions are made out, there may be public interest reasons for refusing relief.

21.2.7　PROCEDURE

The claimant issues a claim form against the facilitator, claiming disclosure of the identity of the wrongdoer. An interim application seeking disclosure of the wrongdoer's identity is then made supported by written evidence. Once the identity of the wrongdoer is disclosed, the proceedings started against the facilitator have achieved their aim and fresh proceedings should be commenced against the wrongdoer.

In *Loose* v *Williamson* [1978] 1 WLR 639, Goulding J held the order may be granted without notice if this is justifiable on the facts. The claimant sighted three fishing boats poaching on his shell fishery. He noted the identification numbers of two of the boats. He sought *Norwich Pharmacal* orders without giving notice against the owners of those two boats for disclosure of the identities of those on board their boats and for the identity of the third boat. The order was made because the claimant would suffer irreparable harm if the fishing continued, whereas the defendants would suffer no harm by disclosing.

21.2.8　COSTS

A claimant will normally be required to pay the legal costs and any other expenses incurred by a blameless defendant in complying with a *Norwich Pharmacal* order. It may be possible to recover such costs and expenses from the wrongdoer if liability is eventually established, provided it was foreseeable that the claimant would need to make a *Norwich Pharmacal* application before bringing the substantive proceedings.

21.3　Pre-action Disclosure

21.3.1　JURISDICTION

Under SCA 1981, s. 33(2) and CCA 1984, s. 52(2), the court has power to make an order for pre-action disclosure against the likely defendant. Such an order can only be made if four conditions are fulfilled:

(a) the applicant appears likely to be a party to subsequent proceedings;

(b) the defendant appears likely to be a party; and

(c) the defendant appears likely to have or to have had relevant documents in his or her possession, custody or power; and

(d) advance disclosure is desirable to dispose of the anticipated proceedings fairly, or to prevent the need to commence proceedings, or to save costs.

21.3.2   WHAT IS MEANT BY 'LIKELY'

In *Dunning* v *Liverpool Hospital Board* [1973] 1 WLR 586, CA, the applicant, who was previously of good health, developed a cough and was admitted to hospital for investigations. After 17 weeks she left hospital in poor health, with impaired memory and difficulty in walking. A consultant who reported on the applicant's medical condition to her solicitors said that his assessment had been considerably hampered by the absence of the applicant's medical notes, which the hospital refused to disclose. On appeal, a majority in the Court of Appeal ruled in favour of disclosure of the notes under what is now s. 33(2). Lord Denning MR said the word 'likely' should be construed: '. . . as meaning "may" or "may well be made" dependent on the outcome of the discovery'. In *Burns* v *Shuttlehurst* [1999] 1 WLR 1449, however, the Court of Appeal preferred the test propounded by James and Stamp LJJ, namely whether the applicant could establish a worthwhile action or a reasonable basis for the intended action.

In *Shaw* v *Vauxhall Motors Ltd* [1974] 1 WLR 1035, CA, Buckley LJ said that s. 33(2) should not '. . . be used to encourage fishing expeditions to enable a prospective plaintiff to discover whether he has in fact got a case at all.' Ormrod LJ said that if a claimant is going to ask the court to exercise its discretion to grant him an order under s. 33(2), it is only fair that he should commit himself by letter or other written evidence '. . . to at least either a description of the accident and how it happened, or a statement that he does not know how it happened.'

21.3.3   PROCEDURE

The procedure for applications under SCA 1981, s. 33(2) and CCA 1984, s. 52(2), is laid down in CPR, r. 31.16, which provides:

> (1)   This rule applies where an application is made to the court under any Act for disclosure before proceedings have started.
> (2)   The application must be supported by evidence.
> (3)   The court may make an order under this rule only where—
>   (a)   the respondent is likely to be a party to subsequent proceedings;
>   (b)   the applicant is also likely to be a party to those proceeding;
>   (c)   if proceedings had started, the respondent's duty by way of standard disclosure, set out in rule 31.6, would extend to the documents or classes of documents of which the applicant seeks disclosure; and
>   (d)   disclosure before proceedings is desirable in order to—
>   (i)   dispose fairly of the anticipated proceedings;
>   (ii)   assist the dispute to be resolved without proceedings; or
>   (iii) save costs.

This means that applications for pre-action disclosure are made by issuing an ordinary application notice supported by evidence in the anticipated substantive proceedings (but before the substantive proceedings are themselves issued).

21.3.4   THE ORDER

If the basic conditions are fulfilled, the court may, not must, order the defendant to disclose the relevant documents and to produce them to the applicant, or to the applicant's legal, medical or professional advisers. Thus, in appropriate cases, the applicant may be precluded from seeing the documents. The order is limited to such documents as the defendant ought to disclose by way of standard disclosure.

The CPR, r. 31.16(4) and (5), provide:

> (4)   An order under this rule must—
>   (a)   specify the documents or the classes of documents which the respondent must disclose; and

> (b)   require him, when making disclosure, to specify any of those documents—
>
> (i)   which are no longer in his control; or
>
> (ii)   in respect of which he claims a right or duty to withhold inspection.
>
> (5)   Such an order may—
>
> (a)   require the respondent to indicate what has happened to any documents which are no longer in his control; and
>
> (b)   specify the time and place for disclosure and inspection.

21.3.5   DIRECTIONS TO COMMENCE SUBSTANTIVE PROCEEDINGS

The CPR, r. 25.2(3), provides that where the court grants an interim remedy before a claim has been commenced, it may give directions requiring a claim to be commenced. A special rule, however, applies to applications for pre-action disclosure, with r. 25.2(4) creating a distinction between s. 33 and s. 52 orders and other types of pre-action orders. Rule 25.2(4) provides that the court need not direct that a claim be commenced where a pre-action disclosure order is made. The reason for the distinction is that pre-action disclosure orders may result in the claimant deciding not to bring substantive proceedings at all, as recognised in *Dunning* v *United Hospitals Board of Governors* [1973] 1 WLR 586, and it would not make sense to require the claimant to bring a substantive claim in such circumstances.

21.3.6   ACCESS TO HEALTH RECORDS

Patients are given a general right of access to their health records by the Access to Health Records Act 1990. Access will not be given:

(a)   Where the record was made before the commencement of the Act (1 November 1991), unless the record was made partly before and after that date, and the post-Act part is not intelligible without the pre-Act notes: s. 5(1)(b), (2).

(b)   Where disclosure is likely to cause serious harm to the patient: s. 5(1)(a).

(c)   Where the patient is a child who does not have sufficient understanding: s. 4.

Where a valid application is made, the holder of the record must allow the patient to inspect it, supply a copy, and provide an explanation of any technical terms used in the notes: s. 3. The holder must comply within either 21 or 40 days, depending on the age of the records. Rules of court may be made providing for applications where it is alleged the holder has not complied with the Act: s. 8.

21.4   Production of Documents Against Non-parties

21.4.1   JURISDICTION

Under SCA 1981, s. 34(2) and CCA 1984, s. 53, the court has power to order a non-party to produce documents before trial. In the absence of this power witnesses could only be required to produce documents in response to a witness summons, which would mean the documents could only be required (in the absence of consent) to be produced at trial.

The SCA 1981, s. 34(2), is similar to s. 33(2), but here the application has to be made after the proceedings are issued, whereas the purpose of s. 33(2) is to decide whether to issue substantive proceedings. Under s. 34(2) the application is made against a witness, whereas under s. 33(2) the application is against a potential defendant.

21.4.2   CONDITIONS

The conditions that must be satisfied are set out in CPR, r. 31.17(3):

The court may make an order under this rule only where—

> *(a) the documents of which disclosure is sought are likely to support the case of the applicant or adversely affect the case of one of the other parties to the proceedings; and*
>
> *(b) disclosure is necessary in order to dispose fairly of the claim or to save costs.*

21.4.3 PROCEDURE

An application for disclosure against a non-party can be made at any time after substantive proceedings have been issued. It is made by application notice, and must be supported by written evidence: CPR, r. 31.17(2).

21.4.4 THE ORDER

The CPR, r. 31.17(4) and (5), provide:

> *(4) An order under this rule must—*
> *(a) specify the documents or the classes of documents which the respondent must disclose; and*
> *(b) require the respondent, when making disclosure, to specify any of those documents—*
> *(i)   which are no longer in his control; or*
> *(ii) in respect of which he claims a right or duty to withhold inspection.*
> *(5) Such an order may—*
> *(a) require the respondent to indicate what has happened to any documents which are no longer in his control; and*
> *(b) specify the time and place for disclosure and inspection.*

21.4.5 JUDICIAL APPROACH

In *O'Sullivan v Herdmans Ltd* [1987] 1 WLR 1047, HL (NI), Lord Mackay LC said that if the conditions under the Northern Ireland equivalent of s. 34 are satisfied the court may refuse the order '. . . if it is of the opinion that the order is unnecessary or oppressive or would not be in the interests of justice or would be injurious to the public interest.' However, generally, '. . . the interests of justice are served by the promotion of settlements and early, complete preparation by both parties for trial.'

Opposing early disclosure under s. 34 when the conditions are satisfied will usually be seen by the courts as an attempt to delay rather than promote the interests of justice.

21.4.6 ACCESS TO HEALTH RECORDS

A possible alternative to an application under s. 34 (or CCA 1984, s. 53) is sometimes to obtain the health records under the Access to Health Records Act 1990.

21.5 Inspection of Property

There are wide powers to order inspection, examination, testing, experimenting on and photographing property which is relevant to proceedings. In contrast to search orders, these powers include in some circumstances jurisdiction to order the respondent to allow the applicant, and the applicant's advisers and experts entry onto the respondent's premises. The rules provide for three separate situations, which are considered below.

21.5.1 BEFORE ISSUE OF PROCEEDINGS

21.5.1.1 Jurisdiction

The SCA 1981, s. 33(1), provides:

> *On the application of any person in accordance with rules of court, the High Court shall, in such circumstances as may be specified in the rules, have power to make an order providing for any one or more of the following matters, that is to say*

(a) the inspection, photographing, preservation, custody and detention of property which appears to the court to be property which may become the subject-matter of subsequent proceedings in the High Court, or as to which any question may arise in any such proceedings; and

(b) the taking of samples of any such property as is mentioned in paragraph (a), and the carrying out of any experiment on or with any such property.

21.5.1.2 Conditions

The only condition that must be fulfilled is that the property may become the subject-matter of subsequent proceedings.

21.5.1.3 Procedure

Pre-action inspection orders are applied for by issuing an ordinary application notice in the anticipated proceedings supported by written evidence, but before those proceedings are issued. The CPR, r. 25.5, provides:

(2) The evidence in support of such an application must show, if practicable by reference to any statement of case prepared in relation to the proceedings or anticipated proceedings, that the property—

(a) is or may become the subject matter of such proceedings; or

(b) is relevant to the issues that will arise in relation to such proceedings.

(3) A copy of the application notice and a copy of the evidence must be served on—

(a) the person against whom the order is sought . . .

Like pre-action disclosure applications (see **21.3.5**), the court will not usually give a direction for commencing the substantive proceedings as the decision to commence will usually turn on the nature of the evidence gathered from the inspection (see CPR, r. 25.2(4)).

21.5.1.4 Relationship between s. 33(1) and s. 33(2)

In *Huddleston* v *Control Risks Information Services Ltd* [1987] 1 WLR 701 the claimants sought an order pursuant to s. 33(1) that the defendant permit the claimants to inspect a study prepared by or on behalf of the defendant on the Anti-Apartheid Movement in a prospectus. The grounds of the application were that the prospectus might become the subject matter of subsequent proceedings, or that a question might arise in such proceedings as to whether it was defamatory of the claimants. Hoffmann J was prepared to accept that a written instrument could be both 'property' within s. 33(1) and a 'document' within s. 33(2). Which it was in a particular case depended on the nature of the question that arose. Section 33(1) is concerned with the physical object itself (e.g. the paper, photograph or computer disk), whereas s. 33(2) is concerned with the message on the instrument. The question raised by the claimants related to the message in the prospectus, so their application was for disclosure, and outside the scope of s. 33(1). Their application could only succeed if the conditions in s. 33(2) were fulfilled.

21.5.2 AFTER ISSUE OF PROCEEDINGS, PROPERTY IN THE POSSESSION OF A PARTY

21.5.2.1 The general rules

In many cases one party will have possession of property which the opponent's expert will need to inspect before an expert opinion can be reached. This problem arises where, for example, a surveyor needs to inspect land in relation to an alleged obstruction of ancient lights, or where an engineer needs to examine and test a machine after a factory accident, or where it is claimed goods are not of satisfactory quality. Thus, among the general interim remedies available to the court set out in CPR, r. 25.1, are powers to make:

(1) . . .

(c) an order—

(i) for the detention, custody or preservation of relevant property;

(ii) for the inspection of relevant property;

(iii) for the taking of a sample of relevant property;

> *(iv) for the carrying out of an experiment on or with relevant property; . . .*
> *(d) an order authorising a person to enter my land or building in the possession of a party to the proceedings for the purposes of carrying out an order under sub-paragraph (c); . . .*
> *(2) In paragraph (1)(c) . . . 'relevant property' means property (including land) which is the subject of a claim or as to which any question may arise on a claim.*

Orders for inspection are commonly sought at the allocation stage. They can be asked for in a covering letter sent with the completed allocation questionnaire (the letter should be disclosed to the other parties at the same time), or in draft consent directions filed with the allocation questionnaire. Otherwise, such orders may be made on the case management conference or on an application issued for the purpose at any time after proceedings have been issued, or, in respect of a defendant, after giving notice of intention to defend. No written evidence is necessary.

21.5.2.2 Restriction on applications

The main restriction on such applications is that the rule is limited to physical things. Consequently, inspection of a party's methods of manufacture and packing was refused in *Tudor Accumulator Co. Ltd* v *China Mutual Co.* (1930) WN 201. However, in *Ash* v *Buxted Poultry Ltd, The Times*, 29 November 1989, Brooke J held he had inherent jurisdiction to order the defendants to allow the claimant to make a video film of the defendant's manufacturing process.

21.5.3 AFTER ISSUE OF PROCEEDINGS, PROPERTY IN THE POSSESSION OF A NON-PARTY

21.5.3.1 Jurisdiction

The SCA 1981, s. 34(3), provides:

> On the application, in accordance with rules of court, of a party to any proceedings, the High Court shall, in such circumstances as may be specified in the rules, have power to make an order providing for any one or more of the following matters, that is to say—
> *(a) the inspection, photographing, preservation, custody and detention of property which is not the property of, or in the possession of, any party to the proceedings but which is the subject-matter of the proceedings or as to which any question arises in the proceedings;*
> *(b) the taking of samples of any such property as is mentioned in paragraph (a) and the carrying out of any experiment on or with any such property.*

The county courts have an identical power under CCA 1984, s. 53(3).

21.5.3.2 Procedure

An order for inspection of property against a non-party is sought by issuing an application notice supported by evidence during the course of the substantive proceedings. The CPR, r. 25.5, provides:

> *(2) The evidence in support of such an application must show, if practicable by reference to any statement of case prepared in relation to the proceedings . . ., that the property—*
> *(a) is . . . the subject matter of such proceedings; or*
> *(b) is relevant to the issues that will arise in relation to such proceedings.*
> *(3) A copy of the application notice and a copy of the evidence in support must be served on—*
> *(a) the person against whom the order is sought; and*
> *(b) in relation to an application under section 34(3) of the Supreme Court Act 1981 or section 53(3) of the County Courts Act 1984, every party to the proceedings other than the applicant.*

Table 21.1   Special disclosure and inspection orders

Type of order	Type of case	Against	Stage	Type of application
Search order, entry and removal	Real possibility of defendant destroying vital material	Defendant	On issue of claim	Without notice
Norwich Pharmacal, identity of tortfeasor	Unknown defendant	Facilitator	Pre-action	Claim form and application on notice
SCA 1981, s. 33(1), inspection of property	General application	Person with possession of property which may become the subject matter of subsequent action	Pre-action	Application notice before issue
SCA 1981, s. 33(2), pre-action disclosure	General application	Likely Defendant	Pre-action	Application notice before issue
SCA 1981, s. 34(2), disclosure of documents	General application	Non-party	After issue	Application notice
SCA 1981, s. 34(3), inspection of property	General application	Non-party	After issue	Application notice
Detention, Custody, Presentation, Inspection, Samples, Observation, Experiments	General application	Party with possession of property	After issue	Allocation directions (generally)

21.6   Interim Delivery-up of Goods

21.6.1   JURISDICTION

The Torts (Interference with Goods) Act 1977, s. 4(2), provides:

> On the application of any person in accordance with rules of court, the High Court shall, in such circumstances as may be specified in the rules, have power to make an order providing for the delivery up of any goods which are or may become the subject matter of subsequent proceedings [for wrongful interference] in the Court, or as to which any question may arise in the proceedings.

21.6.2   PRINCIPLES

A number of guidelines have been suggested by the Court of Appeal in *CBS UK Ltd* v *Lambert* [1983] Ch 37:

(a)   There should be clear evidence that the defendant is likely to dispose of the goods in order to deprive the claimant.

(b)   There must be some evidence that the defendant acquired the goods wrongfully.

(c)   The order should not be made if it will act oppressively against the defendant.

Often, the court needs to balance the claimant's immediate need for the goods against the defendant's grounds for retaining them.

21.6.3   THE ORDER

The order may provide for delivery to the claimant or a person appointed by the court. As an alternative to an order for delivery up, the court may make an order for preservation and detention of the goods.

In *CBS* v *Lambert* the Court of Appeal said the order:

(a)   should clearly specify the chattel to be delivered up;

(b)   should not authorise the claimant to enter the defendant's land without the defendant's permission;

(c)   should make adequate provision for the safe custody of the goods; and

(d)   should give the defendant liberty to apply.

21.6.4   PROCEDURE

Applications under the Torts (Interference with Goods) Act 1977 are among the general interim remedies available under CPR, r. 25.1. Being an interim application, CPR, Parts 23 and 25 apply, so an application notice must be issued, usually on notice, supported by witness statement or affidavit evidence. In urgent cases the application can be made without notice and even before issue of originating process.

21.7   Questions

OBJECTIVES

By the conclusion of this section you should:

(a)   have a sound understanding of the approach to case management normally taken in cases on each of the three case management tracks;

(b)   know the directions commonly given in cases on the three tracks;

(c)   have a sound understanding of the different types of case management hearings;

(d)   have a sound understanding of the procedure relating to the disclosure and inspection of documents;

(e)   understand the principles relating to *Norwich Pharmacal* applications;

(f)   understand the practice and procedure relating to obtaining disclosure before proceedings start and against non-parties; and

(g)   have a sound understanding of the rules relating to service outside England and Wales.

RESEARCH

Read the materials in **Chapters 17** to **21** in advance of Large Group Session 5, and consult **Chapter 7**. You will also need to read the materials in **Chapter 11** in advance of Small Group Class 5.

LARGE GROUP SESSION 5

In advance of Large Group Session 5, read questions 1 to 3, which will be dealt with in the class.

QUESTION 1

Sarah injured her ankle when she tripped over a defective paving stone. She has sued Lawborough City Council, who are the highway authority responsible for the street where the accident happened. A defence has been served. On full liability general damages are likely to be about £800, and there is also a loss of earnings claim worth about £2,500. Advise Sarah on the future progress of her claim.

QUESTION 2

Paul has brought proceedings against James claiming damages for breach of contract. The value of the claim is about £10,000. A defence was filed a few weeks ago. You are advising James in conference. Your instructing solicitor has mentioned that a list of documents was recently received from Paul.

(a) What directions would you expect would apply to this case? How can you be sure?

(b) Is James likely to be in breach of those directions?

(c) What should be done about the list of documents received from Paul?

QUESTION 3

You have been instructed on behalf of Vera, who suffered a severe soft tissue injury to her right wrist when a bottle of home-recipe ginger beer exploded as she was opening its top. She bought the ginger beer at a car boot sale held regularly on a site owned by the local authority near where she lives. The label on the bottle simply reads; 'Rustic Ginger Beer. Not recommended for children under 12. 1 litre.' Vera wants to claim damages for personal injuries, but has never known the identity of the person who sold the ginger beer to her. Your instructing solicitors have made inquiries, and have discovered that the car boot sale was organised by Arthur, who will almost certainly know the identities of everyone who was selling merchandise at the car boot sale, because the local authority require the organisers of car boot sales to keep records of everyone trading at such sales on its property. Your instructing solicitors have approached Arthur, who has refused to name the person who sold Vera the ginger beer. Which one of the following is the advice you should give Vera?

[A] To issue proceedings against Arthur claiming disclosure of the name and address of the person selling ginger beer at the car boot sale on the day in question.
[B] To issue proceedings against Arthur and leave him to issue a Part 20 claim against the person who sold Vera the ginger beer.
[C] To apply for pre-action disclosure against Arthur under the Supreme Court Act 1981, s. 33(2).
[D] That there is no cause of action against Arthur, and in the circumstances there is no appropriate legal remedy available against him.

SMALL GROUP SESSION 5

On the basis of your research, answer questions 4 to 11 in advance of Small Group Class 5.

QUESTION 4

(a) If an order for disclosure of documents is made what type of disclosure will be required?

    (b)   What documents does such an order require the party against whom it is made to disclose?

    (c)   What efforts must a party make in order to locate disclosable documents?

QUESTION 5

Two years ago a cable car which travelled around the perimeter of a theme park and adventure playground, owned and managed by Countryside Leisure plc, collapsed and fell to the ground causing its occupants, all children on a school outing, serious injury. Within days of the accident Countryside Leisure plc instructed its Safety Officer to conduct an investigation with a view to establishing the possible cause of the accident and recommending ways in which such an occurrence could be avoided in the future. It was also expected that the Safety Officer's findings would be of equal assistance to Countryside Leisure plc's solicitors for use in subsequent litigation, which it fully expected would ensue.

You act for Countryside Leisure plc which seeks your advice as to whether it can be compelled to disclose the Safety Officer's report to the victims of the accident.

QUESTION 6

At a case management conference Mark was ordered to serve on Phillip a list of documents within 21 days. Under CPR, r. 31.10(5), the list must include a disclosure statement. Eighteen days later Mark served a list of documents, including a disclosure statement.

On inspection, Phillip finds that one of the documents appearing in the list mentions a file of correspondence on the issues raised in the action. The file has not been mentioned at all in Mark's list of documents. Which one of the following propositions is correct?

[A]   Phillip cannot obtain further disclosure of the file of correspondence because Mark's disclosure statement is conclusive that he has given full disclosure.
[B]   Phillip is restricted to applying for a further disclosure order at a pre-trial review under CPR, Part 29, if one is scheduled, because the parties have a duty to apply for all other directions at such hearings only and not separately.
[C]   Phillip is entitled to make an application for Mark's list of documents to be set aside *ex debito justitiae* on the ground of irregularity.
[D]   Phillip can apply for an order for specific disclosure under CPR, r. 31.12, because he has evidence that documents exist which should have been disclosed.

QUESTION 7

Finola hires light aircraft from an aerodrome in Hampshire to amateur pilots. Last year a plane from Finola's fleet repeatedly flew at hedge-top level over Georgina's farm causing her cattle to stampede and damage fences, hedges and growing crops. The plane flew low over the farmhouse. Georgina suffered serious shock. Neither the police nor the Ministry of Aviation are prepared to take action against the culprit and so far all attempts by Georgina to persuade Finola or the authorities to identify the pilot have failed. Advise Georgina how she can obtain the necessary information from Finola to commence proceedings against the pilot.

QUESTION 8

Michael went into Dorchester Royal Infirmary for a cosmetic operation to his cauli-flower ear. After the operation Michael developed symptoms of brain damage which, it is thought, might be due to the use of an anaesthetic known to have dangerous side effects.

    (a)   Advise Michael whether the Infirmary can be made to disclose its records and, if so, what procedure should be followed.

(b) The Infirmary allege that Michael's symptoms resulted from an operation he had at Lawby General Hospital (which is administered by a different Health Authority) in 1990. Advise Michael whether the General Hospital can be made to disclose its records and, if so, what procedure should be followed.

QUESTION 9

Robert started proceedings against Richard. The case was allocated to the multi-track. Shortly after allocation a trial date was fixed for 6 December 2000. Robert has had difficulties with the firm of solicitors he instructed and has decided to replace them with new solicitors. The new firm of solicitors consider that the case has been very badly run and need time to take stock. In the light of Robert's difficulties Richard is amenable to postponing the date for mutual exchange of expert's reports by four weeks. This will mean that the parties will not be in a position to return their listing questionnaires by the specified date. Which of the following is the correct advice?

[A] Robert must make an application to the court for a variation in the case management timetable.
[B] Because Robert has a good reason for the delay, the parties are free to vary the case management timetable without notifying the court.
[C] So long as Robert notifies the court in writing that the parties have agreed to a variation in the case management timetable the variation will be permitted.
[D] The parties can make any variation to the case management timetable, without notifying the court, so long as the date fixed for trial does not have to be postponed.

QUESTION 10

Jill Young was injured in Dover when she was run over by a Renault Estate driven by Monsieur Dupont who lives in Paris.

Jill has a good case against Monsieur Dupont.

(a) Advise Jill on appropriate procedure.

(b) Would your advice differ if Monsieur Dupont were a French Canadian living in Ottawa?

QUESTION 11

Alan, an importer of glassware, has an ongoing contract of carriage with Bettoni. Bettoni's lorries depart from Naples, and travel through France before crossing to England by ferry. Drivers are often changed at Bettoni's depots in Rome and Paris.

Alan has evidence that Bettoni's staff have been stealing from the goods while in transit. Most of the incidents have taken place in Rome and Paris, but some have happened in London. Total losses exceed £200,000.

Alan wishes to sue Bettoni and the individual culprits. Bettoni is resident in Italy, the others live in Italy, France and England. Where should proceedings be started?

TWENTY TWO

REQUESTS FOR FURTHER INFORMATION

22.1   Introduction

We have already seen how parties can obtain disclosure of documents, and thus, among other things, be in a better position to assess the strengths and weaknesses of the other side's case. Additionally, the judicious (and legitimate!) use of the request for further information, can ensure that your opponent's statement of case has been set out in such a way as to make the issues between the parties absolutely clear. Nevertheless, there may be many times when it would be helpful if you could obtain further information from the other side without being limited to the other side's statement of case. In most cases, one simply has to wait for the exchange of witnesses' statements or wait until the trial — after all, it is then that the evidence is given and examined. However, there are circumstances in which it may be appropriate to ask for further information about matters raised in the witness statements or from documents inspected in the process of disclosure. As discussed at **5.7** above, the process of seeking further information extends to seeking information as the case develops, and there will be many cases where requests for further information are made early on to clarify the statements of case, and also at a later stage to clarify the evidence.

22.2   Procedure

This has already been discussed at **5.7**.

22.3   Principles

PD 18, para. 1.2, provides:

> *A request should be concise and strictly confined to matters which are reasonably necessary and proportionate to enable the first party to prepare his own case or to understand the case he has to meet.*

Until 1999 it was not unusual for parties to serve interrogatories and requests for further and better particulars (the predecessors of the present request for information) which were incredibly long and detailed. It was not unusual to ask 30 or 50 questions, many with several sub-questions. There was always the suspicion that such requests were mainly designed to rack up costs, or to make it difficult for the other party to answer, so that applications for 'unless' orders (orders with sanctions) could be made. Applying the overriding objective, and as PD 18, para. 1.2, makes clear, such an approach is no longer tolerated, and any requests made for information should be reasonably necessary and proportionate.

Between about 1875 and 1999 a body of case law developed setting out certain limits on the old procedure for serving interrogatories. Most of the rules were restrictive, and it is highly unlikely that the courts will be any more generous under the Civil Procedure Rules 1998 than they were under the old system. There will follow a short discussion based on some of the old rules restricting the use of interrogatories which are likely to still be valid when applying the overriding objective under the 1998 Rules.

22.3.1 RELEVANCE TO THE ISSUES

Requests will not be allowed unless they are relevant to the matters in issue. This might allow requests which may open a train of inquiry tending to establish the existence or non-existence of material facts (*Marriott* v *Chamberlain* (1886) 17 QBD 154), but the court will be astute in such a case to apply the overriding objective to ensure the inquiry is kept under control. Requests asked for the purposes of future actions will be refused.

22.3.2 'FISHING' REQUESTS

'Fishing' requests are disallowed.

If the question is asked by a party '. . . in order that he may find out something of which he knows nothing now, which might enable him to make a case of which he has no knowledge at present' it is fishing and will be disallowed (per Lord Esher MR in *Hennessey* v *Wright (No. 2)* (1888) 24 QBD 445, at 448, CA).

22.3.3 QUESTIONS AS TO THE CREDIBILITY OF WITNESSES

Questions going to credibility of witnesses, as opposed to liability or damages, are not allowed: *Thorpe* v *Greater Manchester Chief Constable* [1989] 1 WLR 665, CA.

22.3.4 SCANDALOUS REQUESTS

Scandalous requests are disallowed. These include insulting or degrading questions, as well as those which are irrelevant or impertinent to the issues.

22.3.5 OPPRESSIVE REQUESTS

Oppressive requests are also disallowed.

A question is oppressive if it places an undue burden on the party required to answer. As Collins MR said in *White* v *Credit Reform Association* [1905] 1 KB 653, at 659:

> a question becomes oppressive when it exceeds the legitimate requirements of the particular occasion. Such questions have some relevance to the issues, and the approach of the court is to ask whether the benefit in obtaining an answer counter-vails the inconvenience imposed on the opponent.

Thus, in *Parnell* v *Walter* (1890) 24 QBD 441, the Court of Appeal regarded a question asking for the precise circulation of a newspaper to be oppressive, and limited the required answer to giving the best information available in round figures. Similarly, a question in *Kirkup* v *British Railway Engineering* [1983] 1 WLR 1165, directed to noise levels in the whole of the defendant's operations, was limited by Croom-Johnson J on appeal to the works where the claimant was employed.

Kirkup is also authority for the proposition that a question is oppressive if not precisely formulated.

22.3.6 NECESSARY FOR DISPOSING FAIRLY OF THE CLAIM

For example, a request in a debt action which was designed to compel the defendant to acknowledge a debt under what is now the Limitation Act 1980, s. 29, and thereby defeat an accrued limitation defence, would be disallowed as unnecessary for disposing fairly of the claim: *Lovell* v *Lovell* [1970] 1 WLR 1451, CA.

22.3.7 NECESSARY FOR SAVING COSTS

If witnesses on a subject will be called at trial, it is very unlikely that requests on the same subject will be allowed because they will be unnecessary for 'saving costs'.

In *Griebart* v *Morris* [1920] 1 KB 659, at 666 Scrutton LJ expressed the view that:

> In most accident cases both parties are able to call witnesses, and therefore to interrogate upon small questions of fact relating to the details of the accident cannot be necessary for the fair trial of the action, and interrogatories should not be allowed.

The claimant in *Griebart* had no independent witnesses and had suffered head injuries in the accident, resulting in loss of memory such that she might have been unable to give useful evidence at trial. In those special circumstances the Court of Appeal ordered the driver to answer interrogatories as to the facts of the accident.

Hall v *Selvaco Ltd, The Times*, 27 March 1996, CA, is authority for the proposition that requests to obtain information or admissions which were or likely to be contained in statements of case, medical reports, disclosable documents or witness statements are not generally necessary for saving costs unless, exceptionally, a clear litigious purpose would be served.

22.4 Requests for Further Information and Search Orders and Freezing Injunctions

It is often important in the case of freezing injunctions to obtain information as to where the defendant's assets can be found. The High Court has the power to order disclosure of assets, the jurisdiction being incidental to the power to make the freezing injunction under SCA 1981, s. 37.

In cases where the court orders disclosure of assets, all the court does is to insert an extra clause into the main freezing injunction order.

Similar clauses are also inserted into search orders to obtain further information.

22.5 Collateral Use

The CPR, r. 18.2, says that the court may direct that information provided whether voluntarily or after an order must not be used for any purpose other than for the proceedings in which it is given. Consideration should be given to asking for such a direction whenever sensitive information is to be given in answer to a request for information.

Figure 22.1 Request for further information

IN THE CENTRAL LONDON COUNTY COURT	Claim No. CL00 43762

BETWEEN

ELEANOR JANE WELDON   <u>Claimant</u>

and

(1) JAMES ARTHUR WILLIAMS

(2) D. STOKES (HAULAGE) LIMITED   <u>Defendants</u>

<u>REQUEST FOR FURTHER INFORMATION UNDER PART 18</u>

Made on behalf of Eleanor Jane Weldon (the first party) to D. Stokes (Haulage) Limited (the second party) dated 25th October 2000.

1. Is the first defendant employed or has the first defendant been employed by the second defendant? If yes, say in what capacity, what his principal duties are and have been, and the date his employment with you commenced and, if it be the case, the date his employment with you ended.

2. Was a Leyland commercial vehicle registration number F987 ZYX ('the lorry') owned by the second defendant, and was the said vehicle operated by the second defendant, on 21 December 1998?

3. Was the lorry operating in London N10 on 21 December 1998?

4. Did the first defendant drive the lorry in Newlands Road, London N10 on 21 December 1998?

5. Did the lorry collide with a parked car in Newlands Road, London N10 on 21 December 1998?

TAKE NOTICE that these requests are to be answered no later than 24 November 2000.

AND TAKE NOTICE that Donald Stokes, a director of the second defendants D. Stokes (Haulage) Limited, is required to answer these requests.

Dated the 25th day of October 2000, by Messrs Buchanan & Co. of 23 The Hard, London N10, solicitors for the claimant.

TWENTY THREE

LIMITATION

23.1 Introduction

This chapter deals with the substantive rules on the limitation periods applicable to various classes of proceedings, which are discussed in **23.2** to **23.6**. A reasonable limitation period will not infringe Article 6(1) of the European Convention on Human Rights, nor will it infringe EC law: *Aprile SRL* v *Amministrazione Delle Finanze Dello Stato (No. 2)* [2000] 1 WLR 126, ECJ.

23.2 Limitation: General

Limitation is a procedural defence and if relied upon details must be given in the defence: PD 16, para. 16.1. The expiry of a limitation period will not be taken by the court of its own motion. The basic policy is that defendants should not be perpetually at risk of proceedings being brought, and should not have to defend stale claims. Fixed periods have been laid down for bringing various categories of cases (see **Table 23.1**), although there has been a tendency in more recent legislation towards granting some flexibility (see **23.5**).

Effluxion of time usually has the effect of extinguishing the claimant's remedy. In cases of adverse possession of land and conversion, expiry of the limitation period has the additional effect of extinguishing the claimant's title (see e.g. **23.3.3.3**).

Table 23.1   Limitation periods

The following table sets out the limitation periods for a selection of different categories of cases. It is not comprehensive.

	Class of action	*Limitation period*
1.	Tort, other than 2–3 below	6 years (Limitation Act 1980 (LA 1980), s. 2)
2.	Personal injuries claims in negligence, nuisance or breach of duty (including contract or statute)	3 years (LA 1980, s. 11)
3.	Fatal Accidents Act 1976 claims on behalf of the deceased's dependants	3 years from the date of death or the dependant's date of knowledge
4.	Contract	6 years (LA 1980, s. 5)
5.	Recovery of land	12 years (LA 1980, s. 15(1))
6.	Actions by beneficiaries to recover trust property or in respect of breach of trust	6 years (LA 1980, s. 21(3))
7.	Contribution under Civil Liability (Contribution) Act 1978	2 years (LA 1980, s. 10(1))

23.3   Accrual of Cause of Action

The date on which time begins to run for limitation purposes depends on the nature of the cause of action. Before considering some of the rules relating to specific causes of action, we will deal with some general points.

23.3.1   GENERAL RULES

In *Reeves* v *Butcher* [1891] 2 QB 509, 511, Lindley LJ said '. . . it has always been held that the statute runs from the earliest time at which an action could be brought.' This is the time when facts exist establishing all the essential elements of the cause of action: *Coburn* v *Colledge* [1897] 1 QB 702, 706 per Lord Esher MR. A distinction is drawn between the substantive elements, which must be present, and mere procedural bars which do not stop time running. Sometimes this can be a difficult distinction to draw: see *Sevcon Ltd* v *Lucas CAV Ltd* [1986] 2 All ER 104, HL. Further, there must be a party capable of suing and a party liable to be sued: *Thomson* v *Lord Clanmorris* [1900] 1 Ch 718, 729 per Vaughan Williams LJ (obiter). This will not be so where, for example, goods are converted after the owner has died intestate. Time in such a case runs from after letters of administration are taken out.

23.3.2   CONTRACT

Time runs from breach of the contract.

23.3.3   TORT

23.3.3.1   Trespass and libel
These are actionable *per se*, without proof of damage, so time runs from the wrongful act.

23.3.3.2   Slander, nuisance, negligence and other torts not involving personal injuries or death
These require proof of damage, so time runs from the damage. Formerly, the fact that the damage may not have been discovered until some time later did not prevent time running. See now the rules relating to latent damage (**23.3.4**).

23.3.3.3   Conversion
Time runs from the converting event. Note the following special rules:

(a)   Where a chattel is converted more than once, the original six-year period is not renewed by the subsequent conversions: LA 1980, s. 3(1).

(b)   At the end of the original six-year period, the true owner's title is extinguished: LA 1980, s. 3(2).

(c)   Subject to (d), there is no time limit at all in bringing a claim in respect of a stolen chattel: LA 1980, s. 4(1), (2).

(d)   Where a chattel is converted, then stolen at a later date, proceedings in respect of the theft are barred once the original owner's title is extinguished under s. 3(2) in respect of the original conversion: LA 1980, s. 4(1).

23.3.3.4   Personal injuries: date of knowledge
Time runs from accrual (usually the date of the accident, when the injury was sustained) or, if later, the injured person's date of knowledge: LA 1980, s. 11(4). Under LA 1980, s. 14(1) a claimant's 'date of knowledge' is the first date the claimant knew three (sometimes four) things.

For time to begin to run the claimant must know:

(a)   That the injury was significant i.e. sufficiently serious to justify instituting proceedings for damages against a defendant who did not dispute liability and was able to satisfy a judgment: LA 1980, s. 14(2). The question is whether it would have been reasonable for the individual claimant concerned to consider the injury insufficiently serious. Collateral considerations, such as whether it would be impolitic to sue one's employer, are irrelevant: *McCafferty* v *Metropolitan Police District Receiver* [1977] 1 WLR 1073, CA.

(b) That the injury was attributable to the alleged default. In *Guidera* v *NE I Projects (India) Ltd* [1990] CAT 60 Sir David Croom-Johnson said, 'It is knowledge that attribution is merely possible, a real possibility and not a fanciful one, a possible cause as opposed to a probable cause of the injury' that is required.

The final words of s. 14(1) expressly state that 'knowledge that any acts or omissions did or did not, as a matter of law, involve negligence, nuisance or breach of duty' is irrelevant. Although it is the essence of the allegedly negligent act or omission which must be known by the claimant, there must be a degree of specificity in that knowledge: *Nash* v *Eli Lilly & Co.* [1993] 1 WLR 782, CA.

(c) The identity of the defendant. Time may not run against an injured employee where the exact identity of an allegedly negligent employer is not clear from the employee's contract of employment: *Simpson* v *Norwest Holst Southern Ltd* [1980] 1 WLR 968, CA.

AND

(d) If it is alleged that the act or omission was of a person other than the defendant (e.g. in vicarious liability situations), the identity of that person and the facts supporting an action against the defendant.

The concept of 'knowledge' was considered by the Court of Appeal in *Nash* v *Eli Lilly & Co.* [1993] 1 WLR 782. This depends on the nature of the information the claimant has received, the extent to which the claimant paid attention to such information, and the claimant's capacity to understand it. The court has to assess the intelligence of the claimant in order to determine whether he was able to understand the information available to him. The court has to consider whether the claimant had broad knowledge of the matters discussed above. Knowledge detailed enough to enable the claimant's advisers to draft Particulars of Claim is not required before time begins to run, and is contrary to the final words of s. 14(1): see *Broadley* v *Guy Clapham & Co.* [1994] 4 All ER 439, CA. Consequently, it is quite possible (particularly in the medical negligence field) for a claimant's claim to be time-barred before the claimant appreciates his or her claim may be actionable: *Dobbie* v *Medway Health Authority* [1994] 1 WLR 1234, CA.

Further, s. 14(3) provides that a person's knowledge includes knowledge which he or she might reasonably have been expected to acquire from observable facts and the taking of appropriate expert advice. Whether the claimant is to be fixed with such constructive knowledge often turns on the expert advice it would have been reasonable for the claimant to obtain. Where a serious injury has been suffered as a result of allegedly negligent medical treatment, Stuart-Smith LJ indicated in *Forbes* v *Wandsworth Health Authority* [1997] QB 402, CA, that a period of 12 to 18 months may be reasonable for taking stock before seeking expert advice.

23.3.3.5 Fatal accidents
Time runs from the date of death or, if later, the date of the relevant dependant's knowledge (LA 1980, s. 12), again as defined in LA 1980, s. 14 (see **23.3.3.4**).

23.3.4   LATENT DAMAGE

LA 1980, ss. 14A, 14B, were inserted by the Latent Damage Act 1986. They apply to negligence actions, other than personal injuries cases. They are restricted to negligence claims in tort, and do not include actions for breach of contractual duty founded on allegations of negligent or careless conduct: *Iron Trade Mutual Insurance Co. Ltd* v *J K Buckenham Ltd* [1990] 1 All ER 808. Latent damage is often a problem in relation to defective buildings, but ss. 14A, 14B apply to all types of non-personal injuries negligence cases, such as claims against solicitors for negligent drafting or advice. The practical scope of the provisions has been dramatically reduced by the overruling of *Anns* v *Merton London Borough Council* [1978] AC 728, HL by *Murphy* v *Brentwood District Council* [1991] 1 AC 398, HL.

LA 1980, s. 14A provides for two alternative periods, namely six years from accrual and, if later, three years from the 'starting date' (see **23.3.4.1** and **23.3.4.2**). Both are subject to a 'longstop' of 15 years (see **23.3.4.3**).

23.3.4.1 Six years from accrual

As stated in **23.3**, an action in tort accrues when all the essential elements exist. In an action against a solicitor for negligent advice, the claimant suffers actual damage and has a complete cause of action when the advice is acted on, such as by executing a document: *Forster* v *Outred & Co.* [1982] 1 WLR 86, CA. Contrast *Pirelli General Cable Works Ltd* v *Oscar Faber & Partners (a firm)* [1983] 2 AC 1, HL where consulting engineers designed an addition to the claimant's factory, including a chimney. The chimney was built in 1969. Unsuitable materials were used, and cracking developed in 1970. With reasonable diligence, the claimants could have discovered the cracks in 1972, but in fact only discovered them in 1977. It was held that the action accrued when the damage came into existence in 1970. Acting on the defendants' design, discoverability and actual discovery of the damage were all rejected as dates for the accrual of the action. Whether this is still the law must be open to question. *Pirelli* was interpreted as falling within the *Hedley Byrne & Co. Ltd* v *Heller & Partners Ltd* [1964] AC 485, HL principle in *Murphy* v *Brentwood District Council* [1991] 1 AC 398 at 466, where Lord Keith said that if the claimants had discovered the defect before any damage had occurred their cause of action would have accrued at that stage.

23.3.4.2 Starting date

The alternative period of three years runs from the earliest date the claimant knew:

(a) that the relevant damage was sufficiently serious to justify commencing proceedings;

(b) that the damage was attributable to the alleged negligence; and

(c) the defendant's identity;

(d) if it is alleged that the act or omission was of a person other than the defendant, the identity of that person and the facts supporting an action against the defendant.

These concepts mirror those for determining the claimant's date of knowledge in personal injuries cases (see **23.3.3.4**).

23.3.4.3 Longstop

LA 1980, s. 14B provides a 15-year overriding time limit for negligence actions not involving personal injuries, after which such actions shall not be brought even if the cause of action has not yet accrued or the 'starting date' has not yet arrived. This 15-year period runs from the date of the act or omission which is alleged to constitute the negligence resulting in the claimant's damage.

23.3.5 RECOVERY OF LAND

A number of very detailed rules are set out over four pages in LA 1980, sch. 1.

23.3.6 CONTRIBUTION

Time runs from the date when the amount of the liability in respect of which contribution is sought was fixed (excluding any variation on appeal). Thus, if the amount was determined by a court, time runs from the date judgment was given (LA 1980, s. 10(3)). If settled by compromise, time runs from the date the amount was agreed (LA 1980, s. 10(4)).

23.4 Calculating the Limitation Period

23.4.1 GENERAL RULES

Time runs from the day following the day on which the cause of action arose, as parts of a day are disregarded: *Marren* v *Dawson, Bentley & Co. Ltd* [1961] 2 QB 135. Time normally stops running when the originating process is issued: *Thompson* v *Brown* [1981] 1 WLR 747, HL. The day of issue is included in calculating the period. If the court office is closed on what would otherwise be the last day of the limitation period, proceedings will be in time if issued on the next day on which the court office is open: *Kaur* v *S. Russell & Sons Ltd* [1973] QB 337, CA. If a claim form is received by the court on a day earlier than the date of issue, the claim is 'brought' for the purposes of the Limitation Act on the date of receipt rather than issue: PD 7, para. 5.1. The court will normally date stamp the covering letter to record the date of receipt: para. 5.2.

23.4.2 SETS-OFFS AND COUNTERCLAIMS

By virtue of LA 1980, s. 35(1)(b), sets-offs and counterclaims are deemed to have been commenced on the same date as the original action. This is often called the statutory relation back. As this provision may save claims which might otherwise be time barred, generally no such claim can be made after the expiry of the limitation period unless it is 'an original set-off or counterclaim'. To qualify as such, the set-off or counterclaim must be brought by a party who has not previously made any claim in the action: s. 35(3).

23.4.3 PART 20 CLAIMS

Part 20 claims, other than counterclaims, are deemed to have been commenced on the date the Part 20 claim form was issued: LA 1980, s. 35(1)(a).

23.4.4 DISABILITY

Time does not run against a person under disability on the date the cause of action accrued: LA 1980, s. 28. There are two categories:

(a)   children (persons under the age of 18); and

(b)   persons of unsound mind. These are persons who, by reason of mental disorder within the meaning of the Mental Health Act 1983, are incapable of managing and administering their property and affairs (see LA 1980, s. 38(2), (3)).

Where the claimant suffers injury resulting in immediate unsoundness of mind, limitation does not run for the period of the disability. If, before attaining majority, a claimant becomes of unsound mind, the limitation period will only commence when the later disability ends. But, where a person of full age becomes of unsound mind after the accrual of a cause of action, time continues to run during the period of disability.

23.4.5 FRAUD

By LA 1980, s. 32(1)(a) the limitation period in an action based upon the fraud of the defendant does not run until the claimant either has, or could with reasonable diligence have, discovered the fraud. The action must be actually founded on fraud, as in deceit. The fact the defendant has incidentally been fraudulent or dishonest (as in many conversion cases) is not enough: *Beaman* v *A.R.T.S. Ltd* [1949] 1 KB 550, 558, CA.

23.4.6 CONCEALMENT

Where any fact relevant to the claimant's right of action has been deliberately concealed by the defendant, time does not begin to run until the claimant either discovers, or could with reasonable diligence have discovered, the concealment: LA 1980, s. 32(1)(b). In *Kitchen* v *Royal Air Force Association* [1958] 1 WLR 563, CA, solicitors negligently failed to advise the claimant that she had a possible claim against an electricity company. The section came into operation when, later, the solicitor failed to inform her that the company had offered to pay £100 in compromise, so as not to reveal their earlier negligence. Moreover, s. 32(1)(b) also operates where the defendant conceals facts relevant to the claimant's claim after time has started to run: *Sheldon* v *RHM Outhwaite (Underwriting Agencies) Ltd* [1996] AC 102, HL.

23.4.7 MISTAKE

Where the claimant's action is for relief from the consequences of a mistake, again time does not run until the mistake either is, or could with reasonable diligence have been, discovered: LA 1980, s. 32(1)(c). In *Peco Arts Inc* v *Hazlitt Gallery Ltd* [1983] 1 WLR 1315, the claimant, on the recommendation of a specialist in nineteenth century drawings, bought a drawing from the defendants. It was an express term that it was an original drawing signed by the artist. Six years after purchase it was revalued by an art expert, and no doubts were cast on its authenticity. Five years later it was found to be a reproduction. The claimant claimed for recovery of the purchase price as money paid under a mutual mistake of fact. It was held that 'reasonable diligence' in the context of the claimant's action meant doing that which an ordinary prudent buyer of a valuable work of art would do, and that on the facts the claimant had exercised reasonable diligence.

23.4.8 BREACH OF TRUST

LA 1980, s. 21(1), provides that no limitation period applies to actions brought by beneficiaries either:

(a)   in respect of any fraud by a trustee; or

(b)   to recover from a trustee property converted to the trustee's use.

Time was held to run in favour of the trustee in *Thorne* v *Head* [1894] 1 Ch 599, who had negligently left trust funds with a solicitor who then embezzled it. The trustee was not a party to or privy to the fraud.

23.5   Discretionary Extension of Limitation Periods

23.5.1 GENERAL

Some of the prescribed periods may be extended in the discretion of the court. Thus, the three month period for making an application for judicial review may be extended if the court considers there is good reason for doing so: RSC O. 53, r. 4(1) which is preserved in CPR, sch. 1. In defamation cases, if the claimant discovers the relevant facts after the expiry of the one-year basic period, an action can be brought within one year of the facts becoming known, but only with the permission of the court: LA 1980, s. 32A.

23.5.2 PERSONAL INJURIES CASES

23.5.2.1 Principles
Perhaps more important is the equitable discretion of the court to disapply the primary limitation period in personal injuries cases. LA 1980, s. 33, provides:

(1)   If it appears to the court that it would be equitable to allow an action to proceed having regard to the degree to which —

(a) the provisions of section 11 or 12 of this Act prejudice the plaintiff or any person whom he represents; and

(b) any decision of the court under this subsection would prejudice the defendant or any person whom he represents;

the court may direct that those provisions shall not apply to the action, or shall not apply to any specified cause of action to which the action relates.

. . .

(3) In acting under this section the court shall have regard to all the circumstances of the case and in particular to —

(a) the length of, and the reasons for, the delay on the part of the plaintiff;

(b) the extent to which, having regard to the delay, the evidence adduced or likely to be adduced by the plaintiff or the defendant is or is likely to be less cogent than if the action had been brought within the time allowed by section 11 or (as the case may be) by section 12;

(c) the conduct of the defendant after the cause of action arose, including the extent (if any) to which he responded to requests reasonably made by the plaintiff for information or inspection for the purpose of ascertaining facts which were or might be relevant to the plaintiff's cause of action against the defendant;

(d) the duration of any disability of the plaintiff arising after the date of the accrual of the cause of action;

(e) the extent to which the plaintiff acted promptly and reasonably once he knew whether or not the act or omission of the defendant, to which the injury was attributable, might be capable at that time of giving rise to an action for damages;

(f) the steps, if any, taken by the plaintiff to obtain medical, legal or other expert advice and the nature of any such advice he may have received.

The leading authority on s. 33 is *Thompson v Brown* [1981] 1 WLR 747, where the House of Lords held that the discretionary power to disapply the primary limitation period is unfettered, the court being required to take into account all the circumstances of the case.

If the delay was caused by the claimant's solicitors' negligence, that is a highly relevant factor, because the strength of an alternative claim will directly affect the degree to which the claimant is prejudiced by the time limit in s. 11. However, as Lord Diplock mentions at p. 750, instructing new and strange solicitors may cause some prejudice to the claimant.

The factors set out in the LA 1980, s. 33(3)(a) and (b), are addressing the period between the expiry of the primary limitation period, as extended, if appropriate, by the claimant's date of knowledge under s. 14: *Long v Tolchard, The Times*, 5 January 2000, CA. Wrong advice from the claimant's lawyers is relevant for the purposes of s. 33(3)(a) and (f), and the claimant is not to be criticised for this type of error by his or her lawyers: *Das v Ganju* [1999] PIQR P260, CA. One of the things s. 33(3)(b) requires the court to consider is the extent to which it is possible to have a fair trial of all the issues. If the claimant has a strong, or even a cast iron, case against the original tortfeasor, that is an important factor to place into the balance that has to be struck, but, like all the other factors, is not determinative of the application, which may still be decided against the claimant: *Long v Tolchard.*

Section 33 was further considered by the House of Lords in *Donovan v Gwentoys Ltd* [1990] 1 WLR 472. The claimant was injured at work in 1979 when aged 16. She had received advice from her union representative about sickness pay, but he did not mention claiming damages. The claimant attained her majority on 25 April 1981. She eventually consulted a solicitor on 6 April 1984. Limitation expired on 25 April 1984. The defendants were notified of the claim in September 1984, and proceedings were issued on 10 October 1984. The accident papers in 1979 referred to a wrist injury, but the details of the claimant's injury sent to the defendants in January 1986 revealed the substantial claim was for a knee injury. The defendants set up the Limitation Act in defence, and the claimant applied for a direction under s. 33(1).

Lord Griffith adopted the following passage from the dissenting judgment of Stuart-Smith LJ in the Court of Appeal:

The time of the notification of the claim is not one of the particular matters to which the court is required to have regard under section 33(3), although it may come in under paragraph (e). But to my mind it is an extremely important consideration . . .

Lord Griffith held that the balance of prejudice in the case came down heavily in favour of the defendants. It would not be equitable to require the defendants to meet such a stale claim which they would have the utmost difficulty in defending, whereas the claimant would suffer only the slightest prejudice in being required to sue her solicitors.

23.5.2.2 Procedure

An application under s. 33 to disapply the limitation period is considered to be a final rather than interim matter: see *Hughes* v *Jones, The Times*, 18 July 1996, CA. It should therefore be dealt with by a judge having trial jurisdiction over the claim (which means that District Judges can only deal with these applications in County Court fast track cases). It is incumbent on the claimant to disclose all relevant circumstances at the hearing of the application, and if this is breached, the decision may be set aside: *Long* v *Tolchard, The Times*, 5 January 2000, CA.

Whether to exercise the jurisdiction under s. 33 can come before the court in the following instances:

(a) by way of a cross-application by the claimant if the defendant applies for summary judgment or to strike-out;

(b) on an application by application notice supported by evidence by the claimant;

(c) by way of a trial of limitation as a preliminary issue; or

(d) may be left to be dealt with at trial.

23.5.3 ISSUING A SECOND CLAIM

Where proceedings are issued within the limitation period but those proceedings are informally discontinued (as in *Walkley* v *Precision Forgings Ltd* [1979] 1 WLR 606, HL) or the originating process expires before it can be served in circumstances where it will not be renewed (as in *Chappell* v *Cooper* [1980] 2 All ER 463, CA), the claimant will not be allowed to issue a second set of proceedings after the limitation period has expired and rely on the provisions of s. 33 to disapply the limitation period.

In *Walkley* v *Precision Forgings Ltd* (supra) Lord Wilberforce (at p. 609) said that LA 1980, s. 33(1)(a):

. . . must be contemplating a case in which, because the three years have expired without an action being brought, s. 2A (now s. 11) applies to the prejudice of the plaintiff. But if the plaintiff has brought his action within the three years, how has he been prejudiced by s. 2A (s. 11)? ... He brought his first action within the normal limitation period, and if he has suffered any prejudice, it is by his own inaction and not by the operation of the Act.

Also, as Lord Diplock said in *Deerness* v *John R Keeble & Son* [1983] 2 Lloyd's Rep 260, HL, LA 1980, s. 33 cannot be used to heal such self-inflicted wounds.

The second claim must, however, be the same as the first for the *Walkley* principle to apply. Thus, where the first claim was commenced against the employer of the driver of the other vehicle involved in a road traffic accident as being vicariously liable for the negligence of the driver, and, after that claim was struck out through not being served in time, a second claim was made against the driver personally, it was held the *Walkley* principle did not apply: *Shapland* v *Palmer* [1999] 1 WLR 2068, CA. Accordingly, a direction could be given under the LA 1980, s. 33.

23.5.4 CATEGORISATION OF INJURY CLAIMS

The House of Lords in *Stubbings* v *Webb* [1993] 2 AC 498 was faced with a case where the claimant alleged she had suffered mental illness as a result of being sexually abused and raped by the defendants over a period between 16 and 28 years before the proceedings were issued. It was held that cases of intentional trespass to the person are governed by the six-year limitation period in the LA 1980, s. 2 and not the three-year limitation period for personal injuries cases in the LA 1980, s. 11. Further-more, because a case involving intentional trespass to the person is not an action for 'negligence, nuisance [or] breach of duty' the provisions in the LA 1980, s. 14 relating to the claimant's date of knowledge (see **23.3.3.4**) and in the LA 1980, s. 33 giving the court a discretion to extend the primary limitation period (see **23.5.2**) had no applica-tion to the case. Consequently the case was time-barred, there was no discretion to direct that the primary limitation period should not apply, and the action was struck out. However, the House of Lords approved *Letang* v *Cooper* [1965] 1 QB 232 where the Court of Appeal held that the three-year limitation period in LA 1980, s. 1 and the provisions of LA 1980, ss. 14 and 33 apply to cases of unintentional trespass to the person. Ms Stubbing's application to the European Court of Human Rights claiming violation of her rights under Articles 6(1), 8(1) and 14 of the European Convention on Human Rights failed: *Stubbings* v *UK, The Times*, 24 October 1996.

In *Seymour* v *Williams* [1995] PIQR 470, on facts similar to those in *Stubbings* v *Webb*, it was held that allegations of sexual abuse against the claimant's father were time barred because the action was commenced more than six years after the claimant reached her majority, but that a claim against the claimant's mother, based on breach of the mother's parental duties to the claimant, was an action within s. 11 and could therefore be saved under either the date of knowledge or discretionary rules in s. 14 and 33. A claim by a pyschiatric patient against a female nurse who, instead of giving him proper medical treatment, was alleged to have entered into an intimate sexual relationship with him (allegedly thereby worsening his condition), was held by *Bowler* v *Walker* [1996] PIQR 22, CA, to be a claim for breach of duty under s. 11 and, as it was brought between three and six years after the alleged incidents, could only be saved (on the facts) under s. 33. Similarly, a claim for damages for a failed sterilisation resulting in an unwanted pregnancy is a claim for personal injuries governed by the three-year limitation period in s. 11: see *Walkin* v *South Manchester Health Authority* [1995] 4 All ER 132, CA.

A claim against a driver of a vehicle who may have been uninsured pleaded as a loss of the opportunity to sue the driver's insurer is a claim in respect of personal injuries, and is governed by the three-year limitation period in LA 1980, s. 11: *Norman* v *Ali, The Times*, 25 February 2000, CA. Further, a claim in professional negligence against a solicitor arising out of the firm's handling of a divorce ancillary relief claim, which included a claim for anxiety and stress arising out of the firm's alleged mishandling of her claim, became, for that reason, a claim in respect of personal injuries and subject to a three-year limitation period rather than the usual six-year period in claims in tort and breach of contract: *Oates* v *Harte Reade and Company* [1999] PIQR P120.

23.6 Equitable Remedies

By LA 1980, s. 36(1), the usual time limits do not apply to claims for specific performance, injunctions or other equitable relief. The defences of laches and acquies-cence are preserved by LA 1980, s. 36(2). In considering these defences, the courts assess the hardship caused to the defendant by the delay, any effect upon third parties, and the balance of justice in granting or refusing the relief claimed. In keeping with equitable principles, the court has a wide discretion, and no firm maximum period has been laid down. See generally *Weld* v *Petre* [1929] 1 Ch 33 and *Jones* v *Stones* [1999] 1 WLR 1739.

TWENTY FOUR

AMENDMENT

24.1   Introduction

This chapter considers:

(a)   The procedural rules relating to the amendment of statements of case and misjoinder of parties.

(b)   The rather complex rules that apply when a party seeks to amend after the expiry of a relevant limitation period.

24.2   Amendment: General

In many cases, a party to an action may wish to amend a statement of case after it has been served. Sometimes, a claimant who wishes to add a claim for a new cause of action, or to join a new defendant, will have to amend the claim form, as well as the particulars of claim, or the defendant may wish to amend the defence. Further, it has to be admitted, even lawyers are not perfect, and an occasional slip may have to be amended.

In **24.3** to **24.5** we will first consider the general rules, which can be divided into amendment with and without the permission of the court. We will then, in **24.6**, consider the problems relating to amendment of parties.

24.3   Amendment Without Permission

By CPR, r. 17.1(1), a party is allowed to amend a statement of case at any time before it has been served on any other party. Once it has been served a statement of case can only be amended with the consent of the other parties or the permission of the court. As we have seen previously, the term 'statements of case' is defined as the claim form, particulars of claim, the defence, reply, Part 20 claims and any further information given is relation to them: CPR, r. 2.3(1).

The right to amend without permission is therefore largely restricted to amendments to the claim form and particulars of claim in the period between issue and service, which could be as long as four months. Other statements of case could fall to be amended without permission in the period between filing and service, but in most cases this will be a very short period of time.

A party served with a statement of case amended without permission can object to the amendment by issuing an application notice seeking an order disallowing the amendment pursuant to CPR, r. 17.2. Such an application should be made within 14 days of service of the amended statement of case: r. 17.2(2).

24.4   Amendment by Consent

Any amendment is allowed with the written consent of all other parties: CPR, r. 17.1(2)(a).

24.5   Amendment With Permission

24.5.1   PRINCIPLES

The CPR, r. 17.1(2), provides:

> *If his statement of case has been served, a party may amend it only—*
> *(a)   with the written consent of all other parties; or*
> *(b)   with the permission of the court.*

A court asked to grant permission to amend will base its decision on the overriding objective. Generally, disposing of a case justly should mean that amendments should be allowed to enable the real matters in controversy between the parties to be determined. The usual costs rule is that the party granted permission to amend must pay the other parties their 'costs of and caused by' the amendment (PD 44, para. 2.5). Under the old system it was held that: 'However negligent or careless may have been the first omission, and however late the proposed amendment, the amendment should be allowed if it can be made without injustice to the other side. There is no injustice if the other side can be compensated by costs.' (*per* Brett MR in *Clarapede* v *Commercial Union Association* (1883) 32 WR 262).

However, this is not always the case. Lord Griffiths in *Ketteman* v *Hansel Properties Ltd* [1987] AC 189, HL, has said,

> . . . it is not the practice invariably to allow a defence which is wholly different from that pleaded to be raised by amendment at the end of the trial even on terms that an adjournment is granted and that the defendant pays all the costs thrown away . . . Whether an amendment should be granted is a matter for the discretion of the trial judge and he should be guided in the exercise of the discretion by his assessment of where justice lies. Many and diverse factors will bear upon the exercise of this discretion.

Turning to the facts, during the final stages of the trial it became apparent that the defendants were likely to lose on the merits. During closing speeches they were granted leave to amend their defence to plead a limitation defence. They could have raised the defence at an earlier stage, and the House of Lords agreed with the Court of Appeal that such an amendment should not have been allowed. If the application had been made earlier, preferably before the trial, it is unlikely the defendant would have encountered difficulties in amending.

The principles in these cases were approved in the post-CPR case of *Charlesworth* v *Relay Roads Ltd* [2000] 1 WLR 230, where Neuberger J described them as representing a fundamental assessment of the functions of the court and having a universal and timeless validity.

In *Smith* v *Baron, The Times*, 1 February 1991, CA, after completion of the evidence, the judge invited both counsel into his room where he drew to their attention what he thought the correct issue was. Both sides were then given permission to re-amend their statements of case in open court, and judgment was given to the claimant. On appeal by the defendant it was held that the judge had acted quite properly, as the purpose of the rules on amendment was to permit a judge to allow the formulation of the real issues between the parties if they did not appear from the original statements of case.

The interrelation between the *Clarapede* and *Ketteman* principles was considered by the Court of Appeal in *Easton* v *Ford Motor Co. Ltd* [1993] 4 All ER 257. *Clarapede* governs all applications made in the early stages of litigation through to the period immediately before trial. In the latest stages of litigation, and particularly the closing stages of the trial, *Ketteman* will apply. There is a grey area between the two. So, for example, a substantial, sixth, amendment was allowed on the sixth day of a lengthy trial in *Beoco Ltd* v *Alfa Laval Co. Ltd* [1995] QB 137, CA.

In any case, the court may refuse an amendment if it will serve no useful purpose: *Re Jokai Tea Holdings Ltd* [1992] 1 WLR 1196, CA.

24.5.2   PROCEDURE

A party seeking permission to amend must issue an application notice. Generally no evidence is required in support, but the proposed amended statement of case must be filed with the application: PD 17, para. 1.2(2).

The traditional way of amending is to retype the statement of case showing the original wording in ordinary black type, but with the amendments made in, or underlined in, red. Any words deleted are shown crossed through in red ink. Re-amendments are shown in green ink. Subsequent amendments are shown first in violet and then yellow inks: PD 17, para. 2.4. However, there are two other options:

(a) by using monochrome type face, but with a numeric code indicating the amendments (PD 17, para. 2.2(2)); or

(b) by simply retyping the document incorporating the changes and omitting deleted text (PD 17, para. 2.2). However, the court may, if it thinks it desirable, direct that the amendments be shown in one or other of the ways described above.

If there is a substantial change the document should be re-verified by a statement of truth (PD 17, para. 1.4).

The amended statement of case should be endorsed 'Amended [Particulars of Claim] by Order of District Judge [Chelmsford] dated [15th January 2001]'.

24.6   Addition and Substitution of Parties

24.6.1   THE MAIN RULES

If an amendment involves the removal, addition or substitution of a party the court will consider CPR, Part 19, which provides a code for dealing with such situations (as well as providing a code for intervention by non-parties (see **8.7**)). Permission for such amendments must be sought if the alteration is to be made after service of the claim form: r. 19.4(1).

The main test when considering a change involving the addition or substitution of a party is whether the amendment is 'desirable': see CPR, r. 19.2(2)–(4). Nobody, however, may be added as a claimant unless they consent in writing: CPR, r. 19.4(4).

The CPR, r. 19.2, provides so far as is material:

> (2)   *The court may order a person to be added as a new party if—*
> (a)   *it is desirable to add the new party so that the court can resolve all matters in dispute in the proceedings; or*
> (b)   *there is an issue involving the new party and an existing party which is connected to the matters in dispute in the proceedings, and it is desirable to add the new party so that the court can resolve that issue.*
> (3)   *The court may order any person to cease to be a party if it is not desirable for that person to be party to the proceedings.*

> *(4) The court may order a new party to be substituted for an existing one if—*
>   *(a) the existing party's interest or liability has passed to the new party; and*
>   *(b) it is desirable to substitute the new party so that the court can resolve the matters in dispute in the proceedings.*

Court fees are payable when new parties are brought in.

24.6.2 PROCEDURE FOR MAKING CHANGES IN THE PARTIES

Any change involving the addition or substitution of a party will involve amending the statements of case, and can only be made by order of the court: see CPR, r. 19.2(2)–(4). The application may be made by an existing party or by a person who wishes to become a party: CPR, r. 19.4(2). There is an express provision requiring evidence in support of an application under r. 19.2(4) for the substitution of a new party where an existing party's interest has passed (e.g. on death), and that type of application can be made without notice: r. 19.4(3). Any other type of application for addition or substitution does not strictly have to be supported by written evidence, though the circumstances may make this desirable. Further, any other type of addition or substitution application is usually made on notice to all other parties.

If a proposed change in the parties is agreed by the court, the order must be served on all the parties and also on anyone affected by the order: CPR, r. 19.4(5). An order granting permission to make such an amendment may include consequential directions (r. 19.4(6) and PD 19, para. 3.2) dealing with:

(a) filing and serving of the amended claim form and particulars of claim on any new defendant, usually within 14 days;

(b) serving other relevant documents on the new party;

(c) providing the new defendant with a response pack for the purpose of admitting, defending or counterclaiming;

(d) serving the order on all parties and any other person affected by it; and

(e) the management of the proceedings.

24.6.3 EFFECT OF ADDITION OR SUBSTITUTION OF A NEW PARTY

A person added as a defendant by amendment becomes a party for the first time when the amended proceedings are served: *Ketteman* v *Hansel Properties Ltd* [1987] AC 189, HL.

24.7 Amendment after the Limitation Period

24.7.1 GENERAL RULE

The Limitation Act 1980, s. 35(3), provides:

> *Except as provided by section 33 of this Act or by rules of court, neither the High Court nor any County Court shall allow a new claim . . ., other than an original set-off or counterclaim, to be made in the course of any action after the expiry of any time limit under this Act which would affect a new action to enforce that claim.*

A 'new claim' is defined in s. 35(2) as:

> *any claim by way of set-off or counterclaim, and any claim involving either —*
>   *(a) the addition or substitution of a new cause of action; or*
>   *(b) the addition or substitution of a new party . . .*

Relevant rules of court, made under s. 35(4), are CPR, rr. 17.4 and 19.5.

24.7.2   AMENDMENT AFTER THE LIMITATION PERIOD TO ADD/SUBSTITUTE A NEW CAUSE OF ACTION

The Limitation Act 1980 (LA 1980), s. 35, provides that a new cause of action may be added to existing proceedings after the expiry of the limitation period only if either:

(a)   it is an original set-off or counterclaim made by a party who has not previously made any claim in the action (s. 35(3)); or

(b)   the court disapplies the personal injuries limitation period under LA 1980, s. 33 (s. 33 is explained at **23.5.2** above) (s. 35(3)); or

(c)   it arises out of the same, or substantially the same, facts as are already in issue (s. 35(5)(a)).

An original set-off or counterclaim ((a) above) has been construed as being a set-off or counterclaim raised by an original defendant against an original claimant (Lord Donaldson MR in *Kennett* v *Brown* [1988] 1 WLR 582, overruled on another point by *Welsh Development Agency* v *Redpath Dorman Long Ltd* [1994] 1 WLR 1409).

The writ served in *Brickfield Properties Ltd* v *Newton* [1971] 1 WLR 863 claimed damages against the defendant architect for negligent supervision of certain works. After the limitation period had expired, a statement of claim was served claiming damages both for negligent design and negligent supervision. The defendant applied to strike out the allegation of negligent design. The Court of Appeal held that the statement of claim could not stand without amending the writ. It was further held that the design and supervision claims arose out of 'substantially the same facts' ((c) above), and in its discretion the court allowed the amendment of the writ.

A relatively common situation of a new claim arising out of substantially the same facts is where a building society brings a claim for possession (only), and subsequently applies to amend to add a money claim for the amount outstanding: see *Lloyds Bank plc* v *Rogers* (16 July 1999, CA, unreported).

24.7.3   AMENDMENT AFTER THE LIMITATION PERIOD TO ADD/SUBSTITUTE A NEW PARTY

There are four situations where such an amendment will be allowed. The first is in relation to personal injury cases (s. 35(3)), the remaining three are where it is necessary to add/substitute a new party (s. 35(5)(b)).

24.7.3.1   Limitation Act 1980, s. 33
This is where a new party is added or substituted when the court disapplies the personal injury limitation period under s. 33 (see s. 35(3) and CPR, r. 19.5(4)). The addition of the new party will also be allowed if the decision under s. 33 is left until trial (r. 19.5(4)(b)).

24.7.3.2   Action cannot properly be carried on without new party
The CPR, r. 19.5(3) provides that the addition or substitution of a new party after the expiry of a limitation period may be necessary if:

(b)   the claim cannot properly be carried on by or against the original party unless the new party is added or substituted as claimant or defendant . . .

The rule gives no further guidance on when claims cannot 'properly' be carried on without the amendment. It is possible that the rule gives a general discretion to the court to consider whether evading the provisions of the Limitation Act by amendment would be 'proper'. However, this is unlikely to be what the rule envisages. The former provisions (RSC O. 15. r. 6(6)) giving effect to this part of the LA 1980, s. 35 laid down five categories of cases where errors in naming parties gave rise to a legal bar to obtaining a remedy, and it was only in these five categories where it was considered 'necessary' (the same word used in the present rules in r. 19.5(2)(b) in this context) to add a party once limitation had expired. It is most likely that it will only be 'proper' to add or substitute a party under r. 19.5(3)(b) where a legal impediment such as those set out in the old O. 15, r. 6(6), exists. The old categories were where:

(a) property was vested in the new party at law or in equity and the claimant's claim was in respect of an equitable interest in that property which was liable to be defeated unless the new party was joined; or

(b) the relevant cause of action was vested in the new party and the claimant jointly but not severally; or

(c) the new party was the Attorney General and the proceedings should have been brought by relator proceedings (see **8.2.13**) in his name; or

(d) the new party was a company in which the claimant was a shareholder and on whose behalf the claimant was suing to enforce a right vested in the company; or

(e) the new party was sued jointly with the defendant and was not also liable severally with him and failure to join the new party might have rendered the claim unenforceable.

It will be appreciated that these categories were rather narrow. Joint, but not several, entitlement or liability (grounds (b) and (e) above) may arise where a contract is, by its terms, made jointly with numerous persons. An example is *Roche* v *Sherrington* [1982] 1 WLR 599 where it was alleged that loans were made to the defendant from moneys in a joint account in the names of three persons. In such a case, under CPR, r. 19.3, all three must be made parties to the action, as defendants if they do not consent to acting as claimants unless the court gives permission to the contrary.

24.7.3.3 Alteration of capacity

The third situation is provided by CPR, r. 17.4(4):

> *The court may allow an amendment to alter the capacity in which a party claims if the new capacity is one which that party had when the proceedings started or has since acquired.*

24.7.3.4 Correcting a mistake

The fourth situation is provided by CPR, r. 19.5(3)(a), which allows the correction of the name of an existing party after the expiry of the limitation period even if the effect is to substitute a new party where:

> *(a) the new party is to be substituted for a party who was named in the claim form in mistake for the new party . . .*

Further, by CPR, r. 17.4(3), once the limitation period has expired:

> *The court may allow an amendment to correct a mistake as to the name of a party, but only where the mistake was genuine and not one which would cause reasonable doubt as to the identity of the party in question.*

It would seem from *International Distillers and Vinters Ltd* v *J.F. Hillebrand (UK) Ltd, The Times*, 25 January 2000, that:

(a) CPR, r. 19.5(3)(a), governs applications which involve substituting a new party for the person who was originally named in the proceedings, and the only question from the rules is whether the original person was named in mistake for the new party; and

(b) CPR, r. 17.4(3), governs applications where the amendment does not involve substituting a new party for the misnamed party, but is limited to correcting the name of the original party. Apparently, from the *International Distillers* case, this rather less substantial form of amendment requires more stringent preconditions to be satisfied, as set out in r. 17.4(3), than those required under r. 19.5(3).

This, of course, is unlikely to be true. Instead, a sound interpretation of the rules would be that where the effect of a proposed amendment sought after limitation has expired is to substitute a new party for that originally named, the requirements of both rr. 17.4(3) and 19.5(3) must be satisfied, together with a consideration to the overriding objective. Thus, putting the requirements of both rules together, and including the overriding objective, the conditions that must be satisfied before an amendment can be allowed are that:

(a) the original party was named in mistake for the new party;

(b) the mistake was 'genuine';

(c) the mistake was not such as to cause reasonable doubt as to the identity of the party in question (i.e. the party the claimant intended to name); and

(d) making the amendment would enable the court to deal with the case justly.

There was a great deal of complicated case law on the equivalent provisions under the old rules, which is certainly redundant as there are significant differences between the wording of the old and new rules. Until the new provision is construed by the appellate courts, it is not possible to say whether the courts will be prepared to give this provision a wide or a narrow interpretation. The rule does say, however, that substitution will only be allowed where the original party was named 'in mistake *for* the new party'. This may indicate that the claimant has to have had the new party in mind when drafting the claim form, but through some mistake ended up naming someone else. However, the courts may wish to avoid such a narrow construction of the rule.

24.7.3.5 Applications made just before the expiry of limitation
Provided an application to add a new cause of action or new party by amendment is made, and effected by service of an amended claim form (see **24.6.2**), before the expiry of the limitation period, the rules considered in this section (**24.7.3**) do not apply. However, if an application to add a cause of action or a party is made before the expiry of limitation, but service of the amended claim form is not effected until after the expiry of the limitation period, the amendment will be bad unless it falls within one of the exceptions discussed in **24.7.3.1** to **24.7.3.4**: *Bank of America National Trust and Savings Association* v *Chrismas* [1994] 1 All ER 401. Consequently, if an order to add a new cause of action or a new party is made close to the expiry of limitation where none of the exceptions will apply, the order should impose a condition that service on the additional defendants must be effected before the expiry of the limitation period.

Similarly, where an application for permission to amend to add a party or a cause of action is issued before the expiry of the limitation period, but the application is heard after limitation has expired, the Court can only grant permission to amend if the amendment is permitted by one of the exceptions in **24.7.3.1** to **24.7.3.4**: *Welsh Development Agency* v *Redpath Dorman Long Ltd* [1994] 1 WLR 1409, CA.

24.8 Amendments after the Limitation Period Affecting Accrued Rights

24.8.1 GENERAL RULE

Amendments (usually by the defendant) which would prejudice the rights of the opposite party (usually the claimant) existing at the date of the proposed amendment are not generally allowed. Thus in *Steward* v *North Metropolitan Tramways* (1886) 16 QBD 556, CA, the claimant sued the defendants for personal injuries suffered on a tramway. After expiry of the limitation period the defendants sought permission to amend their Defence to set up a contract pursuant to statute which had the effect of transferring liability for the accident to the local road authority. The amendment was disallowed, because, limitation having expired, the claimant could not be put in the same position as if the proposed defence had been served at the proper time.

24.8.2 EXCEPTIONS

(a) If fresh evidence comes to light after the expiry of the limitation period, and the defendants are not at fault in seeking to amend at that stage, they may be allowed to amend notwithstanding any prejudice caused to the claimant by the expiry of the limitation period: *Weait* v *Jayanbee Joinery* [1963] 1 QB 239, CA.

(b) If an amendment to the Defence introduces facts which the claimant must have known all along, it may be allowed notwithstanding the expiry of the limitation period, provided the defendant seeking to amend was not previously aware of those facts: *Turner* v *Ford Motor Co.* [1965] 2 All ER 583, CA.

TWENTY FIVE

RENEWAL OF PROCEEDINGS

25.1 Introduction

There are two rules, neither of which is very onerous in a usual case, which are designed to prevent unduly stale claims being litigated. They are:

(a) the prescribed periods of limitation for commencing proceedings, after which, with certain exceptions, the proposed defendant will have a Limitation Act defence; and

(b) the periods prescribed by the Civil Procedure Rules 1998 over which an originating process is valid after issue for the purpose of service.

These two rules are cumulative. For example, the limitation period for actions for breach of contract is six years, and the period of validity of a claim form is usually four months. If the claimant uses these periods to the full, the defendant need not be served until six years and four months after the breach.

If the claimant does not serve the originating process during the period of its validity, an application may be made to the court for it to be renewed for an extended period. It is this procedure which will now be discussed in this chapter.

25.2 Period of Validity

25.2.1 HOW LONG DOES A CLAIM FORM REMAIN VALID?

This is best explained by reference to CPR, r. 7.5, which provides:

(1) After a claim form has been issued, it must be served on the defendant.
(2) The general rule is that a claim form must be served within 4 months after the date of issue.
(3) The period for service is 6 months where the claim form is to be served out of the jurisdiction.

Thus, once issued, a claim form is valid and available for service on the defendant within the jurisdiction for four months. A claim form issued on 9 September 2000 expires on 8 January 2001, fractions of a day being disregarded: see *Trow* v *Ind Coope Ltd* [1967] 2 QB 899, decided when writs were initially valid for 12 months.

25.2.2 APPLICATION TO EXTEND THE PERIOD OF VALIDITY

If the claimant does not serve the claim form within the relevant six or four month period an application may be made to the court to have its validity extended. This application should ordinarily be made before the validity of the claim expires, although there is power under CPR, r. 7.6, to make an order extending the validity of the claim form even after it has expired. CPR, r. 7.6, provides:

> *(1) The claimant may apply for an order extending the period within which the claim form may be served.*
>
> *(2) The general rule is that an application to extend the time for service must be made—*
>
> *(a) within the period for serving the claim form specified by rule 7.5; or*
>
> *(b) where an order has been made under this rule, within the period for service specified in the order.*
>
> *(3) If the claimant applies for an order to extend the time for service of the claim form after the end of the period specified by rule 7.5 or by an order made under this rule, the court may make such an order only if—*
>
> *(a) the court has been unable to serve the claim form; or*
>
> *(b) the claimant has taken all reasonable steps to serve the claim form but has been unable to do so; and*
>
> *(c) in either case, the claimant has acted promptly in making the application.*

25.2.3 SERVICE OF AN INVALID CLAIM FORM

Such service is not a nullity, but it is an irregularity. The defendant should acknowledge service in the normal way. Simply acknowledging service does not waive the irregularity.

The defendant should then apply for an order invalidating service of the claim form under CPR, r. 3.10. The application must be supported by evidence verifying the facts on which the application is based. However, if there is delay in acknowledging service, or in seeking to set such service aside, or if the defendant fails to state an intention to defend, such (and similar) conduct may be held to be a waiver of the irregularity in service.

25.3 Principles to be Applied

The form of CPR, r. 7.6, shows that a different approach will be taken depending on whether or not the application to extend the period of validity of the claim form is made while the claim form is still valid.

25.3.1 APPLICATIONS MADE DURING THE PERIOD OF VALIDITY

No criteria are laid down in CPR, r. 7.6, itself indicating how the discretion to extend should be exercised. Accordingly, the application will be decided by applying the overriding objective. Dealing with a case justly will include dealing with it if at all possible, but the court will also be mindful of the need to deal with cases expeditiously and the importance of not side-stepping the effect of the Limitation Act. The old rules also gave the court a general discretion in dealing with applications to extend the validity of originating process, and similar considerations obviously informed the courts in developing principles to be applied in such applications. The old principles, which may be of some use as a guide to applying the overriding objective in this context, are discussed at **25.3.3**.

25.3.2 APPLICATIONS MADE AFTER THE EXPIRY OF THE PERIOD OF VALIDITY

For applications after the claim form has expired, fairly exacting criteria have been laid down by CPR, r. 7.6(3) (see **25.2.2**). It will be seen that there should have been efforts to serve, and that there must be no unexplained delay in making the application (albeit the application is made after the expiry of the period of validity). If the claimant has been making efforts to serve, it is not all that likely that the claimant will simultaneously forget about the period of validity. The rule is most likely to assist claimants who believe the court is effecting service, and later discover this is not the case.

25.3.3 OLD PRINCIPLES

Cases involving disputed extensions for the purpose of service reached the House of Lords on a number of occasions in the 1980s and 1990s. Those cases laid down the following principles:

(a) The primary rule was that the power to extend the validity of a writ under RSC O. 6, r. 8, could only be exercised for good reason. The question whether such good reason existed depended on all the circumstances of any particular case.

(b) Where there were matters which could, potentially at least, constitute good reason for renewal it was a matter for the court's discretion whether or not to grant an extension. In considering this discretion the balance of hardship between the parties was a relevant consideration in deciding whether an extension should be granted or refused. The hardship to the claimant was usually the possibility of being left without a remedy against the defendant if the renewal was refused. The hardship to the defendant was often that of defending a stale claim or in being deprived of a Limitation Act defence.

25.3.4 WHAT CONSTITUTED A GOOD REASON FOR EXTENDING THE VALIDITY OF A WRIT?

Typical cases where there would be good reasons for granting an extension were:

(a) Where there was a clear agreement between the parties not to serve the proceedings.

(b) Where the defendant could not be traced or was evading service.

Delays in service caused by a failure of the legal aid authorities to act or to act reasonably could also amount to good reason (see *Waddon* v *Whitecroft-Scovill Ltd* [1988] 1 WLR 309, HL, as could a failure by a County Court to effect service of County Court proceedings (see *Ward-Lee* v *Lineham* [1993] 1 WLR 754, CA).

25.3.5 WHAT DID NOT CONSTITUTE A GOOD REASON FOR EXTENDING THE VALIDITY OF A WRIT?

Typical situations which were held not to amount to good reasons were:

(a) That service would interfere with ongoing negotiations: *The Mouna* [1991] 2 Lloyd's Rep 221, CA.

(b) Delays by the claimant in applying for legal aid, or in applying for restrictions in the legal aid certificate to be lifted.

(c) Difficulty in obtaining evidence.

25.3.6 IF AN EXTENSION IS DESIRED, BUT THERE ARE NO GOOD REASONS

In this situation the claimant must serve the claim form, i.e. serve 'protective proceedings'. If there are continuing negotiations, or if the claimant has not completed the necessary inquiries, the best course is then to obtain an extension of time for the service of the particulars of claim, either by agreement with the defendant or by order of the court.

25.3.7 PERSONAL INJURIES CASES

In *Waddon* v *Whitecroft-Scovill Ltd* [1988] 1 WLR 309, HL, it was made plain that in personal injury cases the question of renewal should be decided using the same principles as are applied in other applications for renewal, and not by the principles governing applications to extend the primary limitation period under LA 1980, s. 33 (for which, see **23.5.2**).

25.3.8 PERIOD OF ANY EXTENSION

In *Baly* v *Barrett, The Times*, 19 May 1989, HL, it seemed there was a local practice of granting initial extensions for periods of 12 months. Lord Brandon said that that practice was wrong — it is always for the claimant to show that the period of extension sought is justified.

25.4 Procedure on Renewal

An application to extend the period of validity is made by issuing an application notice, which is dealt with without giving notice: CPR, r. 7.6(4)(b). The application must be supported by evidence which must include:

(a) all the circumstances relied on;

(b) the date of issue of the claim;

(c) the expiry date of any previous extension; and

(d) a full explanation as to why the claim has not been served.

Once the order has been made, the application notice and evidence in support must be served with the order on the party against whom the order was sought, unless the court otherwise orders: CPR, r. 23.9. The order will contain a notice informing the defendant of the right to apply to set aside the order granting the extension, and any application to set aside must be made within seven days of service of the order: r. 23.10.

25.5 How to Challenge an Order Extending the Validity of a Claim

The first the defendant will know about the order will be when the claim form is served.

The claim should be acknowledged in the usual way, stating an intention to defend. An application should then be made on notice supported by written evidence for an order to setting aside the order extending the validity of the claim form.

25.6 Questions

OBJECTIVES

By the conclusion of this section you should:

(a) be able to identify cases where requests can usefully be made for further information;

(b) understand the relationship between making requests for further information and other procedures for finding out more about an opponent's case;

(c) know the limitation periods governing the main types of cases;

(d) know the main rules on how limitation periods are calculated, including the main rules on discretionary extension of limitation periods;

(e) know the rules on amending statements of case;

(f) know the principles governing discretionary amendments of statements of case;

(g) understand the principles governing application to amend after limitation has expired; and

(h) understand the procedure and principles relating to applications to extend the period of validity of originating process.

RESEARCH

Read the materials contained in **Chapters 22** to **25** of this Manual.

Note: These topics, especially limitation, are often found to be difficult. You may find it helpful, in relation to limitation problems, to prepare a brief chronology of the relevant dates and to take the following four steps (in the order in which they are set out):

(a) Given the cause of action, ascertain the date from which time began to run — in some cases, it runs from the date of the alleged wrongful act; in others from the date when some damage occurred; in yet others from the date of the claimant's knowledge of certain facts; in the case of a combination, from the date on which judgment was given in the main action or, if there was no judgment, from the earliest date on which the amount of compensation was agreed between the person compensated and the person now seeking a contribution.

(b) Once you have discovered the date from which time began to run, apply the ordinary time limit appropriate to the cause of action and ascertain the date of expiry.

(c) Were the proceedings started before the date of expiry? In a straightforward C v D action 'starting' means issuing a claim form. But remember that if C v D proceedings have already been started (within time) and C is seeking to add a new party, C should have served the amended claim form on the new party before the date of expiry. See also the special rules about Part 20 claims.

(d) If you are out of time, ascertain whether the circumstances are such that you are entitled to apply to extend the ordinary time limit.

LARGE GROUP SESSION 6

In advance of Large Group Session 6, read questions 1 to 3, which will be dealt with in class.

QUESTION 1

Julia has issued a claim form against Catherine claiming damages for trespass and an injunction to restrain Catherine from building a garden wall on Julia's land. Julia and Catherine are neighbours. The particulars of claim refer to Catherine having carried out certain works on Julia's 'side of the boundary' between the two properties. You are instructed on behalf of Catherine, who states that the boundary has never been clearly marked and that in her view she has kept within her own property. How can the issues be more clearly defined?

QUESTION 2

On 28 February 1996 Charles was knocked unconscious whilst crossing the High Street at Barchester by a vehicle travelling at an excessive speed. The driver failed to stop. While Charles knows he was hit by a vehicle he cannot remember anything about the vehicle. In August 1997 David approached Charles in the High Street and said he witnessed the accident, and had been feeling guilty about not having come forward sooner. He identified the driver and identified the vehicle as one owned by the Barchester Argus, a local newspaper. In June 1998 Charles consulted your instructing solicitors, who advised him he had a good case in negligence against the Barchester Argus. The person dealing with the case at that time noted the accident as having occurred 'in February'. That person has since left the firm, and in error the person taking over the file thought that the accident date was February 1998. By the time the mistake was realised some time had passed and in the circumstances, rather than comply with any pre-action protocol, a claim form was issued in November 2000. The Argus filed a defence relying on the Limitation Act. You have been asked to advise Charles. Which one of the following is the best advice to give him?

[A] The limitation period is three years from the date of the accident, so by November 2000 it was too late to issue the claim form.

[B] The limitation period began to run when Charles discovered the identity of the defendant in August 1997, so the claim form was issued three months late.

[C] The limitation period started to run in June 1998 when Charles was advised he had a cause of action against the defendant, so the claim form was issued in time.

[D] Although the limitation period is three years from the date of the accident, the error made by your instructing solicitors would amount to a good reason for extending the limitation period under the Limitation Act 1980, s. 33.

QUESTION 3

Charles was seriously injured at work in October 1997. He consulted solicitors who contacted Charles' employers and their insurers and in their communications with them complied with the spirit of the pre-action protocol. Charles' solicitors issued a claim form in June 2000, but they decided not to serve it because they were negotiating with the employer's insurers with a view to settling the claim. In September 2000 the insurers paid £10,000 to Charles which, it was agreed, would be treated 'as if made by way of interim payment'.

It is now November 2000. Charles' solicitors have been unable to reach a settlement and seek your advice as to the steps they should take to continue the action.

SMALL GROUP SESSION 6

On the basis of your research, answer questions 4 to 11 in advance of Small Group Class 6.

QUESTION 4

You are instructed by Theatre Products plc who are being sued by Bobo the clown who had used grease paint sold by Theatre Products plc. This product is alleged to have caused severe dermatitis. Bobo's medical report says that he has used a number of face cleansers and spot removers but his condition has deteriorated.

Theatre Products plc suspect that Bobo's condition may have been exacerbated by the face cleansers but do not know precisely which brands he has used.

Advise Theatre Products plc.

QUESTION 5

Mark has commenced proceedings against Tina claiming damages for personal injuries sustained when he was run down at a light controlled junction. Tina has served a defence claiming that the lights were 'red' for pedestrians. Mark would like the following further information from Tina:

(a) Where she had left before commencing the journey in which the accident happened.

(b) The colour showing at the traffic lights controlling Tina's line of traffic:

    (i) when she was 15 yards in front of the junction of Howard Street and Firs Lane, Macclesfield on [the day of the accident];

    (ii) as she entered the junction.

(c) How fast she was travelling when she struck Mark.

Advise Mark as to the procedure for obtaining the information and whether Tina will have any grounds for objecting to any of these requests.

QUESTION 6

Catherine lost three fingers in an accident at work on 9 January 1997 when her hand got caught in an industrial guillotine. Contrary to safety regulations the machine was unfenced. Catherine was born on 3 September 1979. She instructed solicitors to sue for compensation in July 1997. A letter before action was sent the next month. Medical reports were obtained in 1999, and unsuccessful negotiations were conducted until March 2000. In her statement to her solicitors Catherine indicated that she may not have been concentrating on her job at the time of the accident. The solicitor dealing with Catherine's case left the firm in April 2000, and the file was overlooked until 1 November 2000. A claim form was issued on 2 November.

Will the action be allowed to continue?

QUESTION 7

Michelle, who is aged 28, started proceedings two months ago claiming damages for personal injuries suffered when, seven years ago, the defendant, Clive, is alleged to have battered her with his fists and a heavy mantlepiece ornament. Five years ago Michelle was admitted to hospital suffering from mental illness which Michelle alleges was brought on by Clive's attack. Although she was discharged from hospital after six weeks, Michelle was officially diagnosed as suffering from mental illness until 12 months ago.

Will Michelle's action be allowed to continue?

QUESTION 8

Pike (Groundworks) Ltd sue David for breach of a contract made three years ago. David files a defence which says that at all material times he made it known to Pike that he was acting as agent for Trevor. Advise Pike, who wish to dispute the allegation, but, as the person who contracted on their behalf has left the company, Pike also wish to safeguard their position in case David's case proves to be correct.

QUESTION 9

In August 1994 Norman purchased certain goods from 'Oval Manufacturers' which proved defective. Between 1997 (when the defective nature of the goods was discovered) and last year his solicitors were in correspondence with Surrey Manufacturing plc who had answered the letter they initially wrote to 'Oval Manufacturers'. In July 2000 his solicitors issued a claim form against Surrey Manufacturing plc. A defence was delivered in September 2000 to the effect that the order was not placed with the defendants but with a subsidiary company 'Surrey Industrial Manufacturing plc'. It is now December 2000.

Advise Norman.

QUESTION 10

By a claim form issued on 21 June 1999 Rutland Engineering Company Ltd brought proceedings against Sturdy Compressors plc to recover damages in respect of equipment delivered in September 1994. By its defence Sturdy Compressors admits the contract but denies it was in breach. On 22 November 2000 Sturdy Compressors issued an application notice for permission to amend its defence so as to allege that it was not a party to the contract but merely acting (to the knowledge of Rutland) as agents for another company, Sturdy Valves Ltd.

It is now December 2000.

Advise Rutland Engineering Co. Ltd.

QUESTION 11

Hugh was injured in a road traffic accident 34 months ago allegedly caused by the negligent driving of Julia. Within eight months of the accident solicitors had been instructed and negotiations for a settlement were commenced with solicitors representing Julia. During correspondence Hugh's solicitors told Julia's solicitors that a claim form had been issued in the Christchurch County Court for service by Hugh's solicitors. Julia's solicitors replied, 'At this stage there would appear to be no reason for incurring costs involved in serving proceedings. Please would you give us 14 days' notice of your intention to effect service'. Hugh's solicitors replied giving their consent. Hugh and Julia were unable to agree to the appointment of a single joint expert but gave voluntary mutual exchange of medical reports. Julia (on advice from her solicitors) has viewed Hugh's injuries as being far less serious than the view taken by Hugh. Julia's offers in settlement (the most recent being six weeks ago) have been refused.

Four weeks ago Hugh's solicitors gave notice that they were about to serve proceedings. The claim form was in fact served 10 days ago. It was issued on 27 April 2000 and has been endorsed with a note that it was extended on 11 September 2000 by District Judge Howard for a period of eight months expiring at 4 pm on 26 April 2001. Advise Julia on whether service was effective, and how any application she could make would be considered in the light of the overriding objective.

TWENTY SIX

SECURITY FOR COSTS

26.1   Introduction

There are circumstances where a defendant who has been sued feels that, given the strength of the defence, there is a good chance of defeating the claim, but is worried that, in the event of winning, the claimant would be unable to meet any order for costs made at trial. It can also happen that an impecunious claimant can begin a 'nuisance action', which has little prospect of success, but which is guaranteed to cause inconvenience and annoyance to the defendant, whatever the eventual result.

In order to protect a defendant in this situation, there is provision to make an application that the claimant provide security for costs. If this application is granted, the claimant will be required to pay a specific amount of money into court within a specified time period.

Normally the proceedings will be temporarily halted until the claimant complies with the order. The money will be held to provide a fund out of which the defendant's costs can be paid, in the event of the defendant being successful.

26.2   Conditions for Granting Security for Costs

Security for costs can only be ordered if one of the conditions set out in CPR, r. 25.13(2), is satisfied. The conditions are:

(a)   the claimant is an individual—

    (i)   who is ordinarily resident out of the jurisdiction, and

    (ii)   is not a person against whom a claim can be enforced under the Brussels Convention or Lugano Convention;

(b)   the claimant is a company or other incorporated body—

    (i)   which is ordinarily resident out of the jurisdiction, and

    (ii)   is not a body against whom a claim can be enforced under the Brussels Convention or Lugano Convention;

(c)   the claimant is a company or other body (whether incorporated inside or outside Great Britain) and there is reason to believe that it will be unable to pay the defendant's costs if ordered to do so;

(d)   the claimant has changed his or her address since the claim was commenced with a view to evading the consequences of the litigation;

(e)   the claimant failed to give his or her address in the claim form, or gave an incorrect address in that form;

(f) the claimant is acting as a nominal claimant, other than as a representative claimant under Part 19, and there is reason to believe that he or she will be unable to pay the defendant's costs if ordered to do so;

(g) the claimant has taken steps in relation to his or her assets that would make it difficult to enforce an order for costs against him or her.

Sub-paragraphs (ii) of conditions (a) and (b) are based on the decision of the Court of Appeal in *Fitzgerald* v *Williams* [1996] QB 657. Under the old rules there was no equivalent to sub-paragraphs (ii), so security for costs could, potentially, have been ordered merely because the claimant was outside the jurisdiction. In *Fitzgerald* v *Williams* it was held that this potentially offended against what is now the EC Treaty, Article 12 (ex 6), as being covertly discriminatory against EC residents on the grounds of nationality. As EC nationals protected by Article 12 will more or less coincide with the persons against whom judgments can be enforced under the Brussels Convention, this should no longer be an issue. Sub-paragraphs (ii) of conditions (a) and (b) also aim to rectify the problem identified in *De Bry* v *Fitzgerald* [1990] 1 WLR 522, which is that, as it is relatively cheap and easy to enforce English judgments under the Brussels and Lugano Conventions in the courts of other contracting States, there is little reason for granting security for costs against claimants residing in such countries purely on the basis that the claimant is resident outside the jurisdiction. For similar reasons, it has been held since *Raeburn* v *Andrews* (1874) LR 9 QB 118 that security for costs should not be ordered purely on the basis of residence outside the jurisdiction against claimants resident in Scotland. The result is that security for costs under conditions (a) and (b) is limited to claimants residing outside western Europe.

Ground (c) above is based on the Companies Act 1985, s. 726(1), which provides:

Where in England and Wales a limited company is plaintiff in an action or other legal proceeding, the court having jurisdiction in the matter may, if it appears by credible testimony that there is reason to believe that the company will be unable to pay the defendant's costs if successful in his defence, require sufficient security to be given for those costs, and may stay all proceedings until the security is given.

It is noteworthy that impecuniosity is of itself a ground for granting security for costs against a party in the position of a claimant only if that party is a limited company.

In *Re Little Olympian Each Ways Ltd* [1995] 1 WLR 560, Lindsay J was only prepared to hold that a Jersey registered limited company was 'ordinarily resident out of the jurisdiction' after a detailed analysis of its activities, and on the basis that its central control and management was exercised in Jersey and hence outside the jurisdiction.

26.3 Parties to an Application for Security for Costs

Normally, applications for security for costs are made by defendants against claimants. They can also be made by claimants against defendants in respect of the costs of any counterclaim (but if the counterclaim is a set-off it is most unlikely that security will be ordered: *Ashworth* v *Berkeley-Walbrook Ltd, The Independent*, 9 October 1989, CA). Further they may be made by a Part 20 defendant against the defendant making a Part 20 claim, or against an appellant to an appeal (or a respondent who cross-appeals): see CPR, r. 25.15.

By CPR, r. 25.14, an order for security for costs may also be made against someone other than a claimant if the court is satisfied that the person against whom the order is sought either:

(a) assigned the claim to the claimant with a view to avoiding the possibility of a costs order being made against him or her; or

(b) has contributed or agreed to contribute to the claimant's costs in return for a share of any money or property which the claimant may recover in the proceedings.

26.4 Discretion to Grant Security for Costs

Once it has been established that the case comes within one of the conditions set out in **26.2** or **26.3** above, the court has a general discretion whether to grant an order for security. In exercising this discretion the court will have regard to all the circumstances of the case, and consider whether it would be just to make the order: see CPR, rr. 25.13(1)(a) and 25.14(1)(a).

As can be seen from the case of *Parkinson (Sir Lindsay) and Co. Ltd* v *Triplan Ltd* [1973] QB 609, [1973] 2 All ER 273, CA, in exercising its discretion whether or not to grant the order the court should consider:

(a) The genuineness of the claimant's claim.

(b) The claimant's prospects of success (although the court should not normally embark upon an in-depth analysis of the merits of the case: *Porzelack K.G.* v *Porzelack (UK) Ltd* [1987] 1 WLR 420.

(c) Whether the defendant has made any admissions of the claimant's claim.

(d) Whether the defendant has made any payment into court.

(e) Whether the claimant's impecuniosity has been brought about by the defendant's conduct.

(f) The stage at which the application is made.

(g) Whether the application is being made oppressively and is therefore designed to stifle a claim which has reasonable prospects of success: *Aquila Design (GRB) Products Ltd* v *Cornhill Insurance plc* [1988] BCLC 134, CA.

Further, special considerations need to be given to cases where the claimant is resident outside the jurisdiction. The courts tend to be reluctant to order security for costs against a claimant resident out of the jurisdiction if there are one or more co-claimants resident within the jurisdiction. It is, however, a question of discretion and a defendant being sued by joint claimants, some of whom are resident inside the jurisdiction, some outside, may be able to obtain security for costs against those outside the jurisdiction. In particular, this may be appropriate, following *Slazengers Ltd* v *Seaspeed Ferries Ltd* [1987] 1 WLR 1197, where either:

(a) each claimant is likely to be liable only for an *aliquot* share of the defendant's costs; or

(b) the claimants do not rely on identical causes of action; or

(c) it is impossible, taking into account the court's wide discretion as to costs at trial, to predict the likely costs outcome.

Conversely, where:

(a) foreign and English claimants all rely on the same cause of action; and

(b) it is certain that each claimant will be held liable for all the defendant's costs if unsuccessful; and

(c) at least one of the claimants has funds within the jurisdiction sufficient to cover the whole of the defendant's costs, the court will generally refuse an application for security for costs: *Winthorp* v *Royal Exchange Assurance Co.* (1755) 1 Dick 282 as explained by *Slazengers Ltd* v *Seaspeed Ferries Ltd* [1987] 1 WLR 1197.

26.5 Procedure

26.5.1 APPLICATION

The defendant issues an application notice which is heard by a Master or District Judge. The application must be supported by evidence in writing.

The application may be made at *any stage of the proceedings*, but the defendant should not be dilatory in applying as any delay may count against the defendant when the court considers the application: *Jenred Properties Limited* v *Ente Nazionale per il Turismo, Financial Times*, 29 October 1985, CA.

26.5.2 EFFECT OF THE ORDER

Where the application is successful, the Master will state the amount to be paid and the time within which the claimant must comply with the order. Usually proceedings will be stayed, pending payment of the money. In the Commercial Court the practice is to give the claimant a reasonable time to provide the security, and the defendant liberty to apply for an order dismissing the claim in the event of default (Commercial Guide, appendix 18, para. 6).

26.5.3 AMOUNT OF THE PAYMENT

This is entirely at the court's discretion: *Procon (Great Britain) Ltd* v *Provincial Building Co. Ltd* [1984] 1 WLR 557, CA. However, it is helpful to give the court an estimate of costs of the action, and to that end it is good practice to supply the court with a details of the costs (*T. Sloyan and Sons (Builders) Ltd* v *Brothers of Christian Instruction* [1974] 3 All ER 715), probably in the form of a statement of costs (see **Figure 7.2**).

The order for security can cover both future costs and those already incurred.

The amount of security may be increased by a further application to the court.

26.5.4 THE EFFECT OF NON-COMPLIANCE

The court may dismiss the action, and will do so where it considers that:

(a) the claimant is not pursuing the action sufficiently diligently;

(b) there is no real likelihood of the money being paid; and

(c) the time limit for complying with the order has been ignored: *Speed Up Holdings Ltd* v *Gough and Co. (Handly) Ltd* [1986] FSR 330.

26.5.5 DISCHARGE OR VARIATION OF THE ORDER

It is open to a claimant to apply to discharge or vary an order for security for costs, if the claimant can show the court that there has been a significant change in the circumstances since the making of the order: *Gordano Building Contractors Ltd* v *Burgess* [1988] 1 WLR 890, CA.

26.5.6 AFTER THE TRIAL

If the defendant is successful, as has been said, the money held as security can be used to pay all, or part of his or her costs. Any surplus (unlikely!) must be returned.

If the claimant is successful, the money given as security will be returned, even where there has been a stay of execution pending appeal.

TWENTY SEVEN

PART 36 OFFERS AND PAYMENTS

27.1 Introduction

Part 36 of the Civil Procedure Rules 1998 provides procedures for making 'Part 36 offers' and 'Part 36 payments'. Both procedures provide methods for 'putting pressure' on the other side to bring litigation to a speedy end. By paying in, money is lodged in court, and a notice is served on the claimant of that fact. If the claimant decides to accept the money paid in all proceedings on the action are stayed. If the case goes to trial, the court is not informed about the payment in. If the judgment is for less than the sum paid in, costs since the time of payment in will be awarded against the successful claimant. However, if the judgment is for more, costs will be recovered by the successful party in the normal way. 'Once, therefore, the money has been paid in, the lis between the parties simply is: "Is that sum sufficient to cover the damage which has been suffered?"': *Findlay* v *Railway Executive* [1950] 2 All ER 969 *per* Somervell LJ.

The purpose of payment in is to put the claimant under some pressure. Accordingly, the payment should be pitched somewhere between the minimum and maximum that the claimant is likely to recover. Additional payments in can be made to maintain the pressure to settle.

Part 36 offers have the similar purpose of putting legitimate pressure on the other side to accept a proposal to settle, with costs (and sometimes interest) consequences for non-acceptance. Part 36 offers are expressed to be 'without prejudice save as to costs'. Putting an offer in this form ensures it cannot be used against the offeror on the question of liability if the offer is not accepted, but also allows the court to consider the offer when dealing with costs and interest once liability and quantum have been decided. Part 36 offers used to be called 'Calderbank' offers, following the decision in *Calderbank* v *Calderbank* [1976] Fam 93. Under the Civil Procedure Rules 1998 they fall into two categories depending on whether the offeror is the defendant or the claimant.

27.2 Interrelation between Part 36 Offers and Part 36 Payments

A Part 36 offer can only be made if it is not possible to make a Part 36 payment. A Part 36 payment can only be made once proceedings have started (CPR, r. 36.3(2)) and in respect of money claims. This means that Part 36 offers may be used in the period before proceedings are commenced (in which event they must be replaced by a Part 36 payment within 14 days of service of the claim form: CPR, r. 36.10(3)), and in relation to non-monetary claims, whether or not proceedings have been commenced. An offer to settle a mixed money and non-money claim will only have costs consequences if a Part 36 payment is made in respect of the money part of the claim: CPR, r. 36.4.

27.3 Defendant's Part 36 Offers

27.3.1 THE OFFER

A Part 36 offer must be in writing, and must make clear exactly what it covers. In particular, by CPR, r. 36.5, it must:

    (a)   state whether it relates to the whole claim or to part, or to any issues;

    (b)   state whether it takes any counterclaim into account; and

    (c)   if it does not include interest, give certain details relating to interest. Otherwise it is deemed to include interest until the last day on which it could have been accepted without permission: CPR, r. 36.22.

The defendant's letter setting out the Part 36 offer must say the offer is open for acceptance for 21 days, and should be headed with the words 'without prejudice save as to costs'.

27.3.2   ACCEPTANCE OF THE OFFER

The claimant has 21 days from receiving a Part 36 offer to decide whether to accept, provided the trial has not begun. If the claimant wants to accept more than 21 days after the offer, or in a case where an offer is made less than 21 days before trial, there will be an effective acceptance only if the parties agree costs. If they cannot agree costs, the offer can only be accepted with the permission of the court.

An acceptance that does not need permission results in the claim being stayed (CPR, r. 36.15) and entitles the claimant to his or her costs of the proceedings to the date of serving the notice of acceptance (CPR, r. 36.13), to be assessed on the standard basis if not agreed (these costs concepts are considered in **Chapter 36**).

27.3.3   CONSEQUENCES OF FAILING TO ACCEPT A PART 36 OFFER

If the claimant does not accept a Part 36 offer, and subsequently fails to achieve a judgment which is more advantageous than the terms of the offer, the court will order him or her to pay any costs incurred by the defendant after the time for acceptance, unless it is unjust to do so: CPR, r. 36.20. It is difficult to persuade a court to make any other order.

27.4   Claimant's Part 36 Offers

It is also possible for a claimant to make a 'claimant's Part 36 offer', which may be made and accepted in the same form as a defendant's Part 36 offer. If accepted, the claimant is entitled to recover costs up the date of giving the notice of acceptance: CPR, r. 36.14. If refused, and the claimant gets more at trial than the offer, the court may order interest at a rate 10% above base rate for all or some of the period after the defendant could have accepted, and may order costs on the indemnity basis with interest on costs at 10% above base rate: r. 36.21. Again, these costs concepts will be considered in **Chapter 36**. Care must be taken to ensure that these consequences of failing to beat a claimant's Part 36 offer do not work an injustice or result in a disproportionate advantage to the claimant. If this might be the case, the judge should apply (say) a somewhat reduced rate of interest to reflect the justice of the case: *Little v George Little Sebire and Co.*, *The Times*, 17 November 1999.

27.5   Part 36 Payments

A defendant making a Part 36 payment lodges money in court and serves a notice on the claimant saying that this has been done (see **Figure 27.1**). The purpose is to apply pressure on the claimant, because if the money lodged in court is not accepted by the claimant, and the claimant recovers less than the money paid in, the claimant will almost certainly have to pay the defendant's costs from the last day for accepting the Part 36 payment.

A defendant who has paid money into court under Part 36 must file and serve a Part 36 payment notice which, like a Part 36 offer, must be clear about what it covers. In particular, it must:

(a)   specify the amount paid in;

(b)   specify whether it relates to the whole claim or a part;

(c)   specify whether it takes into account any counterclaim;

(d)   if it does not include interest, give certain details relating to interest. Otherwise it is deemed to include interest until the last day on which it could have been accepted without permission;

(e)   in personal injuries cases the Part 36 payment notice must state the amount of gross compensation, the name and amount of benefits which reduce the gross amount under the Social Security (Recovery of Benefits) Act 1997, and that the sum paid in is the net amount after deduction of the amount of benefit. In such a case the issue on non-acceptance is whether the judgment is greater than the gross sum specified in the notice: CPR, r. 36.23.

The rules for acceptance of Part 36 payments are the same as for Part 36 offers.

A claimant who fails to better a Part 36 payment will be ordered to pay any costs incurred by the defendant after the time for acceptance, unless it is unjust to do so.

27.6   Interest

The CPR, r. 36.22, provides:

(1)   Unless—
(a)   a claimant's Part 36 offer which offers to accept a sum of money; or
(b)   a Part 36 payment notice,
indicates to the contrary, any such offer or payment will be treated as inclusive of all interest until the last date on which it could be accepted without needing the permission of the court.
(2)   Where a claimant's Part 36 offer or Part 36 payment notice is expressed not to be inclusive of interest, the offer or notice must state—
(a)   whether interest is offered; and
(b)   if so, the amount offered, the rate or rates offered and the period or periods for which it is offered.

Therefore, the payment in should include an element of interest from the date of the cause of action until 21 days after the service of payment into court.

This interest factor is an important matter to be borne in mind when advising on the quantum of a payment into court.

27.7   Further Payments In

A defendant can increase the payment into court at any time without permission, but must serve a new notice of payment in on the claimant and any other defendants.

27.8   Clarification

An offeree may be left in some doubt whether to accept a Part 36 payment or Part 36 offer if it is made in an all-encompassing form. Such a party may ask for the Part 36 offer or payment to be 'clarified' by splitting it up between different claimants or different causes of action. This is governed by CPR, r. 36.9, which allows an offeree to write to the offeror requesting clarification. If the offeror fails to provide the requested clarification, an application may be made to the court seeking an order to that effect. The application will be determined applying the overriding objective.

27.9   Late Acceptance

Once the time for acceptance of a Part 36 offer or payment has elapsed, unless the parties agree costs, acceptance is only possible with the court's permission. The old practice was that the court could only allow a late acceptance if there has been no substantial alteration in the risks of the litigation: *Gaskins v British Aluminium Co. Ltd* [1976] QB 524, CA.

27.10   When an Order for Payment Out is Required

There are situations when a Part 36 offer or payment can only be made by an order of the court: CPR, rr. 36.17, 36.18 and 37.4. These are if:

(a)   The money was paid in by some but not all of the defendants (though there are some exceptions, see r. 36.17).

(b)   There is a defence of tender before action.

(c)   The offeror or offeree is a person under disability (i.e. a child or a mental patient).

(d)   The payment is in satisfaction either of causes of action under the Fatal Accidents Act 1976 and the Law Reform (Miscellaneous Provisions) Act 1934, or of a cause of action under the FAA where more than one person is entitled to the money.

27.11   Withdrawal of the Payment In

Withdrawal of money paid in, by the person who paid it in, requires the permission of the court.

The following are examples where withdrawal has been authorised under the old system:

(a)   The discovery of new evidence putting a different complexion on the case.

(b)   A judicial decision changing the relevant law.

(c)   The payment in was made under a mistake.

(d)   The character of the litigation has changed, e.g. by the increase of a counter-claim: *Peal Furniture Co. Ltd v Adrian Share (Interiors) Ltd* [1977] 1 WLR 464, CA.

(e)   Where a global payment in has been clarified, the court may give the defendant permission to revise or withdraw the payment in as an alternative to apportioning the payment in: *Walker v Turpin* [1994] 1 WLR 196, CA.

The claimant is in effect a secured creditor of the defendant for the amount of the payment in. The bankruptcy of the defendant is not in itself a reason for authorising withdrawal: *W.A. Sherratt Ltd v John Bromley (Church Stretton) Ltd* [1985] QB 1038, CA.

Situation (a) above was considered in *W.A. Sherratt Ltd v John Bromley (Church Stretton) Ltd*, where Sir John Donaldson MR said that a change of circumstances justifying a withdrawal of a payment in must result from new facts coming to light, not simply from a change in one's view of already known facts. In *Manku v Seehra* [1985] CILL 224 the defendant made a payment into court based on one expert's report, then, two days later, received a second expert's report from which it was clear that the payment in was too high. Permission to withdraw the payment in was refused because the second expert had simply revalued the claim based on the existing information.

Figure 27.1   Part 36 payment

Notice of Payment into court
(in settlement - Part 36)

In the Central London County Court	
Claim No.	CL9 9388378
Claimant (including ref)	CLIVE SHERRILL
Defendant (including ref)	DORADOWN (MACHINE FITTINGS) LIMITED

To the Claimant ('s Solicitor)

Messrs Younge & Collyer
12 Market Place,
Ponders End,
Enfield
EN7 2AK

Take notice the defendant Doradown (M F) Ltd _____ has paid £ 106,000 _____ (a further amount of £ _____) into court in settlement of
(tick as appropriate)

☐ the whole of your claim
☐ part of your claim *(give details below)*
☐ a certain issue or issues in your claim *(give details below)*

The (part) (issue or issues) to which it relates is(are): *(give details)*

☐ It is in addition to the amount of £_____ already paid into court on

☐ It is not inclusive of interest and an additional amount of £_____ is offered for interest *(give details of the rate(s) and period(s) for which the amount of interest is offered.)*

☐ It takes into account all(part) of the following counterclaim: *(give details of the party and the part of the counterclaim to which the payment relates)*

☐ It takes into account the interim payment(s) made in the following amount(s) on the following date(s): *(give details)*

Note: This notice will need to be modified where an offer of provisional damages is made (CPR Part 36.7) and/or where it is made in relation to a mixed (money and non-money) claim in settlement of the whole claim (CPR Part 36.4).

N242A - w3 Notice of payment into court (in settlement) (4.99)   The Court Service Publications Unit

269

For cases where the Social Security (Recovery of Benefits) Act 1997 applies

The gross amount of the compensation payment is £112,348

The defendant has reduced this sum by £6,346 in accordance with section 8 of and Schedule 2 to the Social Security (Recovery of Benefits) Act 1997, which was calculated as follows:

Type of benefit	Amount
Invalidity Benefit	£6,346

The amount paid into court is the net amount after deduction of the amount of benefit.

Signed [   ]   Position held [   ]
                                  (If signing on
Defendant('s solicitor)   behalf of a firm
                                  or company)

Date [   ]

27.12 Non-disclosure

The fact there has been a Part 36 offer or payment (except in the case of a defence of tender) must not be disclosed to the court until all questions of liability and quantum of damages have been decided: CPR, r. 36.19.

However, when the issue of liability has been decided and the quantum of the damages is to be tried separately any party may bring to the attention of the judge the fact (but not the quantum) of a payment in. This will allow the claimant to be awarded costs on the issue of liability, leaving the costs on the issue of quantum to be determined by the amount of the payment in.

If the claimant's case does not appear to be going well at trial, it may become advisable to accept the amount paid in. This will require the judge's permission, which will not normally be given without the agreement of the defendant.

If the payment into court is disclosed by such an application or by inadvertence, the trial judge has a discretion to continue to hear the case or refer it to another judge. The judge may allow the case to proceed if satisfied that no injustice will be done and the decision on this point is not in itself a ground for appeal: *Millensted* v *Grosvenor House (Park Lane) Ltd* [1937] 1 KB 717.

27.13 Costs and Part 36 Offers and Payments

27.13.1 COSTS WHERE OFFER OR PAYMENT IN ACCEPTED

A party who accepts a Part 36 offer or payment is entitled to costs up to the date of serving the notice of acceptance: CPR, r. 36.13(1). There is also an entitlement to interest on costs from acceptance under the Judgments Act 1838, s. 17.

27.13.2 COSTS WHERE PAYMENT IN NOT ACCEPTED

When a Part 36 offer or payment is not accepted, the question is whether the claimant will recover less than the Part 36 payment, or a less advantageous judgment than the Part 36 offer, or the defendant will be held liable for more than the claimant's Part 36 offer. If the Part 36 offer or payment was the same or 'better' than the judgment eventually obtained from the offeree's point of view, the offeree should have accepted the offer or payment. In such cases, unless the court considers it unjust to do so, it will order the offeree to pay the costs of the offeror from the latest date on which the offer or payment could have been accepted (CPR, r. 36.20(2)), or impose the interest or costs sanctions available under r. 36.21 in the case where the offeree is the defendant. This principle is usually strictly applied. For example, it has been held that where a payment in exactly equals the damages awarded the defendant is entitled to costs after payment in. The trial judge was not entitled to exercise his discretion so as to make no order as to costs after payment in on the basis that he had been considering a slightly larger award: *Wagman* v *Vare Motors Ltd* [1959] 1 WLR 853.

Thus, in *Jones* v *Jones*, *The Times*, 11 November 1999, CA, there had been a payment in of £120,000, and the claimant only recovered damages of £111,000. The amount of damages awarded was probably depressed by a third medical report served by the defendant some six months after the payment in. It was held that the judge erred in principle in awarding the claimant costs up to the disclosure of the last medical report, and the Court substituted an order that (under the present rules would mean) she would only recover her costs to the final date for accepting the payment in. This decision seems somewhat at variance with the ethos of the CPR, and in particular with CPR, r. 44.3, which gives the court wide powers to take into account conduct on questions of costs (see **36.2**). This should be contrasted with *Ford* v *GKR Construction Ltd* (22 October 1999, unreported), where the Court of Appeal affirmed a decision to award the entire costs of the claim to the claimant who was awarded £85,000 despite payments in totalling £95,000. This was because her award was depressed below the level of the payments in by virtue of video surveillance evidence that was introduced in the period of an adjournment between the first and second days of the trial, which was criticised as being late. A decision illustrating the point that r. 44.3 rarely overrides the usual rule where there has been a Part 36 payment exceeding the damages awarded is *Burgess* v *British Steel, The Times*, 29 February 2000. In this case the Court of Appeal overturned a decision to award the claimant costs to the final date for accepting the payment in (which was in the sum of £220,000), and to award no costs thereafter. Before making the payment in, the defendant had disclosed a medical report which asserted that the claimant was malingering and which implied the claimant was pursuing a bogus claim. At trial the claimant established that the claim was genuine, but only recovered £161,000. On appeal it was held this did not justify departing from the usual rule, and the second part of the costs order was altered so that the defendant recovered costs from the last date for accepting the Part 36 payment.

In personal injuries cases the sum taken as the amount paid in includes the amount the defendant is required to withhold under the Social Security (Recovery of Benefits) Act 1997: *Bajwa* v *British Airways plc* [1999] PIQR Q152, CA.

Interest is an important factor in calculating whether or not the judgment exceeds the payment in. The payment in will generally include interest to the last date for accepting the payment in. Interest on the judgment amount to the date of payment in will, therefore, need to be calculated to compare the payment in figure with the judgment figure.

For example, suppose a defendant pays in £70,000 two years after a cause of action has accrued and the judge subsequently awards damages of £60,000. If interest is due on £60,000 for the two years and this exceeds £10,000, the payment in will be less than the total award and costs will be given to the claimant. However, if the interest is less than £10,000, the defendant will be entitled to costs from the date of payment in.

27.14 The Treatment of Money in Court

Money paid into court bears interest at a rate prescribed by the Lord Chancellor.

Money paid into court does not belong to the person claiming damages. Generally, any interest accruing between the date of payment into court and the date of the judgment or order for payment out will go to the party who made the payment in, and any interest accruing thereafter will follow capital payments proportionately.

TWENTY EIGHT

HALTING PROCEEDINGS

28.1   Introduction

This chapter deals with a number of matters which can arise when an action does not proceed smoothly from issue of process to trial. These are:

(a) Striking out, **28.2**, whereby a litigant or the court can attack the validity of a party's statement of case. This may result in part or the whole of a statement of case being struck out, and possibly with judgment being entered.

(b) Sanctions for breach of court orders and directions, **28.3**.

(c) Dismissal, **28.4**, which may be available against a dilatory claimant.

(d) Stays, **28.5**, are temporary halts in proceedings ordered by the court. They are only ordered for good reason, such as where it is likely the action will not proceed to trial, so that further steps will be a waste of costs. In practice, such halts often end up being permanent.

(e) Discontinuing, **28.6**, amounts to a total abandonment of a claim or counter-claim, and entitles the other side to recover its costs incurred up to that time.

28.2   Striking Out

28.2.1   INTRODUCTION

If particulars of claim are struck out, the action will be stayed or dismissed. If a defence is struck out, judgment is entered for the claimant. If the claimant claims damages, then judgment is for damages to be assessed.

28.2.2   GROUNDS FOR STRIKING OUT

The grounds for striking out are contained in CPR, r. 3.4(2), which is set out at **5.9**. Rule 3.4(1) says that the reference to a statement of case in this rule includes reference to part of a statement of case. It is therefore possible for the court to strike out just part of a statement of case where the document is not entirely bad.

The rules in CPR, r. 3.4, do not apply to interim applications, which may only be struck out in the court's inherent jurisdiction: *Port* v *Auger* [1994] 1 WLR 862.

28.2.3   GENERAL PRINCIPLE

Striking out has traditionally been said to be appropriate only in plain and obvious cases, per Lord Templeman in *Williams & Humbert Ltd* v *W. & H. Trade Marks (Jersey) Ltd* [1986] AC 368, HL. Cases requiring prolonged and serious argument are therefore unsuitable for striking out. It is likely, however, that there will now be a greater readiness to use the power to strike out weak cases.

28.2.4 PROCEDURE

The court may exercise its power to strike out on application by a party or on its own initiative, and may do so at any time: PD 3, para. 4.1. However, applications by parties should be made as soon as possible, and generally before track allocation: PD 3, para. 5.1. Many applications to strike out can be made simply by issuing an application notice, there being no need for evidence in support. However, if any facts need to be proved in order to show why a statement of case should be struck out, then written evidence will be needed, and should be filed and served in the usual way: PD 3, para. 5.2. The jurisdiction to strike out is closely related to that governing summary judgment, and in many cases it may be appropriate to seek both in the alternative: PD 3, para. 1.7.

28.2.5 NO REASONABLE CAUSE OF ACTION OR DEFENCE

A number of examples of situations where the power to strike out on the ground of failing to disclose a reasonable cause of action or defence are given by PD 3. A claim may be struck out if it sets out no facts indicating what the claim is about (such as a claim simply saying it is for 'Money owed £5,000'), or if it is incoherent and makes no sense, or if the facts it states, even if true, do not disclose a legally recognisable claim against the defendant. A defence may be struck out if it consists of a bare denial or otherwise fails to set out a coherent statement of facts, or if the facts it sets out, even if true, do not amount in law to a defence to the claim. Many institutional defendants at present are in the habit of filing 8 line defences making blanket denials without stating any positive case. These defences ought to be a thing of the past.

Paragraphs 2 and 3 of PD 3 deal with situations where court officials see, when asked to issue claims or on receipt of defences, that the contents of the relevant document fail to meet these standards. The official may decide to consult the judge, who may on his or her own initiative make an order staying the proceedings or striking out the claim or defence. The judge may or may not give the party a hearing before making such an order, or may make an order under CPR, Part 18 requiring additional information about the defective statement of case with a sanction in default. An order can also be made that the document is to be retained by the court and not served until any stay imposed is lifted.

If a striking out order is made the judge may enter such judgment as the other party may appear entitled to: PD 3, para. 4.2.

If the statement of case could be saved by amendment, then the proper order is for permission to amend rather than striking out: *Republic of Peru* v *Peruvian Guano Co.* (1887) 36 Ch D 489 at 496 (*per* Chitty J); *Brophy* v *Dunphys Chartered Surveyors, The Times*, 11 March 1998, CA.

The fact that the limitation period applicable to a cause of action has expired does not mean that there is no cause of action, but rather that there is a defence to that action. If the particulars of claim discloses that the cause of action arose outside the limitation period the defendant may apply for the particulars of claim to be struck out on the ground they are an abuse of the process of the court, or alternatively seek a preliminary trial of that issue (see **33.2**).

28.2.6 ABUSE OF PROCESS

PD 3, para. 1.5, says a statement of case may be an abuse of process where it is vexatious, scurrilous or ill-founded. An example is where a person seeks to re-litigate a question which has already been adjudicated by a court of competent jurisdiction even though the matter is not strictly speaking *res judicata*: *Hunter* v *Chief Constable of West Midlands Police* [1982] AC 529, HL. Note, however, that *Hunter's* case does not lay down an inflexible rule, and actions have been allowed even though they involve questioning the decision of a court of competent jurisdiction, where fresh evidence has come to light since the earlier decision, or where the later action is against the claimant's solicitors in the earlier proceedings claiming damages for professional negligence: *Walpole* v *Partridge & Wilson* [1994] QB 106, CA. It is clear from cases such as *Bradford & Bingley Building Society* v *Seddon, The Times,* 30 March 1999, that there are two main elements:

(a) that the second claim is one that could have been brought in the first claim, or is in conflict with an earlier claim or evidence; and

(b) an additional element, such as a collateral attack on the earlier decision, or dishonesty, election, or unjust harassment.

It is also an abuse of process to raise in subsequent litigation an issue which should have been raised against someone who was a party to earlier proceedings: *Yat Tung Investment Co.* v *Dao Beng Bank Ltd* [1975] AC 581 (PC) and *Talbot* v *Berkshire County Council* [1994] QB 290, CA.

28.3   Sanctions

The power to impose sanctions for non-compliance with its orders and directions is the means by which the courts can ensure that their case management decisions are complied with, and that they retain control over the conduct of litigation. The most Draconian sanction that may be imposed is striking out. The CPR, r. 3.4(2)(c) (see **28.2.2** above), provides that the court may strike out all or part of a statement of case if it appears that there has been a failure to comply with a rule, practice direction or court order. Striking out the whole of a party's statement of case ought to be reserved for the most serious, or repeated, breaches or defaults. In less serious cases of default or breach the court may be prepared to impose a sanction which, to use a phrase used in some of the recent cases under the old rules, 'fits the crime'. CPR, r. 3.4, itself states that the power to strike out may be exercised over the whole or just a part of a statement of case. For example, a party may be in default of an order to provide further information on a single issue in a case where several issues are raised. A suitable sanction in such circumstances may be striking out the part of the statement of case dealing with that issue.

As alternatives to striking out, the court may impose costs sanctions including ordering a party to pay certain costs forthwith. It may also debar a party in default from adducing evidence in a particular form or from particular witnesses. Alternatively, the court may impose sanctions that limit or deprive a party, if successful, of interest on any money claim, or which increase the amount of interest payable by the party in default.

Further, there are various provisions in the Civil Procedure Rules 1998 and practice directions that automatically impose various sanctions in default of due compliance. For example, CPR, r. 35.13, provides that a party who fails to disclose an expert's report may not use the report at the trial or call the expert to give evidence orally unless the court gives permission. A more severe sanction is imposed by CPR, r. 3.7, which provides for the striking out of claims for non-payment of allocation and listing fees where the claimant fails to pay the fee after the time set by a notice of non-payment. An example from the Practice Directions is PD 32, para. 25.1, which provides that if an affidavit, witness statement or exhibit does not comply with the requirements of CPR, Part 32 or PD 32, the court may refuse to admit it as evidence and may refuse to allow the costs arising from its preparation. This last example differs from the previous two in that it provides for sanctions which the court may choose to impose, whereas the other two provide for sanctions which apply unless the court grants relief.

28.3.1   NON-COMPLIANCE WITH DIRECTIONS

It is to be anticipated that from time to time one or other of the parties to proceedings will be unable to keep to the directions timetable that will have been imposed by the court. This will not generally be a problem provided the parties co-operate and can still keep to the directions relating to the 'key' dates relating to case management conferences, pre-trial reviews, filing listing questionnaires and trial: CPR, rr. 28.4 and 29.5. If the non-compliance is through events outside the control of the defaulting party or is otherwise not deliberate, normally it would be expected that the parties would co-operate in compliance with CPR, r. 1.4(2)(a) and resolve the difficulty by agreeing a new timetable that preserved the 'key' dates. Provided there is no express provision barring variation by the parties, the time specified by any provision of the Civil Procedure Rules 1998 or by the court for doing any act may be varied by the written agreement of the parties: CPR, r. 2.11. If non-compliance cannot be resolved without, say, impinging on one of the 'key' dates, or if the other side insist on compliance, the matter is likely to come before the court.

An 'innocent' party faced with an opponent who has not complied with the court's directions is not permitted to either:

(a)   sit back and wait for the other side's default to get worse by the additional passage of time; or

(b)   make an immediate application for an order.

Instead, the correct procedure is that laid down in PD 28, para. 5 (for fast track cases) and PD 29, para. 7 (which is in identical terms and applies in multi-track cases). The references that follow are to the fast track practice direction (PD 28). The innocent party must first write to the defaulting party referring to the default and warn the defaulting party of the intention to apply for an order if the default is not rectified within a short reasonable period: para. 5.2. This will usually be seven or 14 days. If there is continued default, the innocent party may apply for an order to enforce compliance or for a sanction to be imposed or both: para. 5.1. Any application for such an order must be made without delay: para. 5.2. If the innocent party does delay in making the application, the court may take the delay into account when it decides whether to make an order imposing a sanction or whether to grant relief from a sanction imposed by the rules or any practice direction.

28.3.2   COURT'S APPROACH ON BREACH OF ORDERS OR DIRECTIONS

The general approach that will be adopted where there has been a breach of case management directions is set out in PD 28, para. 5.4 (fast track) and PD 29, para. 7.4 (multi-track) respectively. Paragraphs 5.4 and 7.4 provide as follows:

> *(1)   The court will not allow a failure to comply with directions to lead to the postponement of the trial unless the circumstances of the case are exceptional.*
> *(2)   If it is practicable to do so the court will exercise its powers in a manner that enables the case to come on for trial on the date or within the period previously set.*
> *(3)   In particular the court will assess what steps each party should take to prepare the case for trial, direct that those steps are taken in the shortest possible time and impose a sanction for non-compliance. Such a sanction may, for example, deprive a party of the right to raise or contest an issue or to rely on evidence to which the direction relates.*
> *(4)   Where it appears that one or more issues are or can be made ready for trial at the time fixed while others cannot, the court may direct that the trial will proceed on the issues that are or will then be ready, and order that no costs will be allowed for any later trial of the remaining issues or that those costs will be paid by the party in default.*
> *(5)   Where the court has no option but to postpone the trial it will do so for the shortest possible time and will give directions for the taking of the necessary steps in the meantime as rapidly as possible,*
> *(6)   Litigants and lawyers must be in no doubt that the court will regard the postponement of a trial as an order of last resort. The court may exercise its power to require a party as well as his legal representative to attend curt at a hearing where such an order is to be sought.*

In this connection, PD 28 and 29, paras 4.2(2) and 6.2(2) are relevant, as they provide that the court will assume for the purposes of any later application that a party who did not appeal and who made no application to vary within 14 days of service of any order containing directions was content that they were correct in the circumstances then existing.

As mentioned at **28.3.1**, the court may seek to achieve the aims set out in paras 5 and 7 of PD 28 and 29 by making an order against the defaulting party which may be combined with a sanction. It was accepted principle under the old system that 'unless' orders were not made on the first default of a party, but were a last resort to ensure compliance: see *Hytec Information Systems Ltd* v *Coventry City Council* [1997] 1 WLR 1666. Such an approach is often unworkable under the present system, particularly in cases on the fast track. In these cases there will be a very limited time between any breach and the date or window fixed for the trial, and there simply will not be time for orders without sanctions to be made if trial dates are not to be lost. Consequently, courts are very much more willing to make orders with sanctions, even on a first breach by a defaulting party.

The Court of Appeal in *Biguzzi* v *Rank Leisure plc* [1999] 1 WLR 1926 affirmed a decision to strike out for wholesale disregard for the court's rules. Nevertheless, the Master of the Rolls commented that striking out would not always be the correct approach. Under the Civil Procedure Rules 1998 the court has wide powers which it could use in order to deal with cases fairly without resorting to Draconian remedies such as striking out. These include making orders for indemnity costs, for paying money into court, and awarding interest at higher or lower rates. By a proper exercise of case management powers it should be possible for the courts to ensure parties do not disregard timetables, whilst producing a just result.

However, *Biguzzi* v *Rank Leisure plc* must not be understood as promoting an unduly lenient approach to the imposition of sanctions. Each case has to be considered on its own facts, with the court seeking to do justice between the parties in the light of the overriding objective. There will, accordingly, be a number of cases where there has been serious default where immediate striking out is appropriate: *UCB Corporate Services Ltd* v *Halifax (SW) Ltd* (6 December 1999, CA, unreported); *Purdy* v *Cambran* (17 December 1999, CA, unreported). In *UCB Corporate Services Ltd* v *Halifax (SW) Ltd*, the claimant had repeatedly failed to comply with court directions and provisions in the rules, and there was an unexplained delay of two years, at which point the defendant made an application to strike out. The claimant was regarded as being guilty of a total disregard of court orders, amounting to an abuse of process. Accordingly, the judge was held to have been entitled to strike out the claim rather than imposing a lesser penalty.

Axa Insurance Co. Ltd v *Swire Fraser Ltd*, *The Times*, 19 January 2000, was a case where the Court of Appeal held the judge had been wrong to strike out the claim despite a protracted failure to provide further information. It was said that proof of prejudice is not a requirement for an order for striking out under CPR, r. 3.4(2)(c). That said, prejudice to the innocent party is clearly an important factor, and where it is present, such as in *Purdy* v *Cambran*, where the defendant's expert died in the period of delay, it may offset an argument that striking out would be a disproportionate sanction. Where there is no prejudice, the court may well decide that the default can be characterised as relatively minor, and accordingly impose some lesser sanction.

A party who is late in complying with a direction is well advised to comply before the court considers the consequences of the default. In *Mealey Horgan plc* v *Horgan*, *The Times*, 6 July 1999, the defendants served their witness statements two weeks late. The claimants sought an order requiring the defendants to pay a sum into court as a sanction for late service. Buckley J refused the order, and said a sanction of that nature would be appropriate only in cases of repeated breach of timetables, or where the defaulting party's conduct gave rise to the suspicion it was not acting in good faith. However, the court will almost certainly impose a costs sanction on the defaulting party.

28.3.3   AVOIDING SANCTIONS BEING IMPOSED

The court has a general power to extend and abridge time: CPR, r. 3.1(2)(a). A party who will be unable to comply with an order or direction in time (or who is already in breach) and who has not been able to agree an extension with the other side (perhaps because the Civil Procedure Rules 1998 do not allow such an agreement, such as an extension to the period for service of a Defence beyond 28 days, see CPR, r. 15.5), may make an application under this rule asking the court to extend time for compliance. The discretion given to the court under the rule is unfettered other than by the general requirement to abide by the overriding objective.

On other occasions, a default may arise through the defective performance of the requirements of a rule, practice direction or court order. For example, it may be that the wrong form was used, or that it was sent to the wrong address (but still came to the attention of the other side), or that the document used was not completed correctly. These are errors of procedure. By CPR, r. 3.10, such errors do not invalidate the step purportedly taken, unless the court so orders. The court may make an order invalidating a step if it was so badly defective that the other side were mislead, or where the defects are so great that it would not be right to regard the purported performance as performance at all. Further, by r. 3.10(2), the court may make an order to remedy any error of procedure. A defaulting party should consider seeking such an order where there is an objection made regarding defective performance.

28.3.4   FORM OF ORDER WITH SANCTIONS

Like all other orders, orders with sanctions must specify the time within which the step under consideration must be taken by reference to a calendar date and a specific time: CPR, r. 2.9. The sanction part of the order may take the form of an 'unless' provision. This is to the effect that if the terms of the order are breached, the other party may file a request for judgment to be entered and costs: CPR, r. 3.5. Such an order may read:

> Unless by 4.00 pm on Friday 4th February 2000 the defendant do file and serve a list of documents giving standard disclosure, the Defence shall be struck out and judgment entered for the claimant for damages to be decided by the court.

28.3.5   NON-COMPLIANCE WITH ORDER IMPOSING A SANCTION

If a party fails to comply with a rule, practice direction or court order imposing any sanction, the sanction will take effect unless the defaulting party applies for and obtains relief from the sanction: CPR, r. 3.8. The rule goes on to provide that extensions cannot be agreed between the parties.

28.3.6   RELIEF FROM SANCTIONS

As mentioned in the previous section, a party in breach of a rule, practice direction or order imposing a sanction for non-compliance may apply for relief from the sanction. This is done by issuing an application notice, which must be supported by evidence. On such an application the CPR, r. 3.9, provides that the court will consider all the circumstances, and then sets out a list of the following nine factors which will be considered:

(a) the interests of the administration of justice;

(b) whether the application for relief has been made promptly;

(c) whether the failure to comply was intentional;

(d) whether there is a good explanation for the failure;

(e) the extent to which the party in default has complied with other rules, practice directions, court orders and any relevant pre-action protocol;

(f) whether the failure to comply was caused by the party or his legal representative;

(g) whether the trial date or the likely trial date can still be met if relief is granted;

(h) the effect which any failure to comply had on each party; and

(i) the effect which the granting of relief would have on each party.

In *Woodward* v *Finch* (8 December 1999, unreported), the claimant applied for relief from the consequences of failing to comply with an unless order for service of his witness statements. Proceedings had been issued in April 1994, and there was a history of delay, including a default in serving a schedule of special damages, which was only remedied when the defendant issued an application to strike out. When the claimant failed to serve his witness statements in accordance with directions, the court made the unless order referred to above, expiring on 29 July 1999. On 2 August 1999 the claimant issued an application for relief from the striking out sanction. He explained his delay by pointing to a change in solicitors, and problems in transferring his legal aid certificate. He purported to serve his witness statements the day before his application was heard. The Court of Appeal refused to interfere with the judge's decision to grant relief, despite the history of non-compliance and the fact that the excuse put forward was not a good one. The main reasons were that relief had been applied for promptly; the default was more muddle-headedness than anything else; the trial date could still be met; there was not much effect on either party through the default; and refusing relief would have a devastating effect on the claimant.

28.3.7   NON-COMPLIANCE WITH APPLICABLE PRE-ACTION PROTOCOLS

If, in the opinion of the court, non-compliance with a pre-action protocol that applies to a case leads to the commencement of proceedings which might otherwise not have needed to be commenced, or leads to costs being incurred in the proceedings that might otherwise not have been incurred, PD Protocols, para. 2.3, provides that the orders the court may make include:

> *(1) an order that the party at fault pay the costs of the proceedings, or part of those costs, of the other party or parties;*
> *(2) an order that the party at fault pay those costs on an indemnity basis;*
> *(3) if the party at fault is a claimant in whose favour an order for the payment of damages or some specified sum is subsequently made, an order depriving that party of interest on such sum and in respect of such period as may be specified, and/or awarding interest at a lower rate than that at which interest would otherwise have been awarded;*
> *(4) if the party at fault is a defendant and an order for the payment of damages or some specified sum is subsequently made in favour of the claimant, an order awarding interest on such sum and in respect of such period as may be specified at a higher rate, not exceeding 10% above base rate, than the rate at which interest would otherwise have been awarded.*

Paragraph 2.4 of the same protocol provides that the court will exercise its powers under para. 2.3 with the object of placing the innocent party in no worse a position than he or she would have been in if the protocol had been complied with.

The Personal Injury Pre-action Protocol, para. 1.5, says that if the court has to consider the question of compliance, it will not be concerned with minor infringements, such as the failure by a short period to provide relevant information. A single minor breach will not exempt the 'innocent' party from complying with the protocol.

28.3.8   SECOND ACTIONS

If the claimant's action is dismissed within the limitation period for breach of an unless order, a second action based on the same cause of action would normally be struck out as an abuse of process: *Janov* v *Morris* [1981] 1 WLR 1389, CA.

28.4   Dismissal for Want of Prosecution

28.4.1   INTRODUCTION

There are three types of dismissal for want of prosecution. Two were set out by Lord Diplock in *Birkett* v *James* [1978] AC 297 at 318:

> The power should be exercised only where the court is satisfied either (1) that the default has been intentional and contumelious, e.g. disobedience to a peremptory order of the court or conduct amounting to an abuse of process of the court; or (2)(a) that there has been inordinate and inexcusable delay on the part of the plaintiff or his lawyers, and (b) that such delay will give rise to a substantial risk that it is not possible to have a fair trial of the issues in the action or is likely to cause or to have caused serious prejudice to the defendants either as between themselves and the plaintiff or between each other or between them and a third party.

It is clear that the third type of dismissal for want of prosecution is conduct amounting to an abuse of process of the court (see **28.4.3**).

The first type has been replaced by the system of sanctions discussed at **28.3** above. The other two types should be pretty rare given the heavily case managed environment of litigation under the Civil Procedure Rules 1998. However, there are bound to be cases from time to time that escape regular judicial scrutiny, and which may fall to be dismissed under the principles that will be considered below.

28.4.2   DISMISSAL FOR INORDINATE AND INEXCUSABLE DELAY

28.4.2.1   Principles

For an application for dismissal to succeed under this heading, the defendant must show that the delay satisfies the four following requirements which are derived from *Birkett* v *James* [1978] AC 297, HL, as confirmed by *Department of Transport* v *Chris Smaller (Transport) Ltd* [1989] 1 All ER 897, HL:

(a)   delay must be inordinate. This means 'materially longer than the time which was usually regarded by the courts and the profession as an acceptable period', *per* Cumming-Bruce LJ in *Tabata* v *Hetherington*, *The Times*, 15 December 1983, CA; and

(b)   delay must be inexcusable. Excuses may include such things as the claimant suffering from illness and obstacles created by the defendant. Fault on the part of the claimant's solicitor (or counsel) does not amount to a good excuse for the claimant: *Birkett* v *James*; and

(c)   either:

   (i)   such delay will give rise to a substantial risk that it is not possible to have a fair trial; or

   (ii)   such delay is likely to cause, or to have caused, serious prejudice to the defendant; and

(d)   for an action to be dismissed under this heading, the limitation period must generally have expired. Otherwise the defendant could not say he is prejudiced, since the claimant (who is not in breach of an unless order) could simply issue fresh proceedings: *Birkett* v *James* [1978] AC 297, HL. In exceptional cases, however, it may be appropriate to dismiss an action for want of prosecution even though the limitation period has not expired: *Wright* v *Morris* [1997] FSR 218, CA.

An example of prejudice would be where the evidence the defendant wants to rely upon at trial has become less cogent as a result of the length of time which has elapsed. This applies particularly where the case will depend substantially on oral testimony as opposed to documentary evidence. It is not essential that there should be evidence of particular respects in which potential witnesses' recollections are impaired. The court is entitled to draw an inference that by reason of the delay serious prejudice will be caused as a result of the impairment of witnesses' recollections: *Shtun v Zalejska* [1996] 1 WLR 1270, CA.

The prejudice upon which the defendant can rely is not confined to prejudice in the conduct of the case. In exceptional cases, for example, it can include prejudice to the defendant's business interests: *Department of Transport v Chris Smaller (Transport) Ltd* [1989] AC 1197, HL.

Prejudice may also exist where the delay has increased the amount of the claim, although in such a case it is incumbent upon the defendant to adduce compelling evidence of substantial prejudice before dismissal can be justified: *Hayes v Bowman* [1989] 1 WLR 456, CA. It will only be in a very limited category of cases where the defendant will be able to establish serious prejudice on the grounds of financial prejudice by reason of postponement of judgment: *Gahan v Szerelmey* [1996] 2 All ER 291, CA.

The trial will not be prejudiced if there is no causation between the delay and the prejudice: *Hunter v Skingley* [1997] 3 All ER 568, CA.

28.4.2.2 Delay before issue of process
Although the prejudice to the defendant must be caused by delay after the issue of the proceedings, where there has been a long delay prior to issue, the defendant has only to show something more than minimal additional prejudice as a result of the post-issue delay: *Department of Transport v Chris Smaller (Transport) Ltd* [1989] AC 1197, HL.

28.4.2.3 Defendant's conduct inducing claimant to believe action will proceed
In *Roebuck v Mungovin* [1994] 2 AC 224 the House of Lords overruled a number of decisions, stemming from *County and District Properties Ltd v Lyell* (1977) [1991] 1 WLR 683, which had held that where, after inordinate, prejudicial, delay by the claimant, the defendant induces the claimant to incur further costs in the reasonable belief that the defendant is content for the action to proceed to trial, the defendant will be estopped as a matter of law (not discretion) from seeking the dismissal of the claimant's action. Instead, such conduct by the defendant is only one of the factors the court must take into account in exercising its discretion whether to dismiss the case in hand. The claimant in *Roebuck v Mungovin* delayed for over five years in serving further and better particulars in response to the defendant's request. During the later stages of this delay the defendant's solicitors wrote a number of letters seeking further information and documents from the claimant. The defendant's actions were regarded as being minor compared with the inordinate delay by the claimant, and could not have lulled the claimant into incurring major additional expenditure in the litigation. Accordingly, the action was dismissed.

28.4.3 DISMISSAL FOR ABUSE OF PROCESS

In *Grovit v Doctor* [1997] 1 WLR 640, the House of Lords held that the courts were entitled, under their inherent jurisdiction to prevent abuse of process, to strike out/stay proceedings if the inactivity of the claimant amounted to an abuse of process even if the facts of a case did not fall within the principles of *Birkett v James*.

It was held that the continuation of proceeding when a claimant had no intention of bringing a case to trial could, in appropriate cases, amount to an abuse of process and as such an application could be made to strike out the claim and dismiss the action. The inactivity of a claimant could be the evidence relied upon to establish the abuse of process.

In *Arbuthnot Latham Bank Ltd* v *Trafalgar Holdings Ltd* [1998] 1 WLR 1426, the Court of Appeal stressed the importance of case management by the court and that the consequences of inordinate delay would be a consideration of increasing significance. While it was recognised in *Grovit* v *Doctor* that to continue litigation with no intention to bring it to a conclusion could amount to an abuse of process, it was held that, in the future, the courts could recognise that inordinate and inexcusable delay by a claimant in prosecuting an action which amounted to a wholesale disregard of the rules of the court was an abuse of process which would entitle the courts to dismiss an action. The court explained that while an abuse of process could be within the first category mentioned in *Birkett* v *James*, it was also a separate ground for striking out an action, which did not depend on the need to show prejudice to the defendant or that a fair trial was no longer possible.

The limitation period need not have expired for an application to dismiss under this heading. Further, if a party had one action struck out for abuse of process in these circumstances some special reason would need to be present to justify that party proceeding with a second action commenced within the limitation period: *Arbuthnot*.

28.5 Stays

28.5.1 INTRODUCTION

The SCA 1981, s. 49(3), recognises and preserves the High Court's inherent power to stay proceedings pending before the court either of its own motion, or on the application of any person, whether or not a party to the proceedings. The County Court has the same power by virtue of County Courts Act 1984, s. 38.

A stay is not equivalent to discontinuance or the granting of judgment, and so the proceedings remain in existence. The stay may therefore be removed by the court if proper grounds are shown: *Cooper* v *Williams* [1963] 2 QB 567.

28.5.2 PROCEDURE

Stays are applied for by issuing an application notice. Evidence in support is generally desirable.

28.5.3 GROUNDS

Examples of grounds upon which the defendant may apply for a stay of proceedings are:

(a) Where the claimant in a personal injuries action refuses to undergo a medical examination: *Edmeades* v *Thames Board Mills* [1969] 2 QB 67, CA, which is fully considered at **29.3.2** and **29.3.3**.

(b) Where the action is brought in tort by one spouse against the other and no substantial benefit would accrue from its continuance: Law Reform (Husband and Wife) Act 1962, s. 1(2).

(c) Where the dispute is governed by an arbitration agreement and the defendant wishes the dispute to go to arbitration in accordance with the agreement: Arbitration Act 1996, s. 9.

(d) Where the defendant wishes to argue *forum non conveniens* after permission has been granted without notice for service of originating process outside the jurisdiction.

(e) Where the Civil Jurisdiction and Judgments Act 1982, s. 2, applies, for example, art. 19 (exclusive jurisdiction of courts of another contracting State under art. 16), art. 21 (*lis pendens*).

28.5.4   FURTHER EXAMPLES

The following examples are further situations where a stay may be imposed:

(a)   The usual order on a successful application for security for costs provides for the proceedings to be stayed until the amount specified in the order is paid into court.

(b)   Proceedings are automatically stayed where the claimant accepts a payment into court.

28.5.5   STAY BY CONSENT

An action may be stayed as part of a consent judgment on the joint application of the parties. This applies to 'the stay of proceedings, either unconditionally or upon conditions as to the payment of money' and to 'the stay of proceedings upon terms which are scheduled to the order but which are not otherwise part of it (a "Tomlin order")'. Tomlin orders are considered further at **37.3.2**.

28.6   Discontinuance

28.6.1   INTRODUCTION

Discontinuance means that the claimant gives up entirely all or part of a claim brought against the defendant in an action.

This is to be contrasted with abandonment, which means that the claimant gives up only some particular remedy against the defendant, but wishes to proceed on the rest.

28.6.2   PERMISSION TO DISCONTINUE

In general, a claimant may discontinue without needing to obtain the court's permission: CPR, r. 38.2(1). In the following cases, however, permission is required:

(a)   where an interim injunction has been granted (r. 38.2(2)(a));

(b)   where an undertaking to the court has been given (r. 38.2(2)(a));

(c)   where the claimant has received an interim payment (r. 38.2(2)(b)); or

(d)   where there is more than one claimant (r. 38.2(2)(c)).

Permission may always be given by the court, but in situation (c) above there is the alternative of obtaining consent from the defendant, and in situation (d) above there is the alternative of obtaining consent from the other claimants.

28.6.3   PROCEDURE

Discontinuance is effected by the claimant filing a notice of discontinuance in Form N279 with the court and serving copies on all other parties.

28.6.4   EFFECT

Discontinuing has the effect of bringing the entire claim, or the part of the claim identified in the notice of discontinuance, to an end. It also renders the claimant liable to pay the defendant's costs of the claim, or the part of the claim, that has been discontinued: CPR, r. 38.6. If a claim is discontinued after a defence has been filed, the claimant is not allowed to commence a second claim arising out of the same or substantially the same facts without the court's permission: CPR, r. 38.7.

28.6.5   SETTING ASIDE A NOTICE OF DISCONTINUANCE

A defendant may, within 28 days of service of a notice of discontinuance, apply to have the notice set aside: CPR, r. 38.4. There have been cases in the past where claimants have served notice of discontinuance for tactical purposes, aiming to deprive the defendant of some right or legitimate expectation. Setting aside accordingly may be appropriate where some underhand motive or effect can be identified.

28.7   Questions

OBJECTIVES

By the conclusion of this section you should:

(a)   be able to recognise the circumstances when the court may strike out a statement of case or part of a statement of case on its own initiative;

(b)   understand when an application may be made to strike out an opponent's statement of case or part of a statement of case;

(c)   be aware of other sanctions the court may impose;

(d)   understand the nature of unless orders and when they will be imposed;

(e)   understand the procedure and principles relating to an application for relief from sanctions;

(f)   understand the procedure and principles relating to stays and discontinuance of proceedings.

RESEARCH

Read the materials in **Chapter 28** of this Manual. Refer to **Chapter 37** of this Manual.

LARGE GROUP SESSION 7

On the basis of this research, consider the following questions. It is particularly important to have selected an answer to question 1 in advance of the class.

QUESTION 1

Warren started proceedings against Phillip which were defended and allocated to the fast-track. On allocation directions were made including disclosure of documents by 4 pm on 27 October 2000. Phillip duly sent a list of documents to Warren by the specified date. It is now 13 November 2000 and Warren has failed to send a list of documents. Which one of the following is the best advice to give to Phillip?

[A]   As Warren is in breach of the directions timetable, when a 'key date' is reached, such as return of listing questionnaires, his statement of case will be automatically struck out and he will have to apply for relief from sanctions in order to have his case reinstated.

[B]   Phillip should make an application for an 'unless order' without delay in the terms that unless Warren serve his list of documents by a specified time and date his statement of case will be struck out.

[C]   Phillip should write to Warren, specifying that he has failed to serve his list of documents on time, and warning him that if this default is not remedied within a reasonable period of time, Phillip may apply for an order to enforce compliance or for a sanction to be imposed.

[D]   As this is the first breach of the directions timetable, the court would not make an 'unless order' against Warren, accordingly it would be a waste of costs to do anything about this breach and instead Phillip should wait to see if Warren fails to comply with the next direction before taking any action against him.

QUESTION 2

In an action brought against her, Janet files a defence which simply denies each and every allegation set out in the particulars of claim.

(a) What are the potential consequences of filing such a defence?

(b) At what stage may those consequences have effect?

QUESTION 3

In May 2000 Trevor brought proceedings claiming £120,000, being the price of a quantity of men's overcoats sold by him to Victor. In his defence, Victor stated 'the goods delivered were completely defective'. On 31 July 2000 the Master ordered him to provide further information identifying the alleged defects by 4 pm on 25 August 2000. Victor failed to comply with this order, and on 9 October 2000 the Master ordered that, unless such further information was supplied by 4 pm on 30 October 2000, the defence would be struck out and judgment entered for the claimant. Victor failed to provide the further information and judgment has been entered.

Victor can in fact produce cogent evidence to show the goods were seriously defective. He explains his failure to comply with the court's orders by saying that he had business commitments in Italy, and despite letters from his solicitors, was unable to attend their offices in time to provide them with the information required for them to provide the further information.

Advise Victor as to whether judgment can be set aside and the procedure and principles relating to any application he may make.

QUESTION 4

If an application is made for dismissal for want of prosecution, in what circumstances will such an order be made?

QUESTION 5

Lucy has issued and served a Part 8 claim on Abigail and Martin. Ten days ago Abigail filed in the court office and served on Lucy and Martin a witness statement which shows that Lucy has completely misunderstood the factual position and that there is no basis for granting the relief sought in the action. Lucy accepts that what Abigail says is correct, and asks you to advise her what to do.

QUESTION 6

Margaret has been served by Patricia with a claim form, with particulars of claim attached, claiming damages for seditious blasphemy. Advise Margaret.

TWENTY NINE

EXPERT EVIDENCE

29.1 Introduction

29.1.1 GENERAL RULE

At common law there is a general rule that witnesses must state facts not opinions. To allow witnesses to express their opinions is regarded as an intrusion on the role of the tribunal of fact.

There are effectively two exceptions to this general rule: certain types of evidence given by non-expert witnesses and the evidence given by expert witnesses.

29.1.2 NON-EXPERT WITNESSES

A non-expert witness is allowed to express an opinion or impression where the facts perceived are too complicated or too evanescent in their nature to be recollected or separately and distinctly narrated. The Civil Evidence Act 1972 (CEA 1972), s. 3(2), puts this into statutory form:

> It is hereby declared that where a person is called as a witness in any civil proceedings, a statement of opinion by him on any relevant matter on which he is not qualified to give expert evidence, if made as a way of conveying relevant facts personally perceived by him, is admissible as evidence of what he perceived.

Some examples, which are not intended to be exhaustive, of matters on which a non-expert witness may state an opinion as a compendious way of stating facts are:

(a) Estimations of speed and distance.

(b) The identity of persons or articles.

(c) The state of the weather.

(d) The condition of articles.

(e) The age of persons or articles.

Questions relating to non-expert opinion frequently arise at trial, and CEA 1972, s. 1, expressly extends the hearsay provisions of the Civil Evidence Act 1995 (see **Chapter 31**) to cover statements of opinion.

29.1.3 EXPERT WITNESSES

An expert witness can give opinion evidence in the circumstances referred to in **29.2**.

An expert differs from witnesses of fact in a number of respects in addition to that relating to opinion evidence. An expert witness may rely on published and unpublished material in reaching conclusions, draw on his or her own experience and that of colleagues, and may refer to research papers, learned articles and letters during the course of giving testimony, such documents being themselves admitted in evidence and supporting any inferences which can fairly be drawn from them.

29.2 Admissibility of Expert Evidence

29.2.1 WHEN WILL EXPERT EVIDENCE BE ADMISSIBLE?

As long ago as 1553, Saunders J, in *Buckley* v *Rice-Thomas* (1554) 1 Plowd. 118, at 124, said, '. . . if matters arise in our law which concern other sciences or faculties we commonly apply for the aid of that science or faculty which it concerns.'

In order for expert evidence to be admissible two common law conditions must be satisfied:

(a)   that the matter calls for expertise; and

(b)   that the particular witness is suitably qualified as an expert in the particular field of knowledge.

29.2.2 THE MATTER MUST CALL FOR EXPERTISE

29.2.1.1 Art or science
Regarding the first condition, the inquiry has to be into a matter of art or science which is likely to be outside the experience and knowledge of the tribunal of fact. Expert help is therefore unnecessary on matters relating to normal human nature and behaviour. See the ***Evidence Manual***.

This distinction can be illustrated by *Liddell* v *Middleton* [1996] PIQR 36, CA. This was an action in negligence arising out of a road traffic accident. Stuart-Smith LJ commented that in cases of this type expert evidence from accident reconstruction experts is both necessary and desirable to assist the judge where there are no witnesses capable of describing what happened, where deductions have to be made from circumstantial evidence from the scene, or where deductions are to be drawn as to the drivers' speeds and positions immediately before the collision from the positions of the vehicles after the accident, marks on the road, or damage to the vehicles. In these instances the expert provides the court with the necessary scientific assistance which the court does not possess as an ordinary layman. On the other hand, where the only material available to the expert are the accounts of the eyewitnesses, the expert will be usurping the function of the judge in expressing an opinion about speeds of the vehicles or whether any of the drivers could have done anything to avoid the accident: in these circumstances drawing the necessary inferences and finding the necessary facts are within the ordinary knowledge of the layman, and therefore an expert's opinion on these matters is irrelevant and inadmissible.

29.2.2.2 Handwriting evidence
It is provided by the Criminal Procedure Act 1865, s. 8, that:

> *Comparison of a disputed Writing with any Writing proved to the satisfaction of the Judge to be genuine shall be permitted to be made by Witnesses; and such Writings, and the Evidence of Witnesses respecting the same, may be submitted to the Court and Jury as evidence of the Genuineness or otherwise of the Writing in dispute.*

Despite its title, this statute applies to civil cases as much as it applies to criminal proceedings. It seems to be clear that despite the use of the word 'Witnesses' rather than the phrase 'expert witnesses' that a comparison of handwriting can only be done with the assistance of a handwriting expert: *R* v *Tilley* [1961] 1 WLR 1309, CCA and *R* v *O'Sullivan* [1969] 1 WLR 497, CA. A different point arose in *Lockheed-Arabia Corp.* v

Owen [1993] QB 806 where the disputed writing was the signature on a cheque. By the time of the trial the original had been stolen in a burglary of the claimant's solicitors' offices, but a photocopy of the cheque was available. It was held that the photocopy was a 'disputed writing' within the meaning of the section, and a comparison with a control sample of writing could be undertaken by a handwriting expert at trial. The fact the original was not available only went to weight.

29.2.3 THE WITNESS MUST BE SUITABLY QUALIFIED AS AN EXPERT IN THAT FIELD

As to the second condition, the question is whether the witness has sufficient skill and knowledge in relation to the field in question. See the **Evidence Manual**.

There is no absolute requirement that the witness be professionally qualified, there being several areas where expertise is obtained through experience rather than study. However, generally, the proposed expert must be fully professionally qualified in the relevant area, and should often be to the forefront of those practising in that area. For example, in an ordinary personal injuries action it is usual to obtain the expert opinion of a consultant orthopaedic surgeon rather than a general practitioner.

As to how senior an expert to instruct, the parties will need to bear in mind the costs rules in CPR, Part 44 and r. 35.4(4), and that experts' fees that are unreasonably high will be reduced down to reasonable figures.

Furthermore, an acknowledged expert is only permitted to give an opinion within his or her own science, so, for example, an orthopaedic surgeon will not be allowed to talk about the injuries to a claimant's teeth.

29.2.4 OPINIONS ON ULTIMATE ISSUES

It used to be that a witness was, at common law, prohibited from giving an opinion on an ultimate issue. For example, in a running down action an accident reconstruction expert used not to be able to say that the defendant had driven negligently, that being one of the very issues for the court to decide. This condition has been abolished in civil cases by the CEA 1972, s. 3(1) and (3).

29.3 Obtaining Facilities for Inspection by Experts

29.3.1 NON-MEDICAL CASES

Orders under CPR, r. 25.1(1)(c), (d), for inspection of land and chattels, and for taking samples, conducting tests, etc. are normally sought at the allocation stage, see **7.6** and **21.5.2**. Normally it is obvious from the nature of the dispute that such orders are in the interests of justice, and they are usually made with very little discussion.

29.3.2 MEDICAL CASES

There is no such general power to order a litigant claiming in respect of personal injuries to submit to a medical examination on behalf of the defendant. The reason for this seems to be that any type of medical examination is an infringement of the fundamental human right to personal liberty, and it would be objectionable to make a direct order for such with power to commit if the claimant refused.

However, the court can achieve much the same result by the indirect method of ordering a stay of the proceedings if the claimant refuses a medical examination on behalf of the defendant: see *Edmeades* v *Thames Board Mills* [1969] 2 QB 67, CA.

29.3.3 WHEN WILL A STAY OF PROCEEDINGS BE ORDERED?

The principle laid down by Lord Denning MR in the above case, was that a stay would be ordered if it was just and reasonable to do so. Put another way, the court would order a stay if the conduct of the claimant in refusing a reasonable request was such as to prevent the just determination of the cause. Thus the test is twofold:

(a) Is it reasonable to order an examination?
and, if so,

(b) Is the claimant's conduct in refusing an examination such as to prevent the just determination of the cause?

(See the judgment of Scarman LJ in *Starr* v *National Coal Board* [1977] 1 WLR 63, CA.)

However, whether or not a stay is granted is entirely within the discretion of the court, and it will only grant a stay if the applicant satisfies it that a stay is required in the interests of justice. The facts of each individual case, and the parties' reasons for asking for, or resisting, the proposed medical examination, are all matters which must be taken into consideration; and each party is under a duty to provide the court with the necessary material to enable the proper exercise of its discretion.

29.3.4 WHERE THE EXAMINATION POSES A RISK TO HEALTH

Further problems arise if the proposed medical examination involves risk to health, or may be of an unpleasant nature. In assessing whether or not a refusal is reasonable, the court will 'weigh' the proposed examination on a scale, ranging from examinations involving no serious technical assault but only an invasion of privacy, to examinations involving a risk of injury or to health.

The degree of reasonableness in the claimant's objections to the proposed examination would bear a close correlation to its position on the scale. The test is then to balance the weight of reasonableness of the defendant's request against the weight of reasonableness of the claimant's objections, in order to ensure a just determination of the case: see *Prescott* v *Bulldog Tools Ltd* [1981] 3 All ER 869.

29.3.5 CONDITIONS IMPOSED BY THE CLAIMANT

29.3.5.1 Permissible conditions

As we have seen, whether a stay will be ordered may depend on whether the claimant is being reasonable. Sometimes a claimant is only prepared to submit to a medical examination upon certain conditions. Any or all of the following conditions have been held to be generally permissible:

(a) That the defendant pay the claimant's loss of earnings in attending the examination.

(b) That the defendant pay the claimant any out-of-pocket expenses in attending the examination, such as fares and subsistence.

(c) That the doctor will not discuss the cause of action with the claimant, except in so far as this is relevant for medical purposes.

(d) That the claimant have a friend, relative or a legal executive or partner from his or her solicitors present. (But see *Whitehead* v *Avon County Council, The Times*, 3 May 1995, CA, where the Court of Appeal upheld a decision that the claimant's action be stayed unless she submitted herself to a psychiatric examination without a friend or relation being present throughout the examination.)

It is usually unreasonable for a claimant to refuse examination by a named doctor but it may be reasonable for the claimant to refuse an examination by a named doctor, for example, where:

(a) A female claimant has an injury which she would prefer to have examined by a female doctor (or, perhaps, a male claimant has an injury which he would prefer to have examined by a male doctor).

(b) There are substantial grounds for doubting the competence, honesty or professional honour of the doctor.

(c) There are substantial grounds for doubting whether the doctor will be able to produce a report which is full, complete and not misleading.

From *Starr's* case, it is clear that the courts will only readily entertain objections which are personal to the claimant. Objections as to the bona fides or competence of the defendant's doctor have to be regarded with considerable caution and care, due to the gravity of the allegations.

29.3.5.2 Where the claimant wishes to have a nominated doctor present
Matters become a little more difficult if the claimant wishes to impose a condition that a doctor nominated by him or herself be present at the examination. The reasonableness test will be applied, and in most cases it will be held that the presence of a lay person should be sufficient reassurance for the claimant. It will have to be a very strong case to overcome the disadvantages of increased costs and delay involved in having two doctors present. (See *Hall* v *Avon AHA* [1980] 1 WLR 481, CA.)

The situation is, of course, different, if the parties agree that there should be a joint medical examination of the claimant. In this case both doctors play an active part in the examination, and it is often a useful procedure prior to agreeing medical evidence, or to focus the medical issues.

29.3.5.3 Automatic disclosure of the medical report generally unjustifiable
It can rarely be a justifiable condition to insist on automatic disclosure of the resulting medical report, as this amounts to an advance requirement to waive legal professional privilege: see *Megarity* v *DJ Ryan and Sons* [1980] 1 WLR 1237, CA. An exception was recognised in *Hookham* v *Wiggins Teape Fire Papers Ltd* [1995] PIQR 392, CA, if past delay in the proceedings or the proximity of the trial justifies such a condition in the particular circumstances.

29.3.6 NOT RESTRICTED TO PERSONAL INJURIES CASES

The power to order a stay where a claimant refuses a reasonable request for a medical examination is not restricted to personal injuries cases. In *Jackson* v *Mirror Group Newspapers Ltd, The Times,* 29 March 1994, CA, a libel action was stayed until the claimant submitted to a medical examination by the defendant's medical expert. The action involved an alleged defamatory statement that the claimant's face had been disfigured by cosmetic surgery. Restricting the defendant's expert to comment on the basis of photographic evidence when the claimant's expert had the opportunity of a full examination would have put the defendant at an unfair disadvantage.

29.4   Medical Examination of Defendant

Cosgrove v *Baker* (14 December 1979, CA, unreported) was interpreted by *Lacey* v *Harrison, The Times,* 22 April 1992, as deciding that in exceptional circumstances the court could order a defendant's defence to be struck out unless he or she submitted to a medical examination on behalf of the claimant where the defendant's liability depended on his or her medical condition. The most important consideration is whether the defendant, in refusing a reasonable request, is preventing the just determination of the case.

29.5   Legal Professional Privilege

29.5.1 THE GENERAL RULE REGARDING EXPERTS' REPORTS

Experts' reports, whether medical or non-medical, and whether obtained by the claimant or the defendant, if made for the purpose of pending or contemplated litigation, are privileged. Therefore, the exchange of experts' reports cannot, subject to the exception mentioned at **29.3.5.3**, properly be made the subject of an interim order (*Worrall* v *Reich* [1955] 1 QB 296, CA).

29.5.2 THE CEA 1972, s. 2

The CEA 1972, s. 2, although it does not alter this rule directly, provides under s. 2(3) that rules of court may be made

> *. . . enabling the court in any civil proceedings to direct, with respect to medical matters or matters of any other class . . . that the parties . . . shall . . . disclose to the other or others in the form of one or more expert reports the expert evidence . . . which he proposes to adduce as part of his case at the trial . . .*

Further, by s. 2(5), rules of court may also make provision prohibiting a party who fails to comply with a direction to disclose expert evidence '. . . from adducing, except with the leave of the court, any oral expert evidence whatsoever . . .'.

Relevant rules are contained in CPR, Part 35, and are considered at **29.6** to **29.10**.

29.6 Control of Evidence

The CPR, r. 32.1, provides that the court may control the evidence to be adduced in the course of proceedings, which may involve excluding evidence that would otherwise be admissible, by giving directions as to:

(a) the issues on which it requires evidence;

(b) the nature of the evidence which it requires to decide those issues; and

(c) the way in which the evidence is to be placed before the court.

This power is exercised in accordance with the overriding objective. It has a particular relevance regarding expert evidence, which is often expensive and time intensive. The power may be used to save expense, to ensure cases are dealt with proportionately, and to ensure that the real issues are addressed at trial.

The court can use its power to control evidence to prevent the parties calling unnecessary expert evidence at trial. This is particularly important, because professional experts are entitled to charge fees at commercial rates for the time they are engaged on a case, and these can often run to £1,000 or more per day. It has been held that apparently one-sided expert directions are permissible if they accord with the overriding objective. Thus, in *Baron* v *Lovell, The Times*, 14 September 1999, CA, the court felt there was not a great deal of difference between the two sides' medical reports, and directed that the medical evidence be limited to the claimant's medical reports. It is becoming increasingly common in fast track cases where the injuries are not too severe for directions to be made for the medical evidence to be restricted to the report served by the claimant with the particulars of claim. This is not restricted to personal injuries claims. In *Thermos Ltd* v *Aladdin Sales & Marketing Ltd, The Independent*, 13 December 1999, the judge held that expert evidence was unnecessary in many claims concerning the alleged infringement of registered designs for consumer articles.

Generally, expert evidence is not allowed in small claims track cases, so the discussion that follows is principally aimed at fast track and multi-track cases.

29.7 Directions Regarding Expert Evidence

Directions dealing with expert evidence will usually be made when the case is allocated to the fast track or multi-track, or on the case management conference. The primary rule is that no party may call an expert or put in evidence an expert's report without the court's permission. In the absence of a direction, therefore, expert evidence is inadmissible. In deciding whether to grant permission, and if so to what extent, the court will seek to restrict expert evidence to that which is reasonably required to resolve the proceedings. The primary rules are:

> *35.1 Expert evidence shall be restricted to that which is reasonably required to resolve the proceedings.*

> *35.4—(1) No party may call an expert or put in evidence an expert's report without the court's permission.*

> *35.13 A party who fails to disclose an expert's report may not use the report at the trial or call the expert to give evidence orally unless the court gives permission.*

Traditionally, if expert evidence was permitted, both parties would instruct competing experts. This is still possible, and the most likely approach in multi-track cases. Recently, there has been a move towards the joint instruction of a mutually acceptable expert, who it is intended will produce a report which is objective and not biased towards either side. This is in fact the favoured approach in fast-track cases.

29.7.1   JOINT INSTRUCTION OF EXPERTS

Where two or more parties wish to submit expert evidence on a particular issue, CPR, r. 35.7(1), provides that the court may direct that the evidence on that issue is to be given by one expert only. If the court makes such a direction, unless the parties agree on the expert to be instructed, the court may select an expert from a list submitted by the parties, or direct how the expert should be selected. Once selected, each instructing party may give instructions to the expert, sending a copy to the other instructing parties.

The fast track practice direction (PD 28) provides that where the court is to give directions of its own initiative and it is not aware of any steps taken by the parties other than service of statements of case, its general approach will be to give directions for a single joint expert unless there is good reason not to do so. If the parties agree directions in a fast track case, primarily they will be expected to have agreed to the joint instruction of experts, but they may agree to instruct their own experts, with subsequent mutual exchange of reports. Of course, the court may disagree with separate instruction, and may force the parties into jointly instructing experts.

The multi-track practice direction (PD 29), on the other hand, says that where the court is proposing on its own initiative to make an order that evidence on a particular issue is to be given by a single expert, the court must, unless the parties consented to the order, list a case management conference. This reflects the fact that separate instruction of experts is far more acceptable in multi-track cases.

PD 28 (fast track), para. 3.9, provides:

> *Where the court is to give directions of its own initiative and it is not aware of any steps taken by the parties other than service of statements of case, its general approach will be: . . .*
> *(4)   to give directions for a single joint expert unless there is good reason not to do so.*

PD 28, para. 3.7, provides:

> *Directions agreed by the parties should also where appropriate contain provisions about: . . .*
> *(4)   the use of a single joint expert, or in cases where the use of a single expert has not be agreed the exchange and agreement of expert evidence (including whether exchange is to be simultaneous or sequential) and without prejudice meetings of the experts.*

PD 29 (multi-track), para. 4.13, provides:

> *Where the court is proposing on its own initiative to make an order under rule 35.7 (which gives the court power to direct that evidence on a particular issue is to be given by a single expert) or under rule 35.15 (which gives the court power to appoint an assessor), the court must, unless the parties consented to the order, list a case management conference.*

There will be some reluctance to insisting on the joint instruction of a medical expert if one of the parties in a multi-track case objects to this course being taken: *Knight* v *Sage Group Ltd* (28 April 1999, CA, unreported).

29.7.2   WRITTEN QUESTIONS TO EXPERTS

A party may put to an expert instructed by another party or a single joint expert written questions about the expert's report for the purpose of clarifying the report. Directions given allowing expert evidence to be introduced will usually provide a date by when questions should be put to the experts. The expert's answers to such questions are treated as part of the expert's report. The CPR, r. 35.6 provides:

> *(1)   A party may put to—*
> *(a)   an expert instructed by another party; or*
> *(b)   a single joint expert appointed under rule 35.7,*
> *written questions about his report.*
> *(2)   Written questions under paragraph (1)—*
> *(a)   may be put once only;*
> *(b)   must be put within 28 days of service of the expert's report; and*
> *(c)   must be for the purpose only of clarification of the report,*
> *unless in any case—*
> *(i)   the court give permission; or*
> *(ii)   the other party agrees.*
> *(3)   An expert's answer put in accordance with paragraph (1) shall be treated as part of the expert's report.*
> *(4)   Where—*
> *(a)   a party has put a written question to an expert instructed by another party in accordance with this rule; and*
> *(b)   the expert does not answer that question,*
> *the court may make one or both of the following orders in relation to the party who instructed the expert—*
> *(i)   that the party may not rely on the evidence of that expert; or*
> *(ii)   that the party may not recover the fees and expenses of that expert from any other party.*

29.7.3   WITHOUT PREJUDICE DISCUSSION

The court may, at any stage, direct a discussion between experts for the purpose of requiring the experts to identify the issues in the proceedings and, where possible, reach agreement on the issues. Such a direction will normally also provide that following the discussion the experts must prepare a statement for the court showing:

(a)   those issues on which they agree; and

(b)   those issues on which they disagree with a summary of their reasons for disagreeing.

29.7.4   MUTUAL EXCHANGE

Where directions allow the parties to each instruct their own expert, the usual practice is for mutual disclosure (i.e. exchange of reports) within a specified period.

However, in exceptional circumstances, and to save costs, sequential disclosure may be ordered with disclosure by one party only and the other party permitted to defer disclosure of any reports, e.g. where a defendant has not had a medical examination and it is likely that the claimant's report will be agreed. Another example was *Kirkup v British Railway Engineering* [1983] 1 WLR 1165. In this case the Statement of Claim was in very general terms, and the defendant had decided on policy grounds (in order to reduce costs) not to ask for particulars, as it had been flooded with 8,661 similar claims by its employees. One principal issue in each case was the noise level in the various workshops where the employees had been working, often stretching over the whole working life of the employee. To obviate the need on the part of the defendants of writing a thesis on noise generally in engineering workshops, a sequential disclosure order was made.

29.8   Form of Experts' Reports

It has been held that the practice of drawing up reports in two parts, one for disclosure, the other not, does not comply with the rules. Further, it has been held at first instance in *Kenning v Eve Construction Ltd* [1989] 1 WLR 1189, that:

> The report would only comply if the whole of the opinion was disclosed because it would only then be that it disclosed the substance of the evidence, not just the evidence-in-chief. It was necessary to take the good with the bad and if the party did not like bits of the report then he was free not to use the witness — it was his choice.

Comments to the same effect were made in *Whitehouse v Jordan* [1981] 1 WLR 246 by Lord Denning MR in the Court of Appeal and by Lord Wilberforce in the House of Lords.

By virtue of CPR, r. 35.10 and PD 35, para. 1.2, an expert's report must:

(a)   give details of the expert's qualifications;

(b)   give details of any literature or other materials the expert has relied on in making the report;

(c)   say who carried out any test or experiment which the expert has used for the report and whether or not the test or experiment has been carried out under the expert's supervision;

(d)   give the qualifications of the person who carried out any such test or experiment;

(e)   where there is a range of opinion on the matters dealt with in the report, summarise the range of opinion, and give reasons for the expert's opinion;

(f)   contain a summary of the conclusions reached;

(g)   contain a statement that the expert understands his or her duty to the court and has complied with that duty; and

(h)   contain a statement setting out the substance of all material instructions (whether written or oral). The statement should summarise the facts and instructions given to the expert which are material to the opinions expressed in the report or upon which those opinions are based. By CPR, r. 35.10(4) and PD 35, para. 3, the instructions referred to will not be protected by privilege, but cross-examination of the expert on the contents of his or her instructions will not be allowed unless the court permits it (or unless the party who gave the instructions consents to it).

An expert's report must be verified by a statement of truth in the form:

> I believe that the facts I have stated in this report are true and that the opinions I have expressed are correct.

If an expert changes his or her mind on a material matter after the exchange of reports, that change of view should be communicated to the other parties (and, if reports have been lodged at court, to the court): *National Justice Compania Naviera SA* v *Prudential Assurance Company Ltd* [1993] 2 Lloyd's Rep 68, *per* Cresswell J.

29.9   Choice of Expert

Under the pre-1999 system one of the aims in choosing which experts to instruct was to find experts who would support the version of events most helpful to the instructing party. The Civil Procedure Rules 1998 seek to move away from this, and place a lot of emphasis on the importance of experts remaining independent of the parties, and confirm that the expert's primary duty is to the court rather than the party paying his fees. The CPR, r. 35.3, provides:

> (1) It is the duty of an expert to help the court on the matters within his expertise.
> (2) This duty overrides any obligation to the person from whom he has received instructions or by whom he is paid.

In *Stevens* v *Gullis* [2000] 1 All ER 527, CA, an expert instructed by one of the parties demonstrated by his conduct that he had no conception of the requirements imposed on experts by the Civil Procedure Rules. This included failing to state in his report that he understood his duty to the court and failing to set out his instructions, and also in failing to co-operate with the other experts in signing an agreed memorandum following a without prejudice meeting of experts. It was held that in the circumstances he should be debarred from giving evidence in the case. On the other hand, provided the expert understands his primary duty is to the court, there is no objection to an employee of one of the parties being instructed as an expert witness: *Field* v *Leeds City Council*, *The Times*, 18 January 2000, CA.

29.10   Procedure at Trial

29.10.1   PUTTING EXPERTS' REPORTS IN EVIDENCE

The CPR, r. 35.11, provides that where a party has disclosed an expert's report, any party may use that expert's report as evidence at the trial.

29.10.2   EXPERT TESTIMONY

The following propositions are derived from the judgment of Cresswell J in *National Justice Compania Naviera SA* v *Prudential Assurance Company Ltd* [1993] 2 Lloyd's Rep 68:

(a) Expert evidence presented to the court should be, and should be seen to be, the independent product of the expert uninfluenced as to form or content by the exigencies of litigation: *Whitehouse* v *Jordan* [1981] 1 WLR 246, HL, *per* Lord Wilberforce.

(b) The expert should give objective, unbiased assistance to the court on matters within his or her expertise: *Polivitte Ltd* v *Commercial Union Assurance Co. plc* [1987] 1 Lloyd's Rep 379.

(c) An expert witness in the High Court or County Courts should never assume the role of advocate.

(d) Facts or assumptions upon which the expert's opinion are based should be stated together with material facts which could detract from the opinion.

(e) An expert witness should make it clear when a question falls outside his or her expertise.

(f) Where an opinion is provisional because the facts are not fully available, that should be stated: *Re J* [1990] FCR 193, *per* Cazalet J.

THIRTY

WITNESS STATEMENTS

30.1 Introduction

The rules providing for the exchange of the parties' witnesses' statements are an important element in producing a more open system for trial preparation. They apply to all divisions of the High Court and to the County Court. The provenance of the rules has been confirmed by the CLSA 1990, s. 5.

30.2 Directions for the Exchange of Witness Statements

The main rules relating to the use of witness statements are to be found in CPR, rr. 32.4 and 32.10:

32.4—(1) A witness statement is a written statement signed by a person which contains the evidence which that person would be allowed to give orally.

(2) The court will order a party to serve on the other parties any witness statement of the oral evidence which the party serving the statement intends to rely on in relation to any issues of fact to be decided at the trial.

32.10 If a witness statement or witness summary for use at trial is not served in respect of an intended witness within the time specified by the court, then the witness may not be called to give oral evidence unless the court gives permission.

When directions are made on allocating a case to the fast track or multi-track, or at a case management conference, the court will make provision for the date by when witness statements must be exchanged. Witness statements are not usually exchanged in small claims track cases, so, like **Chapter 29**, the following discussion is largely limited to fast track and multi-track cases.

Normally mutual exchange is required, and it usually takes place a few weeks after disclosure and inspection of documents. Part of the reason why witness statements are exchanged after disclosure of documents is that the witnesses may need to comment on some of the documentation in their statements. If a witness statement is not served within the time specified in the directions, the witness may only be called with permission.

The statements that need to be exchanged are those of the witnesses a party intends to call at trial. There is no obligation to disclose statements from 'witnesses' who will not be called at trial.

30.3 Format of Exchanged Statements

The statement should represent the witness's evidence-in-chief. It will contain a formal heading with the title of the proceedings. In the top right-hand corner it should state the party on whose behalf it is made; the initials and surname of the witness; whether it is the first, second etc. statement of the witness; the references of the exhibits included; and the date it is made. The opening paragraph should give details of the witness's occupation or description, and if relevant state the position he holds and the name of his employer, and should also state if he or she is a party in the proceedings, or employed by a party.

The text of the statement must, if practicable, be in the witness's own words. It should be expressed in the first person. It is usually convenient to follow the chronological sequence of events. Each paragraph should, so far as possible, be confined to a distinct portion of the subject. The statement should indicate sections of its content that are made only from knowledge and belief as opposed to matters within the witness' own knowledge, and should state the sources of any matters of information and belief. All numbers, including dates, should be expressed in figures. Documents referred to in the statement should be formally exhibited. The statement must include a signed statement that the witness believes the facts it contains are true. False statements may be punished as contempt of court. The form of statement of truth is: 'I believe that the facts stated in this witness statement are true.'

Witness statements must be produced on durable A4 paper with a 35 mm margin and typed on one side of the paper only. Wherever possible they should be securely bound in a manner that will not hamper filing. If they are not securely bound each page should bear the claim number and initials of the witness.

30.4   Witness Summaries

A party who is unable to obtain signed statements before the time prescribed for exchange may apply for permission to serve witness summaries instead of witness statements. Witness summaries are simply summaries of the evidence that would have been included in a witness statement. They could be unsigned draft statements, or even just an indication of the issues it is hoped the witness could deal with. Such orders can only be granted if the party is unable to obtain the relevant witness statement. Unless the court orders otherwise, a witness summary must be served within the period in which a witness statement would have had to be served.

30.5   Failure to Comply with a Direction

It was held in *Beachley Properties Ltd* v *Edgar* [1997] PNLR 197, CA, that where a party failed to comply with directions for the exchange of witness statements and then sought permission, before the trial date, to serve further witness statements late, the court would not exercise its discretion in favour of that party in the absence of circumstances justifying the breach (i.e. a good reason for the failure to comply with the rules or directions) and, therefore, the party would be deprived from using that evidence. In *Mortgage Corporation Ltd* v *Sandoes* [1997] PNLR 263, CA, a differently constituted Court of Appeal rejected the argument that 'the absence of a good reason was always and in itself sufficient to justify the Court in refusing to exercise its discretion to extend the period for exchanging witness statements'. *Beachley* was explained as meaning that once a party was in default, then that party had to satisfy the court that despite the default the discretion should nevertheless be exercised. The party in default could do so in reliance on any relevant circumstances.

The general principles and factors relevant to late service under the Civil Procedure Rules are discussed at **28.3.2** and **28.3.6** above.

In *Mealey Horgan plc* v *Horgan, The Times*, 6 July 1999, the defaulting party served its witness statements about two weeks later than required by directions as extended, and six weeks before trial. Buckley J said that making an order depriving the defaulting party of its evidence would be out of proportion to the default. Such a response would be appropriate only if there had been deliberate flouting of court orders, or inexcusable delay which would otherwise result in the adjournment of the trial. In *Cowland* v

District Judges of the West London County Court (20 July 1999, unreported), the claimants were occupiers of premises, and alleged that their goods were taken by the County Court bailiffs pursuant to a judgment against a third party, and then sold at an undervalue. The key issue on liability was whether the original judgment creditor had given notice to the court before the sale that the goods did not belong to the original judgment debtor. On the morning of the trial the claimant sought to introduce evidence from the original judgment creditor's solicitor on the question of whether he had given notice to the court. It was plain that this evidence went to the heart of the main issue, and was likely to be highly persuasive if not conclusive on the issue. The trial judge refused permission. An appeal was allowed. The solicitor was not and had not been retained by either party to the present proceedings, and there was no property in a witness. It had therefore been open to both sides to seek his testimony, and the reality was that both sides were at fault in not seeking his evidence earlier. Excluding his evidence prevented the claimants from adducing evidence crucial to their case, thus preventing justice from being done. The Court of Appeal said the defendants had not been prejudiced in any way, despite referring to the fact that if they knew of the evidence it was possible they could have protected themselves by making a Part 36 payment. This did not generate material prejudice, because it could be guarded against by an appropriate costs order.

On the other hand, permission to serve the statement of one witness late was refused in *Coore* v *Chief Constable of Leicestershire* (10 May 1999, CA, unreported). Although the court made comments to the effect that the case was based on the exercise of the discretion to allow late service, the main reason given is to the effect that the witness did not address the essential issue in the case.

30.6 Privilege

If a statement is made by a person and the party who took the statement decides not to call the maker of the statement at trial or to use the statement at trial then the statement will be privileged if made for the purpose of pending or contemplated litigation. If, however, a person is to be called at trial, their witness statement will have to be disclosed to the other side on the exchange of witness statements. The exchange of such a witness statement created some debate as to whether, after disclosure, the statement remained protected by legal professional privilege so that the party receiving it could not use it without some further act of waiver of privilege. This would be particularly important if the party who disclosed the statement later decided for some reason not to call the maker of the statement at trial. However, there can be no doubt but that once a witness statement has been exchanged the privilege is waived: *Re Rex Williams Leisure plc* [1994] Ch 350, CA. Indeed, CPR, r. 32.5(5), expressly provides that other parties may use a disclosed witness statement as hearsay evidence if they choose to do so.

30.7 Use of Witnesses' Statements at Trial

30.7.1 EXAMINATION-IN-CHIEF

Exchanged witness statements stand as the witnesses' evidence in chief unless the court otherwise orders. A witness may, however, and provided the court considers there is good reason not to confine the witness to the contents of the disclosed statement, amplify his or her witness statement and give evidence in relation to new matters that have arisen since the statement was served: CPR, r. 32.5(3), (4).

The CPR, r. 32.5, provides:

> *(1) If—*
> *(a) a party has served a witness statement; and*
> *(b) he wishes to rely at trial on the evidence of the witness who made the statement,*

> *he must call the witness to give oral evidence unless the court orders otherwise or he puts the statement in as hearsay evidence.*
>
> *(2)   Where a witness is called to give oral evidence under paragraph (1), his witness statement shall stand as his evidence in chief unless the court orders otherwise.*
>
> *(3)   A witness giving oral evidence at trial may with the permission of the court—*
>
> *(a)   amplify his witness statement; and*
>
> *(b)   give evidence in relation to new matters which have arisen since the witness statement was served on the other parties.*
>
> *(4)   The court will give permission under paragraph (3) only if it considers that there is good reason not to confine the evidence of the witness to the contents of his witness statement.*

Unless such additional evidence is to be called, the examination-in-chief of the witnesses can be very short. They will be called, take the oath, and asked for their names and addresses (and often their occupations). They will then be asked to turn to the pages in the trial bundles (for which see **33.7**) where their statements can be found, and asked whether the document they have been shown is their statement, signed by them and that its contents are true to the best of their knowledge and belief. They are then asked to wait in the witness box for cross-examination.

30.7.2   CROSS-EXAMINATION

The CPR, r. 32.11, provides:

> *Where a witness is called to give evidence at trial, he may be cross-examined on his witness statement whether or not the statement or any part of it was referred to during the witness's evidence in chief.*

30.7.3   COPIES FOR THE PUBLIC

Where a direction is made that an exchanged statement shall stand as a witness' evidence in chief, members of the public present in court may not be able to follow the case and the principle that justice should be administered in open court would be undermined. CPR, r. 32.13 therefore enables members of the public to request to inspect such statements, and, if this happens, the court must make them available on payment of a prescribed fee. This right does not, in all probability, extend to documents exhibited to the statements: *GIO Personal Investment Services Ltd* v *Liverpool and London Steamship Protection and Indemnity Association Ltd* [1999] 1 WLR 984, CA. It is also subject to the court refusing to make the statements available for some sufficient reason, such as disclosure being contrary to the interests of justice or national security, or because of the nature of any expert medical evidence in a statement.

30.8   Implied Undertaking

After a statement has been exchanged, CPR, r. 32.12, provides that it may be used only for the purpose of the present proceedings unless and to the extent that:

(a)   the witness gives consent in writing; or

(b)   the court grants permission; or

(c)   it has been put in evidence at a hearing in public.

THIRTY ONE

HEARSAY IN CIVIL CASES

31.1 The Common Law Rule Against Hearsay

The hearsay rule is one of the oldest of the exclusionary rules in the law of evidence, having developed at the same time as the modern form of trial by jury.

At common law, a witness who was testifying could not repeat either:

(a) what he had himself said outside the witness box on an earlier occasion (the rule against narrative); or

(b) assertions of other persons, whether oral, written or by conduct (the strict hearsay rule).

An assertion is hearsay when it is tendered to establish the truth of that asserted. It is not hearsay when tendered to establish the fact that an assertion was made or the manner in which it was made.

It is also necessary to distinguish between hearsay and real evidence. Real evidence consists of physical objects which are produced for inspection by the court. Thus, a watch may be produced to prove it is defective, or a dog to prove it is vicious. An automatic recording, e.g. a tape recording, video recording or computer printout can be an item of real evidence and, if so, will be admissible provided there is *prima facie* evidence that it is authentic and sufficiently intelligible. The question is whether any specific recording is real evidence or hearsay. This turns on whether the recording or printout contains information produced with human intervention: if not, it is real evidence.

31.2 The Civil Evidence Act 1995

31.2.1 THE ADMISSIBILITY OF HEARSAY IN CIVIL CASES

The Civil Evidence Act 1995 (CEA 1995) which came into force on 31 January 1997 has abolished the common law rule against hearsay for civil cases, and the admissibility of hearsay is now governed by statute.

This appears from s. 1(1), which provides:

In civil proceedings evidence shall not be excluded on the ground that it is hearsay.

Hearsay includes multiple hearsay (s. 1(2)(b)). However, hearsay will not be admissible if the maker of the statement would not have been competent as a witness (s. 5), such as through being too young or of unsound mind.

31.2.2 NOTICE PROCEDURE

Section 2 of the CEA 1995 provides, in effect, that Rules of Court may:

(a) specify classes of proceedings in which a party intending to rely on hearsay evidence must give advance notice to the other parties;

(b) make provision for the other parties to request particulars of the hearsay evidence intended to be adduced; and

(c) prescribe the manner and time for complying with the above.

The rules are contained in CPR, rr. 33.2 and 33.3, which provide:

> 33.2—(1) Where a party intends to rely on hearsay evidence at trial and either—
>   (a) that evidence is to be given by a witness giving oral evidence; or
>   (b) that evidence is contained in a witness statement of a person not being called to give oral evidence;
> that party complies with section 2(1)(a) of the Civil Evidence Act 1995 by serving a witness statement on the other parties in accordance with the court's order.
>   (2) Where paragraph (1)(b) applies, the party intending to rely on the hearsay evidence must, when he serves the witness statement—
>   (a) inform the other parties that the witness is not being called to give oral evidence; and
>   (b) give the reason why the witness will not be called.
>   (3) In all other cases where a party intends to rely on hearsay evidence at trial, the party complies with section 2(1)(a) of the Civil Evidence Act 1995 by serving a notice on the other parties which—
>   (a) identifies the hearsay evidence;
>   (b) states that the party serving the notice proposes to rely on the hearsay evidence at trial; and
>   (c) gives the reason why the witness will not be called.
>   (4) The party proposing to rely on the hearsay evidence must—
>   (a) serve the notice no later than the latest date for serving witness statements; and
>   (b) if the hearsay evidence is to be in a document, supply a copy to any party who requests him to do so.
>
> 33.3 Section 2(1) of the Civil Evidence Act 1995 (duty to give notice of intention to rely on hearsay evidence) does not apply—
>   (a) to evidence at hearings other than trials;
>   (aa) to an affidavit or witness statement which is to be used at trial but which does not contain hearsay evidence;
>   (b) to a statement which a party to a probate action wishes to put in evidence and which is alleged to have been made by the person whose estate is the subject of the proceedings; or
>   (c) where the requirement is excluded by a practice direction.

Hearsay evidence is frequently given by witnesses who repeat what they were told on a previous occasion, and, as the witness statements are supposed to set out the evidence the witnesses are intended to say in-chief, hearsay evidence will usually be set out in the exchanged witness statements. The CPR, r. 33.2(1), says that setting out the evidence in the witness statement is a sufficient compliance with the CEA 1995, s. 2(1), so there is only a limited need to use hearsay notices. Hearsay notices will principally be used in relation to business records, see **31.2.6** below.

A single hearsay notice may deal with the hearsay evidence of more than one witness.

The duty to give notice may be waived by the parties (s. 2(3)). A failure to comply with the duty to give notice does not affect the admissibility of the hearsay evidence, but may adversely affect the weight of the evidence and may be penalised in costs (see s. 2(4)).

31.2.3   ADDUCING HEARSAY EVIDENCE AT TRIAL

By s. 6(3), the CEA 1995 does not affect the continued operation of the Criminal Procedure Act 1865, ss. 3, 4 and 5, which relate to impeaching hostile witnesses by cross-examination, and the use of inconsistent statements.

If a party adduces hearsay evidence without calling the maker of the statement, the CEA 1995, s. 3, provides that the other parties may be allowed by the Rules of Court to call the maker, whose hearsay statement will be treated as the witness's evidence-in-chief, and who will be cross-examined by the party calling the witness.

The relevant provision in the rules is CPR, r. 33.4, which provides:

> *(1)   Where a party—*
> *(a)   proposes to rely on hearsay evidence; and*
> *(b)   does not propose to call the person who made the original statement to give oral evidence,*
> *the court may, on the application of any other party, permit that party to call the maker of the statement to be cross-examined on the contents of the statement.*
> *(2)   An application for permission to cross-examine under this rule must be made not more than 14 days after the day on which a notice of intention to rely on the hearsay evidence was served on the applicant.*

The application will need to be made by issuing an application notice. Consideration should be given to supporting the application with evidence in writing, although there is no strict requirement for this.

If the maker of a hearsay statement is called as a witness at trial, the general rule is that the oral testimony of the witness is all that can be adduced, see CEA 1995, s. 6(2). However, this general prohibition does not prevent the introduction of:

(a)   the exchanged witness statement of the witness (see **Chapter 30**); or

(b)   a previous consistent statement made by the witness adduced to rebut an allegation of fabrication; or

(c)   a previous hearsay statement with the permission of the court. Permission is likely to be granted, for example, where, through the passage of time since the events under consideration, or through the onset of some disease, the witness finds it difficult or impossible to remember the relevant events, or otherwise gives confused or incoherent evidence, but did make a statement about the events soon after they occurred (but outside the time allowed for the use of memory-refreshing documents). See, for example, *Morris v Stratford-on-Avon RDC* [1973] 1 WLR 1059, a case under the CEA 1968.

31.2.4   ASSESSING THE WEIGHT OF HEARSAY EVIDENCE

The weight to be attached to hearsay evidence is dealt with by the CEA 1995, s. 4. This provides that in assessing weight, all the relevant circumstances must be considered. These include the ease of calling the maker of the statement, how contemporaneous the statement was with the events it describes, whether it involves multiple hearsay, any editing, and any motive the maker or recorder may have had to conceal or misrepresent matters: CEA 1995, s. 4(2).

By s. 5(2) evidence is admissible to attack or support the credibility of the maker of the hearsay statements introduced at trial, unless under the rules of evidence a denial by the witness would have been final. This means that evidence on collateral matters cannot be introduced to attack a hearsay statement, subject to the usual exceptions, namely that the witness has been convicted of a crime, the fact that the witness is biased in favour of the party calling him or her, and the fact that he or she has made a statement inconsistent with the present hearsay statement.

If a party wishes to attack the credibility of the maker of a hearsay statement, CPR, r. 33.5, provides:

> *(1)   Where a party—*
> *(a)   proposes to rely on hearsay evidence; but*

(b)   does not propose to call the person who made the original statement to give oral evidence; and

(c)   another party wishes to call evidence to attack the credibility of the person who made the statement,

the party who so wishes must give notice of his intention to the party who proposes to give the hearsay statement in evidence.

(2)   A party must give notice under paragraph (1) not more than 14 days after the day on which a hearsay notice relating to the hearsay evidence was served on him.

The court will also take into account any failure to comply with the notice requirements.

31.2.5   PRESERVATION OF CERTAIN COMMON LAW EXCEPTIONS TO THE HEARSAY RULE

The CEA 1995, s. 7, preserves the continued operation of the following five common law exceptions to the hearsay rule:

(a)   Published works dealing with matters of a public nature.

(b)   Public documents.

(c)   Records of certain courts, Crown grants, pardons and commissions.

(d)   Evidence of a person's reputation for good or bad character.

(e)   Evidence of reputation or family tradition for the purposes of proving pedigree, the existence of a marriage, public or general rights, and for identifying persons or things.

Under the CEA 1968, the common law exception to the hearsay rule relating to the proof of informal admissions was preserved by s. 9 of the 1968 Act. Under the 1995 Act, informal admissions are treated in the same way as other forms of general hearsay, and are admissible under s. 1(1) and subject to the notice requirements in s. 2.

31.2.6   BUSINESS AND PUBLIC RECORDS

Under the CEA 1995, s. 9(1), business (which includes any activity regularly carried on over a period of time, whether for profit or not) and public authority (which includes any public or statutory undertaking or government department) records (which are defined in s. 9(4) as records in whatever form) may be received in evidence without further proof. A document will, by s. 9(2), be regarded as such a record if a certificate signed by an officer of the business or authority is produced to the court. A document purporting to be such a certificate is deemed by s. 9(2)(a) to have been duly given by an appropriate officer and signed by him or her. These provisions are designed to facilitate the easy proof of records without the need to call anyone as a witness at the trial. However, if the document contains hearsay a hearsay notice should still be served.

By s. 9(3), the fact of an absence of an entry in the records of a business or public authority may be proved by an affidavit sworn by an officer of the relevant body. This is useful, as it is notoriously difficult to prove a negative.

THIRTY TWO

ADMISSIONS, NOTICES TO ADMIT AND TO PRODUCE

32.1   Introduction

It makes good sense to delimit the areas of conflict, as to do so saves both time and expense. The subject matter of this chapter deals with aspects of the law relating to admissions by the parties to litigation. We will deal first with admissions of fact, and then admissions in respect of documents. The final part of the chapter will deal with notices to the other side to produce documents to the court.

32.2   Admissions of Fact

32.2.1   WHAT ARE ADMISSIONS?

Admissions are statements, whether express or implied, whether oral or written, which are wholly or partly adverse to a party's case. Admissions may be either formal or informal.

32.2.2   FORMAL ADMISSIONS

Formal admissions may be made by the statements of case or otherwise in writing, including admissions made in compliance with a notice to admit (see **32.3**) or on a case management conference or other directions hearing, see **19.3.3**.

Unless the court grants permission to withdraw or amend a formal admission, the party making it is not allowed to adduce evidence at trial to contradict it.

32.2.3   INFORMAL ADMISSIONS

Informal admissions are simply items of evidence and may be disproved or explained away at trial by evidence to the contrary. Although they are hearsay, in that they are assertions made other than by a person while giving oral evidence at trial and are adduced as evidence of the facts asserted, they are admissible in evidence by virtue of Civil Evidence Act 1995, s. 1.

Where the informal admission is made by a party personally, the only conditions of admissibility are:

(a)   that the statement must be at least partly adverse;

(b)   that the statement was made in the same legal capacity as that in which the party is now suing or being sued; and

(c)   that the statement is received in its entirety.

Servants and agents may make admissions which are admissible against a party if they have express or implied authority to talk about the subject in question. It is to be noted that generally servants and agents have a wider authority to act than to speak about what they have done.

A party may be allowed to resile from an admission if the prejudice suffered by the party who made the admission in being deprived of the right to resile outweighs any prejudice to the other side if the admission was withdrawn: *Gale* v *Superdrug Stores plc* [1996] 1 WLR 1089, CA. Note, however, para. 3.9 of the Personal Injury Pre-action Protocol, which says the presumption is that the defendant will be bound by any admission of liability in claims worth up to £15,000.

32.3 Notice to Admit Facts

A party may seek further to limit and define the issues at trial after the directions stage by serving a notice to admit. A specimen notice appears at **Figure 32.1**.

The CPR, r. 32.18, provides:

(1)   A party may serve notice on another party requiring him to admit the facts, or the part of the case of the serving party, specified in the notice.
(2)   A notice to admit facts must be served no later than 21 days before the trial.
(3)   Where the other party makes any admission in response to the notice, the admission may be used against him only—
(a)   in the proceedings in which the notice to admit is served; and
(b)   by the party who served the notice.
(4)   The court my allow a party to amend or withdraw any admission made by him on such terms as it thinks just.

Under the old rules, if the other side failed to make the requested admissions within 14 days after service of the notice and if those facts were later proved at trial, the costs of proving those facts and the costs occasioned by and thrown away as a result of that failure would be borne by him or her unless the court ordered otherwise: see RSC O. 62, r. 6(7). Under the Civil Procedure Rules 1998 there is no express rule dealing with the consequences of not making a positive response to a notice to admit facts. However, the costs rules in Part 44, and in particular r. 44.3(6), are wide enough to achieve the same result.

Notices to admit are a judicially favoured procedure. In *Baden, Delvaux* v *Société Générale pour Favouriser le Développement du Commerce et de l'Industrie en France SA* [1985] BCLC 258, CA, Sir John Donaldson MR said that notices to admit and the costs penalties are of the greatest importance in the administration of justice and ought to be more frequently used. The reason is that judicial time is saved and the costs of litigation reduced if the issues in dispute are sharply defined before trial.

However, the procedure should not be abused by issuing Notice to Admit facts which are at the centre of the dispute. In such circumstances, the court is unlikely to impose any costs penalty for failing to make the requested admissions.

32.4 Deemed Admission of the Authenticity of Disclosed Documents

A party served with a list of documents may find that they are deemed to have admitted the authenticity of documents disclosed by the other side. The relevant rule is CPR, r. 32.19, which provides:

(1)   A party shall be deemed to admit the authenticity of a document disclosed to him under Part 31 (disclosure and inspection of documents) unless he serves notice that he wishes the document to be proved at trial.
(2)   A notice to prove a document must be served—

> (a) by the latest date for serving witness statements; or
> (b) within 7 days of disclosure of the document,
> whichever is the later.

The reference to 'disclosure' in r. 32.19(2)(b) is presumably intended to be a reference to 'inspection'. If a party believes that documents disclosed by the other side are fabricated or have been tampered with, they must serve a notice to prove. There is a prescribed form for the notice, Form N268.

The purpose of the rule is to prevent the necessity and cost of formal notices to admit documents disclosed in a list of documents. In practice this rule catches the vast majority of documents relevant to litigation.

32.5 Proof of Documents

32.5.1 BEST EVIDENCE RULE

There is a very old common law rule that the contents of a document must be proved by primary evidence. The rule is often said to be an aspect of the best evidence rule. The best primary evidence of a document is the original, although it has been held in *Slatterie* v *Pooley* (1840) 6 M & W 664 that an informal admission is primary evidence of the contents of a document against the party making the admission. Thus, under the general rule, a party suing for damages for breach of a covenant for quiet enjoyment will have to prove the covenant by reference to the original lease.

32.5.2 SECONDARY EVIDENCE OF A DOCUMENT

There are a number of exceptions to the general rule. Examples are:

(a) Where the original has been lost and has not been found after due search.

(b) Where it is impossible to produce the original, such as the inscription on a foundation stone.

(c) Where production is legally prohibited, such as a notice in a factory which must be displayed by Act of Parliament.

(d) Public documents.

(e) Documents covered by the Bankers' Books Evidence Act 1879.

When secondary evidence can be given, the contents of the document can be proved by copies of the original, whether these be manuscript copies, or photocopies or some other method, including copies of copies. The only condition is that the witness producing the copies must be able to say that the copies are true copies. Alternatively, the secondary evidence can take the form of oral testimony.

As regards the choice of mode of secondary proof, a copy will obviously in most cases be the most convenient, but there are 'no degrees of secondary evidence', so there is no objection to oral evidence being given where copies are available.

32.5.3 NON-PARTY HAVING POSSESSION OF THE ORIGINAL

In this situation, the party seeking to rely on the contents of the document will, in the High Court, serve the non-party with a witness summons (see **33.12.6**), commanding the witness to attend court and to bring and to produce specified documents.

A witness who fails to produce such documents for no good reason may be punished by the court for the disobedience and become liable in damages, but secondary evidence may not be given. If, however, the witness validly objects to producing the document, as on grounds of privilege, then, by way of exception, secondary evidence is admissible.

32.5.4 OTHER SIDE HAVING THE ORIGINAL

In this situation the old rules allowed a notice to produce the document at trial to be served on the other side. The notice did not compel production, although non-compliance may be grounds for drawing adverse inferences.

However, the primary purpose behind the procedure was that it laid the ground for allowing secondary evidence.

Secondary evidence was admissible where:

(a) there was evidence of due service of the notice to produce; and

(b) there was evidence that the original was in the possession of the party served with notice to produce; and

(c) the party served had not produced the original.

It was held that once secondary evidence had been adduced, the original could not be adduced to contradict the secondary evidence: *Collins* v *Gashon* (1860) 2 F & F 47.

32.5.5 NOTICE TO PRODUCE UNDER THE CIVIL PROCEDURE RULES 1998

There seems to be a strange lacuna in the Civil Procedure Rules 1998 regarding notice to produce. The CPR, r. 32.19, has a side heading 'Notice to admit or produce documents', but its two sub-paragraphs deal only with the deemed admission of the authenticity of documents disclosed by lists and notice to prove such documents if there is a dispute over authenticity. It is suspected that the failure to include specific provisions dealing with notice to produce is an oversight. It will therefore be prudent to continue serving such notices in cases where the originals of documents are in the possession of the other side, although another option is to serve a witness summons.

Figure 32.1   Specimen notice to admit

Notice to admit facts

In the Central London County Court	
Claim No.	CL9 9388378
Claimant (include Ref.)	CLIVE SHERRILL
Defendant (include Ref.)	DORADOWN (MACHINE FITTINGS) LIMITED

I (We) give notice that you are requested to admit the following facts or part of case in this claim:

1. That the machine referred to in paragraph 2 of the Particulars of Claim was designed to be operated with steel guards in place.
2. That the steel guards designed for use with the machine were removed for maintenance on the 2nd March 1998.
3. That the steel guards wree not in place on 16th April 1998.
4. That the accident on the 16th April 1998 was not caused or contributed to by the negilgence of the claimant.

I (We) confirm that any admission of fact(s) or part of case will only be used in this claim.

Signed _____
(Claimant)(Defendant)('s Solicitor)

Position or office held _____
(If signing on behalf of firm or company)

Date _____

- -

Admission of facts

I (We) admit the facts or part of case (set out above)(in the attached schedule) for the purposes of this claim only and on the basis that the admission will not be used on any other occasion or by any other person.

Signed _____
(Claimant)(Defendant)('s Solicitor)

Position or office held _____
(If signing on behalf of firm or company)

Date _____

The court office at

is open between 10 am and 4 pm Monday to Friday. Address all communication to the Court Manager quoting the claim number

N266 - w3 Notice to admit facts (4.99)   *Printed on behalf of The Court Service*

Figure 32.2   Notice to prove documents

Notice to prove documents at trial

In the Central LondonCounty Court	
Claim No.	CL9 9388378
Claimant (include Ref.)	CLIVE SHERRILL
Defendant (include Ref.)	DORADOWN (MACHINE FITTINGS) LIMITED

I (We) give notice that you are requested to prove the following documents disclosed under CPR Part 31 in this claim at the trial:

1. Letter from Messrs. Armstrong & Graham to the Defendant dated the 20th June 1998.
2. Letter from Messrs. Hope, Lewis & Co. to the Defendant dated the 11th August 1998.

Signed _____

(Claimant)(Defendant)('s Solicitor)

Position or office held
(If signing on behalf of firm or company) _____

Date _____

The court office at

is open between 10 am and 4 pm Monday to Friday. Address all communication to the Court Manager quoting the claim number

N268 - W3 Notice to prove documents at trial (4.99)   Printed on behalf of The Court Service

THIRTY THREE

TRIAL

33.1 Introduction

The vast majority of actions commenced in the civil courts of this country never reach trial. Proceedings may fail to reach the trial stage for many reasons. Judgment may be entered in default of an intention to defend or on an application for summary judgment. The proceedings may be struck out as an abuse of process, or as a result of a sanction, or discontinued. Most frequently, however, the parties avoid trial by negotiating a settlement of their dispute. One of the factors constraining the parties to settle their differences is the great cost of trial. The cost of any individual trial depends on a number of matters, including its length, complexity, the seniority of counsel instructed, and the fees of any experts who are required to attend. However, it can be said that the costs of many trials far exceed the costs of all the interim proceedings involved in the case prior to trial.

If the dispute between the parties cannot be resolved by negotiation, either party may seek to have it determined by the court. Although individual litigants may have their own motives for bringing their cases to trial, such as to have their day in court or to vindicate themselves in public, the primary purpose of having a trial is to decide finally the dispute between the parties by a judgment of the court.

33.2 Listing Questionnaires and Fixing the Date of Trial

These topics have already been considered in the context of the discussion of fast track cases (see **18.3**, **18.6** and **18.10**) and multi-track cases (see **19.2**, **19.6** and **19.7**). Essentially, directions made either on track allocation or at a case management conference or other directions hearing will fix a date for filing listing questionnaires, and trial dates will be fixed as soon as possible. In fast track cases this means at the allocation stage. In multi-track cases, fixing the trial date as soon as possible may mean doing this at the allocation stage, but may mean doing so considerably later. If a trial date is given at an early stage it may be altered later perhaps after the court considers the listing questionnaires. Trial dates may either be fixtures, which obviously means that the trial will commence on a specific date, or may be given by means of a trial 'window' of up to three weeks.

The rules give the courts a great deal of flexibility regarding how they will deal with trials. As discussed in **Chapters 18** and **19** the court can lay down trial timetables prescribing how the time available for the trial will be used, and allocating specified, limited times, for examination-in-chief, cross-examination and so on. Another power available to the court is to direct that one or more issues should be dealt with before the others as preliminary issues.

33.3 Preliminary Issues

33.3.1 INTRODUCTION

As a general rule, it is in the interests of the parties and the administration of justice that all issues arising in a dispute are tried at the same time. However, there are a number of rare and exceptional cases where some question or issue can be more conveniently or economically dealt with before or separately from the main trial. There are three main types of order that can be made:

(a)   the trial of a preliminary issue on a point of law;

(b)   the separate trial of preliminary issues or questions of fact; and

(c)   the separate trials of the issues of liability and damages.

33.3.2   PROCEDURE

A party raising a preliminary issue must usually apply by application notice or at a case management conference or pre-trial review. The court may alternatively make such an order of its own initiative. Very occasionally, the trial judge may order a question or issue to be tried first before the main trial.

The order will formulate the question that is to be tried, and must do so precisely so as to avoid difficulties of interpretation. If the issue is one of law, the court will further order the issue to be tried:

(a)   on the statements of case; or

(b)   on a case stated; or

(c)   on an agreed statement of facts.

33.3.3   WHEN IS TAKING A PRELIMINARY ISSUE DESIRABLE?

In *Allen* v *Gulf Oil Refining Ltd* [1981] AC 101, HL, Lord Roskill said:

> The preliminary point procedure can in certain classes of case be invoked to achieve the desirable aim both of economy and simplicity. But cases in which invocation is desirable are few.

His Lordship gave two examples of situations where the procedure may be appropriate:

(a)   Where 'a single issue of law can be isolated from the other issues in a particular case, whether of fact or of law, and its decision may be finally determinative of the case as a whole.'

(b)   Where the 'facts can be agreed and the sole issue is one of law.'

The House of Lords has protested against orders for the trial of preliminary points of law on assumed facts. In *Tilling* v *Whiteman* [1980] AC 1, Lord Scarman said they were '. . . too often treacherous short cuts. Their price can be delay, anxiety and expense.' The danger is that if the court, perhaps on appeal, decides against the point of law, the case has to go back to the court of first instance to be tried.

There appears to be a slightly increased willingness to order the trial of preliminary issues under the Civil Procedure Rules 1998. The way it is put in the Chancery Guide, for example, at para. 5.7, is that costs can sometimes be saved by identifying decisive issues, or potentially decisive issues, and ordering that they be tried first. The decision of one issue, which in itself may not be decisive, may still be appropriate because it may enable the parties to settle the remainder of their dispute.

33.4   Jury Trial

33.4.1   CASES WHERE JURY TRIAL IS APPROPRIATE

In the County Court (CCA 1984, s. 66) and in the Queen's Bench Division of the High Court (SCA 1981, s. 69) a party may apply for the action to be tried by jury if there is in issue either:

(a)   a claim in fraud; or

(b)   a claim in respect of libel, slander, malicious prosecution or false imprisonment.

The *prima facie* right to trial by jury in such cases is subject to the court otherwise being of the opinion that the trial requires prolonged examination of documents or accounts, or any scientific or local investigation which cannot conveniently be made with a jury. Further, the right to a trial by jury must be exercised (usually at the allocation stage or case management conference) before the place and mode of trial are fixed otherwise the right to trial by jury may be lost although the court retains a discretion to order trial by jury: see by analogy *Cropper* v *Chief Constable of the South Yorkshire Police* [1990] 2 All ER 1005, CA.

It is to be noted that even in the cases mentioned at (a) and (b) above there is no *prima facie* right to trial by jury in the Chancery Division.

Both the County Court and Queen's Bench Division have in addition a discretion to allow trial by jury in other cases. However, the usual rule is that all other cases are tried by judge alone: *Williams* v *Beesley* [1973] 1 WLR 1295, HL.

33.4.2   MAJORITY VERDICTS

Juries in the County Court are eight strong. If they fail to agree on a verdict within a reasonable period of time a majority verdict of 7:1 may be accepted. See Juries Act 1974, s. 17. In the High Court juries are 12 strong, and majority verdicts of 11:1 and 10:2 are permissible (and 10:1 and 9:1 after the discharge of jurors on the ground of evident necessity).

33.4.3   RELEASING JURORS IN LENGTHY TRIALS

Judges in jury trials should inquire of prospective jurors whether they will suffer inconvenience or hardship by having to serve for the estimated length of the trial, and excuse those who will be so affected: *Practice Direction* [1981] 1 WLR 1129.

33.5   Rights of Audience

Counsel, solicitors and (when the Access to Justice Act 1999, s. 40(2), is implemented) legal executives, have rights of audience subject to the terms of the Courts and Legal Services Act 1990 (CLSA 1990) as amended and the regulations of their professional body. At present counsel have unrestricted rights of audience, but it is anticipated that practising certificates will be introduced at some stage: see Access to Justice Act 1999, s. 46. Solicitors have to comply with the Law Society advocacy qualifications to conduct High Court trials. Employed advocates will have their rights of audience increased when ss. 37 and 38 of the 1999 Act are implemented (this particularly affects lawyers employed by the Crown Prosecution Service and the Legal Services Commission).

The following persons are given rights of audience under the CLSA 1990:

(a)   Parties. Litigants can conduct their cases in person.

(b)   Counsel. Members of the Bar are deemed to have been granted rights of audience exercisable in all proceedings in the High Court and County Courts by the General Council of the Bar, and are further deemed to be subject to approved rules of conduct: CLSA 1990, s. 27(2)(a) and s. 31.

(c)   Solicitors. Under CLSA 1990, s. 27(2)(a) and s. 32 all solicitors have full rights of audience in the County Courts and High Court hearings in chambers. Since December 1993 solicitors have, subject to obtaining certain qualifications, been able to apply for rights of audience for High Court and appeal hearings in open court.

(d) Solicitors' responsible representatives. They can only appear in proceedings, whether in the High Court or County Court, which are heard in chambers: CLSA 1990, s. 27(2)(e).

(e) Persons given express leave by the court: CLSA 1990, s. 27(2)(c).

(f) Persons given an express right of audience under any enactment: CLSA 1990, s. 27(2)(b). An example is the right given to local authority officers in respect of rent and possession actions involving local authority housing under CCA 1984, s. 60(2).

33.6 Pre-trial Matters

In advance of trial the parties should use their best endeavours to agree on the issues or the main issues, and it is their duty so far as possible to reduce or eliminate the expert issues. A list of agreed issues should be delivered with the skeleton arguments (for which see **33.8**).

Also, in multi-track cases a pre-trial review may be held. This is usually conducted by the trial judge, is held usually about eight weeks before the start of the trial, and should be attended by the advocates who are to represent the parties at trial. Its functions include ensuring all parties will be ready for trial, to avoid the need for late adjournments or adjournments after the trial begins, to ensure the main issues are identified, and to provide directions for the efficient conduct of the hearing, including a trial timetable.

33.7 Trial Bundles

Trial bundles should be filed by the claimant not more than seven and not less than three days before the start of the trial (CPR, r. 39.5(2)), although the fast track Practice Direction rather inconsistently says trial bundles in fast track cases should be filed at least seven days before the hearing. The responsibility for preparation of the trial bundles rests with the legal representative of the claimant. PD 39, para. 3, lays down detailed rules for trial bundles. Unless the court otherwise orders, the trial bundle should include:

(a) the claim form and all statements of case;

(b) a case summary and/or a chronology where appropriate;

(c) requests for further information and responses to the requests;

(d) all witness statements to be relied on as evidence;

(e) any witness summaries;

(f) any notices of intention to rely on hearsay evidence under r. 33.2;

(g) any notices of intention to rely on evidence (such as a plan, photograph etc.) under r. 33.6 which is not:

  (i) contained in a witness statement, affidavit or expert's report,

  (ii) being given orally at trial,

  (iii) hearsay evidence under r. 33.2;

(h) any medical reports and responses to them;

(i) any expert's reports and responses to them;

(j)   any order giving directions as to the conduct of the trial; and

(k)   any other necessary documents.

The trial bundle should normally be contained in ring binders or lever arch files. It should be paginated continuously throughout, and indexed with a description of each documents and the page number. If any document is illegible a typed copy should be provided and given an 'A' number. The contents of the bundles should be agreed if possible. If there is any disagreement, a summary of the points in dispute should be included. Bundles exceeding 100 pages should have numbered dividers. Where a number of files are needed, each file should be numbered or distinguishable by different colours. If there is a lot of documentation a core bundle should also be prepared containing the most essential documents, and which should be cross-referenced to the supplementary documents in the other files. Identical bundles with the same colour coded files have to be supplied to all the parties plus the bundle for the court and a further one for the use of the witnesses at the trial.

33.8   Skeleton Arguments, Reading Lists and Authorities

Skeleton arguments are compulsory in the High Court (*Practice Direction* [1995] 1 WLR 262) and in the Court of Appeal (see Court of Appeal PD, para. 3). They are used partly in order to enable the judges to do effective pre-reading, and are not used as a substitute for oral argument in court. Their purpose is to identify, not to argue points. They should therefore be as succinct as possible, concisely summarising that party's submissions in relation to each of the issues, and citing the main authorities relied upon (which may be attached). They should be lodged at Court and served on the other parties three days before the hearing. (In the Court of Appeal different time periods for service of skeleton arguments apply.)

In all QBD and Ch.D. claims where bundles must be lodged, the claimant or applicant must at the same time lodge:

(a)   a reading list for the judge who will conduct the hearing;

(b)   an estimated length of reading time; and

(c)   an estimated length for the hearing.

This must be signed by all the advocates who will appear at the hearing. Each advocate's name, business address and telephone number must appear below his or her signature. In the event of disagreement about any of these matters, separate reading lists and estimates must be signed by the appropriate advocates. See *Practice Direction (R.C.J. Reading Lists and Time Estimates)* [2000] 1 WLR 208.

Lists of any authorities which will be relied on at trial must be given to the court by 5 pm on the day before the hearing and to counsel for the other side in good time before the hearing. If an extract from Hansard is to be used in accordance with the principles in *Pepper* v *Hart* [1993] AC 593, copies should be served on the other parties and the court, together with a brief summary of the argument based on the extract, five working days before the hearing: *Practice Direction (Hansard: Citations)* [1995] 1 WLR 192.

33.9   Hearing in Public or in Private

The general rule, buttressed by Article 6(1) of the European Convention on Human Rights, is that all trials are heard in open court. The general rule does not, however, impose an obligation to make special arrangements for accommodating members of the public. By way of exception to the general rule, the CPR, r. 39.2(3), provides that hearings may be conducted in private if:

(a)   publicity would defeat the object of the hearing;

(b)   it involves matters relating to national security;

(c)   it involves confidential information (including information relating to personal financial matters) and publicity would damage that confidentiality;

(d)   a private hearing is necessary to protect the interests of any child or patient;

(e)   it is a hearing of an application made without notice and it would be unjust to any respondent for there to be a public hearing;

(f)   it involves uncontentious matters arising in the administration of trusts or in the administration of a deceased's estate; or

(g)   the court considers this to be necessary, in the interests of justice.

Further, the court may order that the identity of any party or witness must not be disclosed if it considers non-disclosure necessary in order to protect the interests of that party or witness: CPR, r. 39.2(4).

Even though a hearing may be in private, the judgment given will normally not be a secret document and thus will usually be considered a public document: *Forbes* v *Smith*, *The Times*, 14 January 1998.

33.10 Adjournment

The CPR, r. 3.1(2)(b), gives the court and general power to adjourn.

Whether or not a litigant should be granted an adjournment is a matter within the judge's discretion, but the discretion must be exercised judicially and in accordance with the overriding objective. For example, in *Joyce* v *King*, *The Times*, 13 July 1987, CA, the defendant was granted one adjournment, but was unable to obtain legal aid in time for the rearranged hearing. Without legal aid she was unable to get her expert, whose testimony was essential if she was to defend the action, to attend. Even though Mrs King was acting in person, the judge decided to refuse a second adjournment because Mrs King had been given several weeks' notice of the hearing and had applied to adjourn at a late stage. The Court of Appeal set aside the judgment for the claimant and remitted the case for a fresh hearing, because it was clear that it was not possible for Mrs King to obtain justice without the adjournment.

Other sufficient reasons for granting adjournments would include vital witnesses being unavoidably out of the country or too ill to attend trial.

Late adjournments, even with the consent of the other parties, may be visited by costs sanctions and wasted costs orders.

33.11 Non-attendance

If both parties fail to attend the hearing the action is likely to be struck out: CPR, r. 39.3.

If one side fails to attend, the court may allow the trial to proceed in the absence of that party. If it is the claimant who fails to attend, the claim and any defence to any counterclaim will usually be struck out, and judgment will almost certainly be entered for the defendant. If the defendant is absent, the claimant will usually still need to prove the claim to the satisfaction of the court although the court may strike out the defence and any counterclaim under CPR, r. 39.3(1)(c). Any judgment obtained in the absence of one party may be set aside: CPR, r. 39.3(3) and *Shocked* v *Goldschmidt* [1998] 1 All ER 372, CA.

The main factors that are considered on an application to reinstate following striking out for non-attendance are (CPR, r. 39.3(5)):

(a) whether the application to reinstate has been made promptly;

(b) whether there is a good excuse for not attending. Claimants, in particular, are expected to keep in contact with their solicitors, and so have limited grounds for saying they were unaware of a hearing date (*Neufville* v *Papamichael* (23 November 1999, CA, unreported)); and

(c) whether the absent party has a reasonable prospect of success if the trial is reconvened.

Where a party fails to appear, or fails to give due notice to the court of any inability to appear, the court may summon that party to explain the failure, and may impose a fine not exceeding level 3: CLSA 1990, s. 12.

33.12 Witnesses

33.12.1 ORAL TESTIMONY

The general rule is that evidence is to be given orally and in public: CPR, r. 32.2.

33.12.2 HEARSAY

Generally, the evidence of witnesses who cannot attend trial may be adduced at trial under the provisions of the Civil Evidence Act 1995. However, in these circumstances the evidence will not usually be under oath nor will it have been tested in cross-examination.

33.12.3 EVIDENCE BY DEPOSITION

Where the potential witness is too old, frail or ill to attend trial, or is likely to give birth at about the time of the trial, or will leave the country before the trial, it may be appropriate to apply for an order that the witness's evidence be taken on oath before trial under CPR, rr. 34.8–34.12. The examination, which includes cross-examination, is conducted before a judge, examiner of the court or such other person as the court may appoint. The examination can be conducted at any place, including, for instance, the witness's bedside. The evidence is reduced into writing in the form of a deposition which is signed by the witness. The examiner may make a special report as to the conduct of the witness during the examination, reporting matters such as whether the witness fainted or became violent.

A deposition is receivable in evidence at trial, but the party relying on it should serve notice of the intention to rely on it at least 21 days before the trial. The court retains a power to require the deponent to attend trial and give oral evidence: CPR, r. 34.11(4).

33.12.4 EXAMINATION OUT OF THE JURISDICTION

The High Court has power on its own behalf under CPR, r. 34.13, and on behalf of a County Court under CCA 1984, s. 56, to order:

(a) the examination of a witness outside the jurisdiction before the British Consular Authority as a special examiner; or

(b) the issue of a letter of request to the judicial authorities of the relevant country to take a witness's evidence. Evidence obtained under a letter of request may be given either orally or in answer to written questions. A letter of request may alternatively, according to *Panayiotou* v *Sony Music Entertainment (UK) Ltd* [1994] Ch 142, be confined to the production of specified documents in the possession of a person outside the jurisdiction.

33.12.5 TELEVISION LINK

The court may allow a witness to give evidence through a video link or by other means: CPR, r. 32.3.

33.12.6 WITNESS SUMMONS

If a witness is reluctant to attend trial, for example, if the witness has a job and is not prepared to take leave, attendance can be compelled by issuing and serving a witness summons (CPR, rr. 34.2 to 34.7), see **Figure 33.1**. Issuing a witness summons is purely administrative, and a fee must be paid. Service must be effected personally and not less than seven days before the witness is required to attend court. Conduct money, namely a sum sufficient to cover the witness's expenses in travelling to and from court and compensation for loss of time, must be tendered on service of the witness summons if the witness is to be liable to committal proceedings for failing to attend court.

There are two types of witness summons:

(a) to attend court to give oral testimony; and

(b) to produce documents at court. A witness summons is to be used for obtaining documentary evidence, not for the purpose of obtaining disclosure which might lead to the obtaining of evidence after enquiries are made: *Macmillan Inc* v *Bishopsgate Investment Trust* [1993] 1 WLR 1372, CA. The documents to be produced must be sufficiently described, although classes of documents may be described compendiously: *Panayiotou* v *Sony Music Entertainment (UK) Ltd* [1994] Ch 142. The CPR, r. 34.2(4)(b), allows the court to direct that a witness summons may require a witness to produce documents on such date as the court may decide, which may be substantially earlier than the main trial. This device enables a witness summons to operate in a manner similar to disclosure, but against a witness as opposed to a party.

Witness summonses are issued to ensure that witnesses who are able to give relevant evidence are available in court. A person who is served with a witness summons, but is unable to give relevant evidence, may apply to have the witness summons set aside.

33.13 The Day of the Hearing

33.13.1 THE USUAL SEQUENCE OF EVENTS

Provided the claimant has the burden of proof on at least one issue, the claimant will start. The sequence is as follows:

(a) Claimant's opening speech (opening speeches should be succinct).

(b) Claimant's evidence. Witnesses are called and—

(i) sworn (or affirm);

(ii) examined in chief by the claimant (but it is likely that the witness statements shall stand as the evidence in chief of the witness);

(iii) cross-examined by the defendant;

(iv) re-examined by the claimant.

Witnesses may be asked questions by the judge. They are sometimes ordered to leave the court at the start of the hearing so they do not hear the evidence given by other witnesses, unless they are experts or parties. However, it is quite common for witnesses to be present throughout the trial if the legal representatives for both sides do not object.

(c) If the defendant elects not to adduce evidence, the claimant then makes a closing speech, followed by the defendant's statement of his or her case. The next stage would then be (h) below. Otherwise:

(d) Defendant's opening speech (if any).

(e) Defendant's evidence.

(f) Defendant's closing speech.

(g) Claimant's closing speech.

(h) Judgment, which is often given immediately or is sometimes given after an adjournment for consideration.

(i) Consideration of costs. Normally, the party obtaining judgment has its own costs paid by the other side. Consideration is also given to the appropriate basis of assessment of costs, or the costs may be assessed summarily.

Where there are two or more defendants who are separately represented, they open their cases and adduce their evidence in the order their names appear on the record. Their closing speeches are then made in the same order.

If a point of law is raised or an authority is cited for the first time in a final closing speech, the other side is permitted to reply (confining the reply to the relevant point or authority).

The traditional sequence of events may be altered at the discretion of the trial judge, and may be subject to the rigours of a trial timetable.

33.13.2 SECOND SPEECHES

The judge may make a direction dispensing with opening speeches in non-jury trials. In such cases stages (a) and (d) in **33.13.1** would not apply. Nevertheless, it should be noted that a judge has a broad discretion as to the order of speeches at the trial. Even if the judge in question usually only allows counsel a single speech, an application may be made to allow second speeches if, for example, the case is one of complexity or importance.

33.13.3 SUBMISSION OF NO CASE TO ANSWER

A submission of no case to answer can be made by the defendant at the conclusion of the case for the claimant. However, in cases tried by a judge sitting alone, this has been regarded as an inconvenient course to take. First, the judge is the trier of both fact and law, and it is embarrassing for the judge to be asked to express a view on the evidence while it is still incomplete. Secondly, if the judge rules in favour of the submission, there would be the expense of a retrial if the ruling were to be reversed by the Court of Appeal. Consequently, if the defendant intended to make a submission the judge would usually require the defendant to elect whether to call evidence, and would only hear the submission if the defendant elected to call no evidence. See generally *Alexander v Rayson* [1936] 1 KB 169 and *Young v Rank* [1950] 2 KB 510. However, a deputy High Court judge in *Mullan v Birmingham City Council*, *The Times*, 29 July 1999, decided to hear a submission of no case to answer without putting the defendant to its election, because at the end of the claimant's case there were grounds for contending the claim had no reasonable prospect of success.

Figure 33.1 Witness summons

Witness Summons

In the Central London County Court	
Claim No.	CL9 9388378
Claimant (including ref)	CLIVE SHERRILL
Defendant (including ref)	DORADOWN (MACHINE FITTINGS) LIMITED
Issued on	

To

> Mr. Jonathan Collins,
> 38 Belsize Road,
> Edmonton,
> London N18

You are summoned to attend at *(court address)* 13-14 Park Crescent, London W1N 3PD

10.30 (am)(pm) on 25th   of March 2000   at

Court 38

(and each following day of the hearing until the court tells you that you are no longer required.)

☐ to give evidence in respect of the above claim

☐ to produce the following document(s) *(give details)*

Salary details and pay slips for Clive Sherrill from 1st October 1997 to 25th March 2000

The sum of £ 50   is paid or offered to you with this summons. This is to cover your travelling expenses to and from court and includes an amount by way of compensation for loss of time.

This summons was issued on the application of the claimant (defendant) or the claimant's (defendant's) solicitor whose name, address and reference number is:

Messrs. Younge & Collyer, 12 Market Place, Ponders End, Enfield, EN7 2AK, ref. GSP/773

Do not ignore this summons

If you were offered money for travel expenses and compensation for loss of time, at the time it was served on you, and you

- fail to attend or produce documents as required by the summons; or
- refuse to take an oath or affirm for the purpose of answering questions about your evidence or the documents you have been asked to produce

you may be liable to a fine or imprisonment and may in addition be ordered to pay any costs resulting from your failure to attend or refusal to take an oath or affirm.

The court office at 13-14 Park Crescent, London W1N 3PD

is open between 10 am and 4 pm Monday to Friday. When corresponding with the court, please address forms or letters to the Court Manager and quote the claim number.

N28 - w3 Witness Summons (4.99)   *Printed on behalf of The Court Service*

Neither of the two factors mentioned above apply to civil cases tried by jury, and in such cases the judge, who again has a discretion, is much more likely to hear the submission of no case to answer without putting the defendant to the election whether to call evidence.

33.13.4   STANDARD OF PROOF

The civil standard of proof is proof on a balance of probabilities. It must be borne in mind that the degree of probability required to establish proof may vary according to the allegation to be proved: *Hornal* v *Neuberger Products Ltd* [1957] 1 QB 247. The only exception is contempt of court, which must be proved beyond all reasonable doubt.

33.13.5   NOTING JUDGMENT

If the judge gives a reasoned judgment, counsel must take a note of those reasons. This note should be as full as possible. If the court has facilities for mechanically recording judgments, counsel's notes will be used for advising on the merits of any appeal and drafting any necessary notice of appeal. If the judgment is not mechanically recorded, counsel's notes may also form the basis of the note of the judgment used in the Court of Appeal.

Whenever judgment has been given counsel will endorse their briefs with a short note of the orders made by the court before returning their papers to their instructing solicitors. Instructing solicitors may use this as the basis for drawing up the orders. Accuracy in noting the judgment is therefore of real importance. If the orders are at all complex, it is often prudent to consult counsel for the other side immediately after the hearing to ensure both parties are clear on what the court has ordered.

33.14 Conclusion

In addition to being the most expensive stage of most civil proceedings, the trial is usually the most important. Almost all aspects of civil litigation are focussed on the ultimate trial of the case. It is tempting to think that once judgment has been obtained (by trial or otherwise) the case is finished. However, in exceptional cases it may be appropriate to appeal all or part of the judge's decision. This is discussed in **Chapter 39**. Also, in many cases it will be necessary to enforce the judgment (see **Chapter 38**), and, unless there is agreement as to the amount of costs to be paid or a summary assessment of costs, the costs order will have to be assessed (see **Chapter 36**).

THIRTY FOUR

REFERENCES TO THE EUROPEAN COURT

34.1 Introduction

If in the course of litigation before our national courts a question arises as to the interpretation of the Treaties establishing the European Community, or as to the interpretation or validity of any act of the institutions of the EC, that question can be referred to the European Court of Justice for a preliminary ruling if the English court considers that a decision on that particular question is necessary in order to enable it to give judgment. Article 234 (ex 177) of the EC Treaty provides:

> *(1)   The Court of Justice shall have jurisdiction to give preliminary rulings concerning:*
> *(a)   the interpretation of this Treaty;*
> *(b)   the validity and interpretation of acts of the institutions of the Community and of the ECB;*
> *(c)   the interpretation of the statutes of bodies established by an act of the Council where those statutes so provide.*
> *(2)   Where such a question is raised before any court or tribunal of a Member State, that court or tribunal may, if it considers that a decision on the question is necessary to enable it to give judgment, request the Court of Justice to give a ruling thereon.*
> *(3)   Where any such question is raised in a case pending before a court or tribunal of a Member State, against whose decisions there is no judicial remedy under national law, that court or tribunal shall bring the matter before the Court of Justice.*

It also applies to interpretation of the Brussels Convention (Civil Jurisdiction and Judgments Act 1982) and the Rome Convention (Contracts (Applicable Law) Act 1990).

(Similar provisions are contained in Article 150 of the Euratom Treaty and Article 41 of the European Coal and Steel Community Treaty.)

34.2 Mandatory References: Article 234(3)

The only court that is bound to refer a question to the European Court of Justice is a final court against whose decisions there is no judicial remedy under national law. This will usually be the House of Lords, because it is the final court in the land from which no further appeal lies but there may be circumstances where the Court of Appeal or the High Court may be a final court: see *Chiron Corp.* v *Murex Diagnostics Ltd* [1995] All ER (EC) 88.

However, a court against whose decision there is no judicial remedy is not obliged to refer a question to the European Court of Justice if either:

(a)   the point has already been decided by the European Court (but a further reference can be made if the national court wishes the European Court to reconsider the point); or

(b) the correct application of Community law is obvious. The national court must, however, be convinced that the point is equally obvious to the courts of other Members States and the European Court: see *CILFIT (Srl)* v *Italian Ministry of Health* (Case 283/81) [1982] ECR 3415 and *Practice Direction (ECJ)* [1997] All ER (EC) 1.

Further, a final court is only obliged to refer a point if it is necessary to consider that point, i.e. if it is relevant: *CILFIT (Srl)* v *Italian Ministry of Health.*

34.3 Discretionary References: Article 234(2)

References under Article 234(2) (ex 177(2)) are not confined to final courts but are appropriate where a court or tribunal considers a decision on a point within Article 234(1) (ex 177(1)) is 'necessary to enable it to give judgment'. The courts generally have a wide discretion whether or not to refer a point to the European Court. However, while national courts are able to find that acts of Community institutions are valid, if a national court intends to question the validity of an act of a Community institution it must refer that question to the European Court: see *Foto-Frost* v *Haupzollamt Lubeck-Ost* (Case 314/85) [1987] ECR 4199 and *Practice Direction (ECJ)* [1997] All ER (EC) 1.

In deciding whether a decision by the European Court on a point is 'necessary to enable it to give judgment' Lord Denning in *H.P. Bulmer* v *J. Bollinger S.A.* [1974] Ch 401, CA, took a narrow view of the word 'necessary' in that the point would be 'necessary' if it was conclusive of the case whichever way it was decided. This view has been subsequently disapproved. In *Polydor Ltd* v *Harlequin Record Shops Ltd* [1982] CMLR 413, for instance, it was said by Ormrod LJ that 'necessary' meant 'reasonably necessary' in ordinary English and not 'unavoidable'.

The discretion to refer a point is a wide discretion: see **Remedies Manual** for some of the factors which have been considered in some cases to be relevant in the exercise of that discretion.

34.4 Procedure

Similar procedures apply in the County Courts (CCR O. 19, r. 15) and High Court (RSC O. 114) both of which are preserved in the schedules to the Civil Procedure Rules 1998. Only a judge or the Court of Appeal may make an order of reference. The order of reference may be made by the court upon application by a party to the proceedings or on its own initiative. It can be made either at or before the trial or hearing. Usually the proceedings before the national court will be stayed until the question which has arisen is determined by the European Court.

34.5 What Happens Once an Order of Reference is Made?

The request for a preliminary ruling must be set out in a schedule and the question(s) requiring resolution must be drafted with sufficient precision as to enable the European Court to answer simply and completely.

The Senior Master is responsible for sending the request to the European Court.

Upon receipt of the reference, the European Court will deal with it according to its own procedural rules, and once it has made a decision that will be communicated to the national court by the Registrar of the European Court. The parties to the proceedings will also receive a copy.

It must be noted, however, that the European Court does not decide the case in which the question arose. That remains to be done by the national court.

34.6 Costs

The question of costs will normally be reserved to the ultimate hearing of the case before the national court, after the European Court had provided its ruling: see *The Boots Co. plc* v *Commissioners of Customs and Excise* [1988] 1 CMLR 433 and *R* v *Dairy Produce Quota Tribunal, ex parte Hall and Sons (Dairy Farmers) Ltd* [1988] 1 CMLR 592.

34.7 Questions

OBJECTIVES

By the conclusion of this section you should have a sound understanding of:

(a) the principles underlying the general exclusionary rule in relation to evidence of opinion and the main exceptions to that rule, i.e., (i) where an opinion is a shorthand for several factual observations and (ii) where it is necessary to seek the opinion of experts;

(b) the special rules relating to the opinion evidence of experts — including the definition of an expert, the need for the court's permission before a party can rely on expert evidence, the general form and content of expert evidence (secondary facts etc.), the appointment of a single joint expert, the duty of the expert to the court, directions regarding expert evidence;

(c) the practice and procedure relating to the exchange and use of witness statements;

(d) the law and procedure relating to the admission of hearsay evidence in civil trials;

(e) the procedure relating to notices to admit facts and to produce documents;

(f) the procedure relating to obtaining evidence sworn out of court;

(g) the use of witness summonses;

(h) the procedure on the trial of civil actions;

(j) the procedure and principles governing references to the European Court.

RESEARCH

Read the materials contained in **Chapters 29** to **34** of this Manual.

LARGE GROUP SESSION 8

On the basis of this research, consider the following questions. It is particularly important to have selected answers for questions 2 and 5 in advance of the class.

QUESTION 1

You are instructed to advise Barkis, who was injured on 1 December 1998 whilst operating machinery at the Murdstone Ltd factory in Blackfriars. The parties have failed to reach any settlement. Following compliance with the pre-action protocol procedure, a claim form has been issued against the company claiming damages for negligence and breach of statutory duty under the Factories Act 1961. Murdstone's insurers have refused to allow your engineer to inspect the machine.

What advice should you give?

QUESTION 2

Samantha is claiming damages against Daniel for serious personal injuries she suffered in a road accident. The parties were unable to agree to the instruction of a single joint expert before Samantha started proceedings. A claim form has been served together with particulars of claim and a copy of a medical report by a consultant instructed on Samantha's behalf. Case management directions permit the parties to rely on expert evidence. Liability is admitted on Daniel's behalf, but his insurers want Mr Jones, another consultant, to express a second opinion on Samantha's injuries. Her condition has now stabilised after lengthy treatment, and she will not consent to the further medical examination sought by Daniel's solicitors. Having been instructed for the defence, which one of the following is the advice you should give?

[A] That it is for Samantha to prove her claim, and in practice the court will place little reliance on the opinion of a single medical witness in a serious case, so it is better not to seek a second opinion.

[B] That an application should be made to stay Samantha's action unless she consents to a medical examination by Mr Jones.

[C] That an application should be made for an order requiring Samantha to consent to a medical examination by Mr Jones.

[D] That because Samantha's condition has now stabilised after treatment, and the proposed examination by Mr Jones serves no clinical purpose for her recovery, Samantha is entitled to refuse to be examined.

QUESTION 3

(a) Is an expert report privileged?

(b) If a case is allocated to the multi-track, can the court order the parties to instruct a single joint expert?

(c) Is there any mechanism whereby a party can seek to find out more about an opponent's expert's report before trial?

(d) What are the responsibilities of an expert who is instructed to prepare a report for the purposes of litigation?

QUESTION 4

You have been instructed on a case where one of the case management directions made by Master Wym was for the mutual exchange of witness statements by a specified date. Such exchange duly took place on the specified date. The day before the trial one of the defendant's witnesses informed your Instructing Solicitors that they had suddenly remembered a vital piece of evidence. Your Instructing Solicitors believe it is necessary to use this evidence at the trial. They want to know whether they will be allowed to adduce it. Advise them.

QUESTION 5

Early in proceedings relating to a contract dispute, your client, Joan, seeks your advice with regard to evidence contained in her witness statement where she states that she heard Mark say 'I did not inspect the goods'. You intend to call Joan as a witness at trial and believe this comment will assist her case. The correct procedure to enable your client to rely on this evidence is which one of the following?

[A] Serve a hearsay notice on the other side within 14 days of the trial date.

[B] Serve a hearsay notice on the other side within 7 days of the trial date.

[C] Exchange Joan's witness statement with the other side in accordance with directions.

[D] Ask for the permission of the court to adduce the evidence.

QUESTION 6

Patrick is suing Dora for damages for late delivery under a contract for the sale of goods. Dora's defence is that the contractual date for delivery was 23 April 1999, not 3 April as alleged by Patrick. On disclosure, Patrick includes in his list the original of Dora's letter dated 15 March 1999 containing her offer (which he accepted by a letter dated 16 March). Having inspected Patrick's documents, Dora states that the delivery date stated in her letter has been tampered with by removing the '2'. Advise Dora, who wishes to dispute the authenticity of the letter of 15 March, as it now stands.

QUESTION 7

In an action between Ann and Ben directions have been given, and a trial date has been fixed. Ann has served a notice to admit facts. Your client, Ben, is reluctant 'to help Ann win her case'. Advise Ben.

QUESTION 8

Twenty minutes before the scheduled start of an action in the Coventry County Court you are told that your independent witness (your only other witness being the lay client) has just telephoned your instructing solicitor's office to say she is ill in bed and unable to attend. What do you do?

QUESTION 9

You have been instructed on behalf of Cook & Wilson (Chemists) Ltd, the defendants in an action brought by Michael in the High Court claiming damages for false imprisonment following his detention for suspected shop lifting. Directions have been complied with and a trial date has been fixed. Michael serves an application notice on Cook & Wilson seeking an order that the action be tried by a jury. You suspect that this has been done principally in the hope that a jury will award a greater sum in damages than a judge. Are there any grounds on which the application can be opposed?

QUESTION 10

George, who can give relevant evidence at a trial due to start in the next few weeks has been admitted to hospital with a debilitating, possibly terminal, illness. He is in full command of his powers of communication, and is ready to assist the claimant in whatever way is necessary. What should be done on behalf of the claimant?

QUESTION 11

Your client believes that on a matter concerning the interpretation of European Community law any court considering the matter must refer the matter to the European Court of Justice. Is your client correct? If not, what is the position?

THIRTY FIVE

COMMUNITY LEGAL SERVICE AND FINANCING LITIGATION

35.1 Introduction

How a case will be paid for is always a major issue in any litigation. In this respect public funding is an important area to consider as is also who will ultimately pay the costs of litigation. The expensive nature of litigation often means that funding the costs of litigation is almost as important as the relief or remedy sought. There are a number of alternative ways of financing litigation, which will be considered in this chapter. However, the bulk of the chapter will be devoted to public funding.

35.2 Traditional Retainer

The traditional method is for the client to pay the solicitor's costs of conducting a case at an agreed hourly rate. Until recently, arrangements between solicitors and clients were often very lax, with little or nothing said about charging rates or the incidence of billing for the solicitor's charges. Solicitors often simply relied on being able to charge at reasonable rates for the work they did. If they delayed in billing their clients, the first bill could come as a big shock to the client. The Solicitors' Practice Rules now require solicitors to provide their clients with client care letters which should include at least basic information about rates and when bills are likely to be sent and, if possible, an estimate of the future costs. The Solicitors' Costs Information and Client Care Code (1999) also requires solicitors to consider which of the various options on funding is best suited to the client's circumstances.

Charge out rates are based on the salaries of the staff and fee earners working at the solicitor's office together with an element representing the firm's profits. The modern approach is to fix a single hourly rate for each fee earner (or grade of fee earner) in the firm taking these factors into account. A variation on this approach is to adopt widely accepted regional rates for different grades of fee earner. Grade 1 covers partners and solicitors with over four years' post-qualification experience. Grade 2 covers more junior solicitors and senior legal executives. Grade 3 covers legal executives and senior para-legals. Grade 4 covers trainees and junior para-legals. An alternative method has been to quote a lower hourly rate, but to add a mark-up of a variable percentage (say 50% for ordinary litigation). Clients tend to find being quoted a simple hourly rate easier to understand. In addition, the client will be expected to pay for disbursements. These are sums paid by the firm during the course of litigation in respect of experts' and counsel's fees, the cost of making copies of photographs, and similar expenditure. It is normal for solicitors to ask for sums on account of costs when they are first retained, and periodically during the course of litigation.

35.3 Conditional Fee Agreements

As an alternative to a traditional retainer, the client and the solicitor's firm may agree to enter into a conditional fee agreement. Since 1998 it has been possible to enter into these agreements in all types of civil litigation other than family work. The basic idea of these agreements is that the client will not have to pay anything to the firm acting for him or her if the case is lost, but if it is successful the lawyer will be entitled to charge the client at the lawyer's usual rate plus a success fee. The success fee will be a percentage, up to 100%, of the costs otherwise chargeable to the client. It should be related to the risks involved in the litigation, and should in general be subject to being no more than 25% of the sum recovered.

Statutory authorisation for conditional fee agreements ('CFAs') was conferred by the CLSA 1990, s. 58. Before the introduction of this provision any form of fee agreement under which a lawyer is paid depending on the success of the claim was illegal and unenforceable. The illegality in the funding arrangement also meant that a successful party with an illegal funding arrangement could not recover costs from the losing party. Any concern that a CFA might be attacked by the opposite side as savouring of maintenance or champerty was removed by *Hodgson* v *Imperial Tobacco Ltd* [1998] 1 WLR 1056. To be effective under the CLSA 1990, a CFA has to be in writing and comply with the requirements set out in the Conditional Fee Agreements Regulations 2000 (SI 2000 No. 692). In cases where counsel is instructed, there will be a CFA between the client and the solicitor, and a second CFA between the solicitor and counsel. Model forms of CFAs have been drafted in consultation between the Law Society and Bar Council.

Although entering into a CFA means that the client will not have to pay his or her own lawyer's costs if the case is lost, a major concern for most clients is whether they will then be liable to pay the other side's costs. The answer is that, in accordance with the rule that costs normally follow the event, they usually will. However, there are several insurance companies that provide policies designed precisely to cover this situation at reasonably modest cost. A further question is whether the client or the solicitor should meet the disbursements payable (such as court and experts' fees). This will be dealt with in the CFA between the client and the solicitor. The result is that most clients entering into CFAs will have to pay a modest premium for insurance against the risk of paying the costs of the other side, and may (depending on their agreement with the solicitor) have to pay the disbursements.

At the end of the case, if it is successful, the client would hope to recover damages from the other side and also the base costs, but will have to pay the success fee out of the damages. The client may challenge both the base costs and the level of the success fee by asking the court to assess these sums under CPR, r. 48.9.

The mechanics of conditional fee agreements is under review. One of the elements under review is whether an unsuccessful defendant should be limited to paying the successful claimant's base costs, or whether in addition he or she should pay the success fee: see CLSA 1990, s. 58A(6), as amended by the Access to Justice Act 1999 (AJA 1999). Another is whether any insurance premium should be recoverable from the unsuccesful party: AJA 1999, s. 29.

35.4　Legal Expenses Insurance

Some clients have the benefit of legal expenses insurance, often as part of their motor or home insurance policies. In these cases the costs incurred on behalf of the client will be met by the legal expenses insurer. Often these insurers require the client's lawyers to provide advice on the merits of the claim from time to time so they can assess whether continuing the litigation can be justified under the terms of the insurance.

35.5　After the Event Insurance

A client needs to be told about the potential liability for the other side's costs if the case is unsuccessful. The usual rule is that the unsuccessful party in the proceedings is ordered to pay the successful party's costs: CPR, r. 44.3(2). The other side's costs generally have to be paid out of the losing party's personal resources. It may be possible for the client to arrange 'after the event' insurance to cover the other side's costs. With the exception of insurance designed for use with CFAs, such insurance is usually quite expensive.

35.6 Legal Aid

Under the Legal Aid Act 1988 (LAA 1988) a person could qualify for legal advice, assistance or representation, the cost of which was effectively payable out of public funds through the Legal Aid Board. Legal aid was replaced by the Community Legal Service from 1 April 2000. The legal aid system will, however, continue to be important for some years because there will continue to be several thousands of cases with legal aid certificates progressing through the legal system. A litigant who is legally-assisted in this way and is unsuccessful in the proceedings will not normally be ordered to pay the costs of the successful party. Particular consideration must be given to this factor when conducting proceedings against a legally-assisted person.

Legal aid may be divided into two categories. First, initial advice and assistance could sometimes be provided under the Green Form Scheme, a topic considered at **35.7**. Secondly, civil legal aid provided funding for the bringing or defending of civil proceedings. This is discussed at **35.8**.

35.7 Legal Advice and Assistance under the Green Form Scheme

35.7.1 THE GREEN FORM SCHEME

Under LAA 1988, s. 8 a person could receive advice and/or assistance on English law given by a professionally qualified lawyer: R v *Legal Aid Board, ex parte Bruce* [1992] 1 WLR 694, HL. This granted an applicant two hours of a solicitor's time (three hours in matrimonial cases) for preparation, correspondence and an initial interview. It was intended to provide preliminary help and consultation and did not cover representation.

35.7.2 ASSISTANCE BY WAY OF REPRESENTATION (ABWOR)

This covered the cost of a solicitor preparing the client's case and, if assigned, counsel's fees on representing him or her in most civil cases in the magistrates' courts (e.g. hearings in respect of separation, maintenance, defended adoption proceedings) and before a Mental Health Review Tribunal. ABWOR was only available with prior approval of the Legal Aid Board.

35.7.3 ELIGIBILITY

Clients receiving income support, family credit and disability working allowance were automatically entitled to both Green Form advice and assistance and ABWOR. Limits on eligibility were set yearly and depended on the applicant's income and capital.

35.8 Civil Legal Aid

35.8.1 COURTS AND CLAIMS WHERE CIVIL LEGAL AID WAS AVAILABLE

Civil legal aid was available for proceedings in the House of Lords, the Court of Appeal, the High Court, the County Court, the Employment Appeal Tribunal and, for certain domestic proceedings, the magistrates' court. See LAA 1988, s. 14 and sch. 2. Certain types of proceedings, such as defamation actions, were outside the scope of legal aid. Further, legal aid was only available to individuals, not companies.

35.8.2 THE APPLICANT'S FINANCIAL RESOURCES: THE MEANS TEST

Legal aid was granted only if the financial resources of the applicant were within the prescribed income and capital limits: LAA 1988, s. 15(1). An assisted person would be required to pay a contribution towards the costs of his or her representation if his or her financial resources (i.e. income and/or capital) exceeded figures specified in the Assessment of Resources Regulations (amended each year). Income contributions continued for the duration of the proceedings.

35.8.3 THE MERITS OF THE CASE: THE MERITS TEST

Under the LAA 1988, s. 15, entitlement to legal aid was also dependent on the merits of the case. If legal aid was to be granted it had to be shown that there were reasonable grounds for taking, defending or being a party to the proceedings. Counsel instructed to advise in legal aid cases had to assess the prospects of success according to the following categories: A, very good (80%); B, good (60–80%); C, reasonable (50–60%); D (less than 50%); and E, impossible to say.

35.8.4 GENERAL DISCRETION: THE REASONABLENESS TEST

Under this heading the following grounds would be considered:

(a) Would only trivial advantage be gained by the applicant in bringing the proceedings? That is to say he or she would win a moral victory but not much money! Legal aid would be refused in such circumstances.

(b) If a solicitor would not normally be employed in such proceedings (e.g. small claims track claims), then legal aid would be refused.

(c) Was finance available from some other source (e.g. if a trade union offers legal representation as one of the benefits of membership)? Legal aid would then be refused.

35.8.5 THE LEGAL AID CERTIFICATE

A Legal Aid Certificate was granted if the application was successful. Notice of issue of the Legal Aid Certificate had to be given to the other side once the action was commenced, and a copy of the certificate had to be filed at court, and also subsequent amended certificates.

Legal Aid Certificates could be granted subject to limitations: LAA 1988, s. 15(4). Thus, a certificate could impose a limit on the legal aid granted, e.g. limited to all steps up to and including the issue of the claim form, but excluding the obtaining of counsel's opinion on the merits of the case. Certificates could also contain conditions that approval had to be obtained from the Area Office to continue once the costs incurred reach £5,000. Counsel and solicitors would not be paid for any work not authorised by the certificate.

35.8.6 COSTS WHEN THE LEGALLY-AIDED PARTY WINS THE CASE

The usual rule as to costs was that the successful party recovered costs against the loser. If the legally-aided party sued an unassisted party and won, the unassisted party would have to pay the costs incurred by the legally-aided party. Not surprisingly, any costs between the parties which were ordered by the court to be paid in favour of the legally-aided party had to be paid to the Legal Aid Board: see LAA 1988, s. 16(5).

However, if it was the case that both parties were legally aided then the usual form of order in respect of costs was either: (a) 'no order as to costs', i.e. each side bore its own costs (which meant in practice that the Legal Aid Fund paid the costs of both sides, subject to the statutory charge, as to which, see below) or (b) the successful party was awarded its costs but the order was 'not to be enforced without permission of the court' (as to which see **35.8.8**).

35.8.7 THE STATUTORY CHARGE

A legally-aided person was liable to pay for the legal costs of the proceedings incurred on his or her behalf under a Legal Aid Certificate. This liability arose under LAA 1988, s. 16(6). It was discharged from (i) contributions, (ii) any award of costs made in favour of the legally-aided person in the proceedings, or (iii) out of any property recovered or preserved as a result of the proceedings. This liability also arose where there was an agreement for costs and where property was recovered or preserved as a result of the settlement of the case.

'The proceedings' were not restricted to the actual proceedings in which the preservation or recovery took place, but extended to all the proceedings covered by the Legal Aid Certificate: *Hanlon* v *The Law Society* [1981] AC 124, HL. The costs of earlier proceedings could therefore be recoverable by the Legal Aid Board out of property recovered or preserved in later proceedings if the Legal Aid Certificate for the earlier proceedings was amended to cover the later proceedings: *Watkinson* v *Legal Aid Board* [1991] 1 WLR 419, CA.

Any money obtained through an order or agreement for costs, and any property recovered or preserved as a result of the litigation (be it by settlement or judgment), was therefore made subject to a first charge for the benefit of the Legal Aid Board for a sum equal to the legal costs which had been paid out of the Legal Aid Fund on behalf of the legally-aided person. Thus, there was some truth in the saying that the provision of legal aid to a successful litigant was more in the way of a loan than a grant.

The effect of the statutory charge was mitigated in some circumstances by the Civil Legal Aid (General) Regulations 1989 which provided that in some cases enforcement of the charge could be postponed. If money recovered from proceedings under the Married Women's Property Act 1882, or the Matrimonial Causes Act 1973, or the Inheritance (Provision for Family and Dependants) Act 1975, or sch. 1 to the Children Act 1989 was to be used for the purchase of a home for the applicant and/or dependants, or property was preserved or recovered for use as a home by the applicant and/or dependants, then the enforcement of the statutory charge would be postponed by the Board. In such a case the charge was registered against the land in question and was only enforced when the land was sold. If the proceeds of sale were used to buy the next home for the applicant and/or dependants, the charge could be transferred, if the Board consented, to the new home. The charge carried simple (as opposed to compound) interest at the rate of 8% per annum. Further, the first £2,500 recovered or preserved in matrimonial proceedings was exempt from the charge, as were periodical maintenance payments.

The statutory charge could be enforced in much the same way as any other charge.

A solicitor could be made liable for costs if sums recovered in the action were released to the assisted person before the charge had been enforced.

35.8.8 AWARD OF COSTS AGAINST A LEGALLY-AIDED PERSON

The general rule was that costs would not be ordered against an unsuccessful legally-aided person. The LAA 1988, s. 17(1), provided:

> *The liability of a legally assisted party under an order for costs made against him with respect to any proceedings shall not exceed the amount (if any) which is a reasonable one for him to pay having regard to all the circumstances, including the financial resources of all the parties and their conduct in connection with the dispute.*

Although it was unusual for an unsuccessful assisted party to be ordered to pay the whole of the successful unassisted party's costs, sometimes the court would decide that the financial resources of the assisted party were such that it was reasonable to order a small payment towards the successful party's costs, or for the costs to be paid by instalments.

Although the assisted party might not have had the financial resources to pay the successful party's costs in full at the date of the trial, it might be that the assisted party would come into funds in the future. In order to do equity between the parties the court usually awarded the successful party its costs 'not to be enforced without the permission of the Court'. This complied with LAA 1988, s. 17, since the 'liability of a legally assisted party' was construed as meaning a liability to pay. This form of order allowed the successful party to return to court for a variation of the costs order if there was a change in the assisted party's financial circumstances, e.g. if he or she won the football pools or the lottery.

An alternative form of order achieving a similar result was approved by the Court of Appeal in *Parr* v *Smith* [1995] 2 All ER 1031, namely making an order for costs in favour of the successful party, but with the determination of the assisted party's liability postponed in accordance with the Civil Legal Aid (General) Regulations 1989, reg. 127, for such time as the court thought fit.

35.8.9   COSTS PAYABLE BY THE LEGAL AID BOARD

The LAA 1988, s. 18, provided:

> (1)   *This section applies to proceedings to which a legally assisted person is a party and which are finally decided in favour of an unassisted party.*
> (2)   *In any proceedings to which this section applies the court by which the proceedings were so decided may, subject to subsections (3) and (4) below, make an order for the payment by the Board to the unassisted party of the whole or any part of the costs incurred by him in the proceedings.*
> (3)   *Before making an order under this section, the court shall consider what order for costs should be made against the assisted party and for determining his liability in respect of such costs.*
> (4)   *An order under this section in respect of any costs may only be made if—*
>   (a)   *an order for costs would be made in the proceedings apart from this Act;*
>   (b)   *as respects the costs incurred in a court of first instance, those proceedings were instituted by the assisted party and the court is satisfied that the unassisted party will suffer severe financial hardship unless the order is made; and*
>   (c)   *in any case, the court is satisfied that it is just and equitable in all the circumstances of the case that provision for the costs should be made out of public funds.*

Thus, the successful unassisted party could recover some or all of their costs from the Legal Aid Board in proceedings where the other party was a legally-aided person if six conditions were satisfied:

(a)   The court first considered whether any order for costs should be made against the assisted party under s. 17.

(b)   The unassisted party would normally have been entitled to costs.

(c)   The proceedings for which costs were sought were instituted in the court of first instance by the legally-aided party.

(d)   The proceedings were 'finally decided' in favour of the unassisted party (e.g. appeal was no longer possible).

(e)   The court was satisfied that the unassisted party would suffer 'severe financial hardship' unless the order was made.

(f)   The court was satisfied that it was just and equitable in all the circumstances of the case that costs should be paid from public funds.

35.8.9.1   Unassisted party
An order under LAA 1988, s. 18, could only be made in favour of an unassisted party. However, such an order could be made in favour of a party who obtained legal aid part

way through proceedings, the order being restricted to the costs incurred before the issue of the legal aid certificate: *In Re H (Minors) (Abduction: Custody Rights) (No. 2)* [1992] 3 WLR 198, HL.

35.8.9.2 The severe financial hardship requirement

Severe financial hardship had to be likely to result from non-recovery of costs from the Legal Aid Board. In *Hanning v Maitland (No. 2)* [1970] 1 QB 580, Lord Denning MR suggested almost any litigant could prove 'severe financial hardship', except commercial concerns in a considerable way of business, insurance companies and 'wealthy folk' who would not feel the cost of litigation. However, this *dictum* must not be misunderstood as meaning that the threshold was exceptionally low: *Jones v Zahedi* [1993] 4 All ER 909, CA.

The financial resources of the spouse of the unassisted person would not normally be taken into account in deciding whether 'severe financial hardship' was likely: see *Adams v Riley* [1988] QB 372.

If an order was made under LAA 1988, s. 18, it could be for part only of the unassisted party's costs.

35.8.9.3 Procedure

If the court was persuaded to entertain an application under LAA 1988, s. 18, it had to adjourn to give the Legal Aid Board an opportunity to intervene. The unassisted party was required to file an affidavit of means and resources (which was used to assess whether 'severe financial hardship' would be suffered) in advance of the hearing. The hearing could be ordered to be before a Master or District Judge, or could be conducted by the trial judge.

35.9 Community Legal Service

As from 1 April 2000 the Legal Aid Board was replaced by the Legal Services Commission, and legal aid by help under the Community Legal Service. The new system has many features based on the old legal aid system, but has been designed to ensure that public funds are used to support claims that most need assistance in this way. This is reflected in wider categories of excluded cases, and also in greater prescription of the criteria for granting public funding. In particular, there is a greater emphasis on cost-benefit considerations in deciding whether to grant help under the Community Legal Service.

35.9.1 LEVELS OF SERVICE

There are six 'levels of service' under the Community Legal Service. The idea is that the amount of public funding given to a case should be commensurate with its needs, so that limited funding will be given if that is all that is needed, but that full public funding will be given to the most deserving cases.

35.9.1.1 Legal help

This broadly replaces the Green Form Scheme, providing help on how the law applies to a particular case etc.

35.9.1.2 Help at court

This authorises legal representation for the purposes of a particular hearing, without the lawyer becoming the client's legal representative in the proceedings. This is similar to ABWOR.

35.9.1.3 Legal representation

This will cover individuals contemplating legal proceedings or who are parties to proceedings, and will fund 'litigation services'; 'advocacy services'; all the legal assistance usually given before and during proceedings and in achieving or giving effect to any compromise. Legal representation is not a level of service in itself, but is subdivided into two levels:

(a) 'investigative help', which is aimed at cases which require substantial investigation before an assessment can be made whether legal proceedings are justified; and

(b) 'full representation', which is the equivalent of full civil legal aid.

35.9.1.4 Support funding
In a departure from the old system, which did not allow a lawyer to seek a top up on fees by charging the client as well as obtaining legal aid, 'support funding' will provide public funds to supplement funding from other sources for high cost claims. The idea is that there will be some high cost claims which lawyers in private practice will be unwilling to take on CFA terms on the grounds of cost, but which they may be willing to take if the cost is shared with the government. Support funding, like legal representation, is not a level of service in itself, but is sub-divided into two levels:

(a) 'investigative support', which will be in effect partial funding for investigative help; and

(b) 'litigation support', which will be partial support for what would otherwise be full representation.

'High cost' in relation to 'investigative support' will be £5,000 in solicitors' costs and £1,000 in disbursements; and in relation to 'litigation support', high cost will be solicitors' fees exceeding £20,000 or disbursements exceeding £5,000.

35.9.1.5 Specific directions
Other services will not be strictly levels of service covered by the main Community Legal Service scheme, but there will be some public funding of other cases if a specific order or direction is made by the Lord Chancellor. It is contemplated that this may happen in important test cases and possibly also for certain class actions.

35.9.2 EXCLUDED CATEGORIES

Public funding under the Community Legal Service is not available in damages claims for personal injuries, death or damage to property (except that clinical disputes will still be within the scheme, but only through franchised solicitors' firms). Also excluded are:

(a) conveyancing;

(b) boundary disputes;

(c) wills;

(d) matters relating to trust law (which is presumably intended to include constructive trust claims);

(e) defamation and malicious falsehood;

(f) matters relating to partnership law; and

(g) matters relating to the carrying on of a business.

35.9.3 FINANCIAL ELIGIBILITY

Help under the Community Legal Service is only available to clients who are unable to afford to litigate. Rules laying down the financial criteria are to be found in the Community Legal Service (Financial) Regulations 2000 (SI 2000 No. 516). Effectively, State assistance remains available only for the very poor.

35.9.4 INDIVIDUAL

It remains a requirement for public funding that the assisted party must be an individual, so help under the Community Legal Service is not available to limited liability companies.

35.9.5 CRITERIA FOR FUNDING

There are detailed rules setting out the criteria for granting the six levels of help under the Community Legal Service. These are intended to reflect the requirements of the different levels of service, and also to ensure that public money is targeted at the cases that deserve or need it. For example, there are nine criteria for granting full representation, the first six applying to both types of 'legal representation', and the last three being specific to full representation:

(a) funding may be refused if there is alternative funding (other than by way of CFAs, but see (g) below) available;

(b) funding may be refused if there is a complaint system or ombudsman which should be tried first;

(c) funding may be refused if the application is premature;

(d) funding may be refused if another level of service is more appropriate;

(e) funding may be refused if it is unreasonable, for example, in the light of other proceedings;

(f) funding will be refused if the claim is likely to be allocated to the small claims track;

(g) funding will be refused in cases where funding under a CFA is suitable and if the client is likely to be able to enter into such an arrangement;

(h) funding will be refused if the prospects are unclear (for which investigative help may be appropriate); or the prospects are borderline (unless there are public interest reasons or overwhelming importance to the client reasons for funding); or if the prospects are poor;

(i) funding will or may be refused on cost-benefit grounds.

35.9.6 COST-BENEFIT CRITERIA

Funding will be refused if the benefit to be gained does not justify the level of costs likely to be incurred.

In money claims, help under the Community Legal Service may, in general, only be granted if:

(a) the prospects are very good (80% plus, category A), and the value of the claim exceeds the likely level of the costs;

(b) the prospects are good (60–80%, category B), and the value of the claim is at least twice the likely level of costs;

(c) the prospects are moderate (50–60%, category C), and the value of the claim is at least four times the likely level of costs.

In non-money claims the test is whether the likely benefits justify the likely costs, such that a reasonable private paying client would be prepared to litigate.

Funding may be allowed despite costs outstripping the benefits given the risks, if there is a wider public interest or if there is overwhelming importance to the client.

35.9.7 STATUTORY CHARGE

The AJA 1999, s. 10(7), is in similar terms to that previously provided under the legal aid scheme by LAA 1988, s. 16(6) (see **35.8.7**). Under AJA 1999, s. 10(7), the sums expended by the Legal Services Commission in providing help under the Community Legal Service shall be a first charge on any property recovered or preserved for the assisted party. The principles discussed at **35.8.7** almost certainly apply equally to cases funded under the new scheme.

35.9.8 PROTECTION AGAINST COSTS

The AJA 1999, s. 11(1) and (2), provide:

(1) Except in prescribed circumstances, costs ordered against an individual in relation to any proceedings or part of proceedings funded for him shall not exceed the amount (if any) which is a reasonable one for him to pay having regard to all the circumstances including—
  (a) the financial resources of all the parties to the proceedings, and
  (b) their conduct in connection with the dispute to which the proceedings relate;
and for this purpose proceedings, or a part of proceedings, are funded for an individual if services relating to the proceedings or part are funded for him by the Commission as part of the Community Legal Service.
(2) In assessing for the purposes of subsection (1) the financial resources of an individual for whom services are funded by the Commission as part of the Community Legal Service, his clothes and household furniture and the tools and implements of his trade shall not be taken into account, except so far as may be prescribed.

These provisions are almost identical to the similar provisions found under the legal aid scheme in LAA 1988, s. 17 (see **35.8.8**). It is anticipated that where an assisted party under the Community Legal Service loses a claim, that will generally be reflected by a costs order not to be enforced without permission, in much the same way as under LAA 1988. Where a costs order is made under s. 11(1), the court must follow the detailed procedure laid down by the Community Legal Service (Costs) Regulations 2000 (SI 2000 No. 441), regs 9 and 10.

35.9.9 COSTS ORDERS AGAINST THE LEGAL SERVICES COMMISSION

In exceptional cases it is possible to obtain a costs order against the Legal Services Commission, where an assisted party loses a claim. Details of the requirements for making such an order are spelt out in the Community Legal Service (Costs Protection) Regulations 2000 (SI 2000 No. 824), reg. 5, which lays down requirements similar to those applicable under the legal aid scheme by virtue of LAA 1988, s. 18, for which see **35.8.9**.

35.9.10 REGULATIONS

By AJA 1999, s. 11(3) and (4), regulations may be made regulating much of the system. The relevant provisions from s. 11 provide:

(3) Subject to subsections (1) and (2), regulations may make provision about costs in relation to proceedings in which services are funded by the Commission for any of the parties as part of the Community Legal Service.
(4) The regulations may, in particular, make provision—
  (a) specifying the principles to be applied in determining the amount of any costs which may be awarded against a party for whom services are funded by the Commission as part of the Community Legal Service,
  (b) limiting the circumstances in which, or extent to which, an order for costs may be enforced against such a party,

(c)   as to the cases in which, and extent to which, such a party may be required to give security for costs and the manner in which it is to be given,

(d)   requiring the payment by the Commission of the whole or part of any costs incurred by a party for whom services are not funded by the Commission as part of the Community Legal Service,

(e)   specifying the principles to be applied in determining the amount of any costs which may be awarded to a party for whom services are so funded,

(f)   requiring the payment to the Commission, or the person or body by which the services were provided, of the whole or part of any sum awarded by way of costs to such a party, and

(g)   as to the court, tribunal or other person or body by whom the amount of any costs is to be determined and the extent to which any determination of that amount is to be final.

THIRTY SIX

COSTS

36.1 Introduction

Costs in small claims track cases was dealt with in **Chapter 17**. The special rules dealing with fast track costs were considered at **18.11**. It will be recalled that the overriding objective requires the courts to deal with cases in ways that will save expense and which are proportionate to the nature of the case (see **1.4.1** above and CPR, r. 1.1(2)). The extent to which these aims have been achieved will become evident when the costs of the litigation come to be assessed at the end of the case. This chapter will consider the specific rules relating to costs in the Civil Procedure Rules 1998. It will then discuss interim costs orders, and then the system for quantifying costs in cases where there is a detailed assessment of costs.

36.2 General Principles

The two main principles when it comes to deciding which party should pay the costs of an application or of the whole proceedings are:

(a) the costs payable by one party to another are in the discretion of the court (SCA 1981, s. 51 and CPR, r. 44.3(1)); and

(b) the general rule as stated in CPR, r. 44.3(2), is that the unsuccessful party will be ordered to pay the costs of the successful party ('costs follow the event' in the pre-1999 terminology).

The second of these rules is prefaced by the phrase 'If the court decides to make an order about costs . . .'. Case law under the old system (*Gupta* v *Klito*, *The Times*, 23 November 1989) established that a successful party in normal circumstances was entitled to have an order for costs against the loser, with limited exceptions, such as cases where a successful claimant recovered no more than nominal damages, or where the successful party acted improperly or unreasonably (*Re Elgindata Limited (No. 2)* [1992] 1 WLR 1207) or where the issue on which a party succeeded was raised for the first time by amendment at a very late stage (*Beoco Ltd* v *Alfa Laval Co. Ltd* [1995] QB 137). *Re Elgindata Limited (No. 2)* has been one of the pre-CPR cases most frequently referred to in post-CPR cases. Different judges have placed greater or lesser reliance on the principles laid down in that case, but the general consensus is that those principles remain valid, although they should not be taken as binding the discretion of the court. The result is that the starting point when considering the question of costs is that the winner ought to recover costs from the unsuccessful party, although there may be other factors which require some deviation from a simple application of that rule. Further, there are many cases where some detailed analysis is required to determine who has been 'successful', and to what extent.

In exercising its discretion on costs the court is required to have regard to all the circumstances, and in particular to the following matters (CPR, r. 44.3(4) and (5)):

(a) the extent to which the parties followed any applicable pre-action protocol;

(b) the extent to which it was reasonable for the parties to raise, pursue or contest each of the allegations or issues;

(c) the manner in which the parties pursued or defended the action or particular allegations or issues;

(d) whether the successful party exaggerated the value of the claim;

(e) whether a party was only partly successful; and

(f) any payment into court or admissible offer to settle.

The first of these factors is one of the methods by which pre-action protocols will be enforced, albeit indirectly (the other being by a less tolerant attitude on applications by defaulting parties for more time and for relief from sanctions). Factors (b) and (e) require the court to take into account the extent to which the overall winner was in fact successful on the various issues, heads of claim etc. raised in the case. This is intended to support the aspects of the overriding objective relating to identifying the real issues in the case, and only pursuing those issues to trial: see CPR, r. 1.4(2)(b), (c). Factor (c), which covers unreasonable conduct, could also be used against parties who fail to conduct litigation in accordance with the overriding ethos, such as those who are unreasonably unco-operative: see CPR, r. 1.4(2)(a). Exaggeration of the value of a claim (factor (d)) will obviously be relevant where the claim is inflated for the purpose of bringing it in the High Court or to have the case allocated to a higher track than it deserves. It could also be used in cases where exaggeration of the claim makes it difficult for the defendant to assess its true value for the purposes of making an offer to settle or a payment into court.

In *Grupo Torras SA* v *Al-Sabah* (5 July 1999, unreported) a claim had been made against a number of defendants in conspiracy, dishonest assistance in breach of trust and related causes of action. The claims against the fourth, sixth and tenth defendants failed because the claimant failed to prove the essential element of dishonesty as against them. Mance LJ, who was the trial judge, held the fourth defendant would only recover 50% of his costs because, although he did not realise there was a fraud, he was involved in deliberately backdating relevant documentation. The sixth defendant only recovered one-third of his costs. He was the finance director of one of the companies, and had deliberately deceived the auditors and gave untrue evidence at trial. The tenth defendant was a professional man who had created false documentation, misled the auditors and gave untruthful evidence at trial. He too only recovered one-third of his costs.

36.3   Interim Costs Orders

If an order makes no reference to costs, none are payable in respect of the proceedings to which the order relates: CPR, r. 44.13(1) and PD 23, para. 13.2. Usually, however, the court will make some form of order saying who will pay the costs of any interim application. **Table 36.1** sets out in tabular form the meanings of commonly used interim costs orders.

Table 36.1   The meanings of common interim costs orders

Term	Effect
Costs in any event or 'costs'	The party in whose favour the order is made is entitled to the costs in respect of the part of the proceedings to which the order relates whatever other costs orders are made in the proceedings.
Costs in the case/costs in the application	The party in whose favour the court makes an order for costs at the end of the proceedings is entitled to his costs of the proceedings to which the order relates.

Costs reserved	The decision about costs is deferred to a later occasion, but if no later order is made the costs will be costs in the case.
Claimant's/defendant's costs in the case/ application	If the party in whose favour the costs order is made is awarded costs at the end of the proceedings, that party is entitled to his or her costs of the part of the proceedings to which the order relates. If any other party is awarded costs at the end of the proceedings, the party in whose favour the costs order is made is not liable to pay the costs of any other party in respect of the part of the proceedings to which the order relates.
Costs thrown away	Where, for example, a judgment or order is set aside, the party in whose favour the costs order is made is entitled to the costs which have been incurred as a consequence. This includes the costs of: (a) preparing for and attending any hearing at which the judgment or order which has been set aside was made; (b) preparing for and attending any hearing to set aside the judgment or order in question; (c) preparing for and attending any hearing at which the court orders the proceedings or the part in question to be adjourned; (d) any steps taken to enforce a judgment or order which has subsequently been set aside.
Costs of and caused by/costs of and arising from	Where, for example, the court makes this order on an application to amend a statement of case, the party in whose favour the costs order is made is entitled to the costs of preparing for and attending the application and the costs of any consequential amendment to his or her own statement of case.
Costs here and below	The party in whose favour the costs order is made is entitled not only to his or her costs of the proceedings in which the court makes the order but also to his or her costs of the proceedings in any lower court.
No order as to costs/each party to pay his or her own costs	Each party is to bear his or her own costs of the proceedings to which the order relates whatever costs order the court makes at the end of the proceedings.

The choice of order depends on the court's view of who won the interim application, and on the other factors set out in CPR, r. 44.3. Case management hearings usually result in orders for costs in the case, as there is no 'winner'. An adversarial application won by the claimant will usually result in an order for 'claimant's costs'. Applications made without notice, and interim injunctions granted on the basis of the balance of convenience, usually result in 'costs reserved' (see *Desquenne et Giral UK Ltd* v

Richardson (23 November 1999, unreported), and *Picnic at Ascot Inc* v *Derigs* (9 February 2000, unreported).

36.3.1 SUMMARY ASSESSMENT OF INTERIM COSTS

The costs of interim hearings likely to last less than a day are likely to be dealt with by way of summary assessment there and then. The parties are required to file and serve statements of their costs not less than 24 hours before the hearing to assist with this process. Summary assessment should not be made of the costs of parties who are assisted by legal aid or acting under a disability. Nor is summary assessment normally appropriate where an interim application lasts more than a day.

36.3.2 DETAILED ASSESSMENT OF INTERIM COSTS

Orders for costs will be treated as requiring detailed assessment unless the order specifies the sum to be paid or states that fixed costs are to be paid: PD 44, para. 4.2. Detailed assessments generally take place after the proceedings are concluded.

36.3.3 REPRESENTATION BY COUNSEL

PD 44, para. 2.7, allows the court when making a costs order (including both interim costs orders and final costs orders made at trial) to state an opinion as to whether or not the hearing was fit for representation by one or more counsel. Counsel appearing, particularly on interim applications and in any type of hearing where there is more than one counsel, should consider asking the judge to include such a statement in the costs order.

36.3.4 NOTIFYING CLIENT

Where a costs order is made against a legally-represented client who is not present in court when the order is made, the solicitor representing the client is under a duty to inform the client of the costs liability within seven days of the order being made: CPR, r. 44.2. The court may ask for proof that this has been done.

36.4 Final Costs Orders

36.4.1 VARIATIONS FROM WINNER RECOVERING COSTS

Under the CPR, r. 44.3(6), there are seven possible variations from the main rule that the unsuccessful party should pay the whole of the successful party's costs. These variations are:

(a) that a party must pay only a proportion of another party's costs;

(b) that a party must pay a specified amount in respect of the other side's costs;

(c) that a party must pay costs from or until a certain day only;

(d) that a party must pay costs incurred before proceedings have begun;

(e) that a party must pay costs relating only to certain steps taken in the proceedings, although an order of this type can only be made if an order in either of the forms set out at (a) or (c) would not be practicable (CPR, r. 44.3 (7));

(f) that a party must pay costs relating only to a certain distinct part of the proceedings; and

(g) that a party must pay interest on costs from or until a certain date, including a date before judgment.

36.4.2 ORDER FOR COSTS IN CASES INVOLVING MULTIPLE PARTIES

Where the claimant sues two defendants and is successful against one defendant but not the other, if costs were to follow the event, the unsuccessful defendant would have to pay the claimant's costs in respect of the claim against the unsuccessful defendant and the claimant would have to pay the costs incurred in respect of the claim against the successful defendant. However, if it was reasonable to join both defendants to the action, the court in its discretion may make a special order enabling the claimant to recover the costs paid to the successful defendant or for them to be paid by the unsuccessful defendant direct to the successful defendant. There are two types of order: *Bullock* and *Sanderson.*

36.4.2.1 *Bullock* order
This is derived from *Bullock* v *London General Omnibus* [1907] 1 KB 264, CA. The claimant is ordered to pay the costs of the successful defendant and once paid the claimant is then allowed to recover these costs from the unsuccessful defendant in addition to the claimant's costs incurred in respect of the claim against the unsuccessful defendant. This is known as a *Bullock* order.

36.4.2.2 *Sanderson* order
This is derived from *Sanderson* v *Blyth Theatre Co.* [1903] 2 KB 533, CA. The unsuccessful defendant is ordered to pay the successful defendant's costs direct to the successful defendant. Also, the unsuccessful defendant will have to pay the claimant's costs incurred in respect of the claim against the unsuccessful defendant. This order is appropriate where the claimant is legally-aided or insolvent as the order will ensure that the successful defendant is able to recover his or her costs. This order is known as a *Sanderson* order.

36.4.2.3 The choice of order
The choice of order is a matter for the discretion of the court, although the court will normally want to protect the successful defendant first against the risk of irrecoverable costs: see *Mayer* v *Harte* [1960] 1 WLR 770, CA. Nevertheless, likely hardship to a claimant and a desire to spread the burden of irrecoverable costs more equitably are justifiable considerations: see *Bank America Finance Ltd* v *Nock* [1988] AC 1002, HL.

36.4.3 ORDER FOR COSTS IN CASES INVOLVING PART 20 PROCEEDINGS

The court has power to make such order as it thinks just. The following is a general guideline:

(a) Generally, if the claimant wins against the defendant, who then succeeds against the third party, the third party will be liable for the defendant's costs, including those that the defendant will have had to pay the claimant.

(b) However, if the defendant is considered to have defended the claimant's claim for his or her own benefit, the defendant may only be able to recover the costs of the third party action, against the third party.

(c) If the claimant loses against the defendant, and the defendant thus loses against the third party, it does not *necessarily* follow that the claimant will have to pay the costs of the third party. It may be that the defendant should not have joined the third party in any event.

(d) The claimant will have to pay the whole costs if it was inevitable that the defendant would have to join other parties, when meeting the claimant's claim.

(e) Where, for example, the claimant and the third party *both* lose to the defendant, generally each will be responsible only for the costs of the claim to which they were a party.

It should be noted that as costs between the *immediate* parties normally follow the event if, in case (a) above, the third party proves to be insolvent, the defendant will unfortunately still be responsible for paying the claimant's costs.

36.4.4 JOINDER OF ACTIONS

The joinder of causes of action is encouraged by the Civil Liability (Contribution) Act 1978, s. 4, whereby a claimant who brings successive actions for damages in respect of the same damage is not entitled to costs in any action other than the first action, unless the court is satisfied that there were reasonable grounds for bringing separate actions.

36.4.5 COSTS OF COUNTERCLAIMS AND SET-OFFS

36.4.5.1 Where are separate orders appropriate?

Separate orders for costs are appropriate where the claimant succeeds on the claim and the defendant succeeds on the counterclaim, or where they both fail on their respective claims, according to principles established in *Medway Oil and Storage Co. Ltd* v *Continental Contractors* [1929] AC 88, HL.

Thus, the order might be for judgment for the claimant on the claim with the costs of claim, and judgment for the defendant on the counterclaim with costs of counterclaim. There would then be a division of costs between the claim and counterclaim, with the usual result that the costs relating to the claim would be far greater than the costs exclusively referable to the counterclaim.

36.4.5.2 Alternative orders

A single order for costs might be appropriate where the counterclaim is a set-off or where the issues involved in the claim and counterclaim are so interwoven as to be substantially the same, according to Denning LJ in *Chell Engineering* v *Unit Tool and Engineering Co. Ltd* [1950] 1 All ER 378, CA. In such circumstances the court would make a single judgment for the balance between the claim and the counterclaim and then make a single order for costs.

The approach exemplified by *Medway Oil* was recognised by the Court of Appeal in *Universal Cycles plc* v *Grangebriar Ltd* (8 February 2000, unreported) as being the usual form of order where the claimant is successful on the claim and the defendant is successful on a counterclaim. Where there is a set-off, *Universal Cycles* also approved the *Chell Engineering* approach of awarding the overall winner either the entire costs of the action, or a proportion of those costs. In *Universal Cycles* itself the claim was for the price of goods sold and delivered, and there was a counterclaim that alleged the goods were not of satisfactory quality and not fit for their purpose, it being further alleged that the value of the counterclaim exceeded that of the claim. At trial, judgment was given to the claimant in the sum of £109,000, and judgment for the defendant on the counterclaim in the sum of £25,000. Neither party wanted a costs order in the *Medway Oil* form. The judge awarded the claimant its costs to the date of the defence and counterclaim, and required the claimant to pay half the defendant's costs thereafter. The Court of Appeal held that the judge had erred in placing too much emphasis on the amount of time spent on the substantive issues on which the respective parties had succeeded, and too little emphasis on the fact that the claimant had been the overall winner and the late service by the defendant of its schedule of loss. Further, the order made by the judge stepped over the well-known line that a successful party should not, in the absence of a Part 36 offer and save perhaps in very exceptional cases, be ordered to pay any of the losing party's costs. An order was substituted for the defendant to pay all the claimant's costs, save the costs of the trial itself.

36.4.6 AGAINST NON-PARTIES

Aiden Shipping Co. Ltd v *Interbulk Ltd* [1986] AC 965, HL, is authority for the proposition that the SCA 1981, s. 51, confers a very wide discretion on the court as to costs, which includes a power in appropriate cases to award costs against non-parties. Separate proceedings were taken by a ship owner against its charterers, and by the charterers against its sub-charterers. Although both disputes were almost identical, the proceedings were not consolidated. The House of Lords upheld the judge's costs order that the unsuccessful shipowner should pay the charterer's costs, such costs to include any costs the charterers had to pay the sub-charterers in the second set of proceedings.

Principles governing the exercise of the *Aiden Shipping* doctrine were laid down by the Court of Appeal in *Symphony Group plc v Hodgson* [1994] QB 179. Such orders are always exceptional. *Aiden Shipping* orders have been made in a number of cases, such as where a director has caused an insolvent company to bring or defend proceedings or where the non-party has been found to have maintained the action for the purposes of the law against maintenance and champerty: *McFarlane v EE Caledonia Ltd (No. 2)* [1995] 1 WLR 366. The most common basis for successful applications is where the non-party has funded the litigation: see also *Murphy v Young and Co.'s Brewery Ltd* [1997] 1 WLR 1591 and *Locabail (UK) Ltd v Bayfield Properties Ltd (No. 3), The Times*, 29 February 2000. In *Shah v Karanjia* [1993] 4 All ER 792 an application was refused principally because the non-party had not been separately represented at the trial, and the claim against him for costs had not been formulated against him until after the trial.

The CPR, r. 48.2, lays down a statutory framework for the procedure to be followed on these applications. The person against whom the order will be sought must be added as a party (even though, apparently, there may be no substantive cause of action against that person), and that person must be given a reasonable opportunity to attend the hearing to give reasons why the court should not make the order. The determination of the application is a summary matter, with some relaxation of the normal rules of evidence.

36.4.7   TRUSTEES

Where trustees are involved and the costs they have incurred have not been recovered from any other persons the court should order trustees to recover costs from the trust fund, whatever the result, provided the trustees have acted reasonably, in good faith, and for the benefit of the trust fund.

Similarly, the court will normally order the costs of actions by personal representatives on behalf of an estate to be recoverable from the estate. The same principle also applies to actions by mortgagees to protect mortgaged property.

However, where proceedings between trustees and beneficiaries are adversarial in nature, it is appropriate for the court to refuse to order the trustees' costs from the fund: *Holding and Management Ltd v Property Holding and Investment Trust plc* [1989] 1 WLR 1313, CA.

36.4.8   COSTS OF PRE-COMMENCEMENT DISCLOSURE AND DISCLOSURE AGAINST NON-PARTIES

These applications were considered at **21.3** and **21.4**. The general rule is that the court must award the costs of the application to the person against whom the order is sought: CPR, r. 48.1. The practice has been to add the costs of the application as a head of damages in the case of pre-commencement disclosure. This may no longer be necessary as under the new system the pre-commencement application is made in the same action as the main claim for personal injuries, whereas under the old system the application formed a separate action commenced by its own originating process. In the case of disclosure against a non-party the costs will be part of the costs of the action, and should be dealt with by a specific costs order between the parties. The court retains a discretion to make a different costs order in a particular case, having regard to all the circumstances, including the extent to which it may have been reasonable for the respondent to have opposed the disclosure application: CPR, r. 48.1(3). This may be the case where the respondent has failed to honour its obligations under the Access to Health Records Act 1990 or under any applicable pre-action protocol.

36.4.9 COSTS AFTER TRANSFER

Subject to any order that may have been made by the original court, once a case is transferred the new court will deal with all questions as to costs, including the costs incurred before the transfer: CPR, r. 44.13(3), (4).

36.4.10 COSTS BEFORE TRACK ALLOCATION

The special rules relating to costs in cases on the small claims track and fast track only apply once a claim is allocated to one of these tracks: CPR, r. 44.9(1), (2). This means, for example, that where default judgment is entered on a small value claim the costs restrictions in Part 27 do not apply (although the fixed costs rules in Part 45 would be applied instead).

36.4.11 COSTS ON APPEAL

The recovery of costs by the successful party, which can include both the costs of the appeal and below, is normally subject to the discretion of the court.

Non-recovery of costs by a successful appellant may arise, in full or in part, where:

(a) the appeal is only partly successful; or

(b) the court's time has been wasted; or

(c) the appeal was successful only on a point not raised in the notice of appeal.

Non-recovery of costs by a successful respondent may arise, in full or in part, where:

(a) the appeal raised a novel question of general public importance;

(b) new points were raised which were never raised at the original hearing.

36.5 Quantification of Costs

Once an order has been made as to costs the actual amount of costs a party will be able to recover from the other side will need to be quantified. This can be done in a number of ways.

36.5.1 AGREEMENT BETWEEN THE PARTIES

Agreement between the parties, as to the costs payable by one party to the other, avoids the time and expense involved in the assessment of costs.

It is not possible to agree costs in proceedings brought on behalf of a person under disability without the direction of the court.

36.5.2 FIXED COSTS

Some items of expenditure, particularly solicitors' charges in certain proceedings and on entering default judgments, are recoverable only as fixed costs.

36.5.3 SUMMARY ASSESSMENT

This involves the court determining the amount payable by way of costs immediately at the end of a hearing, usually on a relatively rough and ready basis. The starting point will be the statement of costs (see **Figure 7.2**). Courts sometimes develop conventional figures for specified costs for certain types of proceeding, such as the costs awarded for straightforward landlord and tenant possession proceedings. The courts tend to err on the side of caution when specifying the amount of costs to be paid, but it has been known for the amount specified to be relatively large. The court can call for whatever evidence is available at the time in deciding on the figure to be specified, such as looking at Counsel's Brief to see the brief fee, as well as hearing the advocates on the work involved in the matter. There are proposals for the introduction of 'benchmark costs' in the future. These are intended to impose moderate, standard amounts for costs for common interim applications.

36.5.4   DETAILED ASSESSMENT

A detailed assessment of costs involves leaving the quantification of costs to a costs officer, who will consider the amount to be allowed at an assessment hearing at some stage in the future after the parties have been given the opportunity of setting out the amount claimed and points of dispute in writing. Detailed assessments are carried out mainly by District Judges in the County Courts, and there is a special office, called the Supreme Court Costs Office, for the High Court. Generally the court has a discretion to decide whether to make a summary assessment or to order a detailed assessment if the costs cannot be agreed. However, where money is claimed by or ordered or agreed to be paid to or for the benefit of a child or patient the court in general must order a detailed assessment of the costs payable by the claimant to his or her solicitor: CPR, r. 48.5.

36.5.5   BASIS OF QUANTIFICATION

There are two bases of assessment of costs: the standard basis and the indemnity basis. As its name suggests, the standard basis is the one usually applied in costs orders between the parties in litigation. The indemnity basis is used when a client is paying its own solicitor, and also when a trustee's costs are payable out of the trust fund. It can also be used between competing parties in litigation as a penalty for misconduct, or as a result of a successful claimant's Part 36 offer. Costs orders should identify the intended basis of quantification. On both bases the court will not allow costs which have been unreasonably incurred or which are unreasonable in amount.

On an assessment on the standard basis, which is the least generous basis, the CPR, r. 44.4(2), provides that the court will:

(a)   only allow costs which are proportionate to the matters in issue; and

(b)   resolve any doubt which it may have as to whether costs were reasonably incurred or reasonable and proportionate in amount in favour of the paying party.

On an assessment on the indemnity basis there is no reference to proportionality, and any doubt on whether costs were reasonably incurred or were reasonable in amount is resolved in favour of the receiving party: CPR, r. 44.4(3).

36.5.6   PROCEDURE ON DETAILED ASSESSMENT OF COSTS

Assessment proceedings must be commenced within three months of the judgment, order, award or other determination giving rise to the right to costs: CPR, r. 47.7. This is done by serving on the paying party a notice of commencement in the relevant practice form together with a copy of the bill of costs: CPR, r. 47.6(1). The paying party may dispute any item in the bill by serving the receiving party with points of dispute. These must be served within 21 days after service of the notice of commencement: CPR, r. 47.9. If the paying party fails to serve points of dispute within the permitted time the receiving party may, on filing a request, obtain a default costs certificate: CPR, rr. 47.9(4) and 47.11. The receiving party has the right, but is not obliged, to serve a reply to any points of dispute. Any reply should be served on the party who served the points of dispute within 21 days after service: CPR, r. 47.13. Hearings are relatively informal, with the points in dispute being taken in turn and both sides making submissions and the costs officer making rulings on each point in turn.

36.6 Wasted Costs Order

36.6.1 JURISDICTION

Legal representatives may, by SCA 1981, s. 51(6), be made personally liable for any wasted costs. Costs are 'wasted' if they are incurred either:

(a) as a result of any improper, unreasonable or negligent act or omission by that legal representative; or

(b) before such an act or omission, but the court considers it unreasonable to expect the party to pay in the light of that act or omission.

The wasted costs may be simply disallowed on taxation, or an order may be made that the legal representative must pay the whole or some part of them.

36.6.2 PRINCIPLES

The court must, according to *In Re a Barrister (Wasted Costs Order (No. 1 of 1991))* [1993] QB 293, apply a three-stage test:

(a) Has the lawyer acted improperly, unreasonably or negligently?

(b) If so, did such conduct cause the applicant to incur unnecessary costs?

(c) If so, was it in all the circumstances just to order the lawyer to compensate the applicant for the whole or part of the wasted costs?

Guidelines, particularly on the first stage, were laid down in *Ridehalph v Horsefield* [1994] Ch 205, CA. 'Improper' conduct includes professional misconduct and also conduct considered improper by the consensus of professional opinion, even if it does not contravene the letter of the appropriate professional code of conduct. The acid test for acting 'unreasonably' is whether the conduct admitted of a reasonable explanation. 'Negligent' must be understood in an untechnical way as denoting a failure to act with the competence to be reasonably expected of ordinary members of the profession. Pursuing a hopeless case will not be penalised under s. 51(6) unless it amounts to an abuse of process. The reason is that barristers are subject to the 'cab rank' rule and are not allowed to pick and choose their cases, and many solicitors operate on a similar basis. A solicitor is not permitted to abdicate all responsibility by instructing counsel, but the more specialist the area the more reasonable it will be for a solicitor to rely on counsel's advice.

36.6.3 PROCEDURE

By CPR, r. 48.7, the court is required to give the legal representative a reasonable opportunity to attend a hearing to give reasons why the order should not be made. The court may also direct that notice be given to the legal representative's client. It is also provided that for the purposes of such applications the court may direct that privileged documents are to be disclosed to the court and, if the court so directs, to the other party to the application for the order: CPR, r. 48.7(3). This particular provision (r. 48.7(3)) was held to be *ultra vires* and also to infringe Articles 6 and 8 of the European Convention on Human Rights by Toulson J in *General Mediterranean Holdings SA v Patel* [1999] 3 All ER 673.

The procedure is intended to be summary, without detailed statements of case, formal disclosure of documents or requests for further information unless absolutely necessary. If the court makes an order it must specify the amount to be paid or disallowed. Wasted costs applications should normally be made at the end of the trial, and will generally be considered in two stages:

(a) at the first stage the applicant has to adduce evidence which, if unanswered, would be likely to lead to a wasted costs order, and that the wasted costs application appears to be justified having regard to the likely costs involved;

(b) at the second stage the court will give the legal representative an opportunity of putting forward his or her case.

What is 'summary' depends on the nature of the case. The fact that the costs proceedings may take some time to determine does not stop them being summary: *Robertson Research International Ltd* v *ABG Exploration BV, The Times*, 3 November 1999, Laddie J). However, if the application is speculative or bound to fail the court should summarily dismiss it: *Bristol & West plc* v *Bhadresa (No. 2)* [1999] 2 CPLR 209. The court should limit the issues to be considered, and, if necessary, the length of cross-examination and submissions.

36.7   Questions

OBJECTIVES

By the conclusion of this section you should:

(a) understand the procedure and principles relating to applications for security for costs;

(b) understand the procedure and principles relating to Part 36 offers and Part 36 payments;

(c) be aware of the tactical considerations relevant to Part 36 offers and Part 36 payments;

(d) have a practical knowledge of the operation of legal aid and the Community Legal Service;

(e) be aware of the practical consequences of public funding, including obligations when advising on merits, protection against adverse costs orders, and the effect of the first charge against property or money recovered or preserved by the litigation;

(f) be aware of other methods of funding litigation, and in particular conditional fee agreements;

(g) understand the principles applied when the court is considering orders for costs;

(h) understand the different means through which costs are assessed;

(i) know the various interim costs orders and their effects;

(j) understand the various orders when costs do not follow the event; and

(k) understand the possible effect on the order for costs where

(i)   there is more than one cause of action and one party is not successful on all of them;

(ii) there is a joinder of defendants and the claimant succeeds against some but not all of them;

(iii) one or more of the parties has legal aid;

(iv) there has been a Part 36 payment or Part 36 offer.

RESEARCH

Read the materials in **Chapters 26, 27, 35** and **36** of this Manual.

Consult the Code of Conduct, para. 504.

Legal aid is governed by the Legal Aid Act 1988 and the Civil Legal Aid (General) Regulations 1989 and Community Legal Service by the Access to Justice Act 1999, Part I.

LARGE GROUP SESSION 9

You will need to have read questions 1 to 3 in advance of Large Group Session 9, but there is no need to produce answers to these questions in advance of the large group class as the background material will be explained in the class.

QUESTION 1

Martin and Gillian are neighbours. Martin has started an action in the Chancery Division claiming a declaration that he has a right to take wood from a copse on Gillian's land, and an injunction to restrain Gillian interfering with a right of way that he claims along a track crossing Gillian's land. Gillian disputes these claims, and has made a Part 20 counterclaim seeking injunctions requiring Martin to repair and maintain a section of dry stone wall separating their properties and to restrain Martin from trespassing on her land.

You are instructed on behalf of Gillian. Having considered the evidence you take the view that all the claims and Part 20 counterclaims have some merit, but all have certain weaknesses. In conference, Gillian asks what she can do to protect her position on costs. What advice should you give her?

QUESTION 2

In June 1994 Key Computing Ltd sold and delivered a computing system to Best Retail Ltd. A claim form claiming £20,000, the balance of the price, was issued and served in May 2000. In its defence and Part 20 counterclaim Best Retail has raised a number of issues in defence and has made a Part 20 counterclaim in respect of another matter for £200,000.

It is now January 2001, and you have been instructed on behalf of Key Computing. Best Retail has now ceased trading and cannot pay its debts. On the evidence available to you, you advise that Key Computing has reasonable, but by no means certain, prospects of defeating the Part 20 counterclaim at trial. Which one of the following is the best advice to give Key Computing?

[A] To discontinue its proceedings, which will have the effect of discontinuing the Part 20 counterclaim (which is now statute-barred).
[B] That it should apply for an interim payment in order to become a secured creditor.
[C] That an application for security for costs can be made in respect of the costs of the Part 20 counterclaim on the ground that Best Retail is unable to pay the costs of the Part 20 counterclaim.
[D] That an application for security for costs cannot be made because Best Retail is a defendant.

QUESTION 3

You act for Elaine who recently had a passionate but short-lived affair with Gary. Gary moved in with Elaine, and they lived together in her heavily mortgaged flat in Ruislip for 13 months until their relationship broke up. During their period of cohabitation, Gary gave Elaine sums totalling £1,450, which she regarded as contributions towards board and lodging.

After he moved out, Gary started proceedings in the local County Court claiming a beneficial interest in Elaine's flat and seeking an order for sale. Both Gary and Elaine obtained legal aid for the purposes of these proceedings. At the hearing this morning the judge dismissed Gary's action.

You will shortly be invited to address the court on the question of costs. Elaine's costs of defending the action are likely to amount to £15,000, of which she has contributed £1,200 to the Legal Aid Board.

What will you say on the question of costs, and what are Elaine's prospects of recovering her costs from Gary?

SMALL GROUP SESSION 7

Questions 4 to 15 are for Small Group Session 7. You will need to have notes on each of these questions in advance of the small group class.

QUESTION 4

At the hearing of an application by the claimant under CPR, Part 24 for summary judgment, the defendant attends and produces a witness statement in reply of which he has not given the claimant the necessary seven days' notice. The defendant has no excuse for late production of the witness statement. The Master decides to adjourn the hearing as a result. How should the Master deal with the question of costs?

[A] Make no order as to costs.
[B] Reserve costs to the adjourned hearing.
[C] Order the costs to be the claimant's costs in the case.
[D] Order the defendant to pay the claimant's costs thrown away.

QUESTION 5

Leonard has started proceedings against Timothy, his tenant, claiming damages for breach of various covenants in the lease. The particulars of claim set out that Timothy has breached a covenant against alteration by removing and repositioning some internal walls in 1996; has breached a restricted user covenant by, since 1997, using part of the premises for residential purposes; and has breached a covenant to insure the premises since 1998. In the last few days Timothy has served notice on Leonard that he has made a Part 36 payment into court of £6,000 'in satisfaction of all the causes of action and any claim for interest thereon in respect of which the claimant claims'.

Advise Leonard, who feels that a total of £6,000 is insufficient to cover the whole of his claim, but who thinks that it will be more than enough to cover the insurance covenant and one of the others.

QUESTION 6

Carmel sues Jordan for £10,000 for breach of contract. Four weeks before trial Carmel makes a Part 36 offer to Jordan to settle the claim for £8,000. Jordan rejects the offer and the matter goes to trial. Carmel is successful at trial and is awarded damages of £10,000. Advise Carmel as to the potential consequences of the Part 36 offer in the light of the judgment in her favour.

QUESTION 7

Geoff, who alleges he suffered spinal injuries after an accident at work, is suing his employer, Trendy Textiles plc. On 25 September 2000 the defendant made a Part 36 payment of £15,000 into court. Shortly afterwards it received a report dated 1 October 2000 from its consultant surgeon, which firmly expressed the view that Geoff's symptoms were not attributable to any industrial accident but rather to a latent spinal weakness. As a result of this information, Trendy Textiles issued an application notice seeking to withdraw the Part 36 payment. That application was served on Geoff on 8 October 2000, who later on in the day gave notice of acceptance of the Part 36 payment.

Advise Trendy Textiles plc whether the company will be able to withdraw the Part 36 payment into court.

QUESTION 8

Charles, who is ordinarily resident in California, is suing Global Newspapers plc for libel in respect of an article published in the London edition of the Daily Gazette. Global Newspapers plc intend to plead justification and have duly acknowledged service. Charles' British trading operations are experiencing financial difficulties. Global Newspapers are now applying for security for their costs, which they have estimated will amount to at least £200,000 by trial.

(a) Advise Charles as to the factors the court will take into account, and, if an order is made, the way in which the amount of security will be determined.

(b) What difference would it have made if Celia, who lives in Reading and is the other person named in the article, had been joined as a co-claimant?

(c) What difference would it have made if Charles had been ordinarily resident in Belgium?

QUESTION 9

(a) What is the difference between summary assessment and detailed assessment?

(b) What is the difference between the indemnity and standard basis of quantification of costs?

QUESTION 10

Consider the following. A number of questions on them will be posed in the tutorial.

(a) 'The claimant's costs in the case'.

(b) 'The defendant's costs in the case'.

(c) 'The claimant's costs in any event'.

(d) 'Costs thrown away'.

(e) 'Claimant's costs'.

(f) 'Costs in the case'.

(g) 'Costs reserved'.

QUESTION 11

Richard, a passenger in a car driven by Stephen, sustains serious injuries when the car collides with a lorry driven by Thomas. Richard sues Stephen and Thomas, but the judge finds Stephen alone to blame for the accident. Richard is legally aided with a small contribution. What order may be made as to costs?

QUESTION 12

You are appearing in the Dudley County Court at the trial for the defendant who is being sued by the claimant for the price of goods sold and delivered. The defendant alleges that the goods were defective and counterclaims for damages for breach of the implied condition as to satisfactory quality and fitness for purpose. The judge finds that the claimant is entitled to £16,000 on his claim and that the defendant is entitled to £15,500 on his counterclaim.

The judge now invites you to address him on costs. What will you say, and what are the consequences of your proposals?

QUESTION 13

You have been instructed to advise John for the purposes of an application for help under the Community Legal Service on the merits of defending an action brought by Trusty Motors Ltd in the Alnwick County Court claiming the sum of £5,700 and interest pursuant to s. 57 of the Bills of Exchange Act 1882. In his witness statement John says he agreed to buy a 1995 Wolsey Telstar motor car from the claimants for £6,600. He traded in his old car for £900 and gave Trusty Motors Ltd a cheque for the balance. After taking delivery he gave the car a thorough testing by driving to Peterborough and back, encountering no problems. However, four days and a further 200 miles later the car broke down, and had to be towed to a garage. He stopped payment on the cheque, which had not cleared. He says the garage has provided an estimate for the necessary work at £5,200, and that the mechanic he spoke to said that after the work the car would be worth perhaps £3,500. Also in your papers is a detailed estimate from the garage for the work required on the car. The engine needs replacing, as does the clutch and braking system. There is also a serious problem with the tracking, and the chassis is distorted. The garage suggests that general wear indicates that the car has travelled considerably more than the 31,000 miles indicated on the odometer.

What advice should you give?

QUESTION 14

Edward is suing Windermere Glazing Co. (1957) Ltd ('Windermere') in the Shrewsbury County Court for damages and interest at the rate of 8% per annum in respect of an alleged breach of contract committed on 20 June 1998. Windermere is a small family company with pre-tax profits last year of £12,438. On 31 May 1999 Windermere made a Part 36 payment of £30,000 in satisfaction of all Edward's claims and interest. At trial on 20 December 2000 Edward is awarded damages of £27,000 and interest of £5,400. Edward's standard basis costs up to June 1999 are estimated at £1,500 and thereafter at £6,500. Windermere's standard basis costs up to June 1999 are estimated at £900 and thereafter at £8,000.

Counsel for Edward has applied for costs. You appear for Windermere. What submissions would you make on costs and related matters?

QUESTION 15

If the court awards costs to a successful party after a fast track trial, when are those costs usually calculated?

How are the costs of a case limited on the fast track?

THIRTY SEVEN

JUDGMENTS AND ORDERS

37.1   Introduction

This chapter is concerned with how judgments and orders pronounced in court and in chambers are converted into records which can be enforced. A judgment is a final decision in an action while an order is an interim decision although it may end the action, e.g. a final consent order.

37.2   Drawing Up Orders and Judgments

37.2.1   GENERAL RULES RELATING TO DRAWING UP ORDERS AND JUDGMENTS

The CPR, rr. 40.2(2) and 40.3(1), provide that all judgments and orders have to be drawn up and sealed by the court, unless the court dispenses with the need to do so. Normally the court will take responsibility for drawing up, but:

(a)   the court may order a party to draw up an order; or

(b)   a party may, with the permission of the court, agree to draw up an order; or

(c)   the court may direct a party to draw up the order subject to checking by the court before it is sealed; or

(d)   the court may direct the parties to file an agreed statement of the terms of the order before the court itself draws up the order; or

(e)   the order may be entered administratively by consent, in which event the parties will submit a drawn up version of their agreement for entry.

A party who is required to draw up a judgment is allowed seven days to file the relevant document, together with sufficient copies for all relevant parties, failing which any other party may draw it up and file it for sealing: CPR, rr. 40.3(3) and 40.4(1).

Every judgment or order (apart from judgments on admissions, default judgments and consent judgments) must state the name and judicial title of the judge who made it: CPR, r. 40.2(1).

Once an order has been drawn up the court will serve sealed copies on the applicant and respondent, and also on any other person the court may order to be served: CPR, r. 40.4(2). It will be the court that effects service unless one of the exceptions set out in CPR, r. 6.3, applies. The court is given a specific power by CPR, r. 40.5, to order service on a litigant as well as the litigant's solicitor.

Judgments and orders normally take effect from the day they are given or made, not from the time they are drawn up, sealed or served: CPR, r. 40.7. However, the court is given the power to specify some later date from which the order shall take effect. A judgment for the payment of money (including costs) must be complied with within 14 days of the judgment, unless the court specifies some other date for compliance: CPR, r. 40.11. This will include most orders that include a summary assessment of costs. The order may, instead of requiring immediate payment, impose an order for payment by instalments or defer the date for payment.

37.2.2   SPECIAL FORMS OF JUDGMENT

37.2.2.1   Counterclaims
The court has power to give separate judgments when dealing with cases where there are claims and counterclaims. It also has power to order a set-off between the two claims, and simply enter judgment for the balance: CPR, r. 40.13(2). Where it does so, it retains power to make separate costs orders in respect of the claims and counter-claims: CPR, r. 40.13(3).

37.2.2.2   Interim payments
Detailed rules for the form of judgments given in cases where there have been interim payments are laid down in PD 25 Interim Payments. In a preamble to the judgment in such a case there should be set out the total amount awarded and the amounts and dates of all interim payments. The total amount awarded should then be reduced by the total amount of the interim payments, with judgment being given for the balance. If the interim payments exceed the amount awarded at trial, by virtue of CPR, r. 25.8(2), the judgment should set out any orders made for repayment, reimbursement, variation or discharge, and any award of interest on the overpaid interim payments.

37.2.2.3   Compensation recovery
In personal injuries cases where some or all of the damages are subject to recovery under the Social Security (Recovery of Benefits) Act 1997, the judgment should include a preamble setting out the amounts awarded under each head of damage, and the amount by which it has been reduced in accordance with the Act: PD 40B, para. 5.1. The judgment should then provide for entry of judgment and payment of the balance.

37.2.2.4   Payment by instalments
A judgment for payment by instalments must state the total amount of the judgment, the amount of each instalment, the number of instalments and the date on which each is to be paid, and to whom the instalments should be paid: PD 40B, para. 12.

37.2.2.5   Orders requiring an act to be done ('unless orders')
Orders requiring an act to be done, other than the payment of money, must specify the time within which the act must be done. The consequences of failing to comply with the order must also be set out: PD 40B, paras 8.1 and 8.2. There are two suitable forms of wording, and the first form should be used wherever possible. The second form should be used where the defaulting party does not attend: 'Unless the claimant serves his list of documents by 4.00 pm on Friday, 22 January 2000, his claim will be struck out and judgment entered for the defendant.' 'Unless the defendant serves his list of documents within 14 days of service of this order. . .'

37.2.2.6   Penal notice
Injunction orders, whether prohibitory or mandatory, are intended to have penal consequences and can be punished as a contempt of court. These orders need to be endorsed with a penal notice in the following form (PD 40B, para. 9.1):

> If you the within-named [   ] do not comply with this order you may be held to be in contempt of court and imprisoned or fined, or [in the case of a company or corporation] your assets may be seized.

Undertakings given in lieu of injunctions are treated in the same way. A person giving an undertaking may also be required to sign a statement, which is endorsed on the court's copy of the order, to the effect that he or she understands the terms of the undertaking and the consequences of failure to comply with it: PD 40B, para. 9.3.

37.3   Consent Orders

37.3.1   NATURE OF CONSENT ORDERS

37.3.1.1   Using a consent order

A consent order can record the agreement of the parties in respect of certain interim matters and it may also be used to record the terms of a compromise when an action is settled.

37.3.1.2   The contractual nature of consent orders

As is inherent in the judgment of Buckley LJ in *Chanel Ltd* v *F.W. Woolworth & Co.* [1981] 1 WLR 485, a consent order is based on a *contract* between the parties. The contractual nature of such orders was recognised as long ago as 1840, when in *Wentworth* v *Bullen* (1840) 9 B & C 840 it was pointed out that the contract is contained in what passes between the parties (usually an exchange of correspondence) and that the consent order is simply evidence of that contract. To be effective, strictly the necessary ingredients for a contract need to be present.

37.3.1.3   The consent order as an estoppel

A consent order can act as an estoppel, effective to prevent a party from alleging matters against the other which have been compromised by the agreement: see *Kinch* v *Walcott* [1929] AC 482. However, the wording of each order has to be looked at carefully to determine whether it will act as an estoppel. For example, if it is clear that, in arriving at a consent order, one party expressly reserved the right to proceed against the other on certain allegations, there will be no estoppel by reason of the order: see *Rice* v *Reed* [1900] 1 QB 54.

37.3.1.4   Can a consent order be set aside or varied?

Before the consent order has been drawn up it is possible to apply back to the court to have it set aside or altered. However, good grounds are required for showing that the consent was procured through misrepresentation, mistake or any other ground for setting aside a contract: see *Dietz* v *Lennig Chemicals Ltd* [1969] 1 AC 170.

After the consent order is perfected the court has no power to vary it. In *De Lasala* v *De Lasala* [1980] AC 546 (PC) Lord Diplock said:

> Where a party seeks to challenge, on the ground that it was obtained by fraud or mistake, a judgment or order that finally disposes of the issues raised between the parties, the only ways of doing it that are open to him are by appeal from the judgment or order or by bringing a fresh action to set it aside.

However, there is a distinction between a real contract and a simple submission to an order. In *Siebe Gorman & Co. Ltd* v *Pneupac Ltd* [1982] 1 All ER 377, at 380, Lord Denning MR said:

> It should be clearly understood by the profession that, when an order is expressed to be made 'by consent' it is ambiguous. One meaning is this: the words 'by consent' may evidence a real contract between the parties. In such a case the court will only interfere with such an order on the same grounds as it would with any other contract. The other meaning is this: the words 'by consent' may mean 'the parties hereto not objecting.' In such a case there is no real contract between the parties.

37.3.1.5   Enforcement

Generally, if either party fails to comply with a consent order, the innocent party can seek to enforce it in the same manner as any other court order.

37.3.2   TOMLIN ORDERS

37.3.2.1   The use and nature of a Tomlin order

Where complex terms of settlement are agreed, or terms are agreed which extend beyond the boundaries of the action, or where it is sought to avoid publicity of the terms agreed, the compromise can be embodied in a Tomlin order. The name is derived from a *Practice Note* [1927] WN 290, where Tomlin J said that in a case where terms of compromise have been arranged and it is proposed that the action be stayed on agreed terms to be scheduled to a consent order, the minutes should be drawn so as to read as follows:

> And, the claimant and the defendant having agreed to the terms set out in the annexed schedule, it is ordered that all further proceedings in this action be stayed, except for the purpose of carrying such terms into effect. Liberty to apply as to carrying such terms into effect.

37.3.2.2 Enforcement where the agreed terms are broken

If the agreed terms are broken, enforcement is a two-stage process.

First, the action must be restored under the liberty to apply, and an order obtained requiring the opponent to comply with the scheduled obligation that has been breached.

Secondly, if that order is not complied with it can then be enforced by committal or by levying execution as appropriate.

As is made clear in *E. F. Phillips & Sons Ltd* v *Clarke* [1970] Ch 322, at 325, provisions in the schedule can be enforced even if not part of the original action. As Goff J said:

> . . . provided [a Tomlin] order is in the normally appropriate form with a qualified stay and a liberty to apply, and provided the application is strictly to enforce the terms embodied in the order and the schedule and does not depart from the agreed terms, an order giving effect to the terms may be obtained under the liberty to apply in the original action, notwithstanding the compromise itself goes beyond the ambit of the original dispute and the provision sought to be enforced is something which could not have been enforced in the original action and which indeed, is an obligation which did not exist but arose for the first time under the compromise.

37.3.3 ENTERING CONSENT ORDERS

37.3.3.1 Administrative consent orders

In order to save time and costs, CPR, r. 40.6, allows certain types of consent orders to be entered by a purely administrative process without the need for obtaining the approval of a judge. However, this process may not be used if any of the parties is a litigant in person: r. 40.6(2)(b). The types of orders covered are:

(a) judgments or orders for the payment of money;

(b) judgments or orders for the delivery up of goods (other than specific delivery);

(c) orders to dismiss the whole or part of the proceedings;

(d) orders for stays on agreed terms which dispose of the proceedings, including Tomlin orders;

(e) orders setting aside default judgments;

(f) orders for the payment out of money in court; and

(g) orders for the discharge from liability of any party; and

(h) orders for the payment, waiver or assessment of costs.

The consent order has to be drawn up in the agreed terms, has to bear the words 'By Consent', and be signed by the solicitors or counsel acting for each of the parties. In cases where terms are annexed in a schedule, provisions dealing with the payment of money out of court and for the payment and assessment of costs should be contained in the body of the order rather than in the schedule: PD 40B, para. 3.5.

37.3.3.2 Consent orders approved by the court

If an order is agreed between the parties, but includes a provision going beyond the types of orders referred to in the previous section, or if one of the parties is a litigant in person, it will have to be approved by a judge (often a District Judge or Master). It will be drawn up as above. The name of the judge will not be known, so the draft will have to include a space for the judge's details to be inserted: PD 23, para. 10.3. If all the parties write to the court expressing their consent, the court will treat that as sufficient signing of the consent order: PD 23, para. 10.2. The court will not necessarily make the order in accordance with the agreement between the parties, as the court retains ultimate control, particularly over case management matters. However, it will always take the terms agreed between the parties into account in whatever order it decides to make: see, for example, PD 28, para. 3.8.

In cases where the court's approval must be sought, either party may make the application for approval, and the application may be dealt with without a hearing: CPR, r. 40.6(5), (6).

37.4   In the Court of Appeal

Orders are drawn up by the Court Associate, not by the parties.

37.5   In the House of Lords

House of Lords Practice Direction, para. 22.1 provides:

> *After the House has given judgment, drafts of the final order of the House are sent to all parties who lodged a case. The drafts must be returned to the Judicial Office within one week of the date of receipt (unless otherwise directed) either approved or with suggested amendments. If substantial amendments are proposed, such amendments must be submitted to the agents for the other parties, who shall indicate their approval or disagreement, both to the agents submitting the proposals and to the Judicial Office . . .*

The final order is sent to the agents for the parties.

37.6   Interest on Judgments

Under the Judgments Act 1838, s. 17 and CCA 1984, s. 74, simple interest, currently at 8% per annum, is payable on all High Court money judgments and County Court money judgments of £5,000 and more. In addition, a County Court judgment for any amount of money carries interest at 8% per annum if it is in respect of a debt which is a qualifying debt for the purposes of the Late Payment of Commercial Debts (Interest) Act 1998. A debt is a qualifying debt if it was created by virtue of an obligation under a contract to which the Act applies: s. 3(1). The 1998 Act is being introduced in stages between 1 November 1998 and 1 November 2002. In the first phase it applies to commercial contracts for the supply of goods and services where the supplier is a small business and the purchaser is a large business or a United Kingdom public authority.

Also of significance is *Thomas v Bunn* [1991] 1 AC 362, HL, where it was held that in cases where the claimant enters a judgment for damages to be decided by the court, 1838 Act interest on the main award runs from the date of the damages judgment, not the liability judgment. In personal injuries cases, interest on general damages before judgment, is currently awarded at 2% per annum as opposed to 8% per annum under the Act. One effect of the decision is that it removes the interest rate disincentive on defendants admitting liability at an early stage, even though they still dispute quantum.

Under CPR, r. 40.8, interest on costs runs from the date the judgment is given. As regards interest on costs after a claim is automatically struck out for non-payment of the fees payable at the allocation or listing stages, or after acceptance of a payment in or an offer to settle, or after a claim is discontinued, by virtue of the CPR, r. 44.12, interest runs from the date of the event giving rise to the entitlement to costs (i.e. the date of striking out, acceptance, or the date of service of the notice of discontinuance).

37.7 The Correction of Errors in Judgments or Orders

Errors in judgments or orders as drawn up may sometimes be corrected.

The CPR, r. 40.12, provides:

> (1) *The court may at any time correct an accidental slip or omission in a judgment or order.*
> (2) *A party may apply for a correction without notice.*

The rule extends to accidental slips and errors made both by officers of the court and by the parties and their advisers. But the error must be an error in *expressing* the manifest intention of the court. If the intention of the court is in error, the remedy lies in an appeal.

If the contemplated type of error was made, but it was not 'accidental' as required by r. 40.12, the court retains inherent jurisdiction to correct it. Thus, in *Hatton* v *Harris* [1892] AC 547 at 560, Lord Watson said:

> Where an error of that kind has been committed it is always within the competency of the court, if nothing has intervened which would render it inexpedient or inequitable to do so, to correct the record in order to bring it into harmony with the order which the Judge obviously meant to pronounce. The correction ought to be made on [application], and is not a matter either for appeal or rehearing.

37.8 Register of County Court Judgments

A Register of County Court Judgments is operated by Registry Trust Limited under powers given by the CCA 1984, ss. 73 and 73A and the Register of County Court Judgments Regulations 1985 (SI 1985 No. 1807). County Courts provide periodic returns containing details of unsatisifed judgments to Registry Trust Limited, and the register kept by the company is open to inspection on payment of prescribed fees. The information is regularly used by financial institutions for credit scoring purposes.

THIRTY EIGHT

ENFORCEMENT

38.1 Introduction

A litigant who obtains a judgment or order does not thereby automatically obtain the remedy sought in the proceedings. Leaving aside the possibility of an appeal (a topic considered in **Chapter 39**), there is still the worry that the order will not be obeyed by the other side. Of course, most litigants will abide by the ruling of the court with reasonable promptness. But the court needs powers to enforce compliance by parties who fail to obey judgments and orders made against them, or else public confidence in the legal system would be lost. The rules of court referred to in this chapter can be found in the preserved provisions in Schedules 1 and 2 of the Civil Procedure Rules 1998.

38.2 Oral Examination

It may be that the judgment creditor (the person who has obtained a judgment for the payment of money) knows little or nothing about the judgment debtor's assets. Without further information he will be unable to make an intelligent choice between the methods of enforcement that are available. Informally further information can be obtained either personally or through an inquiry agent.

After judgment the court will provide formal assistance by the process of oral examination. In the County Court, CCR O. 25, r. 3(1), provides that:

> . . . the appropriate court may, on an application made ex parte by the judgment creditor, order the debtor . . . to attend before the court officer and be orally examined as to the debtor's means of satisfying the judgment and may also order the [debtor] to produce any books or documents in his possession relevant to the debtor's means.

The High Court contains a similar provision for examination before a Master, District Judge or other appropriate officer: RSC O. 48, r. 1.

The nature of the examination was considered by the Court of Appeal in *Republic of Costa Rica* v *Stronsberg* (1880) 16 Ch D 8, where Jessell MR said that the judgment debtor 'must answer all questions fairly directed to ascertain from him what amount of debts is due, from whom due, and to give all necessary particulars to enable the plaintiffs to recover under a garnishee order.' And, according to James LJ 'The examination is not only intended to be an examination, but to be a cross-examination, and that of the severest kind.'

38.3 Execution Against Goods

Execution against a judgment debtor's goods is by way of a warrant of execution in the county court, and by way of the writ of *fieri facias* (abbreviated to *fi. fa.*) in the High Court. County Court judgments for £5,000 or more must be transferred to the High

Court if to be enforced by this method. County Court judgments for less than £1,000 must be enforced in the County Court if enforced by this method. For judgments between £1,000 and £5,000 either court can enforce by this method. A judgment creditor seeking to enforce by either of these methods must complete the necessary forms, and pay the prescribed fee: see RSC O. 46 and 47 and CCR O. 26. Actual enforcement is the responsibility of the court bailiff (in the County Court) or the sheriff (in the High Court).

The bailiff, armed with the warrant of execution, or the sheriff, armed with the writ of *fi. fa.*, will call at the judgment debtor's premises and seek to gain entry. They are not entitled to break open outer doors, nor are they allowed to gain entry by putting a foot in the door and pushing their way in. Once lawfully inside the building, they can seize sufficient goods to satisfy the judgment debt. They can seize any type of goods, including money, bills of exchange, promissory notes and bonds, except protected goods. Clothing, bedding, furniture, household equipment and provisions necessary for satisfying the basic domestic needs of the debtor and his or her family, and such tools, books, vehicles and equipment as are necessary for the debtor's use in his or her employment, business or vocation, are protected goods. Goods belonging to other members of the debtor's family, goods on hire purchase, and goods belonging to a limited company which is not the debtor may not be seized.

Once goods have been seized, the bailiff or sheriff will either take them away, or may leave them in the premises having entered into a 'walking possession' agreement with some responsible person in the building. Under the terms of such an agreement the responsible person agrees not to remove or damage the goods, and authorises the bailiff or sheriff to re-enter the premises at any time to complete the enforcement process.

If the goods are taken away, the bailiff or sheriff will provide the debtor with an inventory, and will then arrange for them to be sold by an appointed broker or appraiser through a public auction. Purchasers acquire good title to the goods. Written accounts of the sale, and the application of the proceeds of sale, are then provided to the debtor, and the net proceeds of sale after various expenses are paid to the judgment creditor.

38.4   Garnishee Proceedings

Where a judgment debtor is owed money from a third party ('the garnishee'), the simplest and often most effective method of enforcement is by way of garnishee proceedings. A garnishee order absolute has the effect of transforming the garnishee's obligation to pay money to the judgment debtor into an obligation to pay that money to the judgment creditor. Ideally, the garnishee should be some responsible person, such as a High Street bank, which will readily honour the new obligation to pay the judgment creditor. However, there is no restriction in this respect, and it is equally possible to obtain garnishee orders against trade debts, and loans between friends and family.

An application for a garnishee order follows a two-stage process, see RSC O. 49 and CCR O. 30. The first stage is an application without notice by filing a witness statement or affidavit for a garnishee order to show cause. Certain prescribed information has to be included in the witness statement or affidavit, including details of the judgment being enforced and details of the debt it is proposed to garnish. If an order to show cause is granted, the court will fix a return day for the second stage (a hearing on notice to consider whether the order should be made *absolute*). The order to show cause must be served on the garnishee personally (or in the County Court by first-class post) at least 15 days before the return day, and on the judgment debtor at least seven days after service on the garnishee and at least seven days before the return day. Service of the order to show cause has the effect of binding in the hands of the garnishee any debt due or accruing due from the garnishee to the debtor, up to the amount of the judgment. On the return day the order will normally be made absolute, but it is open, for example, for the garnishee to dispute its alleged liability to the judgment debtor. Once the order is made absolute, the garnishee is obliged to pay the garnished debt to the judgment creditor. Making payment in compliance with the order operates as a valid discharge in relation to the garnishee's debt to the judgment debtor.

38.5 Charging Orders

A charging order, as its name suggests, is an order imposing a charge on specified property of a judgment debtor for the purpose of securing the amount of a judgment debt: see the Charging Orders Act 1979, s. 1(1). The property that can be charged under a charging order includes (by s. 2) a beneficial interest in land, a beneficial interest in government stock or in company shares, debentures or other securities. Charging orders have to be sought in the court where the judgment was obtained, except High Court judgments for less than £5,000 have to be transferred to the County Court for this form of enforcement.

Like garnishee proceedings (see **38.4**), charging order applications follow a two-stage process. The first stage is an application without notice for a charging order to show cause, followed by a hearing on notice for a charging order *absolute.* The evidence in support of the order to show cause must contain certain prescribed information (see RSC O. 50 and CCR O. 31), including the subject matter of the intended charge and the names and addresses of all known creditors of the debtor. If an order to show cause is made in respect of the debtor's interest in land, the order to show cause may be registered as a pending action. A return date will be fixed by the court, and the judgment debtor must be served with the order together with the judgment creditor's witness statement or affidavit in support at least seven days before the return day. The court may also direct service on all or any of the debtor's other creditors, who have an interest in the application because, if the order is made absolute, there will be less in the way of unsecured assets available to the unsecured creditors if the debtor becomes insolvent.

By the Charging Orders Act 1979, s. 1(5), on the return date when the court is deciding whether to make the order absolute, it is required to consider all the circumstances of the case, and in particular the personal circumstances of the debtor and whether any other creditor or creditors are likely to be unduly prejudiced by the making of the order. If the order is made absolute, it operates as a charge on the relevant property, converting the judgment creditor from an unsecured to a secured creditor. It does not provide the judgment creditor with an immediate right to any money, but it does provide a valuable safeguard in the event of the debtor becoming insolvent before paying, and it also provides the foundation for proceedings for enforcement by sale.

38.6 Enforcement by Sale

Proceedings to enforce a charge, whether obtained by a charging order or otherwise, have to be brought by a separate action commenced by Part 8 claim. Evidence is initially given by witness statement or affidavit. If fully contested, the action proceeds to trial, where an order may be made for the sale of the property charged.

38.7 Attachment of Earnings

An attachment of earnings order is the most appropriate method of enforcement where the judgment debtor has no substantial assets other than salary. It is an order directed to the debtor's employer requiring the employer to make periodic deductions from the debtor's salary and to pay the sums deducted (less a £1 collection fee) to the collecting officer of the court. Attachment of earnings orders can only be made by the County Courts in respect of ordinary civil litigation, so a High Court judgment to be enforced in this manner will first have to be transferred to the County Court.

It is a pre-condition for the making of an attachment of earnings order that the judgment debtor has failed to make at least one payment due under the judgment.

Thus, such orders can only be made where the judgment provides for payment by instalments that have fallen into arrears. The 'earnings' that may be attached are wages, salaries, fees, bonuses, commission and overtime payable under a contract of service, and also occupational pensions and statutory sick pay. It does not include State pensions or self-employed income, see the Attachment of Earnings Act 1971, s. 24.

An application for an attachment of earnings order is a simple matter of completing the prescribed form and paying a court fee: CCR O. 27. The court then sends a two-page questionnaire to the debtor asking detailed questions as to the debtor's financial circumstances, and which also contains a box where the debtor can make an offer to pay by instalments. On receipt of the form a court official can make an attachment of earnings order. Either party can object to the official's determination, in which event there is a hearing to consider the form of order that should be made. If the debtor does not co-operate, a 14-day committal order can be made. Often the court will make a suspended order, which will only be served on the employer if the debtor fails to pay the stated instalments.

An attachment of earnings order has two components:

(a) The debtor's protected earnings rate. This is related to the debtor's needs, and is the amount that must be earned each week or month before any money can be deducted under the order; and

(b) The normal deduction rate. This is the weekly or monthly instalment that the employer is required to deduct from the debtor's salary.

38.8 Judgment Summons

This is a procedure under the Debtors Act 1869, s. 5, for punishing a defaulting judgment debtor with a period in prison. It has ceased to be of general application and is now restricted to maintenance orders in family law and arrears of some taxes, see the Administration of Justice Act 1970, s. 11.

38.9 Writs and Warrants of Delivery

Where the claimant obtains a judgment for *delivery of goods*, the means of enforcement is by writ of delivery (in the High Court: RSC O. 45, r. 4) or by warrant of delivery (in the County Court: CCR O. 26, r. 16).

There are two types of writ (and warrant) of delivery, corresponding to the provisions of the Torts (Interference with Goods) Act 1977, s. 3.

A writ (or warrant) to enforce the discretionary relief in s. 3(2)(a) of the Act for delivery of the claimant's goods is known as a *writ (or warrant) of specific delivery*. It requires the sheriff (or bailiff) to seize the goods specified in the judgment. The judgment debtor does not have the alternative of paying the assessed value of the goods.

A writ (or warrant) to enforce the relief in s. 3(2)(b) of the Act requiring delivery of the goods or damages in the alternative is known as a *writ (or warrant) of delivery*. It directs the sheriff (or bailiff) to seize the specified goods or to levy execution against the general goods of the judgment debtor to the assessed value of the specified goods, in the latter case with the result that the claimant's remedy is converted into one for damages.

38.10 Writ or Warrant of Possession

A judgment for the possession of land is *invariably* secured through High Court writs (RSC O. 45, r. 3) (or County Court warrants (CCR O. 26, r. 17(1)) of possession. The claimant applies for the writ or warrant of possession simply by filing forms with the court and paying the court fee. Enforcement is dealt with by the sheriff (High Court) or bailiff (County Court).

It is usual to inform the police before enforcing possession, as entry *may be gained by force*. The claimant will usually need to be on hand in order to make the land secure after possession has been obtained.

In the County Court, CCA 1984, s. 111(1), provides: 'For the purposes of executing a warrant to give possession of any premises, it shall not be necessary to remove any goods from those premises.' In the High Court, on the other hand, execution is not considered to be completed until all the goods and persons in the premises have been removed.

In *R v Wandsworth County Court* [1975] 1 WLR 1314, Lord Widgery CJ said 'it has always been the law that the bailiff, when lawfully enforcing a warrant for possession, turns out everybody he finds on the premises, even though they are not the parties.'

38.11 Receivers by Way of Equitable Execution

Receivership orders are made where it is impossible to use any of the other legal methods of enforcement. By the order the receiver will be authorised to receive rents, profits and moneys receivable in respect of the judgment debtor's interest in specified property. If necessary, the receiver may bring proceedings in the judgment debtor's name to obtain moneys payable to the judgment debtor which do not amount to debts (which could be attached by garnishee proceedings), such as a claim to be indemnified.

By RSC O. 51, r. 1:

> *Where an application is made for the appointment of a receiver by way of equitable execution, the Court in determining whether it is just or convenient that the appointment should be made shall have regard to the amount claimed by the judgment creditor, to the amount likely to be obtained by the receiver and to the probable costs of his appointment and may direct an inquiry on any of these matters or any other matter before making the appointment.*

In *Maclaine Watson & Co. Ltd* v *International Tin Council* [1988] Ch 1 (at first instance), Millett J said that the test is 'that there should be no way of getting at the fund except by the appointment of a receiver.' It operates by removing a hindrance arising out of the nature of the property which prevents execution at law.

The application must be supported by two affidavits or witness statements — the first showing the grounds for making the order deposing to the particulars of the judgment, the amount outstanding, results of execution, and that the judgment debtor has no property which can be taken by other methods of execution and details of the property over which it is proposed to appoint the receiver; the second, made by some responsible person other than the applicant or the applicant's solicitor, deposing to at least five years' knowledge of the proposed receiver and his or her fitness for appointment as a receiver.

38.12 Committal for Breach of an Order or Undertaking

38.12.1 WHAT IS COMMITTAL FOR BREACH?

Defiance of court orders is only one, but the most common, form of contempt of court. Others include contempts in the face of the court and writing works calculated to interfere with the course of justice.

Committal for breach means that the person in breach is sent to prison for a period not exceeding two years: see Contempt of Court Act 1981, s. 14(1). There are two purposes behind doing this. One is to punish for the past contempt, the other to secure compliance with the court order.

As an alternative to committing to prison, by RSC O. 52, r. 9 the court has the power to fine or take security. Further alternatives are to give a strong reprimand; to grant an injunction restraining a repetition of the contempt; and, in an appropriate case, to make a summary award of damages.

38.12.2   PROCEDURE FOR THE ISSUE OF A COMMITTAL ORDER

The application is by claim form or application notice: RSC O. 52, r. 4 and CCR O. 29, r. 1(4).

(a)   The applicant is required to identify the provisions of the order (injuction) that are alleged to have been broken, and the ways in which it is alleged that the injunction has been broken. The acts need not be set out as counts in an indictment.

(b)   The applicant must file affidavit evidence in support.

(c)   The respondent is served by personal service with the notice and affidavits not less than three clear days before the hearing.

(d)   The hearing is before a judge. At the hearing the judge must be satisfied that the breach has been proved *beyond reasonable doubt.*

(e)   If so satisfied, the judge can make an immediate or suspended committal order for a fixed period not exceeding two years.

38.13   Writ of Sequestration

This too is a process for punishing contempt. It has become well known through its use in trade union cases. The writ is addressed to four sequestrators requiring them to enter the contemnor's lands and to seize the contemnor's personal property and to hold the same until the contempt is purged: see RSC O. 46, r. 5.

THIRTY NINE

APPEALS

39.1 Introduction

'Can I appeal?' is a familiar question to any member of the Bar. Frequently clients are anxious to know whether they can appeal in the event of an unsuccessful claim or defence long before their case is even heard. For others, it is the most pressing question after judgment is pronounced. It is therefore vital for you to retain at the very least a working knowledge of the appeals procedure, the grounds (if any) upon which an appeal may be brought, whether permission to appeal is required, and the time limit within which an appeal must be brought.

Some appeals can be brought as of right. Most other decisions can be appealed with permission. However, it is comparatively rare for decisions, particularly after trial, to be appealed. In 1989–90 a total of 1,611 appeals were completed in the Court of Appeal, of which just over 25% were successful. Only 53 appeals were taken to the House of Lords, of which about a third achieved some success.

Counsel has a heavy responsibility when called upon to advise on the merits of an appeal. Lord Donaldson MR, in an annual review, put it in this way:

> The question which the adviser may ask himself is whether, looking at the matter objectively, there are sufficient grounds for believing not only that the case should have been decided differently, but that in all the circumstances it can be demonstrated to the satisfaction of the Court of Appeal that there are grounds for reversing the judge's findings. In considering this question the adviser must never forget the financial risk which an appellant undertakes of having not only to pay his own costs of the appeal, but those of his opponent and, for this purpose, the adviser has two clients if the litigant is [publicly funded]. Nor must he underrate the effect upon his client of the emotional and other consequences of a continued state of uncertainty pending an appeal. In a word, one of the most important duties of a professional legal adviser is to save his clients from themselves and always to remember that, whilst it may well be reasonable to institute or to defend particular proceedings at first instance, a wholly new and different situation arises once the claim has been fully investigated by the court and a decision given.

39.2   Civil Appeals Framework

Table 39.1 shows in outline the possible routes when appealing in civil matters.

Table 39.1

Type of order appealed from	Appeal to	Whether permission is required	Hearing *de novo* or show grounds
1. CC District Judge's interim order	CC judge	No	*De novo*
2. CC District Judge's final order	CC judge	No	Grounds
3. CC judge's order on appeal from 1. or 2.	CA	Yes	Grounds
4. CC judge's interim orders and non-multi-track final orders	HC judge	Yes	Grounds
5. CC judge's final order (multi-track)	CA	Yes	Grounds
6. CC on point of jurisdiction	QBD Div. Ct.	Yes	Grounds
7. HC Master's or District Judge's interim order	HC judge	No	*De novo*
8. HC Master or District Judge's final order (non-multi-track)	HC judge	Yes	Grounds
9. HC Master or District Judge's final order (multi-track)	CA	Yes	Grounds
10. HC judge's order	CA	Yes	Grounds
11. Leapfrog appeal from HC judge	HL	Yes, from both HC judge and HL	Grounds
12. CA	HL	Yes	Grounds

39.3   Appeal Notices

An appellant must file an appeal notice in form N161 in order to initiate an appeal. This must set out the grounds on which it is alleged the judge below went wrong (strictly this is not necessary for appeals from interim orders by Masters and District Judges, but is widely regarded as good practice even for these appeals). If permission to appeal is required (see **39.6**), the appeal notice must include a request for such permission: CPR, r. 52.4(1). If permission to appeal out of time is required (see **39.4** and **39.7**), an application for such permission must be made to the appeal court (r. 52.6(1)), which is usually made in the appeal notice.

39.4 Time for Bringing an Appeal

An appeal is brought by filing the appeal notice. This must be done within 14 days after the date of the decision of the lower court, unless the lower court has directed some other period for bringing the appeal: CPR, r. 52.4(2). Once an appeal notice has been filed it must be served on each respondent as soon as practicable, and in any event within seven days after being filed: r. 52.4(3).

39.5 Respondent's Notice

A respondent may oppose an appeal in one of three ways:

(a) by simply arguing that the decision below was correct for the reasons given by the judge below. In this circumstance there is no need to serve a respondent's notice;

(b) by arguing that the decision below was correct, but for reasons other than those given by the judge below. In this circumstance a respondent's notice should be served (CPR, r. 52.5(2)(b));

(c) by cross-appealing part of the judgment below that went against the respondent. In this circumstance again a respondent's notice is required (see CPR, r. 52.5(2)(a)).

Where a respondent's notice is required, it must be filed (in form N162) within 14 days of the respondent being served with the appellant's notice (if no permission was required) or notification that the appellant has permission to appeal (if permission was required): see CPR, r. 52.5(4), (5). It must then be served on the appellant as soon as practicable, and in any event within seven days after being filed: r. 52.5(6). A respondent's notice should include a request for permission to cross-appeal where permission is required: r. 52.5(3). Both forms of respondent's notice should address the grounds set out in the appeal notice, and should seek to define and confine the scope of the argument on the appeal: PD Court of Appeal, para. 5.6.1.

39.6 Permission to Appeal

Appeals from interim decisions by Masters and District Judges can be made without permission: see CPR, r. 52.3(1). However, with three minor exceptions, permission is required for appeals from decisions of County Court and High Court judges: r. 52.3(1). The exceptions where judges' decisions may be appealed without permission are those from:

(a) committal orders;

(b) a refusal to grant *habeus corpus*; and

(c) secure accommodation orders under the Children Act 1989, s. 25.

If permission to appeal is required it should initially be sought from the court below, and if permission is refused, from the appeal court (by including a request for permission in the appeal notice, see CPR, r. 52.3(2)). In appeals to the Court of Appeal, permission to appeal is first considered on the papers by a single Lord Justice. If permission is refused, the appellant may request the question of permission to be reconsidered at a hearing: r. 52.3(4).

The basic test for granting permission is whether the appeal has a real prospect of success: r. 52.3(6)(a). As discussed at **39.8.1.3** and **39.8.3**, there are restricted grounds for mounting a successful appeal. A fanciful prospect of success is not enough. Another factor is the general importance of the issue raised by the appeal. If the point is not of particular general importance, and if the costs of appealing do not justify the amount at stake, permission is unlikely to be granted. Further, permission may be refused in respect of second appeals (i.e., where an appellant loses at first instance and then on appeal to the judge, and now wishes to appeal further to the Court of Appeal), unless the appeal raises an important point of principle or practice, or there is some other compelling reason for hearing a further appeal: Access to Justice Act 1999, s. 55.

39.7 Extending Time for Appealing

Any application to extend the time for appealing should be made to the appeal court (CPR, r. 52.6), and permission to appeal out of time cannot be granted by agreement between the parties. The general principles discussed at **28.3** on failing to comply with time limits apply on such an application.

39.8 Nature of Appeal Hearings

39.8.1 APPEALS FROM INTERIM ORDERS

39.8.1.1 Initial interim appeals

Appeals from District Judges (see 1. in **Table 39.1**) and Masters (see 6. in **Table 39.1**) in interim matters are by way of complete rehearing. In determining the appeal the judge exercises his or her own discretion unfettered by the decision below. These appeals are identified in the 4th column of **Table 39.1** as those where the appeal hearing is '*de novo*'. One difference is that the appellant opens the appeal, rather than the party who originally made the application.

39.8.1.2 Subsequent interim appeals

A subsequent appeal from the decision of a County Court Circuit Judge (see 3. in **Table 39.1**) or a High Court Judge (see 8. in **Table 39.1**) on an interim matter is to the Court of Appeal. Before the appeal court can interfere with the decision below the appellant must establish grounds, which have to be set out by the appellant in the appeal notice.

39.8.1.3 Discretion

Many, if not most, interim applications turn on the exercise of the court's discretion. In almost all cases the discretion is conferred on the judge. Thus, on appeal from a Master or District Judge, the High Court or County Court judge exercises his or her own discretion independently of the decision below. On further appeal, the Court of Appeal will not, as a rule, interfere with the judge's discretion. The Court of Appeal is only entitled to substitute its own exercise of discretion in such limited circumstances as where the judge:

(a) failed to exercise any discretion at all;

(b) went wrong in principle;

(c) made a mistake of law;

(d) took into account irrelevant matters;

(e) misinterpreted the facts;

(f) exercised the discretion in a way in which no reasonable judge could have exercised it.

39.8.2 APPEALS FROM FINAL ORDERS

An appeal from a final order includes an appeal to a County Court judge (see 2. in **Table 39.1**) (where the County Court judge will act in a similar way to the Court of Appeal) and appeals to the Court of Appeal (see 4., 7. and 9. in **Table 39.1**). Consideration will now be given only to appeals to the Court of Appeal.

The appellant will open. The evidence of witnesses called at the trial will be considered from transcripts of the short-hand note or judge's note of the evidence. In exceptional circumstances the Court of Appeal may receive fresh evidence not available at the trial (see **39.11**), and take into account changes in the law since the trial having retrospective effect. The function of the court is also rather different, and this is considered at **39.8.3**.

39.8.3 GROUNDS FOR ALLOWING AN APPEAL FROM A FINAL ORDER

An appeal court will allow an appeal where the decision of the lower court was either wrong or unjust because of a serious procedural or other irregularity: CPR, r. 52.11(3).

39.8.3.1 Decisions by juries

Juries usually give general verdicts, and usually it is impossible to attack them on appeal. One possible ground is that the verdict, whether on liability or damages, is one which no properly directed jury could reasonably have found upon the evidence. The Court of Appeal has power where the damages awarded are excessive or inadequate to substitute a proper sum for the sum awarded by the jury: CPR, r. 52.10(3).

39.8.3.2 Credibility of witnesses

The trial judge sees the witnesses giving evidence, the Court of Appeal does not. Having the advantage of having seen the demeanour and manner of the witnesses in court, the trial judge's findings on the credibility of witnesses will be upset on appeal only if the Court of Appeal is convinced that the judge was plainly wrong: *Powell* v *Streatham Manor Nursing Home* [1935] AC 243, HL.

39.8.3.3 Inferences

There is a distinction between:

(a) facts deposed to by witnesses and found by the trial judge; and

(b) inferences of fact drawn from those facts.

The Court of Appeal is not at the same disadvantage as in **39.8.3.2** in drawing inferences. If, on full consideration, the Court of Appeal concludes that the judge's inferences were wrong, it will overrule the decision below.

39.8.3.4 Points not raised below

An appellant cannot, as a rule, raise on appeal points of law or fact not raised at the trial below: *Clouston & Co. Ltd* v *Corry* [1906] AC 122, HL. However, a respondent may seek to support the findings of the trial judge on any ground, including any not raised below, provided such ground is included in the respondent's notice.

39.9 Stay of Execution

Initiating an appeal does not have the automatic effect of staying execution on the judgment or order under appeal: CPR, r. 52.7. Stays can nevertheless be sought, generally either from the court appealed from or the court appealed to.

In considering an application for a stay, the courts act on the principle that in general successful litigants must not be deprived of the fruits of the litigation. A stay may be granted where the applicant files evidence showing that if the amount of the judgment were to be paid, there would be no reasonable probability of getting it back if the appeal were to be successful: *Atkins* v *Great Western Railway* (1886) 2 TLR 400.

This was considered to be too stringent a test and inconsistent with modern practice by the Court of Appeal in *Linotype-Hell Finance Ltd* v *Baker* [1993] 1 WLR 321. Staughton LJ said a stay could be granted if an appellant would face financial ruin without it, provided the appeal had some prospect of success. Although the court has to balance the advantages to the parties and exercise its common sense in deciding whether to grant a stay of execution, the starting principle is that there has to be good reason for depriving the successful party of the fruits of its judgment at first instance: see *Winchester Cigarette Machinery Ltd* v *Payne (No. 2), The Times,* 15 December 1993, CA. The appellant needs to show some special circumstance taking the case out of the ordinary.

39.10 Court of Appeal Appeals Procedure

Within seven days of service of the notice of appeal the appellant must set down the appeal by lodging with the Master of Civil Appeals, copies of the judgment or order and the notice of appeal. The case is then entered in the appropriate list of appeals.

For the detailed procedure dealing with skeleton arguments, appeal bundles and listing arrangements for appeals to the Court of Appeal and the House of Lords see PD (Court of Appeal).

Substantive appeals to the Court of Appeal are generally heard by three-judge courts (SCA 1981, s. 54(2)), but in a number of situations the court is duly constituted if it consists of two judges. These include appeals from interim orders, from County Court orders, and from final orders made by Masters and High Court District Judges: see SCA 1981, s. 54(4). Where a two-judge court is divided, either party may apply for a rehearing before a three-judge court. Fortunately, this is extremely rare.

Before the hearing the judges will have read the notice of appeal, any respondent's notice, the judgment under appeal and the skeleton arguments. At the beginning of the hearing the Presiding Lord Justice will state what other documents and authorities have also been read. Accordingly, it is not usually necessary for counsel to open the facts, but to proceed to the strongest ground of appeal. If, exceptionally, it would be helpful to the court for counsel to open the appeal, the Presiding Lord Justice notifies counsel before the hearing. Counsel should avoid reading passages of transcript *in extenso,* and should go immediately to the relevant passages in the judgments of cases which have been pre-read by the court. Lay clients should be forewarned of these arrangements, so as not to be left with the impression that their cases are not being given a fair hearing: *Practice Direction* [1995] 1 WLR 1191.

39.11 Fresh Evidence

Fresh evidence may be in the form of an affidavit/deposition/witness statement or by oral examination. Where there was a hearing on the merits in the court below, the Court of Appeal may receive fresh evidence (other than as to matters occurring since the date of hearing) only if it is satisfied that such evidence:

(a) could not have been obtained with reasonable diligence for use at the hearing;

(b) would probably have an important influence on the result of the case; and

(c) is apparently credible (see *Ladd* v *Marshall* [1954] 1 WLR 1489).

39.12 Orders for a New Trial

One of the Court of Appeal's powers on appeal is to order a new trial: see SCA 1981, s. 17 and CPR, r. 52.10(2). This is more of a live issue if the case was tried with a jury. Grounds for making such an order include misdirecting the jury; leaving to the jury questions which are for the judge; and irregularities in relation to the jury (such as jurors conversing with strangers after retiring to consider the verdict). Other grounds, such as improper admission or rejection of evidence, could occur in trials by judge alone. Even if such grounds are established, a new trial will generally only be ordered if the Court of Appeal is of the opinion that some substantial wrong or miscarriage has been thereby occasioned. This means that a new trial will not be ordered unless there is a doubt whether the verdict below was correct on either liability or remedy: *Bray* v *Ford* [1896] AC 44, HL.

39.13 Questions

OBJECTIVES

By the conclusion of this section you should:

(a) understand the different methods of enforcing money and other judgments;

(b) have developed, where there is a choice, a tactical sense as to which method or combination of methods of enforcement is appropriate given the circumstances of the judgment debtor;

(c) have a practical knowledge of the principles and procedures governing consent and Tomlin orders; and

(d) have a sound understanding of the principles and procedures governing civil appeals.

RESEARCH

Read the materials contained in **Chapters 37** to **39** of this Manual.

LARGE GROUP SESSION 10

Read the following questions in advance of Large Group Session 10. There is no need ·to have prepared answers in advance of the class, as the background materials will be considered in the class.

QUESTION 1

Fiona obtained judgment some time ago against Sarah in the sum of £5,700. Sarah has ignored requests for payment. Fiona has made an application without notice to the District Judge for, and obtained, a garnishee order against a bank account in Sarah's name held by the Regional Bank plc. What is the effect of the order made on the application without notice on Regional Bank plc once it is served?

[A] It must hold £5,700 or the sum standing to Sarah's credit (whichever is less) pending an application made with notice.
[B] It must pay £5,700 or the sum standing to Sarah's credit (whichever is less) direct to Fiona.
[C] It must pay £5,700 or the sum standing to Sarah's credit (whichever is less) into court within 14 days.
[D] It must pay the whole amount standing to Sarah's credit into court within 14 days.

QUESTION 2

Pickwick Mail Order plc has obtained judgment for £3,782 in the Dewsbury County Court against Diane. Diane's home is jointly owned with her husband. Enquiries have indicated that there are two cars at the address, and the ground floor rooms appear to be furnished to a high standard with numerous items of household electrical equipment.

Advise Pickwick Mail Order plc as to the appropriate method of enforcing the judgment.

QUESTION 3

After judgment has been obtained in the High Court, which one of the following methods of enforcement is not executed by the sheriff?

[A] Seizure and sale of the judgment debtor's goods in satisfaction of a money judgment.
[B] Seizure of listed and identified goods for delivery to the claimant.
[C] Removal of persons from land and giving possession to the claimant.
[D] Attaching a debt due from a third party to the judgment debtor so that the third party is required to pay the debt direct to the judgment creditor.

QUESTION 4

P & Co. have obtained separate judgments against Anne, Ben and Colin. P & Co. are experiencing difficulty in enforcing each of these judgments.

How can they enforce them and what procedure must be followed if:

(a) Anne has no assets but earns £150 per week as a bus driver employed by London Buses?

(b) Ben is retired and receives a pension from his former employers?

(c) Colin works as a self-employed brick-layer. He owns a van, various bricklayers tools, and is owed money for work he has done as a sub-contractor?

QUESTION 5

Your client Murdstone, who lives next door to the celebrated singer Johnny Hopeless, has obtained an injunction prohibiting him from rehearsing during the hours between midnight and 7 o'clock in the morning. Last night Johnny was heard practising his latest number until 3 o'clock.

Advise.

QUESTION 6

Michael has brought proceedings in the Queen's Bench Division against Cathy in respect of a liquidated claim (for £64,000). Some weeks before the trial is due to start Cathy makes a without prejudice offer to Michael, in full and final satisfaction of Michael's claim against her, to pay Michael £48,000 at the rate of £2,000 per calendar month (because Cathy is in some temporary financial difficulties). Michael agrees to a consent judgment in these terms and Cathy's solicitors now seek your advice on how to draft and enter such a judgment.

QUESTION 7

By agreement between the parties Master Scrooge assessed Thelma's damages. The sum he awarded was £7,000. Thelma had expected to recover around £50,000. Advise Thelma.

QUESTION 8

Robert has brought an action against Joe in the Queen's Bench Division. Joe applies to strike out Robert's particulars of claim, on the ground it discloses no reasonable grounds for bringing the claim. Master Muddle grants the application and dismisses Robert's action. Advise Robert of any right of appeal.

QUESTION 9

Your client disagreed with the interim order made by a County Court District Judge and appealed to the Circuit Judge. The Circuit Judge has just given her decision on this appeal. The decision has gone against your client. Your client wants to appeal this decision. Which one of the following states the correct position?

[A]   An appeal lies to a High Court judge without permission.
[B]   An appeal lies to the Court of Appeal without permission.
[C]   An appeal lies to the Court of Appeal with permission.
[D]   An appeal lies to the High Court judge with permission from the County Court judge or a High Court judge.

INDEX